The Earthscan Reader in Risk and Modern Society

Edited by Ragnar E Löfstedt and Lynn Frewer

EARTHSCAN

Earthscan Publications Ltd, London

First published in the UK in 1998 by
Earthscan Publications Ltd

Copyright © Ragnar E Löfstedt and Lynn Frewer, 1998

A catalogue record for this book is available from the British Library

ISBN: 1 85383 504 8 (paperback)
ISBN: 1 85383 499 8 (hardback)

Typesetting by Composition & Design Services, Minsk, Belarus
Printed and bound by Biddles Ltd, Guildford and King's Lynn
Cover design by Andrew Corbett
Cover photograph © Brett Elof/Panos Pictures

For a full list of publications, please contact:

Earthscan Publications Ltd
120 Pentonville Road
London N1 9JN
Tel: 0171 278 0433
Fax: 0171 278 1142
email: earthinfo@earthscan.co.uk
http://www.earthscan.co.uk

Earthscan is an editorially independent subsidiary of Kogan Page Ltd and
publishes in association with WWF-UK and the International Institute for
Environment and Development

This book is printed on elemental chlorine free paper

Contents

List of Tables and Figures

Tables

Figures

List of Acronyms

AIDS	acquired immune deficiency syndrome
BPEO	best practicable environmental option
DDT	dichlorodiphenyltrichloroethane
DEP	Department of Environmental Protection (US)
DNA	deoxyribonucleic acid
DOE	Department of Energy (US)
DTI	Department of Trade and Industry (UK)
EDB	ethylene dibromide
ELM	elaboration likelihood model
EPA	Environmental Protection Agency (US)
EU	European Union
G7	group of seven leading industrialized nations
GPA	generalized Procrustes analysis
MAU	Multiattribute Utility Theory
NFI	Normed Fit Index
NGO	non-governmental organization
PET	polyethylene terephthalate
PLS	partial least squares
PPI	patient package insert
PUC	public utility commissions
RAPA	Risk Assessment and Policy Association (US)
SPSS	Statistical Package for the Social Sciences
SRA	Society for Risk Analysis
TMI	Three Mile Island (US)

Sources of Information

Chapter 2: The Psychometric Paradigm

Slovic, P (1987) 'Perception of Risk' *Science*, vol 236, 17 April, pp280–285

Chapter 3: The Social Construction of Risk

Shrader-Frechette, K (1990) 'Scientific Method, Anti-Foundationalism and Public Decision Making' *Risk: Health Safety and Environment*, vol 1, no 1, pp23–41

Chapter 4: Risk Comparisons

Freudenburg, W R and Rursch, J A (1994) 'The Risks of "Putting Numbers in Context": A Cautionary Tale' *Risk Analysis*, vol 14, no 6, pp949–958
Roth, E, Morgan, G M, Fischhoff, B, Lave, L and Bostrom, A (1990) 'What Do We Know About Making Risk Comparisons?' *Risk Analysis*, vol 10, no 3, pp375–387

Chapter 5: Cultural Theory

Rayner, S and Cantor, R (1987) 'How Fair is Safe Enough? The Cultural Approach to Societal Technology Choice' *Risk Analysis*, vol 7, no 1, pp3–9
Sjöberg, L (1997) 'Explaining Risk Perception: An Empirical Evaluation of Cultural Theory' *Risk Decision and Policy*, vol 2, no 2, pp113–130
Wildavsky, A and Dake, K (1990) 'Theories of Risk Perception: Who Fears What and Why?' *Dædalus*, vol 119, no 4, pp41–60

Chapter 6: From Risk Perception to Risk Communication

Fischhoff, B (1995) 'Risk Perception and Communication Unplugged: Twenty Years of Process' *Risk Analysis*, vol 15, no 2, pp137–145

Chapter 7: The Importance of the Media and the Social Amplification of Risk

Burns, W J, Slovic, P, Kasperson, R, Kasperson, J X, Renn, O and Emani, S (1993) 'Incorporating Structural Models into Research on the Social Amplification of Risk: Implications for Theory Construction and Decision Making' *Risk Analysis*, vol 13, no 6, pp611–623

Kasperson, R E, Renn, O, Slovic, P, Brown, H S, Emel, J, Goble, R, Kasperson, J X and Ratick, S (1988) 'The Social Amplification of Risk: A Conceptual Framework' *Risk Analysis*, vol 8, no 2, pp177–187

Chapter 8: Trust

Frewer, L J, Howard, C, Hedderley, D and Shepherd, R (1996) 'What Determines Trust in Information About Food-Related Risks? Underlying Psychological Constructs' *Risk Analysis*, vol 16, no 4, pp473–486

Slovic, P (1993) 'Perceived Risk, Trust and Democracy' *Risk Analysis*, vol 13, no 6, pp675–682

Chapter 9: Mental Models

Bostrom, A, Fischhoff, B and Morgan, G M (1992) 'Characterizing Mental Models of Hazardous Processes: A Methodology and an Application to Radon' *Journal of Social Issues*, vol 48, no 4, pp85–100

Jungermann, H, Schütz, H and Thüring, M (1988) 'Mental Models in Risk Assessment: Informing People About Drugs' *Risk Analysis*, vol 8, no 1, pp147–155

Chapter 10: Optimistic Bias or Unreal Optimism

Weinstein, N D (1989) 'Optimistic Biases About Personal Risks' *Science*, vol 246, 8 December, pp1232–1233

Chapter 11: Examples of What Social Scientists Can Do

Löfstedt, R E and Renn, O (1997) 'The Brent Spar Controversy: An Example of Risk Communication Gone Wrong' *Risk Analysis*, vol 17, no 2, pp131–136

Renn, O, Webler, T and Kastenholz, H (1996) 'Procedural and Substantive Fairness in Landfill Siting: A Swiss Case Study' *Risk: Health Safety and Environment*, vol 7, no 2, pp145–168

Preface

The purpose of this reader is to provide an up-to-date account of the recent research work within the risk field. It is a research area that has grown very rapidly over the last seven years, since the publication of the well-received *Readings in Risk* edited by T S Glickman and M Gough at Resources for the Future (Glickman and Gough, 1990). Since then, three new major risk journals (*Journal of Risk Research, Risk Decision and Policy* and *Risk: Health, Safety and Environment*) have been launched, and various risk organizations such as the US-based Risk Assessment and Policy Association (RAPA) have been established. Over these seven years, the field has expanded in a large number of different directions. In this book we have reprinted what we believe are some of the most influential articles of the past seven years, as well as several other articles which we believe are more practical in nature and which illustrate how the theoretical knowledge about risk analysis can be applied to real-life settings. The first chapter gives an overview of the social dimensions to risk management and summarizes some of the conceptual directions that the field has taken over the past ten years.

This overview is not all-encompassing. The debate about the term 'acceptable risk' versus 'tolerable risk' has been omitted (although the reader is referred to Pidgeon et al, 1992, for a good summary. We have also chosen not to review the discussion about the relative importance of 'perceived' versus 'real' risk (see Hood and Jones, 1996).

It is fair to say that the field has been dominated by the search for a 'holy grail': that is, research has been directed toward finding and applying a formula that can explain as well as predict the public's perceptions of different hazards. To date, the existence of such an explanatory model has been increasingly questioned. Various schools of thought have addressed the question at least in part. The psychometric paradigm provides explanations of some of the factors underlying public perceptions of risk, and has a certain amount of descriptive value. The social amplification of risk framework offers an explanation why some risks are amplified (that is, an increase in the perceived threat) but others are attenuated (that is, become less threatening). However, no theory or model, or indeed school of thought, has succeeded in adequately predicting how the public will perceive a particular hazard, or type of hazard. This is clearly the next theoretical goal in social risk research, a goal for risk researchers as we enter the new millennium. The question remains as to whether this goal will be achieved in the near future. Another research need is to be able to explain people's reactions by way of more sophisticated analyses of the social meanings of events involving risks of various kinds.

Ragnar E Löfstedt and Lynn Frewer
July 1998

Part One
Introduction

Chapter 1

Introduction

One of the most disputed issues in the modern-day social scientific approach of risk management revolves around the topic of when and where the first research in this area was published, marking the beginning of academic achievement in this exciting new area. One view is that social scientists began to find interest in the risk field following the pioneering work on the psychometric paradigm by Fischhoff, Lichtenstein and Slovic in the mid-1970s. This research was the psychologists' response to the engineer Chauncey Starr's seminal article 'Social benefit versus technological risk' (Starr, 1969). The research by Fischhoff and colleagues was underpinned by theories from within cognitive psychology, more specifically theories associated with heuristics (or decision rules) and cognitive biases (or selective processing of incoming information – Kahneman et al, 1982).

An alternative view is that the field is, in fact, considerably older. Its roots can be found in the 'Chicago School' of geography developed by White and later Burton and Kates (eg Burton et al, 1978; White, 1945). It was White who, in his doctoral thesis of 1945, tried to explain why flood damage on flood plains was increasing year after year, despite large financial investments in protective measures. The results showed that people's previous experience of floods directly influenced their behaviour when they were again under threat from a possible flood. Those who were living on a flood plain and who experienced floods year after year perceived a new and possibly increased flood threat as becoming less serious as time went on. Their reasoning was in line with the saying 'lightning never strikes twice'; local people discounted the threat from the hazard since the prospective flood was believed either not to happen, or could not be as devastating as the floods previously experienced. On the other hand, those with little or no previous experience of floods perceived the threat to be greater than those already exposed, and also expected more serious consequences from hazard exposure.

These findings led researchers to theorize that reactions to hazards were based on experiential factors. Human groups with different social, economic and cultural background characteristics, living in diverse geographical areas, would perceive risks in ways reflecting their knowledge and environment (Burton and Kates, 1964a and b; Burton et al, 1978; White, 1945 and 1961). People's responses were dependent both on their perception of the hazard and their knowledge of the ability of society, and the individual, to deal with that hazard (Burton et al, 1978).

The results and criticisms of this work have been discussed at length and will not be repeated here (eg Blaikie et al, 1994; Burton et al, 1992; Hewitt, 1983). However, the natural hazards school of thought has had considerable influence on the seminal work on technological hazards and should be considered in any discussion of the research area.

The Psychometric Paradigm

The next step of research into risk perception might be identified in the work of Starr, who employed historical analysis to gain an understanding of the degree of risk acceptance of different hazards. His research was driven by the need to understand society's previous responses to risk. A critical issue was whether or not responses to risk were considered voluntary and whether this factor of voluntary exposure had a significant relationship with the extent to which a hazard was accepted by the public (Starr, 1969).

Several psychologists criticized Starr's approach and developed an alternative model, that of 'expressed preferences'. Contrary to Starr's analysis, this approach did not 'reveal' what the societal response to risks could potentially be in the future through the process of direct historical investigation. Instead the emphasis was on the measurement of individual perceptions of risk, and judgements associated with different risk-related options. The research findings illustrated the importance of contextual factors such as perceived controllability, catastrophic potential, and dread as factors of risk perception, although perceived voluntariness of exposure was still deemed to be important (Fischhoff et al, 1978; Renn, 1990; Slovic, 1987).

The Social Construction of Risk

The results from this body of research dispelled a series of assumptions which had become prevalent in risk research. Experts themselves may be biased or at least motivated by self-serving interests and values. Thus the risk judgements of experts could not be regarded as 'absolute', and the beliefs of lay people could not be discounted in favour of expert opinions. Most participants in the risk debate have fundamentally different types of values and priorities which shape their definitions and judgements of risk and acceptability (Gould et al, 1988, p54), and this is likely to vary according to whether they are lay citizens or experts (Freudenburg, 1988; Lichtenstein and Fischhoff, 1977; Mazur, 1985). The hitherto strongly defended belief that there was such a thing as objective risk, and that the focus of risk communication must be to align public perceptions with this objective risk 'reality', was demonstrated to be inappropriate. Risk perception was now argued to be socially constructed (ie factors other than technical risk estimates guide the behaviours and actions of individuals regarding particular hazards (see Bayerische Ruck, 1993)).

Various factors such as perceived fairness, morality and meanings drive demand for risk mitigation and inform public policy on risk reduction.

Secondly, risk perception and risk-taking behaviour can be characterized and more fully understood if they are seen as judgements under uncertainty. The identification of an individual's best choice from several alternatives could be treated as the result of the application of rationalist or reductionist models of the world. Social constructionists, however, argue that the perceptions of risk are not 'irrational', but rather reflect the wider context of risk, such as a prioritized need to reduce the negative environmental effects of hazard exposure (Flynn et al, 1993; Jasanoff, 1993; Shrader-Frichette, 1990 and 1991; Wynne, 1992 and 1996).

Research on risk perception has been criticized for its lack of integration in the social and cultural context, and its impact on the institutional sphere (Hadari, 1987; Kunreuther et al, 1985). The use of survey methodology necessitates the use of questions thought to be important to the researchers. Respondents are forced to express opinions utilizing the rating scales provided in the questionnaire that employ psychological constructs which might seem strange or implausible, about which they know very little (Gould et al, 1988). In addition, some researchers feel that although the psychometric paradigm is well grounded empirically, there has been little theoretical advancement since the early 1980s (Pidgeon et al, 1992; Sjöberg, 1998).

Research within the psychometric paradigm has also been criticized as being based on too small sample sizes, leading to unrepresentative results, both within and between populations or groups. The theory was conceptually tested on various samples in different cultural settings and achieved similar results, most notably by Gould et al in 1988 (sample 1021) and Vleck and Stallen in 1981 (sample 679). The model is based on the firmly established psychological theory on cognition, founded in heuristics and biases (Kahneman and Tversky, 1974; Kahneman et al, 1982). Finally, the model is easily tested, an important characteristic for reliability of results, and possesses a pleasing plausible face validity. The strength of the model is its explanatory capacity. However, there is a need to develop predictive risk perception models, and it is this lack of predictive capacity which is the model's weakness.

Risk Comparisons

Another idea that has emerged from the psychometric research relates to the inappropriateness of making risk comparisons between different types of hazard. Such risk comparisons attempt to place unfamiliar risks in context by comparing them with more familiar risks. Problematically, this approach to risk research ignores one of the most important findings from the psychometric paradigm – that risk decisions are not driven by estimates of probabilities alone. Roth et al (1990) have criticized the use of such comparisons since they neglect the critical dimensions of risk-taking decisions. Such risk comparisons tend to reduce risks to relative positions along one single dimension (eg loss of life expectancy), whereas lay conceptualization of risk encompasses much more complex considerations. Freudenburg and Rursch (1994) have criticized the use of simple unidimensional risk comparisons on the basis that the wider social context in which risks are embedded is excluded. For example, opposition to controversial technologies to a large extent is driven by trust in those responsible for regulating the risks, not by relative risk estimates.

Furthermore, there is a growing body of evidence that the underlying concerns of the public which underpin risk perceptions may be uniquely linked to a particular hazard type or domain (Slovic et al, 1987). For example, perceptions of unnaturalness or 'tampering with nature' are one of the most important determinants of public reactions to genetic engineering – there is little point in making risk comparisons with the probability of 'being struck by lightning' if the determinants of what is fearful are very different for each of the two hazards (Frewer, Howard and Shepherd, 1997).

Given the problems of this type, risk researchers were looking beyond the psychometric paradigm by the end of the 1980s. The model, by now, had been replicated in many parts of the world and scientists were looking for new conceptual avenues to reach further understanding and knowledge. Risk research, since the empirical work performed by Starr in 1969, had been largely dominated by psychologists who were familiar with the normative methodology favoured by the psychometric paradigm, and had strong backgrounds in cognitive psychology. While the input into the area from anthropology continued, students with other disciplinary backgrounds began to contribute to the area. Social psychology, political science, sociology and geography now started to shape the directions that research into risk were taking. As the field progressed, and as more scientists (particularly in the United States) became involved in various research programmes, the multidisciplinarity of the area began to become more apparent and also more integrated. Researchers began to apply theories and ideas from other disciplines. Kasperson and his colleagues, for example, were inspired by political scientists such as Putnam (see Putnam, 1993; eg Kasperson et al, 1998), philosophers working on uncertainty provided inputs into the area (Funtowicz and Ravetz, 1990; eg Slovic, 1993) as did economists (eg Renn, 1998). Slowly, risk research has progressed away from the psychometric paradigm, incorporating insights from many disciplines (for an in-depth discussion on the type of work funded by the US-based National Science Foundation and how it progressed, the reader is referred to Golding, 1992).

It was at this stage that some of the theories that had been neglected during the rise of the psychometric paradigm began to reappear and be reconsidered as important. In particular, cultural theory has re-emerged as the focus of attention.

Cultural Theory

Cultural theory was originally developed by Mary Douglas, an anthropologist at University College, London, and her colleagues in the late 1970s and early 1980s. Cultural theory is seen as a way of categorizing people based on the notion of one of the areas that they value most, namely 'the set of social arrangements or institutions that they strongly identify or participate in' (Pidgeon et al, 1992, p112), in order to maintain a particular way of life. The theory of cultural bias, it is argued, predicts personal dispositions in the assessment of technological risks (ie which individuals view technology and emerging technology as largely benign, and which individuals perceive threat or risk to be associated with technology in general). These attitudes form a series of cultural biases. The individual differentially selects certain hazards as greater or lesser risks so that they are consistent with their predominant worldview (or perspectives on interpersonal relationships). Cultural biases (ie hierarchists, fatalists, individualists, egalitarians and those particularly concerned with the environment) reflect the different worldviews held by individuals (eg see Thompson et al, 1990). Ways of life are not necessarily stable through an individual's lifetime, but may be subject to change. However, if the predominant cultural bias of an individual can be quantified at any given time, it should be possible to predict what that individual perceives as risky at that juncture.

Individualists are in favour of self-regulation and the free market economy. Theoretically, they are more willing to accept the risks taken by society (which include development, expansion and regulation at the level of both industry and government) with respect to both technological advances and their potential impact on the environment. Individualists should distrust and dislike organizations, and oppose the development of technology on the basis of potential risks to society.

Hierarchists prefer a social organization where the maintenance of authority within the framework of social relationships is paramount. They should be predicted to be supportive of technological risk-taking at a societal level, provided that these risks are backed and controlled by the appropriate authority structures. From this, it follows that individuals scoring high in hierarchy should trust information provided by sources which are seen to maintain and support such authority structures.

Egalitarians value equality of outcome in the sense of diminishing distinctions between individuals in terms of economic inequalities and external characteristics (eg ethnicity and gender). They are predicted to perceive the dangers associated with technology to be great, both in environmental and socio-economic terms. Societal risk taking (eg in the application of potentially risky new technologies) will be rejected by those individuals with an egalitarian perspective. Trust in information sources should be biased towards those organizations or institutions that are seen to be primarily concerned with positive environmental or collective outcomes rather than with the expansion of market economies, and that are not perceived to hold vested interests that conflict with individual or organizational benefit.

Fatalists perceive societal and technological changes to be independent of any socially derived perspective. It has been hypothesized that individuals who are high in fatalism are excluded (or see themselves as excluded) from any formal organization of social life. Thus fatalists are unlikely to differentiate between potential hazards on the basis of the characteristics associated with the hazard (eg whether the hazard is highly technological or not).

The environment and technology worldview relates to the individual's attitude to the interaction between technological change and development, and environmental impact. Those individuals scoring high on this subscale express concern about the environmental effects of technological development, and oppose economic expansion if they perceive a likelihood of environmental damage. The predominant worldview can then be used to make predictions about an individual's tendency to fear technological risks – 'who fears what and why?'

The cultural theory of risk received quite a deal of curiosity and attention following the publication of the book *Risk and Culture* (Douglas and Wildavsky, 1982; for a good overview, see Rayner and Cantor, 1987 and Thompson et al, 1990). However, for several years after its publication, conceptual problems and difficulties in operationalizing the theory resulted in the cultural theory of risk getting an unfavourable reception by academia and policy makers. There are several reasons for this response. Firstly, there is no real reason why the model (typology) should be limited to four or five cultural biases; why can there not be six, eight or 18? (Johnson, 1987). Secondly, until the early 1990s no adequate empirical test of the theory had been carried out, although there had been several illustrative studies (eg Rayner, 1990). Thirdly, the concepts are said to be too unclear and vague to be efficiently tested. Fourthly, individuals, social groups or institutions can have more than one bias, thus making predictions regarding risk perception derived from membership of one group difficult (Johnson and Covello, 1987).

Empirical work from the late 1980s challenged this critique (Wildavsky and Dake, 1990). New results appeared to indicate that cultural theory was quantitatively testable, and the field received new interest within academia. In 1991, Dake published the results of such a test of the theory which showed a positive correlation between the cultural biases of hierarchists and individualists and the perception of taking risks. A positive correlation was uncovered between egalitarians who had a tendency to oppose technological risks (Dake, 1991). The results of the research seem to indicate a cleavage between egalitarian bias and the others.

The resulting interest in the theory, particularly in the United Kingdom, culminated in the publication of a new book on risk by John Adams which gave cultural theory another favourable review (Adams, 1995). The book sold well (more than 3000 copies) and resulted in a series of articles being published on the subject (eg Adams, 1997). In March 1997, the Royal Society organized a meeting in London on risk and society where cultural theory played a pivotal role. Since the mid 1990s, industry and environmental regulators have become increasingly interested in theoretical perspectives that could help to improve their understanding of public perception of risk. Cultural theory has now begun to be utilized in research within an industrial context, with what can only be described as mixed practical results (Wilkinson, 1997). Regulators have used cultural theory to explain public trust and distrust associated with the Environment Agency (Slater, 1997), and researchers in UK-based think-tanks such as Demos believe it useful for the understanding of poverty (6, 1997).

Outside the UK, the response to cultural theory has also been varied. In the United States there is some evidence of positive correlation between different cultural biases and risk perception (Peters and Slovic, 1996; Slovic et al, 1992). However, the evidence is not conclusive worldwide. In Norway the cultural theory of risk perception has been tested in two separate studies utilizing items referring to cultural bias in questionnaires. The explanatory power of cultural bias for public risk perception was only 5 per cent in the first study and 9 per cent in the second study (Grendstad, 1990; Grendstad and Selle, 1994). In France, several researchers have also attempted to operationalize the theory using these questionnaire items. In this case, the cultural items explained only 10 per cent of the total variance (Brenot et al, 1996).

Swedish research has also failed to demonstrate the predictive capacity of the theory. A series of studies conducted at the Stockholm School of Economics has shown that cultural bias items do not predict perceptions of technological risks better than other attitude scales such as environmental concern (eg see Sjöberg, 1996 and 1997). Finally, a critique of the theory from an anthropological point of view is provided by Boholm (1996), who identifies serious flaws in the theory itself.

Based on these recent findings, it is unclear whether cultural theory will aid researchers in answering the question 'who fears what and why?' Some North American and UK researchers are highly optimistic that cultural theory can add something to the understanding of public perception of technological risk, while others believe it is more of a trend that may appear interesting owing to intuitively perceived common sense but which is of little practical relevance.

From Risk Perception to Risk Communication

The natural outcome of understanding risk perception is the development of effective risk communication about different potential hazards. There are certain ethical constraints in the area of risk communication which must be addressed during programme development. For some potential hazards (eg lifestyle behaviours such as smoking) there is no ethical reason for using persuading methods to get people to reduce risk exposure. For other types of hazard (eg the introduction of genetically modified food) such persuasive tactics are inappropriate – ideally the emphasis should be on effective risk–benefit communication which allows members of the public to make informed choices about risk exposure.

During the late 1980s, many researchers began to experiment with the application of some of the findings of risk perception research to risk communication (see National Research Council, 1989; Stern, 1991). While risk communication cannot be defined as an independent discipline, it is perhaps best described as 'the flow of information and risk evaluations back and forth between academic experts, regulatory practitioners, interest groups, and the general public' (Leiss, 1996, page 86). At its best, risk communication is not a top-down form of communication from expert to the lay public, but rather a constructive dialogue between all those involved in a particular debate about risk.

Risk communicators are represented by two broad categorizations – practitioners and theoreticians. The practitioners develop ideas based on theories of risk perception to provide practical advice to industry and government on how they can effectively communicate with the concerned public about particular hazards. In order to develop such practical guidelines, it is necessary first to develop a conceptual framework which can assimilate the various factors which determine effective risk communication.

Outcomes of Risk Communication Studies: Conceptual Angles

To date, the outcomes of the various risk communication programmes implemented in Europe and the United States have been ineffective. The public tend to remain hostile to the local siting of waste incinerators and nuclear waste dumps, a public reaction which has not been influenced by the implementation of risk communication programmes (Adler and Pittle, 1984; Cvetkovich et al, 1986; Slovic and MacGregor, 1994). While in part such responses might be attributable to the practical problems associated with the lack of funding of risk communication programmes and, from this, failure to conduct proper evaluations (Kasperson and Palmlund, 1987; Chess et al, 1995a and b), due account must also be taken of the inability of practitioners to understand that they have to work together with the public rather than simply 'educate' them (Fischhoff, 1995; Leiss, 1996).

Researchers, frustrated by the lack of both practical and academic success of the various risk communication initiatives, have tried to identify underlying conceptual reasons why these programmes have failed. Among the factors that have received the greatest attention are those of the social amplification of risk, the role of trust and the importance of mental models held by those to whom risk communication is directed (for excellent reviews, see Fischhoff, 1995; Leiss, 1996). The potential impact of these factors is discussed in the next section.

The Importance of the Media and the Social Amplification of Risk

The relationship between media representation of risks and associated public perceptions of these same risks (and their impact on behaviour) is complex. For example, the health and risk communication literature suggests that mass-media channels are more likely to influence judgements about risks for society, as opposed to personal level risk judgements (Coleman, 1993). The theory of 'agenda setting' assumes that the media do not directly influence what the public think, but are successful in making issues salient or significant. An elaboration of the agenda setting theory, called the 'quantity of coverage theory', assumes that increased coverage not only makes the risk salient, but also turns public opinion in a negative direction, independent of the nature of the risk reporting itself. 'Cultivation theory' predicts that media exposure will increase the fear of hazards in proportion to the degree of exposure (Gerbner and Gross, 1976). Many communication campaigns have assumed that subjective perceptions will accommodate scientific perspectives and judgements as a result of media exposure (Liu and Smith, 1990). However, contextual, content and social factors also play a part in mediating responses to risk information.

There are two major issues associated with the coverage of hazards and associated information in the media. These issues reflect both the assessment of the extent of the coverage as well as the risk content itself. It is essential that both these issues are addressed if the relationship between the media and risk perception is to be understood fully.

Mazur and Lee (1993) argue that negative public reactions are not the result of critical reporting or negative bias in news coverage, but rather of the sheer amount of coverage in the media. The theory of 'agenda setting' assumes that the media do not directly influence what the public thinks, but are successful in making issues salient to the public. In support of this hypothesis, Mazur (1987) noted that the intensity of public concern is directly related to the amount of reporting, even if the overall tone of the coverage is positive. From a cognitive psychological perspective, simple but frequently repeated messages are likely to result in the formation of an 'availability heuristic', or establishment of an internal rule that signifies potential danger (Tversky and Kahnemann, 1984).

The theory about the social amplification of risk (Kasperson et al, 1988) takes into account the integration of different models of risk perception and risk communication. 'The social amplification of risk is based on the thesis that events pertaining to hazards interact with psychological, social, institutional and cultural processes in ways that can heighten or attenuate individual and social perceptions of risk and shape risk behaviour' (Renn, 1991). The social amplification process itself is made possible by the occurrence of a risk-related event (an event of physical nature) or by a potential for a risk-related event, which has some kind of substantive or hypothetical reality (Kasperson et al, 1988). The risk-related event is selected by a 'transmitter', in most cases the mass media or an interpersonal network, which amplifies or attenuates the risk. The transmission is then continued by members of, or institutions within, society who may also attenuate or amplify the risk into a message (the so-called 'ripple effect'). Such messages lead to secondary effects, which might be financial, such as rises in insurance rates; affective, such as anti-technology feelings; or economic, such as a decline in tourist activity.

Social amplification is underpinned by theoretical models which seek to identify factors that determine what society actually defines as a risk, what society does not define as a risk, and the resulting rationality of the public's response to the risk-related event and associated transmission of risk relevant information.

At the time of publication of this Reader, the contribution of social amplification concepts to risk research is only beginning to be understood fully, as the theoretical perspective is comparatively new, although new research is identifying key issues driven by the initial concept (eg Burns et al, 1993). There have, however, been at least three empirical tests of the social amplification model, which suggests that at least some of the underlying causes and factors influencing social response can be explained within its framework (Freudenburg, 1992; Machlis and Rosa, 1989; Renn et al, 1992). The concept has also been applied in a more qualitative way to help explain a series of past crises. For example, risk amplification is succinctly demonstrated by the case of the localized radioactive contamination experienced in Goiânia, Brazil. The erroneous and illicit opening of a cesium 137 canister from a cancer therapy machine caused 250 people to be contaminated by radiation. Of these, four died. However, the incident led to a social amplification effect which had far greater economic and social impacts and reached beyond the radioactive contamination itself. One effect was a 50 per cent decline in agricultural output in the area resulting from decreased market demands. Cars with Goiânia licence plates were stoned as being readily identifiable as potentially contaminated by radiation (Kasperson and Kasperson, 1996).

Risk attenuation has also been observed and recorded. A vivid account of how risks can be attenuated socially is provided by the case of the Sahel famine in Ethiopia. This catastrophe was all but ignored by the media and, indeed, the wider public, until the height of the crisis in 1984 when it was finally recognized on an international level (Kasperson and Kasperson, 1996).

The model has received some criticism, primarily related to the simplicity of the mechanisms of risk amplification and risk attenuation. Firstly, the occurrence of a risk-related event itself is partially determined by a series of interactive processes (Pidgeon et al, 1992, p115) while others argue that the model is far too mechanistic and ignores the importance of social construction of risk (Boholm, 1998). Furthermore, the process of amplification or attenuation in itself is likely to provoke further responses. 'Feedback' within the processes in attenuating or amplifying an event also needs to be explored further (Renn, 1991).

Freudenburg et al (1996) question whether the mass media do, in fact, 'blow risks out of proportion'. The alternative argument is that the media minimize the kinds of reporting that may disturb the operation of large-scale industries. The authors report that, in terms of the actual coverage of different hazards, the most important effect in increased coverage derives from the levels of objective information, such as the numbers of casualties or the actual level of damage. However, 'keynote' effects, such as headlines and photographs, which are relatively independent of 'objective' risk information, are more influential in influencing the emotional tone of the risk report and, by implication, the risk perception of the hazard. It should also be noted that political orientation and co-existing attitudes may determine individuals' selection of risk messages (Eiser et al, 1990). Thus it is likely that public responses to media reporting of risk will depend on individual differences in already held risk perceptions, as well as what actually is reported.

Trust

One of the most likely explanations for the failures of risk communication initiatives is that reactions to risk communication are not only influenced by message content (ie what is communicated about risks (and indeed benefits) of particular hazards) but also by trust in those responsible for providing the information (Earle and Cvetkovich, 1995; Kasperson et al, 1992; Leiss, 1996; Renn and Levine, 1991; Slovic, 1993; Slovic and MacGregor, 1994). Failure to implement risk communication programmes successfully often results from public distrust of policy makers and industrial officials owing to credibility problems, past history or social alienation (see Löfstedt and Horlick-Jones, 1998). Owing to the recent theoretical developments in the trust area, risk researchers are arguing that the entire field has entered a new dimension (Fischhoff, 1995 and 1996; Leiss, 1996).

Leiss points out that in the early stages of risk communication, between 1975 and 1984, the main concern of the technical experts was to provide accurate numerical information. It was believed that if correct risk estimates were made, the public would believe in what the experts had to say and in what they did recommend solely on the basis of their expertise. However, significant public opposition to risk-based decision making resulted in experts expressing an 'open contempt toward the public perception of risk', which was discounted as being irrational (Leiss, 1996, p88). This would result in further distrust in these experts by the public, who would view their actions as arrogant, self-serving and reflecting a 'hidden agenda' of vested interests. Today, experts realize that public trust is extremely important if they are to achieve effective risk communication, and indeed the area has received much attention from both theoreticians and practitioners in the field.

Trust, once lost, is very difficult to regain (Slovic, 1993). It is far easier to destroy trust than to build it, particularly as negative (trust-undermining) events tend to take the form of specific events or accidents, whereas positive (trust-building) events are more often fuzzy or indistinct. Concern about the loss of public trust in risk regulators, risk communicators, and indeed science in general, has resulted in increased interest in the role more generally of trust and distrust in society. Barber (1983) has identified some of the reasons that he thought contributed to a decline in trust in science (and the professions more generally). He suggested, for example, that the increased influence that professions have over people's welfare, a greater value placed on equality and a better educated public all contributed to this trend. The political issue of who makes important decisions for others is central to recent discussions of reactions to potential technological hazards (Beck, 1992). There appears to be belief within the policy-making community that a greater understanding of the trust causing/destroying phenomena could contribute to resolving social, environmental and political problems.

A lack of trust towards policy makers and industrial officials is seen to cause difficulties in siting hazardous industrial plants and installations (eg the siting of a nuclear waste dump in Nevada (Rosa et al, 1993)), and in managing environmental crises (eg chemical spills and the proposed decommissioning of Brent Spar). Research indicates that the public believe that governments work closely with industry, and the latter may be seen as possessing a vested interest in putting forward a particular point of view. This in turn causes public distrust in regulation and legislative controls (Kunreuther et al, 1993; Linnerooth-Bayer and Fitzgerald, 1996; Macfarlane, 1993). Inappropriate handling of crises may lead to further loss of trust in the risk regulators. Failure to develop the most effective risk-communication strategies clearly has profound financial implications, as well as a 'policy cost'. In fact, researchers have shown that controversies such as Brent Spar decrease the public's trust and confidence in policy makers (Löfstedt and Renn, 1997), and the cumulative effect of the crises is an increasing inability of policy makers to handle situations effectively (Freudenburg, 1996).

These controversies have caused serious problems for the waste and chemical industries in North America and Europe. It is becoming increasingly difficult to site and build a wide array of installations, including hazard waste-disposal facilities and ordinary waste incinerators (eg Löfstedt, 1997; Petts, 1995), sewage treatment plants and power stations. These difficulties, to some extent, may be explained by a decline in public trust. In the United States, where around 300 million tons of hazardous waste are produced per year (Field et al 1996), no large free-standing hazardous waste facility has been sited anywhere since 1980 (Piller, 1991; Rabe, 1994).

It is even becoming difficult to site and build renewable energy plants in some nations owing to public opposition (Hargreaves, 1996).

Several explanations have been provided for the increase in distrust in society today. Among the more interesting reasons are the importance of globalization, the development of the 'risk society', civic engagement and the role of credibility.

Globalization and the Risk Society

There is a long history in the relationship between capitalism, individualism and trust. Macfarlane points out that as early as in the 13th century in England, the area was characterized by 'rampant individualists, highly mobile both geographically and socially, economically "rational", market oriented and acquisitive, and ego-centred in kinship and social life' (Macfarlane, 1979, p58, quote taken from Seligman, 1997). For the market to work, trust had to be present. Individuals who are no longer part of their traditional social groupings have to trust each other in order to ensure that the market transactions that they are involved in are successful (Seligman, 1997, p89). Hence, the growth of modernity was dependent on mutual trust.

In more recent years, the studies conducted in the field of trust have increasingly focused on the role of globalization. There is a notion that the role of globalization has made society more complex and more difficult to understand, forcing individuals to rely more on policy makers, industrial officials and other authorities. The public of today are forced to trust various types of experts in order to cope. These ideas are brought to the forefront by Giddens in his book *The Consequences of Modernity*. According to Giddens, modernity refers to 'modes of social life or organisation which emerged in Europe from about the seventeenth century onwards and which subsequently became more or less worldwide in their influence' (Giddens, 1990, p1). He argues that the factors that make up modernity include:

- The separation of time and space which leads to individuals being able to break free from local habits and conditions, as well as to the setting up of organizations and the formation of history owing to standardized dating systems (Giddens, 1990, pp20–21).
- The importance of disembedding: which refers to the 'lifting out of social relations from local contexts and their restructuring across indefinite spans of time-space' (Giddens, 1990, pp21–29).
- The role of reflexive reappropriation of knowledge based on the continuous influx of new information (Giddens, 1990, p15).

When these three factors are taken together, trust, Giddens argues, has to play an important role. No longer can the individual fall back on tradition as was once possible in a pre-modern society (Giddens, 1994a and b). Tradition was associated with pervasive order (see Etzioni, 1996, ppxvi–xx), where individuals had few rights and no real individual autonomy as they were governed by church, war lords and nobility. In such situations honour and faith were seen as of the utmost importance (see Seligman, 1997, p54) and trust was not needed. Today, individuals have rights and exercise autonomy. Religion plays little role and the nobility has been largely disempowered. There is no strict order, but rather a loose one based on democratic principles, to which each one of us has to abide. In such societies, trust must play a large role. Giddens argues that no longer can the individual rely on the knight in the village, as in feudal days, to protect him or her. Rather the individual must establish his or her social networks and establish trust with the members of these networks, and with a series of experts and policy makers who maintain present-day order (an effect termed 'disembedding'). This becomes further complicated by the fact that as modernity has progressed, so has the large amount of communication available increased the knowledge of the lay person. This lay knowledge, argues Giddens (1990, pp130–131), leads to an individual's awareness that they have limited expertise and that they must trust experts who act on their behalf (see also Shapiro, 1987). However, doing so creates the danger of experts monopolizing knowledge. Experts do not always know what is right or wrong and care should be taken when such responsibility is conferred to such individuals (Beck, 1994). Barber is not worried that experts will take complete control, as he believes that the public has ultimate power. In a democratic system, policy makers can only rule and experts can only be experts if the public has a vested trust in them. Barber takes the view that the more trust the public has in policy makers, the more power is possessed by policy makers (Barber, 1983; see also Gamson, 1968, Parsons, 1969).

Similarly, in pre-modern societies response to events, or reflexivity, was limited to interpreting and reinterpreting the tradition within that society (Giddens, 1990, pp36–45). However, the reflexivity of present-day social life, human practices, including technological intervention, are constantly changing forms and patterns as new information becomes available. In modern-day society the public has to shift its trust or belief from one set of ideas or notions to another in a short period in order to be in touch with society (eg changing from writing letters to sending faxes, to communicating by e-mail). Consequently, there has been a growing interest in the new as it is seen as better, at the expense of tradition, cultural values and history, although in effect the new is based in some form of cumulative knowledge, which is continuously revised.

Many researchers are worried that modernity is going too quickly. Beck, in his seminal book, *Risk Society*, argues that today risk is once again increasing as technology, largely owing to reflexive modernity, becomes inherently complex. Accidents and crises largely become unpredictable, and governments lose control of the regulatory structures which contain such accidents and crises (Beck, 1992). In such situations, some researchers state, and many policy makers have been led to believe, that there will be some form of backlash to modernity toward traditionalism, whereby society is less complex and trust relations are easy to formulate.

Civic Engagement

There is a belief among some academics that an increase in public engagement in the decision-making process is the ground for an improved civic society in which trust toward local and national governments is increased, as is economic growth (Fukuyama, 1995; Putnam, 1993). Civic societies are seen as 'agents of social reintegration' (Misztal, 1996, p211) where civic engagement may be likened to a cement that makes both democracy and the market work (Wolfe, 1989). Whether civic engagement is important for developing a trustworthy society is a hypothesis currently being tested in the United States by Putnam (Putnam, 1995a and b).

Credibility and Trust

Trust relies on competence and credibility. If policy makers are seen as competent and credible, there is a high likelihood that they are also trusted (Barber, 1983; Lee, 1986; Renn and Levine, 1991). Barber points out that the public are rational when they distrust policy makers, professionals or industry that act incompetently. Rational distrust toward policy makers is therefore a way of maintaining democratic control of authority (Barber, 1983, pp169–170). For policy makers to be seen as credible they have to have an acquired reputation (Arrow, 1974; Dasgupta, 1988; Fukuyama, 1995; Putnam, 1993; Seligman, 1997).

Renn and Levine have identified five crucial specific components that determine people's trust: competence, objectivity, fairness, consistency and faith (Renn and Levine, 1991, pp179–180). The basis of these five components is that trust is largely based on historical experience. An individual will trust a regulatory body or industry depending on how it has acted in the past. If a company has a good track record in terms of safety, reliability and public relations, the chances are high that the public trusts the company; this was clearly depicted in a case study in Sweden. The majority of the public in Malmö largely felt that the nearby nuclear power station was safe as they 'trusted Swedish industry' (Löfstedt, 1996), implying that the plant is safe because Swedish industry as a whole is seen to be trustworthy.

There is some evidence that the formative factors related to trust are very different from those associated with distrust (Frewer et al, 1996). Trusted sources are perceived to be both knowledgeable and concerned with public welfare. Distrusted sources are perceived to distort information, to have been proven wrong in the past, and to provide biased information. Trust is also associated with moderate accountability. Too much accountability and the source is perceived to be prevented from 'telling the truth'. Too little accountability, and the source is perceived to sensationalize risk information. Improved credibility is likely to result from increased transparency in the regulatory process, as in so doing it disassociates from potential vested interests.

The social psychological literature provides various models of attitude change which offer some theoretical explanation of the effect of trust. Petty and Cacioppo (1984) have extensively studied the area of persuasion and the impact of information and communication on attitude change. The elaboration likelihood model (or ELM) represents an extremely influential social psychological theory of persuasive communication. The model proposes that there are two routes to persuasion – the 'central' route and the 'peripheral' route. The central route involves the receiver of risk communication engaging in in-depth processing of the incoming information. Utilization of the peripheral route is influenced by the external cues surrounding the information. These external cues may result in the receiver of the information making assumptions about the accuracy of the informational content, and discounting the information, without recourse to processing.

There is considerable support within the social psychological literature to support this model (Eagly and Chaiken, 1993). Perceived honesty of the source has been shown to be a factor providing accurate message contents. Communicator bias might be perceived to be associated with 'knowledge' where the source is perceived to have known too little about the 'facts' to provide accurate information, but is essentially perceived to be honest or associated with 'reporting' (where there is a perception that information is systematically distorted to promote a particular view or self-interest of the communicator) (Eagly et al, 1978). From this it can be predicted that source credibility may play an important part in determining whether central or peripheral processing occurs (Liska, 1978). High credibility is likely to facilitate central processing; low credibility will act as an external cue, resulting in peripheral processing and failure to change attitudes. The utility of the model as applied to risk communication has been demonstrated; reactions to risk information have been found to be dependent on perceived hazard characteristics as well as source characteristics (Frewer et al, 1997).

Other researchers question the importance of trust and credibility in risk communication. Margolis, in his critical analysis of the research done in the field of social science on risk, points out that public perception of government institutions with high credibility, such as the US Food and Drug Administration and the USEnvironmental Protection Agency (EPA), does not differ significantly from government institutions with low credibility, such as the US Department of Energy (Margolis, 1996, pp29–30). Although public opinion polls show that there are high levels of trust toward doctors and scientists (Davis and Smith, 1994), the public are still highly sceptical of reports from these bodies regarding the regulation of various risks.

There are several problems with such arguments. Firstly, it is unclear whether the public are able to differentiate between different government departments in the US. There is also some confusion as to whether the US EPA really is seen as a very credible institution. As Landy et al (1994) point out, the agency has made a series of mistakes in risk communication in the past 20 years. Even if the agency maintains high credibility with the public, effective risk communication will only result if the communication is about hazards which the agency is perceived competent to communicate about. Furthermore, the discussion surrounding public trust of doctors and scientists is not straightforward. Some types of scientists are trusted more than others (eg scientists working for non-governmental organizations such as Greenpeace are seen to be more trustworthy than scientists working for industry). The perceived credibility of scientists and governments greatly influences the effectiveness of communicating complex information on hazards to lay people. Scientific risk information may also need to be supplemented by situational knowledge that is relevant to the specific subpopulation affected by the hazard (Shrader–Frichette, 1990 and 1991; Wynne, 1992). Account should also be taken of the general decline in trust in science which has occurred since the 1950s and the series of incidents that have occurred indicating that technology is out of control. For example, the catastrophes involving DDT, thalidomide, Three Mile Island and Chernobyl also have symbolic values suggestive of the inherent dangers of advanced technologies as an apocalyptic threat to humanity – eg Beck, 1992 and 1995.

In addition, information on hazards which are associated with controversy, and where scientific opinion is divided (eg global warming or genetic modification), tends to be perceived as less trustworthy. Source characteristics are seen to align with public perceptions about the hazard, rather than these perceptions being determined by trust in the source itself (Frewer et al, in press).

Mental Models

Papers addressing the task of integrating methodologies to help the designer of risk communication choose and analyse the content, structure and organization of communication began to appear in the late 1980s (eg see Bostrom et al, 1992; Bostrom et al, 1994; Jungerman et al, 1988 and Roth et al, 1990). Research in this area was largely derived from theoretical perspectives on text comprehension and mental models. In particular, the effort was made to avoid the problems associated with attempts of technical experts to make predictions in any systematic way about the informational needs and gaps in the technical knowledge of lay people.

The three most important factors associated with this approach are, firstly, that the recipient of a communication needs a certain amount of basic information regarding technical risk in order to make decisions regarding exposure or risk mitigation. Existing beliefs about risks are likely to influence how information is interpreted. The text structure which surrounds the information is itself important in the process of interpretation (Atman et al, 1994). This was probably the first research which addressed the importance of text structure, and made reference to the more general psychological and linguistic literature on text comprehension. It was recognized that effective risk communication must both identify what information is missing from the mental model held by lay people and also state clearly what is wrong in terms of beliefs about the science underpinning risk evaluation and exposure. The research was important in that it addressed the issue of information salience – unless risk communication addressed both the underlying and realistic concerns of people's beliefs about risks, people were likely to discount information as either being salient to themselves personally or as rather uninteresting. This strand of risk research is developing, and promises to yield fruitful results in the future in terms of identification of misconceptions regarding various kinds of risks, as well as with regard to the development of methodologies for identifying appropriate text formats for conveying risk information.

Optimistic Bias or Unreal Optimism

A further area of great interest in predicting individual responses to particular risks and hazards involves the investigation of the phenomenon of 'optimistic bias' or 'unreal optimism'.

Weinstein (1980) identified this risk-related phenomenon, whereby individuals believe that while risk events do occur with some degree of negative effect, these events are relatively unlikely to harm them personally. People perceive that they themselves are relatively invulnerable to a particular hazard, but that others are more likely to be effected (Weinstein, 1989). Individuals appear to have a low estimate of the probability of an occurrence of the negative outcomes of risks affecting the self. This effect is reversed for positive events, where perceived probability is increased. This biased understanding of the personal applicability of risk appears to affect only the self, or indeed, may be reversed when it is applied to other people. The relationship between anxiety (and depression) and perceptions of perceived lack of personal control have been long established (Seligman, 1975).

It has been argued that optimistic bias is better explained as the need by an individual for control over a situation; perceived personal control over a potential hazard reduces the subjective probability of personal risk associated with the hazard. This effect has been termed the 'illusion of control'.

McKenna (1993) notes that there is a problem with this concept, since an individual may hold an optimistic view about the occurrence of a particular hazard, while exercising no personal control over the probability of the event occurring. This indicates that for those hazards where personal control is not conceptually feasible, the 'illusion of control' is conferred on to regulatory or external organizational structures within society. For societal risks of this type, personal risk perceptions should be the same as for other people, as there is no evidence available to the individual which could suggest that such regulatory structures protect them especially. However, the concept of societal risk may involve effects, such as environmental impact, which do not necessarily adversely influence the well-being of individuals.

'Optimistic bias' has been identified as one of the most important barriers to effective risk communication, particularly for risk communication directed at health. Clearly people will not attend to messages about health if they believe that these messages are directed towards vulnerable others who are really at risk. Even for a lifestyle hazard like smoking, for example, people tend to maintain an optimistic bias by selecting other more vulnerable smokers as their comparison group.

However, the true impact of 'optimistic bias' on risk-related decision making is not really understood and the actual impact that such optimistic biases have on lifestyle decisions merits further investigation. In any case, the underlying psychological determinants of personal risk perception may be very different from the perceptions of risk to the average person, and these need to be understood before the causes and likely effects of 'optimistic bias' can be truly identified.

How Can Social Scientists Contribute to Risk Management?

Over the past ten years, a new industry has developed with the aim of providing advice to policy makers and industry on how to manage risks better, and how to avoid controversies and conflict with the public on risk issues. Increasingly the research base for this work emerges from within academia and implies direct transfer of research skills from risk communication theory to risk communication practice.

Thus the conceptual work being conducted by social science risk researchers at the present time has a high degree of practical relevance for both industry and governments. It is highly likely that foundations such as the UK Economic Social Research Council and research bodies of the European Union will continue to demand more practical oriented work with positive benefits for UK/European economic competitiveness, work that will make the ties between social science risk researchers, industry and government even tighter. However, it is important that the social scientific theory underpinning the understanding of risk perception and risk communication can be refined and developed further. This is a necessary condition if technology transfer to the real world of policy formulation and industrial risk management is to continue to be as effective as it was in the past.

A good example of such work revolves around what Stirling calls 'crisis of confidence' (eg Stirling, 1997 and 1998) where risk assessment and risk management techniques have to be improved in order to make them publicly acceptable. The reason for this crisis is that the public are becoming increasingly distrustful of industry and government (see Credibility and Trust, pp15–17) and today are unwilling simply to accept the use of expert judgements in the formulation of risk assessments. Such techniques are currently being developed and they include the wider use of both citizen juries and citizen panels (eg Renn et al, 1995 and 1996), as well as the greater use of risk characterization with inputs from the public, non-governmental organizations and scientists in the formulation of the criteria for the risk assessment process itself (National Research Council, 1996). These types of techniques are increasing in popularity, especially in countries such as Germany where it is becoming increasingly difficult to build and site 'noxious facilities' (Renn et al, 1995), and to a certain extent the use of citizen panels and juries has resulted in increased public trust in the siting process (eg Löfstedt, 1998).

Conclusion: What is the Future of Risk Research?

We believe that the field of social science research will continue to develop in various different conceptual directions, both of theoretical relevance and applied importance. These concerns are identified below.

The model of the social amplification of risk, long heralded as one of the most interesting innovative theoretical frameworks of the late 1980s, needs to be further tested empirically to examine the practical relevance and conceptual usefulness of the model. It has been noted that 'the framework will ultimately stand or fall on its ability to generate specific hypotheses that can be subject to empirical test, and its ability to provide new insights on risk perception and communication' (Pidgeon et al, 1992, p116).

The issue of trust still merits a great deal of further empirical investigation. It is not currently known to what extent trust can explain the variance observed in public responses to risk communication interventions, nor to what extent these effects exhibit cross-cultural variability. The impact of credibility is also likely to vary between different types of hazard and intuitively will be more important for those hazards where risk control is conferred on to risk regulators, rather than being the responsibility of individual members of the community. The issue of distrust is also important. The question arises as to whether we should have a certain level of distrust in society, as this focuses public attention on the problems of risk management. Does distrust lead to better, safer, less hazardous societies? Finally, within the area of trust, further tests of the civic engagement hypothesis need to be carried out. Are societies that are more 'civic' also more likely to trust regulators and policy makers?

Citizen panels and juries as well as the National Research Council's risk characterization process need to be further applied to present-day siting problems, particularly in countries such as the UK where these techniques have been largely ignored. Of particular concern is whether increasing the input of the general public and other stakeholders with the use of such methodologies can lead to more efficient as well as fairer and more equitable siting procedures.

There is also scope for extending research on social amplification effects. In particular, more research is needed in order to understand the dynamic shifts in perception and attitudes during crises. Such research must include an empirical examination of the relative importance of trust in those who are responsible for dealing with the risk crisis, which also emphasizes the need to explore further the issues of social trust. Two clear strands of research can be identified: the influence of the characteristics of information on effective communication about different types of potential hazard, and an empirical investigation of the importance of trust in those responsible for regulating risks associated with various kinds of hazards. Trust is likely to be particularly important where risk regulators and the providers of risk information are identical.

There are specific areas where further research into risk perception and risk communication is needed. In particular, little is known about the extent to which perceptions of risk generalize across cultures. This has clear implications for understanding public responses to transboundary risks, an area which merits further investigation, particularly for potential hazards such as the genetic modification of crops, where there are clear implications for the further exploration of intercultural differences (and indeed mutual views of risk perception) across cultures.

A further area which might well prove fruitful in the future is the relative importance of risk-related attitudes in decision-making processes. It is possible that some social environments tend to make decisions based on perceptions of risk avoidance (ie individuals have a preference for attainment of zero-risk exposure). In other cultures there might be a preference for decision making which maximizes benefits, and risk perceptions become less important. Research addressing these issues is likely to have a direct bearing on the development of effective risk communication within these different social environments.

Many disparate strands of risk research have been identified in our introductory chapter. These strands should be integrated into higher order models which can unify models of risk perception with models of risk communication. Such models on a higher level of abstraction must integrate different attitudinal factors and examine the relative impact of attitudinal components on risk perceptions and risk-taking behaviours. As well as assessing 'optimistic bias' effects, other beliefs salient to the self must be integrated with attitudinal data relating to risk perceptions (including the perceptions of risk deriving from not engaging in a particular behaviour or not developing a particular technology). Such models cannot ignore the perceived potential benefits associated with risk exposure (or avoidance). In addition, it is vital to identify and take account of other attitudinal factors of relevancy. Such models clearly need to be tested through the demonstration of their utility in a practical context and further refined in a 'real world' context.

Acknowledgements

We would like to thank Ian Christie, Tom Horlick-Jones, and Richard Shepherd for bringing various articles to our attention. We are particularly indebted to Åsa Boholm, Lennart Sjöberg and Andrew Stirling, who read through an earlier draft of this manuscript and who gave us numerous insightful and most useful comments. The remaining errors are our own.

References

Adams, J (1995) *Risk*, University College London Press, London
Adams, J (1997) 'What do mad cows, Brent Spar, the NHS, and contaminated land have in common?', in Bate, R (eds) *What Risk? Science, Politics, and Public Health*, Butterworth–Heinemann, London
Adler, R S and R D Pittle (1984) 'Cajolery or command: Are educational campaigns an adequate substitute for regulation?' in *Yale Journal on Regulation*, vol 1, pp159–193
Arrow, K (1974) *The Limits of Organization* Norton, New York
Atman, C J, A Bostrom, B Fischhoff and M G Morgan (1994) 'Designing risk communications: completing and correcting mental models of hazardous processes' Part 1 in *Risk Analysis*, vol 14, no 5, pp779–788

Barber, B (1983) *The Logic and Limits of Trust* Rutgers University Press, New Brunswick, New Jersey

Bayerische Ruck (1993) *Risk is a Construct* Bayerische Ruck, Munich, Germany

Beck, U (1992) *Risk Society* Sage, London

Beck, U (1994) 'The reinvention of politics: towards a theory of reflexive modernization' in U Beck, A Giddens, and S Lash (eds) *Reflexive Modernization: Politics, Tradition and Aesthetics in the Modern Social Order,* Polity Press, Cambridge

Beck, U (1995) *Ecological Politics in the Age of Risk* Polity Press, Cambridge

Blaikie, P, T Cannon, I Davis and B Wisner (1994) *At Risk: Natural hazards, people's vulnerability and disasters* Routledge, London

Boholm, A (1996) 'Risk perception and social anthropology: Critique of cultural theory' in *Ethnos,* vol 61, no 1–2, pp64–84

Boholm, A (1998) 'Visual images and risk messages: commemorating Chernobyl' forthcoming in *Risk Decision and Policy*

Bostrom, A, B Fischhoff and M G Morgan (1992) 'Characterizing mental models of hazardous processes: A methodology and an application to radon' in *Journal of Social Issues,* vol 48, pp85–100

Bostrom, A, C J Atman, B Fischhoff, and G M Morgan (1994) 'Evaluating risk communications: Completing and correcting mental models for hazardous processes, Part 2' in *Risk Analysis,* vol 14, pp789–799

Brenot, J, S Bonnefous, and C Mays (1996) 'Cultural theory and risk perception: Validity and utility explored in the French context' in *Radiation Protection Dosimetry,* vol 68, pp239–243

Burns, W J, P Slovic, R E Kasperson, J X Kasperson, O Renn, and S Emani (1993) 'Incorporating structural models into research on the social amplification of risk – implications for theory construction and decision-making' in *Risk Analysis,* vol 13, no 6, pp611–623

Burton, I and R W Kates (1964a) 'The perception of natural hazards in resource management' in *Natural Resources Journal,* vol 3, pp412–441

Burton, I and R W Kates (1964b) 'The flood plain and the seashore: A comparison analysis of a hazard zone occupance' in *Geographical Review,* vol 54, pp366–385

Burton, I, R W Kates and G F White (1978) *The Environment as Hazard,* Oxford University Press, New York

Burton, I, R W Kates and G F White (1992) *The Environment as Hazard* (2nd edition) Oxford University Press, New York

Chess, C, K L Salomone, B J Hance, A Saviile (1995a) 'Results of national symposium on risk communication: Next steps for government agencies' in *Risk Analysis,* vol 15, pp115–125

Chess, C, K L Salomone and B J Hance (1995b) 'Improving risk communication in government: Research priorities' in *Risk Analysis,* vol 15, pp127–135

Clarke, L and J F Short (1993) 'Social organization and risk: Some current controversies' in *Annual Review of Sociology,* vol 19, pp375–399

Coleman, C L (1993) 'The influence of mass-media and interpersonal-communication on societal and personal risk judgements' in *Communication Research,* vol 20, pp611–628

Cvetkovich, G T, G B Keren and T C Earle (1986) 'Prescriptive considerations for risk communications', paper presented at the meeting of the International Research Group on Risk Communication

Dake, K (1991) 'Orientating dispositions in the perception of risk: An analysis of contemporary worldviews and cultural biases' in *Journal of Cross Cultural Psychology*, vol 22, no 1, pp61–82

Dasgupta, P (1988) 'Trust as a commodity' in Gambetta, D (ed) *Trust: Making and Breaking of Cooperative Relations* Basil Blackwell, Oxford

Davis, J A and T W Smith (1994) *General Social Survey, 1972-1994: Cumulative Codebook* National Opinion Research Centre, Washington

Douglas, M and A Wildavsky (1982) *Risk and Culture*, University of California Press, Berkeley CA

Eagly, A H and S Chaiken (1993) *The Psychology of Attitudes*, Harcourt Brace Jovanovich, New York

Eagly, A, W Wood, and S Chaiken (1978) 'Causal inferences about communications and their effect on opinion change' *Journal of Personality and Social Psychology*, vol 36, pp424–435

Earle, T, and G Cvetkovich (1995) *Social Trust: Toward a Cosmopolitan Society* Praeger, Westport, CT

Eiser, J R, B Hannover, L Mann, M Morin, J Van Der Pligt, and P Webley (1990) 'Nuclear attitudes after Chernobyl: A cross-national study' in *Journal of Environmental Psychology*, vol 10, pp101–110

Etzioni, A (1996) *The New Golden Rule: Community and Morality in a Democratic Society* Profile Books, London

Field, P, H Raiffa and L Susskind (1996) 'Risk and justice: Rethinking the concept of compensation' in *The Annals of the American Academy of Political and Social Scienlce*, vol 545, pp156–164

Fischhoff, B (1995) 'Risk perception and communication unplugged: Twenty years of process' in *Risk Analysis*, vol 15, pp137–145

Fischhoff, B (1996) 'Public values in risk research' in *The Annals of the American Academy of Political and Social Science*, vol 545, pp75–84

Fischhoff, B, P Slovic, S Lichtenstein, S Read and B Combs (1978) 'How safe is safe enough? A psychometric study of attitudes towards technological risk and benefits' in *Policy Studies*, vol 9, pp127–152

Flynn, J, P Slovic and C K Mertz (1993) 'The Nevada initiative: A risk communications fiasco' in *Risk Analysis*, vol 13, no 5, pp497–502

Freudenburg, W R (1988) 'Perceived risk, real risk: Social science and the art of probabilistic risk assessment' in *Science* vol 242, pp44–49

Freudenburg, W R (1992) 'Nothing recedes like success? Risk analysis and the organizational amplification of risk' in *Risk: Issues in Health, Safety and Environment*, vol 3, no 1, pp1–35

Freudenburg, W R (1996) 'Risky thinking: irrational fears about risk and society' in *The Annals of the American Academy of Political and Social Science*, pp 44–53

Freudenburg, W R, C L Coleman, J Gonzales and C Helgeland (1996) 'Media coverage of hazard events – analysing the assumptions' in *Risk Analysis*, vol 16, pp31–42

Freudenburg, W R and J A Rursch (1994) 'The risks of putting the numbers in context – a cautionary tale' in *Risk Analysis*, vol 14, no 6, pp949–958

Frewer, L J, C Howard, D Hedderley and R Shepherd (1996) 'What determines trust in information about food-related risks? Underlying psychological constructs' in *Risk Analysis*, vol 16, no 4, pp473–486

Frewer, L J, C Howard, D Hedderley and R Shepherd (1997) 'The use of the elaboration likelihood model in developing effective food risk communication' in *Risk Analysis*, vol 17, no 6, pp269–281

Frewer, L J, C Howard and R Shepherd (1997) 'Public concerns about general and specific applications of genetic engineering: Risk, benefit and ethics' in *Science, Technology and Human Values,* vol 22, pp98–124

Frewer, L J, C Howard and R Shepherd (in press) 'The importance of initial attitudes on responses to communication about genetic engineering in food production' in *Agriculture and Human Values*

Fukuyama, F (1995) *Trust: Social Virtues and the Creation of Prosperity,* Free Press, New York

Funtowicz, S O and J R Ravetz (1990) *Uncertainty and Quality in Science for Policy,* Kluwer, Dordrecht

Gamson, W A (1968) *Power and Discontent* Dorsey Press, Homewood, Ill

Gerbner, G and L Gross (1976) 'Living with television: The violence profile' in *Journal of Communication,* vol 26, pp173–179

Giddens, A (1990) *The Consequences of Modernity,* Polity Press, Cambridge

Giddens, A (1991) *Modernity and Self-Identity,* Polity Press, Cambridge

Giddens, A (1994a) *Beyond left and right,* Polity Press, Cambridge

Giddens, A (1994b) 'Living in a post-traditional society' in U Beck, A Giddens and S Lash (eds) *Reflexive Modernisation,* Polity Press, Cambridge

Glickman, T S and M Gough (1990) *Readings in Risk,* Resources for the Future, Washington DC

Golding, D (1992) 'A social and pragmatic history of risk research' in S Krimsky and D Golding (eds) *Social Theories of Risk* Praeger, Westport, CT

Gould, L C, G T Gardner, D R DeLuca, A R Tiemann, L W Dobb and J A J Stolwijk (1988) *Perceptions of Technological Risks and Benefits* Russell Sage Foundation, New York

Grendstad, G (1990) *Europe by Cultures. An Exploration in grid/group analysis* Department of Comparative Politics, Bergen

Grendstad, G and P Selle (1994) *Comparing Theories of Political Culture in Explaining Environmental Attitudes* Norwegian Research Centre in Organisation and Management, Bergen

Hadari, S A (1987) 'What are preference explanations? The interpretive core of economic modelling' in *Social Science Quarterly,* vol 68, no 2, pp340–357

Hargreaves, D (1996) *An investigation into risk communication issues surrounding a proposal to site a 20MW straw-burning, electricity generating plant at Calne, Wiltshire* Department of Psychology, University of Surrey, Guildford

Hewitt, K (1983) *Interpretations of Calamity* Allen & Unwin, Boston

Hood, C and D K C Jones (1996) *Accident: and Design: Contemporary Debates in Risk Management* University College London Press, London

Jasanoff, S (1993) 'Bridging the two cultures of risk analysis' in *Risk Analysis,* vol 13, no 2, pp123–129

Johnson, B B (1987) 'The environmentalist movement and grid/group analysis: A modest critique' in B B Johnson and V T Covello (eds) *The Social and Cultural Construction of Risk* D Reidel Publishing Company, Dordrecht

Johnson, B B (1987) and V T Covello (1987) *The Social and Cultural Construction of Risk* Reidel, Dordrecht

Jungermaft, K, H Schutz and M Thuring (1988) 'Mental models in risk assessment: Informing people about drugs' in *Risk Analysis,* vol 8, no 1, pp147–155

Kahneman, D and A Tversky (1974) 'Judgment under uncertainty: Heuristics and biases' in *Science,* vol 185, pp1124–1131

Kahneman, D, P Slovic and A Tversky (1982) *Judgment Under Uncertainty: Heuristics and Biases,* Cambridge University Press, Cambridge

Kasperson, R E and J X Kasperson (1996) 'The social amplification and attenuation of risk' in *The Annals of the American Academy of Political and Social Science* vol 545, pp95–105

Kasperson, R E and I Palmlund (1987) 'Evaluating risk communication' in V T Covello, D B McCallum and M T Pavlova (eds) *Effective Risk Communication: The role and Responsibility of Government and Non-Government Organisations* Plenum, New York

Kasperson, R E, O Renn and P Slovic et al (1988) 'The social amplification of risk: A conceptual framework' in *Risk Analysis,* vol 6, pp177–187

Kasperson, R E, D Golding and S Tuler (1992) 'Siting hazardous facilities and communicating risks under conditions of high social distrust' in *Journal of Social Issues,* vol 48, pp161–172

Kasperson, R E, D Golding and J X Kasperson (1998) 'Risk, trust, and democratic theory' in G Cvetkovich and R E Löfstedt (eds) *Social Trust* Earthscan, London

Kunreuther, H C, W Sanderson and R Vetschera (1985) 'A behavioral model of the adoption of protective activities' in *Journal of Economic Behaviour Organisation* vol 6, pp1–15

Kunreuther, H, K Fitzgerald and T D Aarts (1993) 'Siting noxious facilities: A test of the siting credo' in *Risk Analysis,* vol 13, pp301–318

Landy, M K, M C Roberts and S R Thomas (1994) *The Environmental Protection Agency: Asking the Wrong Questions from Nixon to Clinton* Oxford University Press, New York

Lee, T R (1986) 'Effective communication of information about chemical hazards' in *The Science of the Total Environment,* vol 51, pp149–183

Leiss, W (1996) 'Three phases in the evolution of risk communication practice' in *Annals of the American Academy of Political and Social Science,* vol 545, pp85–94

Lichstenstein, S and B Fischhoff (1977) 'Do those who know more also know more about how much they know?' in *Organisation Behaviour and Human Performance,* vol 20, pp159–183

Linnerooth-Bayer, J and K B Fitzgerald (1996) 'Conflicting views on fair siting processes: Evidence from Austria and the US' in *Risk: Health, Safety and Environment* vol 7, pp119–134

Liska, J (1978) 'Situational and topical variations in credibility criteria' in *Communication Monographs* vol 45, pp85–92

Liu, J T and V K Smith (1990) 'Risk communication and attitude change: Taiwan's national debate over nuclear power' in *Journal of Risk and Uncertainty,* vol 3, pp331–349

Löfstedt, R E (1996) 'Risk communication: The Barsebäck nuclear plant case' in *Energy Policy,* vol 24, no 8, pp689–696

Löfstedt, R E (1997) 'Evaluation of two siting strategies: The case of two UK waste tire incinerators' in *Risk: Health, Safety and Environment,* vol 8, no 1, pp63–77

Löfstedt, R E (1998) *The role of trust in the north Blackforest: an evaluation of a citizen panel process* Centre for Technology Assessment in Baden-Württemberg, Stuttgart

Löfstedt, R E and Renn, O (1997) 'The Brent Spar controversy: An example of risk communication gone wrong' in *Risk Analysis,* vol 17, no 2, pp131–136

Löfstedt, R E and Horlick-Jones, T (1998) 'Environmental regulation in the UK: Politics, institutional change and public trust' in G Cvetkovich and R E Löfstedt (eds) *Social Trust* Earthscan, London

MacFarlane, A (1979) *The Origins of English Individualism: The Family, Prosperity, and Social Transition* Cambridge University Press, New York

MacFarlane, R (1993) 'The consumer voice in food safety' in FNA/ANA, vol 8/9, pp17–23

Machlis, G E and E A Rosa (1989) 'Desired risk and the social amplification of risk framework' in *Risk Analysis*, vol 10, pp161–168

Margolis, H (1996) *Dealing with Risk* Chicago University Press, Chicago

Mazur, A C (1985) 'Bias in risk-benefit analysis' in *Technology Society.* vol 7, pp25–30

Mazur, A (1987) 'Putting Radon on the public's risk agenda' in *Science, Technology and Human Values,* vol 23, no 12, pp86–93

Mazur, A and J Lee (1993) 'Sounding the global alarm: Environmental issues in the US national news' in *Social Studies of Science,* 23, pp681–720

McKenna, F P (1993) 'It won't happen to me: Unrealistic optimism or illusion of control?' in *British Journal of Psychology,* vol 84, pp39–50

Misztal, B A (1996) *Trust in Modern Societies* Polity Press, Cambridge

National Research Council (1989) *Improving Risk Communication* National Academy Press, Washington DC

National Research Council (1996) (P Stern and H Fineberg eds) *Understanding Risk* National Academy Press, Washington DC

Parsons, T (1969) *Politics and Social Structure* Free Press, New York

Peters, E and P Slovic (1996) 'The role of effect and worldviews as orienting dispositions in the perception and acceptance of nuclear power' in *Journal of Applied Social Psychology,* vol 26, pp1427–1453

Petts, J (1995) 'Waste management strategy development: A case study of community involvement and consensus-building in Hampshire' in *Journal of Environmental Planning and Management,* vol 38, pp519–536

Petty, R E and J T Cacioppo (1984) 'Source factors and the Elaboration Likelihood Model of persuasion' in *Advances in Consumer Research,* vol 11, pp668–672

Pidgeon, N, C Hood, D Jones, B Turner and R Gibson (1992) 'Risk perception' in *Risk: analysis, perception and management* Royal Society, London

Piller, C (1991) *The Fail-Safe Society: Community Defense and the End of American Technological Optimism* Basic Books, New York

Priester, J R and R E Petty (1995) 'Source attributions and persuasion: Perceived honesty as a determinant of message scrutiny' in *Personality and Social Psychology Bulletin,* vol 21, pp637–654

Putnam, R D (1993) *Making Democracy Work: Civic traditions in modern Italy* Princeton University Press, Princeton

Putnam, R D (1995a) 'Bowling along: America's declining social capital' in *Journal of Democracy,* vol 6, no 1, pp65–78

Putnam, R D (1995b) 'Tuning in, tuning out: The strange disappearance of social capital in America' in *PS: Political Science and Politics,* pp664–683

Rabe, B G (1994) *Beyond NIMBY: Hazardous waste siting in Canada and the United States* Brookings Institution, Washington DC

Rayner, S (1990) 'Management of radiation hazards in hospitals: plural rationalities in a single institution' in *Social Studies of Science,* vol 16, pp573–591

Rayner, S and R Cantor (1987) 'How fair is safe enough – the cultural approach to societal technology choice' in *Risk Analysis,* vol 7, no 1, pp3–9

Renn, O (1990) 'Risk perception and risk management: A review, part 1: risk perception' in *Risk Abstracts,* vol 7, pp1–9

Renn, O (1991) 'Risk communication and the social amplification of risk' in R E Kasperson and P M Stallen (eds) *Communicating Risks to the public: International Perspectives* Kluwer, Dordrecht

Renn, O (1998) 'Three decades of risk research: accomplishments and new challenges' in *Journal of Risk Research* vol 1, pp49–71

Renn, O and D Levine (1991) 'Credibility and trust in risk communication' in R E Kasperson and P M Stallen (eds) *Communicating Risks to the public: International Perspectives,* Kluwer, Amsterdam

Renn, O, W J Burns, J X Kasperson, R E Kasperson and P Slovic (1992) 'The social amplification of risk: Theoretical foundations and empirical applications' in *Journal of Social Issues,* vol 48, pp137–160

Renn, O, T Webler and P Wiedemann (eds) (1995) *Fairness and Competence in Citizen Participation* Kluwer, Dordrecht

Renn, O, T Webler and H Kastenholz (1996) 'Procedural and substantive fairness in landfill citing' in *Risk: Health, Safety and Environment,* vol 7, no 2, pp145–168

Rosa, E A, R E Dunlap and M E Kraft (1993) 'Prospects for public acceptance of a high-level nuclear waste repository in the United States: Summary and implications' in R E Dunlap, M E Kraft and E A Rosa (eds) *Public Reactions to Nuclear Waste: Citizens' Views of a Repository Siting,* Duke University Press, Durham NC

Roth, E, M G Morgan, B Fischhoff, L Lave and A Bostrom (1990) 'What do we know about making risk comparisons' in *Risk Analysis,* vol 10, no 3, pp375–387

Seligman, A B (1997) *The Problem of Trust,* Princeton University Press, Princeton

Seligman, M E P (1975) *Helplessness* Freeman, San Francisco

Shapiro, S (1987) The social control of impersonal trust, in *American Journal of Sociology* vol 93, no 3, pp623–658

Shrader-Frechette, K S (1990) 'Scientific method, antifoundationalism and public decisionmaking' in *Health, Safety and Environment* vol 1, pp23–41

Shrader-Frechette, K S (1991) *Risk and Rationality: Philosophical Foundations for Populist Reforms,* University of California Press, Berkeley.

Sjöberg, L (1996) 'A discussion of the limitations of the psychometric and Cultural Theory approaches to risk perception' in *Radiation Protection Dosimetry,* vol 68, pp219–225

Sjöberg, L (1997) 'Explaining risk perception: An empirical evaluation of cultural theory' in *Risk Decision and Policy,* vol 2, pp113–130

Sjöberg, L (1998) 'Perceived competence and motivation in industry and government as factors in risk perception' in G Cvetkovich and R E Löfstedt (eds) *Social Trust* Earthscan, London

Slater, D (1997) 'Sound science and the public perception of risk' paper presented to the Environment Agency Board, 4 September

Slovic, P (1987) 'Risk Perception' in *Science,* vol 236, pp280–285

Slovic, P (1993) 'Perceived risk, trust, and democracy' in *Risk Analysis,* vol 13, no 6, pp675–682

Slovic, P and D MacGregor (1994) *The Social Context of Risk Communication* Decision Research, Eugene, Oregon

Slovic, P, D MacGregor and N N Kraus (1987) 'Perception of risk from automobile safety defects' in *Accident Analysis and Prevention,* vol 19, pp359–373

Slovic, P, J Flynn, C K Mertz and L Mullican (1992) *Health Risk Perception in Canada* Decision Research, Eugene, Oregon

Starr, C (1969) 'Social benefit versus technological risk' in *Science*, vol 165, pp1232–1238

Stern, P C (1991) 'Learning through conflict: a realistic strategy for risk communication' in *Policy Sciences*, vol 24, pp99–119

Stirling, A (1997) 'Limits to the value of external costs' in *Energy Policy*, vol 25, pp517–540

Stirling, A (1998) 'Risk at a turning point?' in *Journal of Risk Research*, vol 1, no 2, pp97–109

Thompson, M, R Ellis and A Wildavsky (1990) *Cultural Theory* Westview Press, Boulder, Colorado

Tversky, A and D Kahneman (1984) 'Choices, Values and Frames' in *American Psychologist*, vol 39, pp341–350

Vieck, C J H and P J M Stallen (1981) 'Judging risk and benefits in the small and in the large' in *Organisational Behaviour and Human Performance*, vol 28, pp235–271

Weinstein, N D (1980) 'Unrealistic optimism about future life events' in *Journal of Personality and Social Psychology*, vol 39, pp806–820

Weinstein, N D (1989) 'Optimistic biases about personal risks' in *Science*, vol 244, pp1232–1233

White, G F (1945) *Human Adjustment to Floods: A Geographical Approach to the Flood in the United States* Department of Geography, University of Chicago Press, Chicago

White, G F (1961) 'The choice of use in resource management' in *Natural Resource Journal*, vol 1, pp23–40

Wildavsky, A and K Dake (1990) 'Theories of risk perception. Who fears what and why?' in *Daedalus*, vol 119, no 4, pp41–60

Wilkinson, A J (1997) 'Improving risk based communications and decision making', paper presented at the Society of Petroleum Engineers European Environmental Conference

Wolfe, A (1989) *Whose Keepers? Social Science and Moral Obligation* University of California Press, Berkeley CA

Wynne, B (1992) 'Sheep farming after Chernobyl: A case study in communicating scientific information' in B V Lewenstein (ed) *When Science Meets the Public*, American Association for the Advancement of Science, Washington, pp43–67

Wynne, B (1996) 'May the sheep safely graze?' in S Lash, B Szerszynski and B Wynne (eds) *Risk Environment and Modernity: Toward a New Ecology* Sage, London, pp44–83

6, P (1997) *Escaping poverty: From safety nets to networks of opportunity*, Demos, London

Part Two
Risk Perception

Perception of Risk

Paul Slovic

The ability to sense and avoid harmful environmental conditions is necessary for the survival of all living organisms. Survival is also aided by an ability to codify and learn from past experience. Humans have an additional capability that allows them to alter their environment as well as respond to it. This capacity both creates and reduces risk.

In recent decades, the profound development of chemical and nuclear technologies has been accompanied by the potential to cause catastrophic and long-lasting damage to the earth and the life forms that inhabit it. The mechanisms underlying these complex technologies are unfamiliar and incomprehensible to most citizens. Their most harmful consequences are rare and often delayed, hence difficult to assess by statistical analysis and not well suited to management by trial-and-error learning. The elusive and hard to manage qualities of today's hazards have forced the creation of a new intellectual discipline called risk assessment, designed to aid in identifying, characterizing, and quantifying risk (1).

Whereas technologically sophisticated analysts employ risk assessment to evaluate hazards, the majority of citizens rely on intuitive risk judgements, typically called 'risk perception'. For these people, experience with hazards tends to come from the news media, which rather thoroughly document mishaps and threats occurring throughout the world. The dominant perception for most Americans (and one that contrasts sharply with the views of professional risk assessors) is that they face more risk today than in the past and that future risks will be even greater than today's (2). Similar views appear to be held by citizens of many other industrialized nations. These perceptions and the opposition to technology that accompanies them have puzzled and frustrated industrialists and regulators and have led numerous observers to argue that the American public's apparent pursuit of a 'zero-risk society' threatens the nation's political and economic stability. Wildavsky commented as follows on this state of affairs (3).

> How extraordinary! The richest, longest lived, best protected most resourceful civilization, with the highest degree of insight into its technology, is on its way to becoming the most frightened.

Reprinted with permission from *Science* 236, 17 April 1987, pp280–285. Copyright © 1987 American Association for the Advancement of Science.

Is it our environment or ourselves that have changed? Would people like us have had this sort of concern in the past? ... Today, there are risks from numerous small dams far exceeding those from nuclear reactors. Why is one feared and not the other? Is it just that we are used to the old or are some of us looking differently at essentially the same sorts of experience?

During the past decade, a small number of researchers has been attempting to answer such questions by examining the opinions that people express when they are asked, in a variety of ways, to evaluate hazardous activities, substances, and technologies. This research has attempted to develop techniques for assessing the complex and subtle opinions that people have about risk. With these techniques, researchers have sought to discover what people mean when they say that something is (or is not) 'risky', and to determine what facts underlie those perceptions. The basic assumption underlying these efforts is that those who promote and regulate health and safety need to understand the ways in which people think about and respond to risk.

If successful, this research should aid policy-makers by improving communication between them and the public, by directing educational efforts, and by predicting public responses to new technologies (for example, genetic engineering), events (for example, a good safety record or an accident), and new risk management strategies (for example, warning labels, regulations, substitute products).

Risk Perception Research

Important contributions to our current understanding of risk perception have come from geography, sociology, political science, anthropology and psychology. Geographical research focused originally on understanding human behaviour in the face of natural hazards but it has since broadened to include technological hazards as well (4). Sociological (5) and anthropological studies (6) have shown that perception and acceptance of risk have their roots in social and cultural factors. Short (5) argues that response to hazards is mediated by social influences transmitted by friends, family, fellow workers, and respected public officials. In many cases, risk perceptions may form afterwards, as part of the ex post facto rationale for one's own behavior. Douglas and Wildavsky (6) assert that people, acting within social groups, downplay certain risks and emphasize others as a means of maintaining and controlling the group.

Psychological research on risk perception, which will be my focus, originated in empirical studies of probability assessment, utility assessment and decision-making processes (7). A major development in this area has been the discovery of a set of mental strategies, or heuristics, that people employ in order to make sense out of an uncertain world (8). Although these rules are valid in some circumstances, in others they lead to large and persistent biases, with serious implications for risk assessment. In particular, laboratory research on basic perceptions and cognitions has shown that difficulties in understanding probabilistic processes, biased media coverage, misleading personal experiences and the anxieties generated by life's gambles cause uncertainty to be denied, risks to be misjudged (sometimes overestimated and sometimes underestimated), and judgements of fact to be held with unwarranted confidence. Experts' judgements appear to be prone to many of the same biases as those of the general public, particularly when experts are forced to go beyond the limits of available data and rely on intuition *(8, 9)*.

Research further indicates that disagreements about risk should not be expected to evaporate in the presence of evidence. Strong initial views are resistant to change because they influence the way that subsequent information is interpreted. New evidence appears reliable and informative if it is consistent with one's initial beliefs; contrary evidence tends to be dismissed as unreliable, erroneous, or unrepresentative *(10)*. When people lack strong prior opinions, the opposite situation exists – they are at the mercy of the problem formulation. Presenting the same information about risk in different ways (for example, mortality rates as opposed to survival rates) alters people's perspectives and actions *(11)*.

The Psychometric Paradigm

One broad strategy for studying perceived risk is to develop a taxonomy for hazards that can be used to understand and predict responses to their risks. A taxonomic scheme might explain, for example, people's extreme aversion to some hazards, their indifference to others, and the discrepancies between these reactions and opinions of experts. The most common approach to this goal has employed the psychometric paradigm *(12, 13)*, which uses psychophysical scaling and multivariate analysis techniques to produce quantitative representations or 'cognitive maps' of risk attitudes and perceptions. Within the psychometric paradigm, people make quantitative judgements about the current and desired riskiness of diverse hazards and the desired level of regulation of each. These judgements are then related to judgements about other properties, such as (1) the hazard's status on characteristics that have been hypothesized to account for risk perceptions and attitudes (for example, voluntariness, dread, knowledge, controllability); (2) the benefits that each hazard provides to society; (3) the number of deaths caused by the hazard in an average year, and (4) the number of deaths caused by the hazard in a disastrous year.

In the rest of this article, I shall briefly review some of the results obtained from psychometric studies of risk perception and outline some implications of these results for risk communication and risk management.

Revealed and Expressed Preferences

The original impetus for the psychometric paradigm came from the pioneering effort of Starr *(14)* to develop a method for weighing technological risks against benefits in order to answer the fundamental question, 'How safe is safe enough?' His 'revealed preference' approach assumed that, by trial and error, society has arrived at an 'essentially optimum' balance between the risks and benefits associated with any activity. One may therefore use historical or current risk and benefit data to reveal patterns of 'acceptable' risk-benefit trade-offs. Examining such data for several industries and activities, Starr concluded that (1) acceptability of risk from an activity is roughly proportional to the third power of the benefits for that activity, and (2) the public will accept risks from voluntary activities (such as skiing) that are roughly 1000 times as great as it would tolerate from involuntary hazards (such as food preservatives) that provide the same level of benefits.

The merits and deficiencies of Starr's approach have been debated at length (15). They will not be elaborated here, except to note that concern about the validity of the many assumptions inherent in the revealed preferences approach stimulated Fischhoff et al (12) to conduct an analogous psychometric analysis of questionnaire data resulting in 'expressed preferences'. In recent years, numerous other studies of expressed preferences have been carried out within the psychometric paradigm (16–24).

These studies have shown that perceived risk is quantifiable and predictable. Psychometric techniques seem well suited for identifying similarities and differences among groups with regard to risk perceptions and attitudes (Table 2.1). They have also shown that the concept 'risk' means different things to different people. When experts judge risk, their responses correlate highly with technical estimates

Table 2.1 *Ordering of perceived risk for 30 activities and technologies (22). The ordering is based on the geometric mean risk ratings within each group. Rank 1 represents the most risky activity or technology.*

Activity or Technology	League of women voters	College Students	Active Club Members	Experts
Nuclear power	1	1	8	20
Motor vehicles	2	5	3	1
Handguns	3	2	1	4
Smoking	4	3	4	2
Motorcycles	5	6	2	6
Alcoholic beverages	6	7	5	3
General (private) aviation	7	15	11	12
Police work	8	8	7	17
Pesticides	9	4	15	8
Surgery	10	11	9	5
Fire fighting	11	10	6	18
Large construction	12	14	13	13
Hunting	13	18	10	23
Spray cans	14	13	23	26
Mountain climbing	15	22	12	29
Bicycles	16	24	14	15
Commercial aviation	17	16	18	16
Electric power (non-nuclear)	18	19	19	9
Swimming	19	30	17	10
Contraceptives	20	9	22	11
Skiing	21	25	16	30
X-rays	22	17	24	7
High school and college football	23	26	21	27
Railroads	24	23	29	19
Food preservatives	25	12	28	14
Food colouring	26	20	30	21
Power mowers	27	28	25	28
Prescription antibiotics	28	21	26	24
Home appliances	29	27	27	22
Vaccinations	30	29	29	25

of annual fatalities. Lay people can assess annual fatalities if they are asked to (and produce estimates somewhat like the technical estimates). However, their judgements of 'risk' are related more to other hazard characteristics (for example, catastrophic potential, threat to future generations) and, as a result, tend to differ from their own (and experts') estimates of annual fatalities.

Another consistent result from psychometric studies of expressed preferences is that people tend to view current risk levels as unacceptably high for most activities. The gap between perceived and desired risk levels suggests that people are not satisfied with the way that market and other regulatory mechanisms have balanced risks and benefits. Across the domain of hazards, there seems to be little systematic relationship between perceptions of current risks and benefits. However, studies of expressed preferences do seem to support Starr's argument that people are willing to tolerate higher risks from activities seen as highly beneficial. But, whereas Starr concluded that voluntariness of exposure was the key mediator of risk acceptance, expressed preference studies have shown that other (perceived) characteristics such as familiarity, control, catastrophic potential, equity and level of knowledge also seem to influence the relation between perceived risk, perceived benefit, and risk acceptance (12,22).

Various models have been advanced to represent the relation between perceptions, behaviour, and these qualitative characteristics of hazards. As we shall see, the picture that emerges from this work is both orderly and complex.

Factor-Analytic Representations

Many of the qualitative risk characteristics are correlated with each other, across a wide range of hazards. For example, hazards judged to be 'voluntary' tend also to be judged as 'controllable'; hazards whose adverse effects are delayed tend to be seen as posing risks that are not well known, and so on. Investigation of these relations by means of factor analysis has shown that the broader domain of characteristics can be condensed to a small set of higher older characteristics or factors.

The factor space presented in Figure 2.1 has been replicated across groups of lay people and experts judging large and diverse sets of hazards. Factor 1, labelled 'dread risk', is defined at its high (right-hand) end by perceived lack of control, dread, catastrophic potential, fatal consequences and the inequitable distribution of risks and benefits. Nuclear weapons and nuclear power score highest on the characteristics that make up this factor. Factor 2, labelled 'unknown risk', is defined at its high end by hazards judged to be unobservable, unknown, new and delayed in their manifestation of harm. Chemical technologies score particularly high on this factor. A third factor, reflecting the number of people exposed to the risk, has been obtained in several studies. Making the set of hazards more or less specific (for example, partitioning nuclear power into radioactive waste, uranium mining and nuclear reactor accidents) has had little effect on the factor structure or its relation to risk perceptions (25).

Research has shown that lay people's risk perceptions and attitudes are closely related to the position of a hazard within this type of factor space. Most important is the horizontal factor 'dread risk'. The higher a hazard's score on this factor (the further to the right it appears in the space), the higher its perceived risk, the more people want to see its current risks reduced, and the more they want to see strict regulation employed to achieve the desired reduction in risk (Figure 2.2). In con-

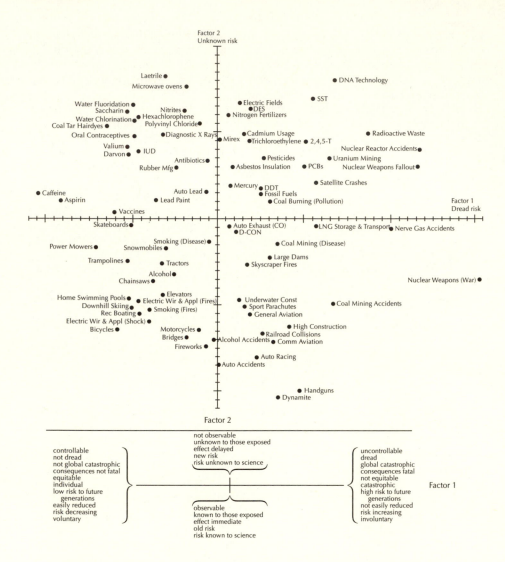

Figure 2.1 *Location of 81 hazards on factors 1 and 2 derived from the relationships among 18 risk characteristics. Each factor is made up of a combination of characteristics, as indicated by the lower diagram (25).*

trast, experts' perceptions of risk are not closely related to any of the various risk characteristics or factors derived from these characteristics (25). Instead, as noted earlier, experts appear to see riskiness as synonymous with expected annual mortality (26). As a result, conflicts over 'risk' may result from experts and lay people having different definitions of the concept.

The representation shown in Figure 2.1, while robust and informative, is by no means a universal cognitive mapping of the domain of hazards. Other psychometric methods (such as multidimensional scaling analysis of hazard similarity judgements), applied to quite different sets of hazards, produce different spatial models

(13, 18). The utility of these models for understanding and predicting behaviour remains to be determined.

Accidents as Signals

Risk analyses typically model the impacts of an unfortunate event (such as an accident, a discovery of pollution, sabotage, product tampering) in terms of direct harm to victims – deaths, injuries and damages. The impacts of such events, however, sometimes extend far beyond these direct harms and may include significant indirect costs (both monetary and non-monetary) to the responsible government agency or private company that far exceed direct costs. In some cases, all companies in an industry are affected, regardless of which company was responsible for the mishap. In extreme cases, the indirect costs of a mishap may extend past industry boundaries, affecting companies, industries and agencies whose business is minimally related to the initial event. Thus, an unfortunate event can be thought of as analogous to a stone dropped in a pond. The ripples spread outward, encompassing first the directly affected victims, then the responsible company or agency, and, in the extreme, reaching other companies, agencies and industries.

Some events make only small ripples; others make larger ones. The challenge is to discover characteristics associated with an event and the way that it is managed that can predict the breadth and seriousness of those impacts (Figure 2.3). Early theories equated the magnitude of impact to the number of people killed or injured or to the amount of property damaged. However, the accident at the Three Mile Island (TMI) nuclear reactor in 1979 provides a dramatic demonstration that factors besides injury, death and property damage impose serious costs. Despite the fact that not a single person died and few, if any, latent cancer fatalities are expected, no other accident in our history has produced such costly societal impacts. The accident at TMI devastated the utility that owned and operated the plant. It also imposed enormous costs (27) on the nuclear industry and on society, through stricter regulation (resulting in increased construction and operation costs), reduced ope-

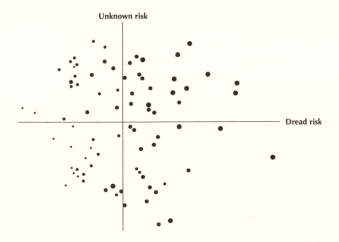

Figure 2.2 *Attitudes toward regulation of the hazards in Figure 2.1.*
The larger the point, the greater the desire for strict regulation to reduce risk (25).

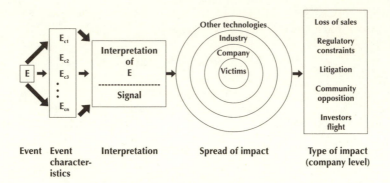

Figure 2.3 *A model of impact for unfortunate events.*

ration of reactors worldwide, greater public opposition to nuclear power, and reliance on more expensive energy sources. It may even have led to a more hostile view of other complex technologies, such as chemical manufacturing and generic engineering. The point is that traditional economic and risk analyses tend to neglect these higher order impacts, hence they greatly underestimate the costs associated with certain kinds of events.

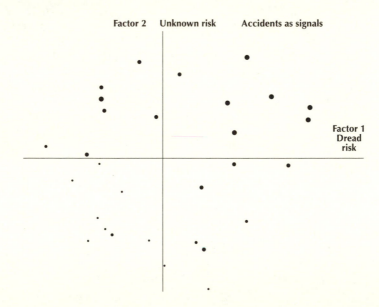

Figure 2.4 *The relation between signal potential and risk characterization for 30 hazards in Figure 2.1. The larger the point, the greater the degree to which an accident involving that hazard was judged to 'serve as a warning signal for society, providing new information about the probability that similar or even more destructive mishaps might occur within this type of activity'. Media attention and the higher order costs of a mishap are likely to be correlated with signal potential (28).*

Although the TMI accident is extreme, it is by no means unique. Other recent events resulting in enormous higher order impacts include the chemical manufacturing accident at Bhopal, India, the pollution of Love Canal, New York, and Times Beach, Missouri, the disastrous launch of the space shuttle Challenger, and the meltdown of the nuclear reactor at Chernobyl. Following these extreme events are a myriad of mishaps varying in the breadth and size of their impacts.

An important concept that has emerged from psychometric research is that the seriousness and higher order impacts of an unfortunate event are determined, in part, by what that event signals or portends (28). The informativeness or 'signal potential' of an event, and thus its potential social impact, appears to be systematically related to the characteristics of the hazard and the location of the event within the factor space described earlier (Figure 2.4). An accident that takes many lives may produce relatively little social disturbance (beyond that experienced by the victims' families and friends) if it occurs as part of a familiar and well-understood system (such as a train wreck). However, a small accident in an unfamiliar system (or one perceived as poorly understood), such as a nuclear reactor or a recombinant DNA laboratory, may have immense social consequences if it is perceived as a harbinger of further and possibly catastrophic mishaps.

The concept of accidents as signals was eloquently expressed in an editorial addressing the tragic accident at Bhopal (29).

> What truly grips us in these accounts is not so much the numbers as the spectacle of suddenly vanishing competence, of men utterly routed by technology, of fail-safe systems failing with a logic as inexorable as it was once – indeed, right up until that very moment – unforeseeable. And the spectacle haunts us because it seems to carry allegorical import, like the whispery omen of a hovering future.

One implication of the signal concept is that effort and expense beyond that indicated by a cost-benefit analysis might be warranted to reduce the possibility of 'high-signal accidents'. Unfortunate events involving hazards in the upper right quadrant of Figure 2.1 appear particularly likely to have the potential to produce large ripples. As a result, risk analyses involving these hazards need to be made sensitive to these possible higher order impacts. Doing so would likely bring greater protection to potential victims as well as to companies and industries.

Analysis of Single Hazard Domains

Psychometric analyses have also been applied to judgements of diverse hazard scenarios within a single technological domain, such as railroad transport (30) or automobiles (21). Kraus (30) had people evaluate the riskiness of 49 railroad hazard scenarios that varied with respect to type of train, type of cargo, location of the accident, and the nature and cause of the accident (for example, a high-speed train carrying passengers through a mountain tunnel derails due to a mechanical system failure). The results showed that these railroad hazards were highly differentiated, much like the hazards in Figure 2.1. The highest signal potential (and thus the highest potential for large ripple effects) was associated with accidents involving trains carrying hazardous chemicals.

A study by Slovic, MacGregor, and Kraus (*31*) examined perceptions of risk and signal value for 40 structural defects in automobiles. Multivariate analysis of these defects, rated in terms of various characteristics of risk, produced a two-factor space. As in earlier studies with diverse hazards, the position of a defect in this space predicted judgements of riskiness and signal value quite well. One defect stood out much as nuclear hazards do in Figure 2.1. It was a fuel tank rupture upon impact, creating the possibility of fire and burn injuries. This, of course, is similar to the notorious design problem that plagued the Ford Pinto and that Ford allegedly declined to correct because a cost-benefit analysis indicated that the correction costs greatly exceeded the expected benefits from increased safety (32). Had Ford done a psychometric study, the analysis might have highlighted this particular defect as one whose seriousness and higher order costs (lawsuits, damaged company reputation) were likely to be greatly underestimated by cost-benefit analysis.

Forecasting Public Acceptance

Results from studies of the perception of risk have been used to explain and forecast acceptance and opposition for specific technologies (*33*). Nuclear power has been a frequent topic of such analysis because of the dramatic opposition it has engendered in the face of experts' assurances of its safety. Research shows that people judge the benefits from nuclear power to be quite small and the risks to be unacceptably great. Nuclear power risks occupy extreme positions in psychometric factor spaces, reflecting people's views that these risks are unknown, dread, uncontrollable, inequitable, catastrophic, and likely to affect future generations (Figure 2.1). Opponents of nuclear power recognize that few people have died thus far as a result of this technology. However, long before Chernobyl, they expressed great concern over the potential for catastrophic accidents.

These public perceptions have evoked harsh reactions from experts. One noted psychiatrist wrote that 'the irrational fear of nuclear plants is based on a mistaken assessment of the risks' (*34*, p. 8). A nuclear physicist and leading advocate of nuclear power contended that '...the public has been driven insane over fear of radiation [from nuclear power]. I use the word "insane" purposefully since one of its definitions is loss of contact with reality. The public's understanding of radiation dangers has virtually lost all contact with the actual dangers as understood by scientists' (*35*, p. 31).

Risk perception research paints a different picture, demonstrating that people's deep anxieties are linked to the reality of extensive unfavourable media coverage and to a strong association between nuclear power and the proliferation and use of nuclear weapons. Attempts to 'educate' or reassure the public and bring their perceptions in line with those of industry experts appear unlikely to succeed because the low probability of serious reactor accidents makes empirical demonstrations of safety difficult to achieve. Because nuclear risks are perceived as unknown and potentially catastrophic, even small accidents will be highly publicized and may produce large ripple effects (Figure 2.4).

Psychometric research may be able to forecast the response to technologies that have yet to arouse strong and persistent public opposition. For example, DNA technologies seem to evoke several of the perceptions that make nuclear power so hard to manage. In the aftermath of an accident, this technology could face some of the same problems and opposition now confronting the nuclear industry.

Placing Risks in Perspective

A consequence of the public's concerns and its opposition to risky technologies has been an increase in attempts to inform and educate people about risk. Risk perception research has a number of implications for such educational efforts (36).

One frequently advocated approach to broadening people's perspectives is to present quantitative risk estimates for a variety of hazards, expressed in some unidimensional index of death or disability, such as risk per hour of exposure, annual probability of death, or reduction in life expectancy. Even though such comparisons have no logically necessary implications for acceptability of risk (15), one might still hope that they would help improve people's intuitions about the magnitude of risks. Risk perception research suggests, however, that these sorts of comparisons may not be very satisfactory even for this purpose. People's perceptions and attitudes are determined not only by the sort of unidimensional statistics used in such tables but also by the variety of quantitative and qualitative characteristics reflected in Figure 2.1. To many people, statements such as 'the annual risk from living near a nuclear power plant is equivalent to the risk of riding an extra 3 miles in an automobile', give inadequate consideration to the important differences in the nature of the risks from these two technologies.

In short, 'riskiness' means more to people than 'expected number of fatalities'. Attempts to characterize, compare and regulate risks must be sensitive to this broader conception of risk. Fischhoff, Watson, and Hope (37) have made a start in this direction by demonstrating how one might construct a more comprehensive measure of risk. They show that variations in the scope of one's definition of risk can greatly change the assessment of risk from various energy technologies.

Whereas psychometric research implies that risk debates are not merely about risk statistics, some sociological and anthropological research implies that some of these debates may not even be about risk (5, 6). Risk concerns may provide a rationale for actions taken on other grounds or they may be a surrogate for other social or ideological concerns. When this is the case, communication about risk is simply irrelevant to the discussion. Hidden agendas need to be brought to the surface for discussion (38).

Perhaps the most important message from this research is that there is wisdom as well as error in public attitudes and perceptions. Lay people sometimes lack certain information about hazards. However, their basic conceptualization of risk is much richer than that of the experts and reflects legitimate concerns that are typically omitted from expert risk assessments. As a result, risk communication and risk management efforts are destined to fail unless they are structured as a two-way process. Each side, expert and public, has something valid to contribute. Each side must respect the insights and intelligence of the other.

References

1   For a comprehensive bibliography on risk assessment, see V Covello and M Abernathy, in *Technological Risk Assessment*, P F Ricci, L A Sagan, C G Whipple, Eds, Nijhoff, The Hague, 1984, pp283–363

2   'Risk in a complex society', report of a public opinion poll conducted by L Harris for the Marsh and McClennan Company, New York (1980)

3   A Wildavsky, *American Scientist* 67, 32 (1979)
4   I Burton, R W Kates, G F White, *The Environment as a Hazard* Oxford University Press, Oxford, 1978
5   J F Short, Jr, *American Sociology Revue* 49, 711 (1984)
6   M Douglas and A Wildavsky, *Risk and Culture* University of California Press, Berkeley, 1982
7   W Edwards, *Annual Revue of Psychology* 12, 473 (1961)
8   D Kahneman, P Slovic, A Tversky, Eds *Judgment Under Uncertainty: Heuristics and Biases* Cambridge University Press, New York, 1982
9   M Henrion and B Fischhoff, *American Journal of Physics,* in press
10 R Nisbett and L Ross, *Human Inference: Strategies and Shortcomings of Social Judgment* Prentice-Hall, Englewood Cliffs, NJ, 1980
11 A Tversky and D Kahneman, *Science* 211, 453 (1981)
12 B Fischhoff *et al, Policy Science* 8, 127 (1978)
13 P Slovic, B Fischhoff, S Lichtenstein, *Actual Psychology* 56, 183 (1984)
14 C Starr, *Science* 165, 1232 (1969)
15 B Fischhoff, S Lichtenstein, P Slovic, S L Derby, R L Keeney, *Acceptable Risk* Cambridge University Press, New York, 1981
16 G T Gardner *et al, Journal of Social Psychology* 116, 179 (1982)
17 D R DeLuca, J A J Stolwijk, W Horowitz, in *Risk Evaluation and Management,* V T Covello, J Menkes, J L Mumpower, Eds, Plenum, New York, 1986, pp25–67
18 E J Johnson and A Tversky, *Journal of Exp. Psychology General* 113, 55 (1984)
19 M K Lindell and T C Earle, *Risk Analysis* 3, 245 (1983)
20 H J Otway and M Fishbein, *The Determinants of Attitude Formation: An Application to Nuclear Power* RM-76-80 Technical Report, International Institute for Applied Systems Analysis, Laxenburg, Austria, 1976
21 O Renn and E Swaton, *Environmental International* 10, 557 (1984)
22 P Slovic, B Fischhoff, S Lichtenstein, in *Societal Risk Assessment: How Safe is Safe Enough?,* R Schwing and W A Albers, Jr, Eds, Plenum, New York, 1980, pp181–216
23 C A J Vlek and P J Stallen, *Organ. Behav. Hum. Perf.* 28, 235 (1981)
24 D von Winterfeldt, R S John, K Borcherding, *Risk Analysis* 1, 277 (1981)
25 P Slovic, B Fischhoff, S Lichtenstein, in *Perilous Progress: Managing the Hazards of Technology,* R W Kates, C Hohenemser, J X Kasperson, Eds, Westview, Boulder, CO, 1985, pp91–125
26 P Slovic, B Fischhoff, S Lichtenstein, *Environment* 21 (no 3), 14 (1979)
27 Estimated at $500 billion [see *Electrical Power Res. Institute Journal* 5 (no 5), 24 (1980)]
28 P Slovic, S Lichtenstein, B Fischhoff; *Management Science* 30, 464 (1984)
29 The Talk of the Town, *New Yorker* 60 (no 53), 29 (1985)
30 N Kraus, thesis, University of Pittsburgh (1985)
31 P Slovic, D MacGregor, N Kraus, *Accident Analysis Preview,* in press
32 *Grimshaw vs Ford Motor Co,* Superior Court, no 19776, Orange County, CA, 6 February 1978
33 P Slovic, B Fischhoff, S Lichtenstein, in *Advances in Environmental Psychology,* A Baum and J E Singer, Eds, Erlbaum, Hillsdale, NJ, 1981, vol 3, pp157–169
34 R L Dupont *Business Week,* 7 September 1981, pp8–9.
35 B L Cohen, *Before It's Too Late: A Scientist's Case for Nuclear Energy* Plenum, New York, 1983
36 P Slovic, *Risk Analysis* 6, 403 (1986)

37 B Fischhoff, S Watson, C Hope, *Policy Science* 17, 123 (1984)

38 W Edwards and D von Winterfeldt, *Risk Analysis,* in press

39 The text of this article draws heavily upon the author's joint work with B Fischhoff and S Lichtenstein. Support for the writing of the article was provided by NSF grant SES–8517411 to Decision Research.

Scientific Method, Anti-Foundationalism and Public Decision Making

Kristin Shrader-Frechette

Introduction

The US Department of Energy (DOE) recently awarded $85,000 to a Washington psychiatrist to help 'counter the public's "irrational fear" about nuclear power'. Robert L DuPont, a former director of the National Institute on Drug Abuse, received the funds for a study that has been described as 'an attempt to demonstrate that opponents of nuclear power are mentally ill' (Holden, 1984).[1]

DOE's fears about public irrationality regarding technological risks, however, are not atypical. At least three groups of persons maintain that citizens' worries about environmental risks, from carcinogenic pesticides to loss of global ozone, are irrational. Industry spokespersons, risk assessors and contemporary social scientists have all attacked the environmental fears of lay people as irrational. Edith Efron, for example, author of *The News Twisters* and *The Apocalyptics: Politics, Science, and The Big Cancer Lie,* maintains that both citizens and scientists have attempted to incriminate industry in the name of 'cancer prevention', even though the evidence that certain substances cause environmental and human harm is typically questionable. Public fear of cancer, she says, derives from 'warring attitudes toward the American industrial system' and 'fantasies' about industrial mass murder.[2]

Risk assessors, often experts in the employ of industries responsible for the hazardous technologies they are paid to evaluate, constitute a second class of persons critical of alleged citizen 'irrationality'. Norman Rasmussen, for example, author of the most famous risk analysis, of commercial nuclear reactors, has accused the public of 'inconsistency' in its attitudes toward hazards.[3] In his view, anyone who travels

---

1 Holden, *Fear of Nuclear Power: A Phobia?* 226 *Science* 814 (1984).
2 Efron, *Behind the Cancer Terror,* 16 *Reason* 23 ff (May 1984). *See also,* Efron, *The News Twisters* (1971) and Efron, *The Apocalyptics: Politics, Science, and The Big Cancer Lie* (1984).
3 US Nuclear Regulatory Commission, *Reactor Safety Study: An Assessment Of Accident Risks in U.S. Commercial Nuclear Power Plants,* Report No Wash-1400, 37 (1975), hereinafter WASH-1400. *See* Braybrooke and Schotch, *Cost-Benefit Analysis under the Constraint of Meeting Needs* [Working paper available from D Braybrooke, Dept Philosophy, University of Dalhousie, Halifax, NS, CANADA B3H 3J5.]

by automobile, but opposes commercial nuclear fission, is inconsistent in accepting a large risk but rejecting an allegedly smaller one.[4]

Contemporary social scientists, especially sociologists, constitute the third main camp of persons who are critical of lay attitudes toward technological and environmental risk. Wildavsky and Douglas argue in their study that Americans are biased, witchhunting opponents of technology. They claim that lay persons are dominated by superstitions about environmental risks and by fundamentalist desires for unrealistic environmental 'purity'. Even more surprising, they allege that these contemporary superstitions and biases are no different in kind from those of pre-scientific, primitive people.[5]

The Failure of Foundationalist Positivism

How legitimate are these three attacks on lay accounts of the acceptability of environmental/technological risk? Dismissing the hazard evaluations of the public is highly questionable both for specific and for general reasons. On the specific level, the attacks are problematic because they are premised on experts' highly stipulative, question-begging definition of risk, as reducible merely to an average annual probability of fatality. Most experts also presuppose, following Bayesian accounts of decision theory, that societal or public risk aversion is a linear function of the average annual probability of fatality associated with the hazard.[6]

Lay people, however, typically do not restrict risk to probability of fatality, but include other factors, such as benefits obtained by taking the risk, in their evaluations. Hence their risk aversion is not a linear function of probability of fatality, since it incorporates numerous other parameters such as degree of knowledge of the

---

4 Lave, *Discussion,* in Symposium/workshop ... Risk Assessment and Governmental Decision Making 541 (1979), hereinafter *Risk Symposium. See* Starr and Whipple, *Risks of Risk Decisions,* 208 *Science* 1116 (1980) hereinafter Starr and Whipple, *Risks;* Okrent, *Panel: Use of Risk Assessment,* in Risk Symposium, *supra,* at 663; Bazelon, *Risk and Responsibility,* 205 *Science* 278 (1979). *See, eg,* Cohen and Lee, *A Catalog of Risks,* 36 *Health Physics* 707 (1979): Hafele, *Energy,* in, Science, Technology, and the Human Prospect, 139 (C Starr And P Ritterbush eds 1979). *See also,* M Maxey, *Managing Low-Level Radioactive Wastes,* in, Low-level Radioactive Waste Management 410, 417 (J Watson, ed 1979). *See also,* Starr, *Benefit-Cost Studies in Sociotechnical Systems,* in, Committee on Public Engineering Policy, Perspectives on Benefit-risk Decision Making 26–27 (1972). Finally, *see* Lave, *Risk Symposium, supra,* at 484.

Although society's intuitive evaluations of given risks do not provide sufficient grounds for arguing that these risks ought to be evaluated in a certain way, many risk assessors maintain that correct societal evaluations arc consistent with tenet (3) and the linearity assumption. Hence, in response to alleged counter examples to this assumption, assessors maintain that high public aversion to certain low probability risks does not provide a counter example to the thesis that 'actual' risk probabilities and the value of risk avoidance are linearly related, since the public's aversion in such cases is generated by 'perceived' (ie incorrect) risk probabilities and not 'actual' ones.

For another example of risk assessors in the employ of industry, assessors who charge the public with being irrational, *see* Nealey, *Excessive Fear of Nuclear Technology,* Human Affairs Research Center, Seattle, WA, 1987 (Unpublished manuscript). For some of the dangers associated with labelling citizens as 'irrational', *see* Sandman, *Getting to Maybe,* in Resolving Locational Conflict, 327 (R. W. Lake ed. 1987).

5 A Wildavsky and M Douglas, *Risk and Culture* (1982).

6 For an overview of risk assessment and its Bayesian foundations, *see* K Schrader-Frechette, 1985a.

hazard, equity of risk distribution, and so on.[7] If one accepts a more inclusive, citizen definition of risk, then there are few grounds for alleging that lay people are irrational simply because they deny that environmental risk aversion is a linear function of probability of fatality.[8]

Experts' dismissing the hazard evaluations of the public is also questionable from a more general point of view because there is no accepted algorithm for theory choice, either in pure science (if there is such a thing) or in assessment of technological or environmental risk. And if there is no algorithm, the possession of which guarantees the certainty of experts' judgments about science and technology, then there is no completely firm basis from which to discredit similar judgements made by lay persons. Ever since the failure of Carnap's enterprise, epistemologists like Sellars and Quine have realized that the positivist goal, of finding a specific rule or method to guarantee the rationality of science or knowledge, is incapable of being achieved.[9] As a consequence, epistemology in the late 1980s has been naturalized. To greater and lesser degrees, philosophers have concluded that there is no absolutely reliable method for delivering certain knowledge, just as alchemists finally concluded, centuries before, that there is no recipe for turning base metal or earth into gold.

But if there is no sacrosanct method that always guarantees certainty, whether in science or environmental policy analysis, then our alternative is to naturalize knowledge. On at least one version of naturalism, this means that we must replace the positivists' question, 'how ought we to arrive at our beliefs?' with the naturalists' question, 'how do we arrive at our beliefs?' since the latter is more tractable.[10] Even Hempel, one of the grand old men of positivism, has moved to a somewhat naturalized epistemology. He has admitted that there is no specific rule or method to guarantee the complete objectivity of theory choice, and he has said that science can be guided only in a general sense and only by attempting to provide theories that embody values such as predictive power and explanatory fertility.[11]

On this naturalized account, although scientific knowledge is not completely relative, it is unavoidably value-laden. No scientific theory can be said to be *wholly objective*, but one theory is *more objective* than another if it leads to better predictions or has more explanatory power. Such judgements of objectivity depend on numerous epistemic value judgements about particular predictions or explanations. Some of these epistemic or methodological value judgements concern, for example, whether the data are extensive enough or representative enough to support a given prediction. Other epistemic value judgements affirm, for example, that ignoring certain parameters does not jeopardize the explanatory power of a particular account.

There is no space here to argue for or against any one of the many variants of naturalized epistemology. Nor is there time to provide an anatomy of the epistemic value judgements whose presence, even in allegedly pure science, has toppled the

---

7 *See* Fischhoff, Slovic, and Lichtenstein, *Fact and Fears*, in Societal Risk Assessment, 270 ff (R Schwing and W Albers eds 1970).

8 For arguments to this effect, *see supra, note* 6, Ch Six.

9 *See* Quine, *Epistemology Naturalized*, in Naturalizing Epistemology, 15 ff (H Kornblith ed 1985).

10 *See id* for discussions of naturalized epistemology. D Shapere, Reason and the Search for Knowledge (1984), also presents a well known naturalistic position.

11 C Hempel, *Aspects of Scientific Explanation* (1965); Hempel, *Scientific Rationality* in Rationality Today (T. Geraets ed. 1979): Hempel, *Science and Human Values*, in Introductory Readings in the Philosophy of Science (E Klemke, R Hollinger, and A Kline eds 1982); and Hempel, *Valuation and Objectivity in Science*, in Physics, Philosophy, and Psychoanalysis (R Cohen and L Laudan eds 1983).

positivist edifice of certain and wholly objective knowledge.[12] What is more important, however, is to trace some of the consequences, for policy about technology, if
the current wisdom about naturalized epistemology is correct.

Most obviously, if there is no specific algorithm for theory choice, then scientific experts have no completely unassailable basis on which to criticize the policy
evaluations of the public. Granted, experts typically have a better grasp of the mathematics and facts relevant to policy about science and technology. The problem,
however, is that even science, and assuredly technology assessment or environmental impact analysis, involve more than mathematics or facts; because they do, there
is room for considerable controversy over the epistemic or methodological values in
terms of which the facts and mathematics relevant to policy analysis are interpreted.[13]

Experts Are Often Wrong

That expert interpretations in the area of science and technology are often questionable, and that there is no positivist rule to guarantee their complete reliability, is
illustrated by a recent study by hazard assessors in the Netherlands. They used
actual empirical frequencies obtained from a study done by Oak Ridge National
Laboratories to calibrate some of the more testable subjective probabilities used in
the famous Rasmussen (1975) Report, WASH-1400, probably one of the most famous and most extensive risk assessments ever accomplished.[14] The Oak Ridge frequencies were obtained as part of an evaluation of operating experience at nuclear
installations. These frequencies were of various types of mishaps involving reactor
subsystems whose failure probabilities were calculated in WASH-1400. The Oak Ridge
study used operating experience to determine the failure probability for seven such
subsystems, and the Dutch researchers then compared these probabilities with the
90 per cent confidence bounds for the same probabilities calculated in WASH-1400.
The subsystem failures included loss-of-coolant accidents, auxiliary feedwater-sys-
tem failures, high-pressure injection failures, long-term core-cooling failures, and
automatic depressurization-system failures for both pressurized and boiling water
reactors. Amazingly, all the values from operating experience fell outside the 90 per
cent confidence bands in the WASH-1400 study. However, there is only a subjective
probability of 10 per cent that the true value should fall outside these bands. This
means that, if the authors' subjective probabilities were well calibrated, we should
expect that approximately 10 per cent of the true values should lie outside their respective bands. The fact that all the quantities fall outside them means that WASH-
1400, the most famous and allegedly best risk assessment, is very poorly calibrated.
Moreover, the fact that five of the seven values fell above the upper confidence bound
suggests that the WASH-1400 accident probabilities, subjective probabilities, are
too low. This means that, if the Oak Ridge data are correct, then WASH-1400 exhibits a number of flaws, including an overconfidence bias.[15]

---

12 Scriven, The Exact Role of Value Judgments in Science, in *Introductory Readings in the Philosophy
of Science* [E Klemke, R Hollinger, and A Kline eds 1982); E McMullin, *Values in Science* (Unpublished
ms available from author, Philosophy Dept, U Notre Dame, Notre Dame, IN 46556).
13 Id For a discussion of epistemic value judgements in science, see K Shrader-Frechette, *Science
Policy, Ethics, and Economic Methodology*, Chs Three and Four (1985).
14 WASH-1400, supra, note 3. This figure is also a per-year, per-reactor probability.

Kahneman and Tversky have uncovered other biases of experts. They corroborated the claim that, in the absence of an algorithm completely guaranteeing scientific rationality, experts do not necessarily or always make more correct judgements about the acceptability of technological risk than do lay persons. Kahneman and Tversky showed that virtually everyone falls victim to a number of characteristic biases in the interpretation of statistical and probabilistic data. For example, people often follow an intuition called representativeness, according to which they believe samples to be very similar to one another and to the population from which they are drawn; they also erroneously believe that sampling is a self-correcting process.[16] In subscribing to the representativeness bias, both experts and lay people are insensitive: to the prior probability of outcomes; to sample size; to the inability to obtain a good prediction; to the inaccuracy of predictions based on redundant and correlated input variables; and to regression toward the mean. Nevertheless, training in elementary probability and statistics warns against all these errors.[17]

Both risk assessors and statistics experts also typically fall victim to a bias called 'availability,' assessing the frequency of a class, or the probability of an event, by the ease with which instances or occurrences can be brought to mind. In subscribing to the availability bias, they forget that they are judging a class on the basis of the retrievability of the instances, and that imaginability is not a good criterion for probability.[18]

Most people also fall victim to the 'anchoring' bias, making estimates on the basis of adjusting values of an initial variable. In so doing, they forget that diverse initial starting points typically yield different results; that insufficient adjustments can skew results; and that probabilities of failures are typically underestimated in complex systems. Although employing each of these biases (representativeness, availability, and anchoring) is both economical and often effective, any of them can lead to systematic and predictable errors.[19]

These systematic and predictive errors are important because technology and:[20]

> ...risk assessment must be based on complex theoretical analyses such as fault trees, rather than on direct experience. Hence, despite an appearance of objectivity, these analyses include a large component of judgment. Someone, relying on educated intuition, must determine the structure of the problem, the consequences to be considered, and the importance of the various branches of the fault tree.

In other words, the risk assessor must make a number of unavoidable, sometimes incorrect, epistemic value judgements.

---

15 See R. Cooke, *Subjective Probability and Expert Opinion*, Ch. Nine (1986) (Manuscript to be published in 1990 by Oxford U. Press.)

16 See Kahneman and Tversky, Subjective Probability in Judgement Under Uncertainty: Heuristics and Biases 46 (D Kahneman, A Tversky, P Slovic eds 1981); *See also* Kahneman and Tversky, (1981) *On the Psychology of Prediction*, id, at 68, where they show that even statistical training 'does not change fundamental intuitions about uncertainty.' See especially, Tversky and Kahneman, *Belief in the Law of Small Numbers*, id, at 23–31.

17 Id, at 4–11.

18 Id, at 11–14.

19 Id, at 14–20.

20 Supra, note 7, at 463.

Kahneman and Tversky warned that 'the same type of systematic errors', often found in the epistemic or methodological value judgements of lay persons, 'can be found in the intuitive judgements of sophisticated scientists. Apparently, acquaintance with the theory of probability does not eliminate all erroneous intuitions concerning the laws of chance.'[21] The researchers even found that psychologists themselves, who should know better, used their feelings of confidence in their understanding of cases as a basis for predicting behaviour and diagnosing ailments, even though there was no correlation between their feelings of confidence and the correctness of the judgements.[22]

Such revelations about the prevalence and causes of expert error are not totally surprising since, after all, the experts have been wrong before. They were wrong when they said that irradiating enlarged tonsils was harmless. They were wrong when they said that X-raying feet, to determine shoe size, was harmless. They were wrong when they said that irradiating women's breasts, to alleviate mastitis, was harmless. And they were wrong when they said that witnessing A-bomb tests at close range was harmless.[23]

For all these reasons it should not be surprising that psychometric analysts have found, more generally, that once experts go beyond the data and rely on value judgements, they tend to be as error-prone and overconfident as lay people. With respect to technological risk assessment, psychometric researchers have concluded that experts systematically overlook many 'pathways to disaster'. These include: (1) failure to consider the way human error could cause technical systems to fail, as at Three Mile Island; (2) overconfidence in current scientific knowledge, such as that causing the 1976 collapse of the Teton Dam; and (3) failure to appreciate how technical systems, as a whole, function. For example, engineers were surprised when cargo compartment decompression destroyed control systems in some airplanes. Experts also typically overlook: (4) slowness to detect chronic, cumulative effects, eg as in the case of acid rain; (5) the failure to anticipate inadequate human responses to safety measures, eg failure of Chernobyl officials to evacuate immediately; and (6) the inability to anticipate 'common-mode' failures simultaneously afflicting systems that are designed to be independent. A simple fire at Brown's Ferry, Alabama, for example, damaged all five emergency core cooling systems for the reactor.[24]

Lessons To Be Learned From Experts' Errors

What all these cases of expert errors indicate, and what the larger failure of the positivists' ideal of complete scientific objectivity suggests, is that we need to reform our policymaking regarding hazardous technology and environmental impacts. This restructuring needs both to protect us from the most dangerous consequences of expert error and to ensure us that the lay people most likely to be affected by a risk have a larger voice in making public policy regarding it. To accomplish this reform, we need to have minimum federal standards for risk abatement and pollution control. In addition, we need to move policymaking out of regulatory agencies and into

---

21 Supra, note 16, at 46.
22 S Oskamp, Overconfidence in Case-Study Judgments, in Kahneman (1981) et al, supra, note 16, at 287–293.
23 See K Shrader-Frechette, *Nuclear Power and Public Policy*, at 98–100 (1983).
24 Slovic, Fischoff, and Lichtenstein, at 475–478.

procedures determined by citizen negotiation or, that failing, adversary assessment.[25] Citizen negotiation and adversary assessment, however, presuppose that experts do not always give us the 'right' or the 'rational' answers about how safe is safe enough. Rather the public themselves must help decide the merits of alternative answers to questions about technological and environmental safety.

Talk about alternative answers, however, suggests that we need to reform technology assessment, environmental impact analysis, and risk management in at least three ways. First, instead of having experts perform a single study, we need to develop alternative technology assessments or environmental impact analyses, weighting them on the basis of different value systems and different epistemic or methodological value judgements. Second, we need to debate the merits of these alternative analyses, each with its own interpretational and evaluative weights. In this way citizens can decide not only what policy they want, but also what value systems they wish to guide their decisions. Third, in areas where assessors obviously have more technical knowledge, eg of probabilities, we need to weight expert opinion on the basis of past predictive successes. In other words, we need to calibrate the scientists and engineers who provide information relevant to policy choices. Let's examine some of the reasons for each of these moves.

Since no necessary connection exists between Pareto optimality (the central concept of benefit-cost analysis) or Bayesian rules and socially desirable policy,[26] it would be helpful if there were some way to avoid the tendency to assume that economic methods or Bayesian rules, alone, reveal socially desirable policy. First, alternatively weighted assessments would enable persons to see that sound policy is not only a matter of economic calculations but also a question of epistemological and ethical analysis, as well as citizens' negotiations.

Second, ethically weighted assessments would provide a more helpful framework for democratic decisionmaking. Weighted policy analyses could show how different measures of social risks, costs, and benefits might respond to changed value assumptions.[27]

Third, because alternative, weighted analyses could explicitly bring epistemic and ethical value judgements into policy considerations at a very early stage of the process, citizens might be able to exercise more direct control over the values to which policy gives assent. To employ a system of alternative, ethically weighted analyses, among which policymakers and the public can decide, would be to recognize (1) that existing assessments already contain implicit ethical weights, and (2) that any proponent of a particular system of ethical and epistemological weights ought to be required to plead his or her case, along with advocates of different value positions, in the public court of reason.

A fourth reason for using alternative, ethically weighted analyses is that it appears more desirable than the procedures likely to be adopted in its place, eg using what economists and risk assessors call 'revealed preferences'.[28] Rather than assuming that past preferences (based on existing economic assumptions) are correct,

---

25 For more information about adversary assessment, *see* Shrader-Frechette, 1985, Ch 9; for discussion of negotiation as related to technology/risk assessment, *see* K Shrader-Frechette, *Risk and Rationality*, Ch 13.

26 D W Pearce, *Introduction, in* The Valuation of Social Cost, 132 (D W Pearce ed 1978). This point is defended in great detail in Shrader-Frechette, *Technology Assessment as Applied Philosophy of Science*, 6 Science, Technology, and Human Values 33–50 (1980).

27 This point is emphasized by Pearce, *supra*, at 134.

using current weighting schemes allows the public to determine what its value and policy choices ought to be.

The purpose of introducing alternative, ethically weighted assessments, of course, would not be to provide a prescription for policy, but to allow the public and other decisionmakers to see how sensitive policy conclusions are to different evaluative assumptions. The work of Kneese et al illustrates dramatically that what policy is said to be technically or economically feasible or unfeasible can change dramatically when different ethical weighing criteria are employed.[29]

Apart from the arguments for experimenting with different ethically weighted systems, there are a number of reasons for mandating that several alternative assessments be done for each project involving the imposition of public or societal risk. First, successful decisionmaking depends in part on knowing all the relevant facts and seeing all sides of a given 'story'. It is more likely that all sides to a story will be revealed if different groups, using different weights, do hazard analyses, than if only one project team performs only one study. The necessity of seeing different 'sides' is borne out by wide divergences among the conclusions of different assessments of the same risk. Various studies of liquefied natural gas risks for Oxnard, California, for example, differed by three orders of magnitude.[30]

Second, consumers have a right to free, informed consent to the technological and environmental risk imposed on them, just as they have analogous rights in the area of medical ethics.[31] If generating alternative analyses helps to ensure that all sides to a policy controversy are heard, then it likely also helps to ensure that public consent to risk is genuinely informed.

Third, all risks are value laden, and all hazard analyses employ judgemental strategies and epistemic or methodological value judgements. As a result, there are no wholly objective risk assessments. But if not, then technology assessment and risk analysis are in part subjective and likely to be highly politicized. And if so, they ought to be accomplished in a political and legal arena where citizens and their representatives are able to recognize the consequences of alternative assessments. Citi-

---

28 Some of the main practitioners of the method of revealed preferences include C Starr, C Whipple, and D Okrent. *See*, eg Starr and Whipple, Risks, *supra*, note 4. *See also* Okrent, *Comment on Societal Risk*, 208 Science 374 (1980). *See also* C Starr, Current Issues in Energy (1979), and D Okrent and C Whipple, Approach to Societal Risk Acceptance Criteria and Risk Management (PB–271–264 US Dept Commerce 1977). Although other means, eg the method of expressed preferences, of assigning measures to RCBA parameters have been discussed, I treat only the methods of market assignment of values and expressed preferences since these two dominate all current RCBA practice.

On the revealed preferences' scheme, society's current revealed preferences are determined on the basis of inductive inferences about what was allegedly preferred in the past. This means, for example, that if, in the past, society 'accepted' X number of automobile fatalities per 100,000 miles driven, then (all things being equal, which they never are) society will accept the same level of fatalities now. Hence, on this theory, society 'reveals' its preferences by means of past behavior which it tolerated.

For a critical perspective on the problems with the method of revealed preferences, *see* Schrader-Frechette, 1985a.

29 Kneese, Ben-David, and Schulze. *The Ethical Foundations of Benefit-Cost Analysis, in* Energy and the Future, 59–74 (D. Maclean and P. G. Brown eds 1982). A V Kneese, S Ben-David, and W D Schulze, A Study of the Ethical Foundations of Benefit-cost Analysis Techniques (unpublished report, to the National Science Foundation, Program in Ethics and Values in Science and Technology, August, 1979).

30 Kunreuther, Linnerooth, *et al, A Decision-Process Perspective on Risk and Policy Analysis, in* Resolving Locational Conflict 261 (R W Lake ed 1987).

31 for an analysis of some problems with consent as related to technology/risk assessment, *see* Schrader-Frechette, 1985a, Ch 4.

zens also need to be able to recognize which assessments are likely to give the most consideration to their interests.

Only if the naive positivists were correct in their belief (that there was a value-free algorithm guaranteeing theory choice) would it make sense to perform only one hazard analysis. Since they are not correct, and since 'acceptable risk' or 'reasonable policy' involves both procedural and ethical dimensions, as well as scientific ones, we need alternative assessments to capture the various ethical and political values informing public policy.[32]

On the new account of technology assessment and risk management that I want to defend, increasing the degree of analytical sophistication is not sufficient either for enfranchising the public or for resolving policy controversies. As environmental conflict over the proposed Cornwall facility demonstrated, expanded research efforts seldom are able to produce dispositive policy information. And if not, then decisionmakers must rely on procedural and democratic, rather than merely scientific, methods of assessing and managing risk.[33]

A fourth reason for performing alternative risk analyses, each with different methodological and ethical assumptions, is that there are numerous uncertainties in hazard assessment. Some of these uncertainties are evident in the wide margins of probabilistic error demonstrated in the Netherlands' study of WASH-1400, already mentioned.

In addition to preparing alternative assessments to represent different citizens' views, another methodological device for improving hazard analysis and technology assessment is to weight expert opinions. This suggestion amounts to giving more credence to experts whose risk estimates have been vindicated by past predictive success. By weighting expert opinions, analysts would have a way to exercise probabilistic control over them. They could attempt to determine whether a hazard assessor (who provides a subjective probability for some accident or failure rate) is 'well calibrated'. (A subjective probability assessor can be said to be well calibrated if for every probability value r in the class of all events to which the assessor assigns subjective probability r, the relative frequency with which these events occur is equal to r.)[34]

The primary justification for checking the 'calibration' of technology and risk assessors is that use of scientific methodology requires 'testing' the risk probabilities estimated by experts, especially since there is a wide divergence of opinion as to their actual values. In the famous WASH-1400 study of nuclear-reactor safety, for example, 30 experts were asked to estimate failure probabilities for 60 components, eg the rupture probability of a high quality steel pipe of diameter greater than three inches, per section-hour. On the WASH-1400 study, the average spread over the 60 components was 167,820. (The spread of these 30 expert opinions, for a given component, is the ratio of the largest to the smallest estimate.) In the same study, another disturbing fact was that the probability estimates of the 30 experts were not independent; if an expert was a pessimist with respect to one component, then there was a tendency for him to be a pessimist with respect to other components as well. Both the spread of expert opinions and their lack of independence suggest that it

---

32 *See* Schrader-Frechette, 1985a, Ch 9.
33 See Barnthouse, *et al, Population Biology on the Courtroom: the Hudson River Controversy,* 34 Bioscience 17–18 (1984).
34 Cooke, *supra,* note 15.

would be important to calibrate them, if we are interested in realistic technology assessment and policy analysis.[35]

A Model for Methodological Improvement and Objectivity in Technology Assessment and Risk Analysis: Scientific Proceduralism

So far, I have argued that we ought to reform technology assessment and quantified risk analysis by using ethical and methodological weighting techniques, performing alternative assessments and calibrating expert opinions. All of these methodological suggestions for improving technology assessment and risk management are predicated in two views: (1) that assessors ought to give up the rigid, anti-naturalistic, naive positivist assumption that expert assessments are wholly objective and value free, and (2) that contemporary technology/risk assessment needs to become more democratic, more open to control by the public, and more responsive to populist and procedural accounts of rational policy analysis and risk management.

What now remains to be established is how to safeguard scientific rationality and objectivity, even though technology assessment/risk assessment methods need to take account of democratic, procedural, ethical and political factors, namely, populist factors allegedly not capable of being handled in purely rational and narrowly objective ways. Such a procedural account of technology assessment and hazard management presupposes that rationality and objectivity, in their final stages, require an appeal to particular cases as similar to other cases believed to be correct. This is what legal reasoning requires, just as Aristotle recognized, rather than an appeal only to scientific method.

The key to this procedural account of technology assessment, policy analysis and risk management is Aristotle's belief that there are no explicit rules for ethical or value judgements. Instead we must use inexplicit and general rules to guide our moral reasoning. Aristotle believed that we came to know these inexplicit rules by relying on the ability of a group of people, similarly brought up, to see certain cases as like others. This is also what Wittgensteinians are disposed to believe about all instances of human learning.

At the final level of technology assessment and risk management, Aristotle and Wittgenstein must be correct. Ultimately even rules must give way, not to further appeals to specific scientific rules, as the naive positivists and many scientists presuppose, but to a shared appreciation of similarities between cases.[36]

As such, this Popperian and Wittgensteinian account (scientific proceduralism) anchors objectivity to a legal, rather than a scientific, model of knowing and to a largely procedural, rather than substantive, account of rational assessment. Criticisms made by the scientific and lay community likely to be affected by a given risk, technology, or environmental impact would help to safeguard the procedural and democratic aspects of rational technology/risk assessment. Calibration of expert opinions and sensitivity analyses would help to safeguard its predictive and scientific components – namely, its rationality and objectivity.

---

35 *Id*, Ch 2.
36 *See* B Williams, Ethics and the Limits of Philosophy 97–98; (1985).

This sketch of the scientific objectivity characteristic of a more populist notion of technology/risk assessment is premised on the Popperian assumption that open, critical and methodologically pluralistic approaches (via citizen participation, alternative assessments, sensitivity analyses, calibration and ethical/methodological weighting schemes) come closest to revealing the theoretical, linguistic and cultural invariants of reality, much as a plurality of experimental perspectives helps reveal the invariants of quantum mechanical systems.

Conclusion

In the view that I am suggesting, what are the relevant variance principles applicable to technology assessment and hazard management? These principles are that risk behaviour or science policy is rational and objective if it survives criticism by various communities of citizens and experts, each with different transformations or evaluations of the same hazard.[37] Arriving at rational policy, on this account, requires an epistemology in which what we ought to *believe* about technology assessment and risk analysis is bootstrapped onto how we ought to act – that is, we ought to *act* in ways that permit open criticism, that recognize due-process rights, that give equal consideration to the interests of all persons, and so on. Acting in this way, however, is a matter of realizing that the constraints or invariants in hazard analysis are in part realized through normative judgements. This is because the constraints must be implemented in institutional forms recognizing values such as equal treatment and informed consent. This means that rational assessment, on the view defended here, is irreducibly political in much the same sense that quantum mechanics is irreducibly statistical. But if so, then any account of rational technology assessment or policy analysis is as much a part of politics as science.[38]

---

37 For a similar view, *see* D G Holdsworth, Objectivity, Scientific Theories and the Perception of Risk (Unpublished paper available from author at Ontario Hydroelectric, Toronto, Canada).
38 *See* D G Holdsworth, Objectivity and Control, (Unpublished paper available from author at Ontario Hydroelectric, Toronto, Canada).

What Do We Know About Making Risk Comparisons?

Emilie Roth,[1] M Granger Morgan,[2,3] Baruch Fischhoff,[2] Lester Lave,[2] and Ann Bostrom[2]

Introduction

A tempting way to describe the risks of hazardous technologies is by comparison with other, better known risks,[2,3] such as: the cancer risk of living at the boundary of a nuclear power plant for five years equals the cancer risk of eating 40 tablespoons of peanut butter (due to aflatoxin).[3] Despite their appeal,[4] such comparisons have come in for considerable criticism.[5-7] There are two major thrusts to this criticism. One is that these comparisons reduce risks to a single dimension (eg loss of life expectancy), whereas many risks are multidimensional. As a result, risks are not fully represented. The second thrust is that risk comparisons are used not just to communicate how large risks are, but also to persuade listeners regarding how large risks should be (eg if you are willing to eat 40 tablespoons of peanut butter over the next five years, then you should be willing to live near a nuclear power plant). Such implicit rhetorical arguments ignore critical elements of people's risky decisions, such as how voluntary the choices are and what benefits they are expected to provide. Because people perceive risks in multiattribute terms, the fact that a risk has a low value on a single focal dimension (eg estimated fatalities in an average year) does not imply its acceptability.[8] As a result of these logical and ethical flaws, it should not be surprising that risk comparisons have provoked anger and mistrust (responses that can only be aggravated by scepticism about how far the risks estimates themselves can be trusted).

In order to help chemical industry spokespeople avoid these pitfalls, Covello et al[1] developed a manual advising plant managers on how to present risk comparisons so that the public will perceive them as useful and legitimate. Their manual has been published and distributed widely by the Chemical Manufacturers Association.

1 Westinghouse Science and Technology Center, Pittsburgh, Pennsylvania 15235.
2 Department of Engineering and Public Policy, Carnegie Mellon University, Pittsburgh, Pennsylvania 15213.
3 To whom correspondence should be addressed.

The manual represents a significant contribution to the risk communication literature. It provides, for the first time, an analysis of the different ways that risk comparison statements have traditionally been employed and offers a framework for evaluating them. Covello et al enumerate 14 commonly used types of risk comparisons, which they then group into five categories, ranked according to their predicted acceptability to lay people (see Table 4.1). The manual recommends that spokespeople select the highest ranking risk comparisons whenever possible, and use low ranking risk comparisons with caution, alert to the possibility that communications using them could backfire.

Because the research base is thin, Covello et al's ranking is based on their accumulated experience and intuitions. Because of its potential significance for guiding risk communication, their proposal warrants empirical evaluation. The present study focuses on how well Covello at al's ranking predicted lay people's judgement of the acceptability of risk comparisons. Its results provide us with a point of departure for a theoretical analysis of Covello et al's proposal.

The Study

The Covello et al manual provides concrete examples of their 14 categories of risk comparisons, set in the context of a specific scenario: A manager of a chemical plant in a small town is faced with the task of communicating to the community about the risk of a chemical produced by the plant (see Appendix). We asked several groups of lay people to evaluate the acceptability of these statements.

Table 4.1 *Risk comparison categorization and ranking system (Covello et al)*

First-rank risk comparisons
  1 Comparisons of the same risk at two different times
  2 Comparisons with a standard
  3 Comparisons with different estimates of the same risk
Second-rank risk comparisons (second choice – less desirable)
  4 Comparisons of the risk of doing and not doing something
  5 Comparisons of alternative solutions to the same problem
  6 Comparisons with the same risk as experienced in other places
Third-rank risk comparisons (third choice – even less desirable)
  7 Comparisons of average risk with peak risk at a particular time or location
  8 Comparisons of the risk from one source of a particular adverse effect with the risk from all sources of that same adverse effect
Fourth-rank risk comparisons (fourth choice – marginally acceptable)
  9 Comparisons of risk with cost or of cost/risk ratio with cost/risk ratio
 10 Comparisons of risk with benefit
 11 Comparisons of occupational with environmental risks
 12 Comparisons with other risks from the same source, such as the same facility or the same risk agent
 13 Comparisons with other specific causes of the same disease, illness, or injury
Fifth-rank comparisons (last choice – rarely acceptable – use with extreme caution!)
 14 Comparisons of unrelated risks.

Such an evaluation requires an operational definition of 'acceptability'. The definition intended by Covello et al is suggested by the following quotation.

> *The highest-ranking comparisons are assumed to be those that put the least strain on the trust relationship between a plant manager and the public. These comparisons tend to strike even skeptical listeners as relevant, appropriate, and helpful information. The lowest-ranking comparisons, on the other hand, are those that have no intuitively obvious claim to relevance, appropriateness, or helpfulness. Such comparisons are more likely to be seen as manipulative or misleading – that is, as efforts to preempt judgments about the acceptability of the risk.*
> *(Source: Covello et al, 1988, p17)*

Thus, there are several distinct elements that contribute to acceptability. As a result, we devised seven rating scales that seemed to tap different elements of Covello et al's definition of 'acceptable'. These scales appear in Table 4.2. Scale 1 asks about how clear and easy to understand the statement is. Scales 2 and 3 consider the perceived relevance and helpfulness of the risk comparison. Scale 4 asks whether the risk comparison seems misleading, in the sense of underemphasizing or overemphasizing the risk. Scales 5 and 6 ask how the risk comparison will affect public trust in the plant manager. Scale 7 provides an overall measure of acceptability, by asking whether the statement should be included in the plant manager's talk. Our subjects' response should reveal how these alternative criteria are correlated with one another as well as with Covello et al's predictions.

Table 4.2 *Scales used to rate Covello et al statements*

1 This statement is clear, easy to understand.	☐ ☐ ☐ ☐ ☐	This statement is unclear, difficult to understand.
2 This statement will help townspeople to better understand the risk.	☐ ☐ ☐ ☐ ☐	This statement will *not* help townspeople to better understand the risk.
3 This statement gives information needed by townspeople in their personal decisions about the risk.	☐ ☐ ☐ ☐ ☐	This statement gives *no* information needed by townspeople in their personal decisions about the risk.

This statement's tone correctly conveys the risk.

4 This statement's tone underemphasizes the risk.	☐ ☐ ☐ ☐ ☐	This statement's tone overemphasizes the risk.
5 This statement is likely to reassure the townspeople.	☐ ☐ ☐ ☐ ☐	This statement is likely to scare the townspeople.
6 This statement is likely to increase the townspeople's trust in the plant manager.	☐ ☐ ☐ ☐ ☐	This statement is likely to decrease the townspeople's trust in the plant manager.
7 This statement should definitely be included in the plant manager's talk.	☐ ☐ ☐ ☐ ☐	This statement should definitely be left out of the plant manager's talk.

Method

Participants

Four groups participated in the study: (A) second-year graduate business students ($N = 13$); (B) members (or their spouses) of a suburban garden club from a middle-to-upper income community ($N = 33$); (C) members of a synagogue ($N = 28$); and (D) members of a Protestant church ($N = 21$) from middle and lower income communities in Pittsburgh. The 95 total participants included a wide range of ages, socioeconomic backgrounds, religions, and both sexes. Participants were either paid $10 or had a $10 donation made to their organization.

Material

In order to introduce the evaluation task, we converted the scenario described in the manual into a cover story which read as follows:

> *Suppose that the manager of a chemical plant that manufactures ethylene oxide in the small midwestern town of Evanston has been asked to give a talk to a local community meeting about risks posed by his plant. The local newspaper plans to reprint the speech in its entirety and make it widely available. People in the town are concerned about the possible risks posed by the plant, but there is no crisis situation or serious confrontational atmosphere.*

> *The plant manager has been a friend of yours for many years. He is concerned about making this speech and, as an old friend, has asked you for your candid advice about some things he is considering saying.*

> *Before starting, here is some background information: ethylene oxide is used in almost all hospitals and other medical facilities as a disinfecting agent. However, it can cause cancer. A risk assessment has shown that the cancer risk that the Evanston plant poses for citizens living in the town is about two additional cancers per year for every million people exposed (there are in fact only 3500 people in Evanston). The plant manager is looking for appropriate and acceptable ways to communicate this risk to the public and to compare it with other risks.*

> *He wants to give a clear honest picture of the risks. He feels that this is both his ethical responsibility and that if he were to misrepresent the situation, eventually that would be discovered and hurt his credibility. He is concerned, however, that even an accurate statement can come out sounding wrong or have the wrong impact. He also wants to keep the talk fairly short and simple, while still doing the topic justice.*

> *The following are 14 different pieces of text that the plant manager is considering using in his talk. Some of them overlap a bit in content. Assume that he will edit them so that they fit together well without much*

overlap. For each statement, please give your advice on the following questions.

This cover story appeared on the front page of a booklet that contained the 14 statements. There was one statement per page. Each statement appeared on the left side of its page, while the seven rating scales appeared on the right.

As indicated in Table 4.2, each rating scale had five points with endpoints labelled. These were coded 1–5 from left to right. With the exception of scale 4 (tone of statement), a lower number indicates a more favourable value. In the case of scale 4, both endpoints of the scale represent unfavourable values (1 = underemphasizes the risk; 5 = overemphasizes the risk).

The order of presenting the 14 statements was varied across participants. Fifteen of group B received the statements in Covello et al's original order, while the remaining 18 received the statements in the reverse order. Two random orders of the 14 statements were also generated. Approximately half of the participants in each of the other three groups received the statements in each of these orders.

Groups A, C and D completed the questionnaires in a group setting at the site of their organization or class. Group B members received brochures by mail.

Results

Results Across Groups

Table 4.3 shows mean responses for each statement on each scale for all 95 participants. With the exception of scale 4, Covello et al's proposal predicts that each successive group of statements will have higher means than its predecessors.[4] This was not found. Spearman rank-order correlations were computed between the mean ratings of each of the 14 statements and the rank order of the class to which it belongs. Table 4.4 presents these correlations, both across all 95 participants and for each of the four groups.[5] None of the seven scales was significantly correlated with Covello et al's order in the direction predicted. For all participants combined, the correlation with scale 7 (whether to include the statement in the plant manager's talk) is close to zero ($r = -0.13$). The only significant correlation ($r = 0.51$, $p < 0.05$) is that with scale 1 (clarity of statement). However, its sign is opposite to that predicted by Covello et al. Each of the four groups produced a similar pattern of results, described more fully below.

Friedman two-way analyses of variance computed on the rank sums across the 95 participants were significant for all seven scales ($p < 0.001$). This non-parametric test indicates that there are reliable differences in the ratings among the 14 statements (not just the differences that were predicted).

---

4 On scale 4 a '3' was the most favourable value. Because all mean responses for scale 4 were less than 3, higher ratings indicate more favourable responses.

5 Analyses were also performed on the rank sums for each statement. The rank sum for each scale was computed by determining each participant's rank ordering of the 14 statements. The rank sums across the 95 participants were highly correlated, with the mean scores appearing in the table (all correlations above 0.85). The results using this measure were essentially the same as when mean scores were examined.

Table 4.3 *Mean responses for the 14 sentences on each scale
(average across all 95 participants)*

		Scales*						
		1	2	3	4	5	6	7
Rank	Statements**	Clarity	Aids understanding	Information needed	Under/over-emphasizes risk	Reassuring	Increases trust	Should be included
First	1	1.71	2.16	2.10	2.77	2.00	1.75	1.82
	2	2.29	2.76	2.55	2.57	2.54	2.50	2.55
	3	3.02	2.73	2.32	2.87	2.95	2.54	2.92
Second	4	2.19	2.67	2.37	2.67	2.94	2.71	2.68
	5	2.10	2.54	2.32	2.66	3.04	2.59	2.98
	6	1.69	2.69	2.58	2.24	2.19	2.33	2.35
Third	7	2.17	2.48	2.24	2.81	2.85	2.71	2.71
	8	2.50	2.51	2.34	2.85	2.76	2.44	2.61
Fourth	9	1.63	2.70	2.37	2.81	2.44	2.44	2.36
	10	1.56	2.81	2.10	2.53	2.65	2.53	2.27
	11	2.08	2.13	1.88	2.66	2.26	2.42	2.37
	12	2.15	3.67	3.47	2.12	3.25	3.44	3.63
	13	1.51	1.98	2.03	2.62	2.44	2.41	2.42
Fifth	14	1.82	2.03	2.18	2.57	2.35	2.48	2.39

* For scales 1–3 and 5–7, 1 is the most favourable response. For scale 4, 1 = underemphasizes risk, 5 = overemphasizes risk.

** The statements are listed in decreasing favourability, according to Covello et al's predictions.

Table 4.4 *Spearman rank-order correlation with the Covello et al ranking*

Scale	All groups	Garden club	MBA students	Synagogue	Church
Clarity	−.51	−.60	−.27	−.19	−.45
Aids understanding	−.24	−.04	−.16	−.12	−.24
Information needed	−.31	−.43	−.04	.03	−.32
Over/underemphasizes risk	−.35	−.36	−.06	−.32	−.18
Reassuring	−.10	−.42	.07	.02	−.09
Increases trust	.01	.23	.29	−.12	.11
Should be included	−.13	−.30	−.09	.08	−.02
	N = 95	N = 33	N = 13	N = 28	N = 21

All correlations at or above .46 are significant at the .05 level. Correlations at or above .65 are significant at the .01 levd.

Table 4.5 presents Pearson correlations among the seven rating scales, computed on mean ratings over all 95 participants. As can be seen, these means tended to be positively and significantly correlated,[6] indicating that statements judged posi-

---

6 As mentioned, higher ratings indicate more favourable responses on scale 4, so that the negative correlations there are consistent with the positive correlations on the other variables.

tively in one respect were also judged positively in others. These results indicate that the weak correlations between scale ratings and the Covello et al ranking cannot be be attributed to their being such poor measures that they cannot correlate with anything. Although all scales correlated with subjects' judgements of whether a statement should be included (scale 7), the strongest predictors were how reassuring it seemed and whether it seemed likely to increase trust.

The statements tended to be rated positively on all scales, with a rating of '1' given in almost 40 per cent of all cases. One possible explanation is that the verbal labels anchoring the scales were too moderate (so that 1 connotes *good* rather than *excellent* performance). The resulting 'ceiling effect' would reduce differences between statements, even though there were still statistically reliable differences in acceptability (see An Ordered Categorical Response Model, p64). A second possibility is that most statements were actually pretty good, even though some were intended to represent seriously flawed risk comparisons (see Risk: Comparisons Deviating from Predictions, p65).

Table 4.5 *Correlation matrix for the seven scales*

	Scale						
Scale	1	2	3	4	5	6	7
1 Clarity	1.00						
2 Aids understanding	0.28	1.00					
3 Information needed	0.22	0.88	1.00				
4 Over/underemphasizes risk	0.32	−0.52	−0.66	1.00			
5 Reassuring	0.56	0.66	0.55	−0.09	1.00		
6 Increases trust	0.29	0.74	0.72	−0.49	0.82	1.00	
7 Should be included	0.53	0.71	0.75	−0.36	0.90	0.91	1.00

Breakdown by Group

The results are similar when the four groups are considered separately. For three groups, there was no significant correlation between mean scale ratings and the Covello et al ordering. For group B, there was a negative correlation ($-0.60; P < 0.05$) between Covello et al's ranking and subjects' clarity ratings.

Every correlation between mean scale ratings of the different groups was positive, indicating a consistent degree of agreement. Correlations ranged between 0.23 and 0.88 with a mean, using Fisher's Z-transformation, of 0.63.

Effects of Order of Presentation

Mean ratings were computed separately for each of the four orders of presentation. Three of the four groups were highly similar to one another and to the overall averages. These were the two groups receiving random orders and the group rating the 14 statements in the order predicted to show decreasing acceptability. These means were all unrelated to Covello et al's prediction order. The ratings of the 15 participants who received statements in Covello et al's original order were significantly correlated ($P < 0.05$) in three cases. Two were in the predicted direction, scales 4 and 6 (–0.57 and 0.52, respectively); while one, scale 5 (–0.52) was in the opposite direction. Overall, the weak and inconsistent pattern with this small group does not shake the general conclusion that order of presentation did not affect subjects' ratings.

An Ordered Categorical Response Model

An ordered categorical response model, specifically a three-level ordered probit model, was used to clarify the differences in ratings among the 14 statements.[9-10][7] The model included the 14 statements, 7 scales, 4 orders of presentation, and 4 groups as predictor variables and the ratings as the dependent variable. Ratings were recoded into three categories, where 0 was 'best' (rating '3' on scale 4; '1' and '2' on other scales), 1 was intermediate ('2' and '4' on scale 4, '3' on others), and 2 was 'worst' ('1' and '5' on scale 4; '4' and '5' on others).[8] The model was estimated in LIMDEP,[11] using maximum likelihood estimation. The base case (represented by the intercept) was item 14, scale 7, order 1 and group 4 (D). This analysis characterizes predictors by beta coefficients that indicate changes in the underlying dependent variable, all else being equal. According to Covello et al hypothesis, the beta coefficients for statements 1–13 should all be negative because each is contrasted with statement 14, which was predicted to be the worst. The coefficients should be increasingly negative as the statements become more attractive and statement number decreases.

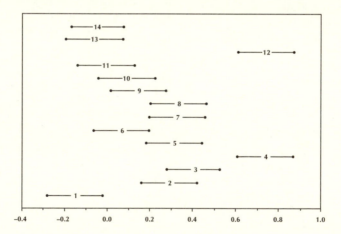

Figure 4.1 Estimated beta coefficients for the statement dummies from the ordered probit regression model, with 95 per cent confidence intervals marked (based on the coefficient's estimated standard deviation). Statement 14 is the base case (intercept).

---

7 An ordered probit model assumes that the observed ratings are discrete and have ordinal properties (ie no interval relation between rating points is assumed), but that the underlying (unobservable) dependent variable (ie statement acceptability) is continuous and normally distributed, conditional on the predictive variables.

8 The original five-point ratings for all scales, except 4, were also fit with an analogous model as was an alternative three-point set of collapsed ratings (0 = 1; 1 = 2,3,4; 2 = 5 for all scales except 4, which was collapsed as above). Similar results were obtained and are available upon request.

The beta coefficients for the 14 statements and their 95 per cent confidence bands are presented in Figure 4.1. They show reliable differences in ratings among the 14 statements that are not captured by the Covello et al ranking system, even when effects of scale, order of presentation, and group are statistically controlled. The beta coefficients typically had the wrong sign (positive). There was no consistent trend over the five ranks.

The analysis yielded significant coefficients for scale and group, but not for order of presentation. The lack of an order effect with this more sophisticated analysis strengthens our inclination to discount the weak differences reported in the previous section. The overall fit of the model is moderately good. The χ^2 statistic from the log-likelihood ratio test is highly significant (727.5, 24 df, p < 0.001) and the model correctly predicts 55 per cent of the observations.

Discussion

Our subjects' ratings reliably distinguished among the statements, but not in the way predicted by Covello et al. This section discusses why Covello et al's predictions might have fared so poorly and offers some alternative perspectives on risk comparison statements.

Risk: Comparisons Deviating from Predictions

One place to look for insight is at those statements whose ratings deviated the most from the Covello et al predictions. As can be seen in Table 4.3, three statements at the top of Covello et al's list were near the bottom of our subjects' ratings, while three of the four worst statements according to Covello et al were rated among the best here.

Comparisons of Risks Across Domains Fared Better Than Expected

According to Covello et al and others,[7] risk comparisons are particularly problematic when they involve risks with very different features. As a result, the examples that Covello et al identify as worst involve risks from different domains. Their statement 13 (representing comparisons that invoke other specific causes of the same consequence) compares the risk of cancer from the chemical ethylene oxide to the risk of cancer from X-rays. Their least favoured statement (14) compares ethylene oxide with other hazards whose consequences did not include cancer (eg lightning). Nonetheless, both statements were in the top half of the set for six of the seven scales. Indeed, they were the highest ranked statements on scale 2 – how much a statement would 'help townspeople to better understand the risk'.

Covello et al's critique of cross-risk comparisons applies most strongly to cases where they are advanced with a rhetorical purpose – of the form 'if you accept Risk A, then you ought to accept (equivalent) Risk B'. Such comparisons have, however, no logical force unless the two risks are equivalent on all their risk features (not to mention their associated benefits and control options). A more modest use of risk comparisons is to convey a feeling for the magnitude of a risk, with no claim of acceptability. Such magnitude comparisons might focus on either the probability of negative consequences (eg as likely as being struck by lightning during an equivalent exposure period) or on their intensity (eg as painful as a root canal without anasthesia). Given their more limited ambitions, magnitude comparisons should be easier to make appropriately than acceptability comparisons.

Conceivably, Covello et al's own sensitivity to these issues kept them from creating truly bad risk comparisons, particularly ones containing indefensible acceptability arguments. As a result, our subjects were able to focus on the magnitude comparisons in the statements. These were, in turn, executed relatively well. If that is the case, then, in effect, Covello et al foiled their own prediction when they created the illustrative statements.

Comparison of Occupational with Environmental Risks Fared Better Than Expected

A second unexpected success was statement 11, which was intended to exemplify comparisons between occupational risks and environmental risks. Rather than emerging near the bottom of the ratings, statement 11 appeared in the top half of all seven scales. It was ranked best on scale 3 ('gives information needed by the townspeople in their personal decisions about the risk') and was one of the top 3 statements on scale 2 ('will help townspeople to better understand the risk'). Covello et al do not explain why they expected such comparisons to be received particularly poorly. One possible reason is that the assumption of occupational risks often implies the acceptance of risk–benefit trade-offs that seem quite inappropriate outside of working life.

However, although Covello et al's statement 11 does refer to occupational and environmental risks, it does not invite risk–benefit comparisons. Rather, its main thrust is that the risk to employees is very small, implying that the risk to the community will be even smaller. Again, the example may have fared unexpectedly well because it lacked the particular feature of its category that people find objectionable.

Comparison with a Standard and Comparisons with Different Estimates of the Same Risk Fared Worse Than Expected

Covello et al stressed the importance of being honest and forthright in providing risk information. Elements of such frankness include indicating uncertainties or disagreements regarding the size of the risk, discussing worst-case estimates as well as best-guess estimates, and noting how a risk compares to various proposed standards of acceptability.

Statements 2 and 3 were intended to exemplify this principle. Statement 2 compares the focal risk to five different emission standards, while statement 3 provides six alternative estimates of the size of the risk, based on different data, different assumptions and different originating sources. Both statements should have been attractive. However, each was ranked in the bottom half of the set on six of the seven scales. They were among the worst three items on scale 1, measuring how 'clear, easy to understand' a statement was. This last result suggests that these statements may have been ranked so poorly because of the quantitative and probabilistic information that they contained. The price paid for such candor may have been confusing recipients. Statement 3 may have been particularly difficult because it included small probabilities presented in decimal form (eg 0,007 cancers per 3500 persons). The Covello et al manual itself explicitly warns against this format. Statement 8, which was designed to reflect a more effective way of communicating small probabilities, had some of the worst ratings on the clarity scale. Apparently, we still have much to learn about presenting such information.

A second possible source of confusion in these statements was the need to integrate the multiple perspectives that they presented. For example, what are recipients to make of a risk that meets one of several standards, especially when they know little about the organization that set each standard or the purpose for which it was set? Similarly, how are they to reconcile competing scientific estimates of a particular risk without understanding the underlying science (and scientists) producing those estimates? Offering multiple perspectives may be a meaningless gesture unless recipients can put them into context. Clearly, more research is needed here as well.

Comparisons of Risk of Doing and Not Doing Something Fared Worse Than Expected

Statement 4, which was intended to illustrate comparing the risks of doing and not doing something, received unexpectedly poor evaluations. It ranked in the bottom half of the set on six of the seven scales, faring particularly poorly on scales 1 (clarity), 5 (reassuring), and 6 (increases trust). It shared the bottom in the ordered probit analysis (Figure 4.1). Here, too, presenting small probabilities in decimal form may have been problematic. In addition, statement 4 notes that the risk could be reduced (by a small amount) by purchasing new equipment, but without indicating whether the plant intends to do so. Silence on that issue may have raised suspicions and reduced ratings related to trust.

Explanations for Failure of Predictions

Reviewing our results in the light of these arguments suggests three reasons why Covello et al's predictions may have failed.

Flaws in Measurement

The first possibility is that Covello et al's theory is correct, but our rating scales failed to measure what they intended by 'acceptability'. As mentioned, we used a variety of rating scales in an attempt to capture the diverse elements of the complex notion of 'acceptability' advanced by Covello et al. It is, of course, possible that none of our rating scales was related to the lay notion of 'acceptability'. However, the fact that so diverse a set of scales failed to correlate with Covello et al's predicted ranking indicates the need to clarify the goals of risk comparisons as well as to study how to reach them.[8]

Flaws in the Examples

A second possible source of failure is that the 14 statements did not capture the essence of the categories that they were meant to represent. The section under Risk: Comparisons Deviating from Predictions, above, raises some such possibilities (eg avoiding the risk acceptability arguments that can make some categories offensive, burdening relatively sound comparisons with unfamiliar decimal probabilities). The fact that recognized experts in this field might encounter such problems suggests the limits to our understanding of risk comparisons.

Flaws in the Underlying Theory

A third possibility is that the theory underlying the ranking system is flawed. It is always difficult to falsify a theory when there is uncertainty about how it should be implemented and evaluated. None the less, it should be troubling to find failures with statements produced by the theory's creators and evaluation scales adapted from their stated objectives.

In Covello et al's theory, there are two obvious places to work on: its classification scheme and the predicted rankings of its categories. Covello et al's classification scheme sorts risk comparisons primarily according to what risks are being compared, and only secondarily according to the purpose of the comparison or the specific information that it contains. Elaborating these features may be a way to improve our understanding of risk comparisons.

Toward a Systematic Classification of Risk Comparisons

One significant contribution of the Covello et al proposal is describing the variety of features of a risk that comparison statements can highlight. Indeed, each category in their system deals with a different aspect of risk. For example, statement 1 describes trends over time, while leaving the communication of absolute and relative magnitude to other statements. It seems unlikely that any criterion of acceptability could apply to messages having such a variety of purposes. Each is legitimate for some purposes and flawed for others, with its acceptability depending heavily on the quality of its implementation.

One way to conceptualize the potential purposes of risk comparisons is according to the roles that they may play in helping people to make decisions about risks. From a decision theory perspective, a decision involves a choice among options, each of which can be characterized by a vector of attributes, representing its pos-

---

8 Any other feature of our measurement procedure might also be called into question. For example, in their thoughtful response to this article, Slovic et al, 1990[12] wonder about what would have happened had we used another cover story. Progress here requires accounting for both those patterns that did emerge in previous studies as well as for those that did not.

sible consequences. With risky decisions, at least some of those attributes involve uncertain negative consequences. When considering decision options (risky or otherwise), one needs to go through three stages: identifying the set of relevant attributes (ie the ones that might matter when one makes a choice), characterizing each option in terms of each attribute, and determining the relative importance of each attribute (in this set of options).

Risk comparisons have a legitimate role to play in supporting each of these stages – that is, they can help people to determine:

1   what attributes merit consideration;
2   how each option rates on each relevant attribute;
3   how those attributes should be weighted.

Evoking Attributes of a Risk

Risk perception research has found that people are capable of rating risks on a large set of attributes (eg voluntariness, equity, dread), which are relevant to their judgements of risk acceptability.[13,14] The fact that these attributes are recognized when they are presented explicitly carries, however, no assurance that will be recalled spontaneously when a risk is mentioned. Indeed, the great number of possible attributes means that it would be hard to bear all in mind at once. A risk comparison might be able to help people by evoking decision-relevant attributes that they might otherwise neglect. Doing so in an unbiased fashion will pose a challenge to the design of communications. Considerations that are out of sight tend to be out of mind.[15,16] Conversely, those comparisons that are made may powerfully shape the attributes that people do consider (eg 'This is the next dioxin' or 'They tell us this is safe, but that's what they said about cigarettes and Agent Orange' or 'They are just like tobacco company scientists').

Determining the Values on Risk Attributes

Once the attributes relevant to a decision have been identified, decision-makers must determine how each option rates on each attribute. Conveying information about the magnitude of consequences is one clear purpose of risk communications. As mentioned, risk comparisons might be a useful tool for doing so, by providing a familiar point of comparison for an unfamiliar hazard – as long as claims of risk acceptability can be avoided.

Crystallizing Preferences

A final role for risk communications is helping people examine and crystallize their own preferences. Simplistic models of decision-making assume a high degree of articulation in people's preferences – namely, they will know how to make all relevant tradeoffs, judging the relative importance of different outcomes. However, with options involving the sort of esoteric consequences involved with many risky decisions, people may welcome non-coercive suggestions of alternative perspectives.[17] Properly qualified risk comparisons might fulfill that role.

Reflections on Category Definition

The analysis above suggests that the details on content may be more important than the form of a risk comparison in determining its acceptability. This may explain some of the lack of predictive power of the Covello et al classification scheme. In some cases, the categories in Covello et al's taxonomy are sufficiently broad to include statements with quite varied character. Conversely, statements that communicate very similar information by different means are sometimes classified separately. For example, statement 11 uses the experience of plant employees as an upperbound estimate of the risk to the townspeople. As such, this statement might arguably belong in category 6 with (other) comparisons that use the risk level experienced by one group as an input to estimating the risk to another.

Category 4 ('comparison of the risk of doing something versus not doing it') provides another example of a category that includes comparisons with varied content. For example, it includes both actions intended to increase risk and actions intended to reduce risks, which may invoke different attitudes. Moreover, all such comparisons invoke risk–benefit tradeoffs, in so far as other consequences accompany these actions. As a result, category 4 overlaps category 9. The fact that these tradeoffs are left implicit in statement 4 may account for some reasons why it was judged more poorly than statement 9, where the tradeoffs are explicit.

Conclusions

Covello et al have enumerated and classified a variety of risk comparisons. They were not, however, able to predict the acceptability of statements generated to represent those categories, at least as measured by our subjects' responses. This failure seems to reflect a combination of (1) difficulty in translating the theory into concrete communications, (2) confounding the different possible purposes of risk comparisons within individual messages, and (3) the absence of adequate research on how to represent different kinds of information credibly. As a result, we need more and better theoretical and empirical research to build on Covello et al's challenging beginning.

Appendix

The following is the text of the 14 specific risk comparison statements, developed by Covello et al (1988), which were evaluated in this research.

Statement 1

'Health risk from emissions of ethylene oxide at our plant are 40 per cent less than a year ago, when we installed exhaust scrubbers. With more equipment coming in, we expect to reduce the risk another 40 per cent by the end of the next year.

'Despite the extremely low health risks to the community from emissions of ethylene oxide at our plant, we are still looking for ways to lower these levels further. These are some of the plans we have under way to accomplish this: (provide specifics). As we implement these steps, we will keep you and the community informed of our progress. We will also continue to monitor our workers and keep track of health statistics within the community to ensure that the risks posed by our plant to our workers and to the community remain in the future as low as, if not lower than, they are today. Since some of you may have further questions about these and other matters concerning our plant operations, as plant manager, I am providing my work and home phone numbers so you can call me. I will do my best to supply you with answers to your questions as quickly as possible.'

Statement 2

'Emissions of ethylene oxide from our plant are half the levels permitted by the US Environmental Protection Agency and by our state's Department of Environmental Protections.

'Emissions of ethylene oxide from our plant are five times lower than the US Environmental Protection Agency's safety standard.

'Plant emissions of ethylene oxide are five times below what was permitted under the old EPA standard, and two times below the level established by the new, stricter EPA standard.'

Statement 3

'Laboratory studies on rats and mice suggest that current exposure to ethylene oxide may cause seven cancers in 1000 generations of residents in this city. This estimate is the maximum that would occur under worst-case conditions. Actual health effects from exposure to ethylene oxide are likely to be lower.

'Let me try to put this number into the context of other numbers. We've said that our worst case prediction is seven-thousandths of one extra cancer within the next 70 years from our plant's emissions of ethylene oxide. Now, no one ever gets seven-thousandths of a cancer. A better way to see the effect is that if 130 different communities the same size as Evanston had a plant just like this one, 129 of those towns would see no effect on their cancer rate. One of the 130 Evanstons might have a single extra cancer.

'Our best estimate of the risk is 0.001 cancers per 3500 persons using what we believe are realistic assumptions. This estimate is based on work done by our own scientists and by researchers at Evanston University. However, you should be aware that the state Department of Environmental Protection (DEP) has calculated a worst-case risk estimate of 0.007 cancers per 3500 persons. DEP made the assumption that all individuals living in Evanston would be exposed to emissions of ethylene oxide 24 hours a day for 70 years. This formula gave DEP a human-lifetime dose. DEP then took the best available laboratory information for ethylene oxide – data obtained from studies on the laboratory mice most likely to develop cancer in response to ethylene oxide – and calculated first the lowest dose that caused adverse health effects in mice and then the equivalent dose in humans. On the basis of these and other pieces of information, DEP concluded that the maximum cancer risk to people in the community is 0.007 cancers per 3500 persons over 70 years.

'Our worst-case estimate of the risk is seven thousandths of a cancer per 3500 persons over the next 70 years. How sure are we that the risk is really this low? The bad news is that we're not as sure as we'd like to be. Risk assessment is a pretty new science, based on models and assumptions rather than hard data. The good news is that we're almost certain the risk is actually smaller than our estimate – we've instructed our scientists to make every assumption on the cautious side, to provide an extra margin of safety. And here's a piece of hard information. We've been manufacturing ethylene oxide in Evanston for 35 years now. We have continually monitored our employees for signs of adverse health effects associated with exposure to ethylene oxide. In all that time, as far as we know, not a single worker or retiree has had the sort of cancer normally associated with ethylene oxide. Please keep in mind that these workers are exposed to consistently higher levels of emissions than the surrounding population is. Therefore, on the basis of our workers' experience so far, the risk is zero. There are also people who think our risk estimate is too low. The Evanston chapter of the Sierra Club estimates seven hundredths of a cancer per 3500 persons over the next 70 years. That's ten times higher than our estimate – but even if they're right, it's still an extremely small potential increase in the cancer rate. And we haven't found anyone with a higher estimate than theirs.'

Statement 4

'If we buy and install the newest and most advanced emission-control equipment available, the worst-case situation is that the maximum total risk will be 0.005 additional cancers per 3500 persons, a very low number. If we don't buy new equipment and keep operating the plant with our current pollution-control system, the worst-case situation is that the maximum total risk will be 0.007 additional cancers per 2500 persons – also a very low number. Please keep in mind that both of these risk estimates are worst-case estimates.'

Statement 5

'The maximum health risk from our plant's emissions of ethylene oxide is 0.007 additional cancers per 3500 persons. We could switch to producing the only known chemical substitute for ethylene oxide. However, the maximum health risk of emissions of that chemical is 50 times higher.'

Statement 6

'We have installed in our plant the most advanced emission control system now operating in the country. Compared with those of older plants, such as the one in Middletown, our emissions are 10 times less.'

Statement 7

'The risk posed by emissions of ethylene oxide is extremely low, no matter where you live or work in Evanston. However, the risk posed by emissions of ethylene oxide for people living two miles from the plant is 90 per cent less than for people living in the nearest home; and the risk for people living in the nearest home is 90 per cent less than for people working within the plant gates. And our workers haven't had a single case of the type of cancer normally thought to be linked to ethylene oxide.'

Statement 8

'Let me see whether these numbers will help. Roughly a quarter of all of us get cancer – a disease caused by smoking, diet, heredity, radon in the soil, pollution, and many other factors. Out of 3500 people, medical data show that one-quarter – or about 875 – are going to get cancer some time in a lifetime. So here's the predicted effect of ethylene oxide emissions from our plant on the overall cancer rate. In 129 of 130 hypothetical Evanstons, no effect – that is, no expected increase in cancer rates at all. In the 130th, cancer rates would rise from 875 to 876. Although this is only a tiny increased risk, it is still an increase. If we can find a way to make it even smaller, we should and we will. The most important thing is for all of us in Evanston to work together to find ways to bring down the total cancer rate, that unfortunate 875 out of 3500. But we at our plant have a special responsibility to be safe neighbors. Much higher risks due to other factors are no reason to ignore a small risk in our facility. Here's what we're doing to make sure we keep the risk from our plant as low as it can possibly get: (provide details).'

Statement 9

'During the next year, our plant will spend more than $2 million to reduce our already small emissions even further. This new investment will hurt us economically but will reduce the risk of cancer in the community by more than 25 per cent when fully operational.'

Statement 10

'If we stopped producing ethylene oxide today, many more people here and throughout the United States might die than could possibly be affected by emissions from our Evanston plant. Ethylene oxide is the best sterilizing agent used by hospitals today. No equivalent substitute for ethylene oxide is available. Continued production of this product will contribute to saving many lives and will ensure that the surgical instruments that doctors and hospitals use are free from infectious agents.'

Statement 11

'One way to look at the data is to compare the risks of emissions of ethylene oxide to plant neighbours with the risks to plant employees. We have been operating this plant for 35 years, with an average employment of 400 people. We therefore have about 10,000 person-years of worker exposure to ethylene oxide at this plant. Health monitoring at our plant indicates that the average workplace concentration of ethylene oxide is 0.5 ppm, a dose 200 times higher than that in the community. The primary health concern about ethylene oxide is its potential for causing certain types of brain cancer. We have not had a single case of brain cancer in our workforce. Moreover, the overall incidence of cancer in our employees is lower than that of the US population as a whole. Nor has Evanston's health department documented any brain cancers among our workers. On the basis of this information, I believe that the health risk posed by the plant to the community is insignificant.'

Statement 12

'I believe that our ethylene oxide emissions do not pose a significant health risk to the community. I also believe that our emissions pose a much less serious problem than our hazardous waste problem, which is daily becoming more serious because the repositories in our state are filled and none are being built.'

Statement 13

'One way to look at the cancer risk from emissions of ethylene oxide in our community is to compare the risk with the cancer risk from the X-rays you get during a health checkup. One chest X-ray per year presents a risk of developing cancer that is twice that of developing cancer from our plant's emissions of ethylene oxide.'

Statement 14

'Another way to get some perspective on the risk of ethylene oxide emissions is by comparing it to some of the risks that we all face in our daily lives, such as the risk of being killed by lightning or the risk of being killed in a car accident. My purpose in making such a comparison is only to put the size of the risk in context. I recognize that such comparisons are like comparing apples and oranges. Still, I think the comparison can help us all understand and gain some perspective on the size of the risk we are talking about. For example, the risk of death by salmonella food poisoning from poultry bought at the local supermarket is at least five limes greater than the risk of cancer from the highest exposure to ethylene oxide in this community.'

'You may be wondering, "But what does that mean to me as a resident of this community? What's the risk to me and my family?" First let me tell you that I am convinced that there is no threat to the health or safety of any member of our community at these extremely low exposure levels. However, I recognize that the data still may be troubling. So it would probably be helpful to put these levels of risk from exposure to ethylene oxide into the context of other risks that we're all exposed to in our daily lives. For example, the risk to the average American of death from lightning is at least 140 times greater than the risk of cancer in Evanston from the highest exposure to ethylene oxide. Hurricanes and tornadoes also pose a risk about 140 times greater. Insect bites pose a risk about 70 times greater. The additional 0.007 cancer risk is about the same as the additional cancer risk you would incur spending four hours in Denver rather than at sea level because of Denver's high altitude and higher radiation level.'

References

1   V T Covello, P M Sandman, and P Slovic, *Risk Communication, Risk Statistics and Risk Comparisons: A Manual for Plant Managers* (Washington, DC, Chemical Manufacturers Association, 1988).
2   B Cohen and I S Lee, 'A Catalogue of Risks,' *Health Physics* 36, 707–722 (1979).
3   R Wilson, 'Analyzing the Risks of Everyday Life,' *Technology Review* 81 40–46 (1979).
4   Environmental Protection Agency, *A Citizen's Guide to Radon: What It Is and What to Do About It, 13 pp* (Washington, DC 1986), 13 pp
5   B Fischhoff, P Slovic, and S Lichtenstein, 'Weighing the Risks,' *Environment* 21 17–20, 32–38, (1979).
6   B Fischhoff, S Lichtenstein, P Slovic, S L Derby and R L Keeney, *Acceptable Risk* (New York, Cambridge University Press, 1981).
7   National Research Council, *Improving Risk Communication* (Washington, DC, The Council, 1989).
8   B Fischhoff, S Watson, and C Hope, 'Defining Risk,' *Policy Sciences* 17, 123–139 (1984).
9   A Agresti, 'Tutorial on Modeling Ordered Categorical Response Data,' *Psychological Bulletin* 105 290–301 (1989).
10 R D McKelvey, and W Zaviona, 'A Statistical Model for the Analysis of Ordinal Level Dependent Variables,' *Journal of Mathematical Sociology* 4 103–120.
11 Greene W H, *Limdep* (Self-published statistical software package and manual, 1985).
12 P Slovic, N N Kraus, and V T Covello, 'Comment: What Should We Know About Making Risk Comparisons,' *Risk Analysis* in press (1990).
13 B Fischhoff, P Slovic, S Lichtenstein, S Read, and B Combs, 'How Safe Is Safe Enough? A Psychometric Study of Attitudes Towards Technological Risks and Benefits,' *Policy Sciences* 8, 127–152 (1978).
14 P Slovic, 'Perception of Risk,' *Science* 336, 280–285 (1987).
15 B Fischhoff, P Slovic, and S Lichtenstein. 'Fault Trees: Sensitivity of Assessed Failure Probabilities to Problem Representation,' *Journal of Experimental Psychology: Human Perception and Performance* 4, 330–344 (1978).

16 A Tversky and D Kahneman, 'Availability: A Heuristic for Judging Frequency and Probability,' *Cognitive Psychology* 5: 207–232 (1973).
17 B Fischhoff, P Slovic, and S Lichtenstein, in T Wallsten (ed), *Cognitive Processes in Choice and Decision Behavior* (Hillsdale, New Jersey, Erlbaum, 1980).

The Risks of 'Putting the Numbers in Context': A Cautionary Tale

William R Freudenburg[1] and Julie A Rursch[1]

Introduction

Risk communication issues are beginning to receive significantly increased attention in the professional meetings and journal pages of the Society for Risk Analysis (SRA), but much of the attention continues to be more anecdotal than quantitative. This situation stands in stark contrast to the treatment of other risk issues, where the norm is for increasingly quantitative precision and sophistication. It was not until Volume 10 (1990) that an issue of *Risk Analysis* carried back-to-back articles dealing quantitatively with risk communication[1,2] and those articles helped to illustrate the risks involved in offering risk communication advice without a sufficiently firm base of systematic research.

Those articles, like this one, focused on the issue of risk comparisons – a technique that often inspires concerns and warnings from risk communication practitioners,[3] but that continues to be employed and advocated by many members of the technical community.[4] Risk comparisons are often advocated in cases where statistical data, alone, appear to have relatively little influence on citizen judgements of the acceptability of risks. The prescription is to put such risks 'in context' by expressing them in comparison against previously quantified risks (eg smoking, driving or eating aflaxotin-tainted peanut butter). The problem, according to risk communication specialists, is that many such comparisons may seem to citizens to be more strategic than scientific, and more akin to propaganda than to public service.

The back-to-back articles in *Risk Analysis* focused on one of the best-known and best-respected sets of warnings from risk communication specialists, a manual produced for the Chemical Manufacturers Association by a group of three authors that includes two former presidents of the Society for Risk Analysis.[5] The specific focus was on a point that would elicit a relatively high level of consensus within the risk communication community – namely, the importance of avoiding inappropriate or so-called apples-and-oranges comparisons. The argument centres around the problems of comparing relatively involuntary risks, such as residential exposure to the emissions from a toxic waste incinerator, against relatively voluntary risks, such as those involved in smoking or driving. The manual offered a hierarchical typology of risk comparisons and identified apples-and-oranges comparisons as the least desirable. While the first article[1] appropriately cautioned readers to keep in mind that

1 University of Wisconsin–Madison, Wisconsin 53706.

this was an initial exploration rather than the final word on the topic, the study produced a striking failure to confirm any of the rankings of the preferences hypothesized by the original manual. The second article[2] responded by amplifying rather than rebutting the first; it noted that 70 per cent of the individuals in another sample initially reduced their estimates of the risks of attending a junior high school containing asbestos fibres when the asbestos risks were compared against other quantified risks (smoking cigarettes, consuming diet soft drinks, having chest X-rays, eating peanut butter and living in a brick house) – but that the effect disappeared when, as often happens in the real world, people were also exposed to a criticism of this risk comparison.[6] As the authors of both studies note, their findings demonstrate the importance of assessing empirically, rather than simply assuming, the actual effectiveness of prescribed techniques. As noted many years ago in a summary of studies of nuclear risk perceptions, 'There is no law of nature...that requires the scientific method to be abandoned merely because questions of human behavior are involved.'[7]

This article extends the empirical examination by using a technique that is complementary to the one employed by Roth et al.[1] The Roth et al study asked subjects to imagine that they were giving advice to the manager of a chemical plant making ethylene oxide (which, the study noted, 'is used in almost all hospitals and other medical facilities as a disinfecting agent'). That study's subjects were also told to assume that this plant manager had 'been a friend of yours for many year', who was not concerned about 'convincing' a potentially hostile audience, but who wanted 'to give a clear, honest picture of the risks' in a talk to a local community meeting where there was 'no crisis situation or serious confrontational atmosphere'. Among the advantages of the Roth et al technique is that it helped to make credible to study participants the task of rating the relative acceptability of 14 risk-comparison statements, a number of which were quite complex. At the same time, however, as noted by Roth et al themselves, this approach (particularly in combination with the extremely limited body of empirical literature to date) places clear limits on the ability to extrapolate from the findings. Perhaps the most obvious limitations include extrapolation to cases *where a significant suspicion already exists*, where the people involved *have not known the risk communicator* for many years, and where individuals are asked not to judge the appropriateness of statements for *other* people, but to judge the acceptability of a risk for *themselves and their own families*. Given that suspicion and lack of thorough personal acquaintanceship are often key characteristics of technological controversies,[8] the importance of these two considerations should be readily apparent. The importance of the third consideration may be less obvious to those who are not social scientists; it involves what research on mass communication has termed 'the third-person effect.'[9] As in the case of 'biased optimism,'[10] or the so-called 'it won't happen to me' assumption, this phenomenon involves systematic differences between what many of us believe about 'other people' and what we believe about ourselves; in general, media messages tend to be judged as likely to exert more of an effect on 'other people' than on study participants themselves.[11]

The study

The present study built on the approach of Roth et al in that the situation was hypothetical rather than current, but in other respects, nearly the opposite approach was used. The focus was on a toxic waste incinerator – a facility intended to be far more controversial than a plant making a hospital disinfectant. The 144 subjects (all of whom were in an introductory social science class at a large, Midwestern university) were asked to put *themselves* in a situation where the facility had been proposed for *their own* community and in which – rather than 'giving advice' to a trusted friend – the subjects were judging the persuasiveness to themselves of a message from someone they did *not* personally know. Unlike Slovic et al,[2] who simulated a courtroom decision context, complete with relatively complex arguments in favour and in opposition, we asked subjects to put themselves in the roles of citizens and voters; arguments were thus stripped down to the kinds of simplified 'sound byte' statements that could be expected on the evening news. The 'story' was presented with an obligatory but oblique reference to the general complaint of 'critics', as in so-called 'even-handed' stories that are common in media reporting on technological controversy.[12] This approach conveyed the information that criticism had arisen but did so while still offering the company relatively direct (if realistically simplified) access to the media, balancing the story by offering only a vague mention of the complaints of critics.

To repeat the oft-heard warning, the subjects in this study were students in a single class, rather than being a statistically representative cross section of the population. To note the most obvious differences from general-population studies, students in this study were younger, better educated, more likely to list occupations as 'student', and lower in current income (albeit somewhat higher in expected future incomes) than a statistically representative sample. Still, in terms of one variable that might have the potential for influencing the credibility of risk communication messages, namely, political orientation, this sample had a decidedly middle-of-the-road cast. As shown in Table 4.5 (Part 1), almost half of the students (44.4 per cent) said that they considered themselves to be political moderates, and the remaining students were divided almost precisely into equal numbers of liberals and conservatives (29.9 and 25.7 per cent respectively).

The subjects in this study were presented with the following scenario:

> *Imagine now that you're living in a small town with many economic problems – a high unemployment rate, stores closed down, and so forth. Along comes a proposal for a new hazardous waste incinerator, which would employ about 45 people, at good wages, for the next 20 years.*
>
> *Critics of the proposal say that this same company's previous incinerators have caused environmental problems, leaking toxic chemicals into the atmosphere. The company says it will do a better job of constructing and maintaining this incinerator, that there are no environmental or health hazards, and that they have done an extensive study that showed your community to be the best site in the slate. State and federal government regulators seem to agree with the company; they support the proposal.*

Subjects were then asked, 'If the matter came to a vote, would you be more likely to allow the company to build the facility in your community, [or] to prevent the company from building the facility?' This is the baseline measure of attitude toward the hazardous waste incinerator.

Next, the subjects were told, 'In the debate that leads up to the election, suppose the company releases a study on the risks created by the facility. According to a company representative, scientists have found that the odds of a really serious accident or health risk from the incinerator "are incredibly small – only about one in a million."' After this, the subjects were asked, 'Would that statement make you more likely to support the facility, not really affect you one way or the other, [or make you] less likely to support the facility?' This second item was obviously intended to convey, with a realistically limited level of detail, the effect of providing statistical probability information alone – permitting an assessment of the effectiveness of the statistical information on the risk of the incinerator, without any explicit risk comparisons, in changing individuals' attitudes toward facility construction.

The risk-comparison information was provided during a third step. After subjects had assessed the effectiveness of the statistical information alone, they were told, 'A lot of people have trouble understanding statistics, so suppose the representative tried to put the risk in context by saying, "That's less than the risk of smoking a couple dozen cigarettes." Would that statement make you more likely to support the facility, not really affect you one way or the other, [or make you] less likely to support the facility?'

Findings

As shown in Table 4.6 (Part 2), a majority of the subjects (63.9 per cent) expressed opposition to the incinerator when they were initially asked how they would vote. When given only the probabilistic risk information, as shown in Part 3 of the table, the majority (54.9 per cent) said that this information would make no difference in their decision about how to vote, but 36.6 per cent said that they would be more likely to support the incinerator; only 8.5 per cent said that the statistical information, alone, would make them less likely to support the facility.

Part 4 of the table shows that, when given the comparison to smoking cigarettes, the majority (62.1 per cent) again said that the statement made no difference in their choice of whether or not to support the facility. Of greater interest is the direction of the effect of the 'risk-comparison' information on those who said that the information would change their views: in comparison with the statistical information, more than twice as high a proportion (19.3 vs 8.5 per cent) said that the analogy to smoking cigarettes would make them likely to *oppose* the building of the hazardous waste incinerator. Similarly, as can be seen by comparing Parts 3 and 4 of the table, the number of those who said that they would be more likely to support the facility was only about half as high (18.6 vs 36.6 per cent) as in the case where only the probabilistic statement was made. In short, the risk comparison involving cigarettes actually produces more hostility toward the incinerator than does the 'one in a million' terminology; if anything, the risk comparison would actually increase the tendency to vote against the proposed incinerator. To determine whether the risk comparison was *significantly* worse than the one-in-a-million assessment, a paired *t* test was done. Both types of risk information were coded so that a 'no difference'

Table 4.6 *Overall frequency breakdowns*

1	In general, do you consider your political views...			
	Responses	*Frequency*	*%*	*Cumulative %*
	Somewhat or strongly liberal	43	29.9	29.9
	Middle of the road	64	44.4	74.3
	Somewhat or strongly conservative	37	25.7	100.0
	Total	144	100.0	

2	How would you vote on the proposed hazardous waste incinerator?				
	Responses	*Value*	*Frequency*	*%*	*Cumulative %*
	Support	.00	52	36.1	36.1
	Oppose	1.00	92	63.9	100.0
	Total		144	100.0	
	Valid cases, 144; missing cases, 0				

3	MILSUPP: What if a company-funded, independent study found risk of 'about one in a million'?				
	Responses	*Value*	*Frequency*	*%*	*Cumulative %*
	Less support	−1.00	12	8.5	8.5
	No difference	.00	78	54.9	63.4
	More support	1.00	52	36.6	100.0
	(No answer)	.	2	Missing	
	Total		144	100.0	
	Valid cases, 142; missing cases, 2				

4	CIGSUPP: What if company spokesperson said, 'That's less than the risk of smoking a few dozen cigarettes'?				
	Responses	Value	Frequency	%	Cumulative %
	Less support	−1.00	27	19.3	19.3
	No difference	.00	87	62.1	81.4
	More support	1.00	26	18.6	100.0
	(No answer)	.	4	Missing	
	Total		144	100.0	
	Valid cases, 140; missing cases, 4				

5 Paired-sample *t* test, where
MILSUPP: What if company-funded, independent study found risk of 10^{-6}?
CIGSUPP: What if spokesperson said risk approximately equal to a 'few dozen cigarettes'?

Variable	*Number of cases*	*Mean**	*SD*	*SE*
MILSUPP	140	.2714	.610	.052
CIGSUPP	140	−.0071	.617	.052

(Difference)				2-tail	*t*		2-tail
mean	SD	SE	Corr.	prob.	value	df	prob.
.2786	.769	.065	.215	.011	4.29	139	.000

* Both variables are coded as follows: +1, more likely to support; 0, wouldn't make any difference; −1, less likely to support.

response takes on the value of 0, while persons reporting that they were 'more likely to support' the facility were coded as +1, and those who reported that they would be 'less likely to support the facility' were coded as –1. As shown in Part 5 of the table, not only is the effect of the one-in-a-million information mildly positive while the risk-comparison results are mildly negative, but the difference between the two means is indeed statistically significant ($t = 4.29$, 139 df, $p < .001$).

Likely Explanation: Problems of Trust and Trustworthiness

How can this result best be understood? As a start, it bears repeating that the cigarette-smoking comparison, while regrettably still common, has many of the characteristics that risk communication practitioners have warned against: it compares the risks of an activity (smoking) that (1) are well documented and (2) can be chosen or avoided by an individual against the risks of a facility that (1) are merely estimated or projected and (2) might in fact be built in a citizen's own neighbourhood, over his or her own objections. Many risk communications specialists' warnings, however, have been based on what they have learned from personal experience – while many other SRA members appear to have learned from *their* own experience that risk comparisons often *are* helpful in conveying information to their own students, colleagues, friends and family members. In informal conversations, a number of these SRA members have explained to us that, based on their one-on-one experiences, they expect risk-comparison approaches to have similarly effective consequences in public debates.

Inconveniently, however, the public debates share almost none of the social characteristics of one-on-one conversational experiences that are friendly, informal and involve an atmosphere of congeniality, trust and presumed good will. In pleasant and unpolarized social contexts, risk comparisons undoubtedly can be useful in conveying information, which in turn is generally meant to inform, not persuade; in technological controversies, the social context and often the intent are likely to be quite different. In spite of the frequent calls from SRA members and the broader technical community for 'educating the public' about technological risks, moreover, empirical evidence provides little support for the assumption that public concerns are due to insufficient or inaccurate information – or that public attitudes will become more favourable as people become 'educated' or better informed. The public that turned against nuclear power, for example, had been subjected to a decades-long, multimillion-dollar public-relations campaign on the benefits of that technology; in one of its *Annual Report(s) to Congress*, for example, the US Atomic Energy Commission[13] noted that nearly 5 million people had seen its exhibits and demonstrations in 1967 alone. To be sure, the increasing scepticism may reflect the potential for what technological proponents might consider 'the wrong kind of education'. Some of the most dramatic declines in public support for nuclear power, for example, took place after headlines featured 'new information', notably including the accident at Three Mile Island.[14] Recent findings suggest, however, that official 'public education' campaigns, focused on overcoming 'irrational' public concerns over controversial facilities such as nuclear waste repositories, appear, if anything, to have been associated with *increasing* levels of public opposition – not just in the United States,[15] but also in nations that are commonly described as being more compliant with the desires of technological elites, such as Japan,[16] Taiwan,[17] and Korea.[18]

Instead, there is a growing body of evidence that levels of information simply are not the significant factors in explaining citizen opposition to controversial technologies. As any number of empirical studies have now shown, differences in knowledge or education levels between supporters and opponents of technologies tend to be either trivial or non existent.[19] In case studies of actual technological controversies, in fact, one of the findings has been a tendency for local *supporters* of controversial technologies to be the ones who, 'by their own accounts, were noticeably and – in many cases – intentionally uninformed' about the issues involved, while the opponents 'took a great deal of initiative in seeking out information'.[20]

In fact, while calls for 'public education' may be well intended, they appear to reflect a fundamental misunderstanding of what it means to live in an advanced, technological society. It is common to assume that life in a technological society means that we 'know more' than did our great-great-grandparents, but in at least one important respect, the assumption is wrong. Collectively, of course, we do know far more, but individually, we tend to know far less about the technology we depend on every day. Instead, we 'depend on' the technology to work properly. At least equally important is the fact that we also depend on people and organizations to perform their specialized tasks with an extremely high level of reliability, competence and trustworthiness. Our great-great-grandparents had almost none of the technology that helps us today, but in general, they could make or repair by hand almost any of the technology upon which they depended. To the extent to which they needed to turn to someone else for assistance, they were relatively likely to be able to call on people whom they knew personally. Today, we have access to far more technology, and our lives are both longer and more prosperous because of it. In the process, however, we have become far more interdependent and, hence, far more vulnerable to institutional actors who are unknown to us – some of whom may be lacking in their performance, whether in terms of competence, dedication or even simply breadth of vision.

The growing interdependence appears to underscore the importance of a factor that is increasingly being identified as significant in explaining public opposition to controversial technologies – the issue of trust and trustworthiness.[21] As noted in an earlier article by the senior author,[22] while the past century has indeed seen a dramatic decrease in the traditional forms of risk – as measured, eg by accidents, death and disease – one of the correlates of this progress has been a dramatic increase in the extent to which the individual needs to depend on the actions of others. One of the correlates of this change, in turn, has been the growth of a different kind of risk – the risk that those 'others' will prove not to be deserving of that trust. In the interest of avoiding some of the emotionally loaded implications of terms such as 'trustworthiness', the senior author has suggested the term 'recreancy',which 'is intended to provide an affectively neutral reference to behaviors of persons and/or of institutions that hold positions of trust, agency, responsibility, or fiduciary or other forms of broadly expected obligations to the collectivity, but that behave in a manner that fails to fulfill the obligations or merit the trust'.[23]

That article's analysis of attitudes towards a proposed low-level nuclear waste facility found, as have other studies,[24] that sociodemographic variables were only weak predictors of attitudes, being associated with differences of only 7–15 per cent in levels of support; even values-based and/or ideological items were associated with differences of only 10–25 per cent. The three recreancy items, in contrast, were associated with differences of 40–60 per cent. In regression analyses, the recreancy variables alone more than tripled the amount of variance that could be explained by the sociodemographic and the ideological variables combined.

Essentially, all risk comparisons – even those that are widely seen as *acceptable* risk comparisons – involve the provision of information by proponents and officials. If those proponents and officials are not trusted, then even 'legitimate' risk comparisons can do more to arouse suspicions than to assuage them; just such a possibility was in fact indicated quite clearly in the present study. One week after the subjects responded to this study's questionnaire, they were provided with a summary of the results. At that time, attention was drawn to the marked ineffectiveness of the risk comparison information, and the persons in attendance were asked how and why it might be that this information would actually have been *less* effective than the uninterpreted information about a one-in-a-million risk. After a brief silence, a voice from the back of the room offered a simple but eloquent interpretation: 'Yeah, we've heard *that* before.' The entire room erupted into laughter, with a number of other subjects expressing their assent.

This focus on trustworthiness is beginning to be mirrored in the social science literature, but agreement on this point is by no means universal. Perhaps the most important alternative interpretation has involved the expectation, consistent with the basic assumptions of neo-classical economics, that citizens will tend to display a kind of rational selfishness or self-interest. This logic suggests that if facilities create problems or 'diseconomies' for nearby residents (noise, pollution, stigma, uncertainty, etc), the residents will oppose the facilities unless they can be adequately compensated.[25] Later in the present study, accordingly, subjects were offered a set of six potential 'mitigation measures' that were intended to help distinguish between what will be called the 'rational selfishness' and the 'trustworthiness/recreancy' arguments. The options included paying every adult $1000; buying insurance against damage; building new parks, schools and recreational facilities; setting up a local advisory board; allowing local officials to shut down the facility; and setting up a locally elected board with the power to close the facility. Study subjects were asked first to identify the measures that would be most helpful in securing support for the proposed incinerator and then to identify those that would be *least* effective.

To guard against any possibility of selective interpretation, the complete list of potential mitigation options was presented to six persons having expertise in the social sciences. These experts were told nothing about the hypothesized effects before providing their reactions; instead, they were told simply that the study involved a proposed hazardous waste incinerator and that the six options were being considered as ways of dealing with the residents' concerns. The experts were then asked to rank-order the six potential mitigation options, arraying them from the option most likely to appeal to 'people who are concerned mainly that they would not otherwise receive enough benefits to compensate them' to the option most likely to appeal to 'people who are mainly concerned that they won't be able to trust the company or agency'.

The results were consistent with the expectations. Of the six experts contacted, five identified the same option – the $1000 payment – as being likely to have the greatest appeal for those who were reacting to the facility in terms of rationally selfish utility maximization. All six agreed that this same option would have the *least* appeal to people who opposed the facility because they genuinely distrusted assurances from the proponents and regulators. For this second group, all six experts agreed instead that a locally elected board with the power to shut down an unsafe facility would serve as the best available mitigation measure.

Table 4.7 *Attractiveness of potential mitigation options by support/opposition to proposed facility*

Item: Suppose the company offered to make some concessions if the community agreed to host the new incinerator. Which of the following would make you, personally, as happy as possible with the idea of the facility? If the company agreed to...

Count row pct	Pay each resident $1000 (1)	Buy prop & health insurance (2)	Build parks, facil's (3)	Set up advisory board (4)	Current ofcls' shutdown (5)	New board shutdown (6)	'None' (volun- teered) (7)	Row total
Position on facility								
Supporters	1	10	5		6	30		52
	(1.9%)	(19.2%)	(9.6%)		(11.5%)	(57.7%)		(36.4%)
Opponents		21	2	2	8	57	1	91
		(23.1%)	(2.2%)	(2.2%)	(8.8%)	(62.6%)	(1.1%)	(63.6%)
Column total	1	31	7	2	14	87	1	143
	(.7%)	(21.7%)	(4.9%)	(1.4%)	(9.8%)	(60.8%)	(.7%)	(100.0%)

Statistic	Value	df	t value	Approximate significance
Chi-square	7.79759	6		.25331
Pearson's R	.04516		.53678	.59226
Kendall's tau-c	.05164		.63816	
Mantel-Haenszel test for linear association	.28959	1		.59048

Item: Which of the options would be least likely to make you any happier with the idea of hosting the proposed facility?

Count row pct	Pay each resident $1000 (1)	Buy prop & health insurance (2)	Build parks, facil's (3)	Set up advisory board (4)	Current ofcls' shutdown (5)	New board shutdown (6)	'None' (volun- teered) (7)	Row total
Position on facility								
Supporters	20	1	7	23	1			52
	(38.5%)	(1.9%)	(13.5%)	(44.2%)	(1.9%)			(36.4%)
Opponents	53	3	17	16	2			91
	(58.2%)	(3.3%)	(18.7%)	(17.6%)	(2.2%)			(63.6%)
Column total	73	4	24	39	3	0	0	143
	(51.0%)	(2.8%)	(16.8%)	(27.3%)	(2.1%)	(0.0%)	(0.0%)	(100.0%)

Statistic	Value	df	t value	Approximate significance
Chi-square	11.92483	4		.01792
Pearson's R	−.23471		−2.86717	.00478
Kendall's tau-c	−.24373		−2.84802	
Mantel-Haenszel test for linear association	7.82290	1		.00516

The results from the original sample are reported in Table 4.7. As can be seen, the option of 'benefit sharing' in the form of a $1000 payment was selected as the preferred option by only 1 of the 143 persons who responded to this question, and that person happened already to be a supporter of the proposed incinerator. It was singled out as the worst option by more than a third of the supporters, and by an outright majority of the opponents. Supporters and opponents did not differ significantly in the mitigation options they preferred; agreement extended to the option that had the greatest appeal to both groups – namely, the setting up of a locally elected board that would have the power to shut down the facility – an option chosen by roughly 58 per cent of the supporters and 63 per cent of the opponents as the best one available. The supporters and opponents did differ significantly in terms of the options they saw as *least* desirable, although not a single person in either group identified the shutdown option for this distinction. Instead, the option most often singled out as undesirable by facility supporters in this sample is one that has often been explored by the actual operators of existing or planned facilities – establishing a local committee with the responsibility of offering advice but without any actual authority to shut down the facility. Overall, this option was almost as unpopular as the cash payment, although the advisory board was supported by two subjects who were at least among those who had expressed opposition; it was singled out as the least-appealing option by roughly 18 per cent of the opponents and by nearly three times as high a proportion (44.2 per cent) of the supporters.

Discussion

Risk communication specialists have long warned against assuming that risk comparisons will persuade citizens to accept controversial facilities. Many of the 'more technical' members of SRA, however, have awaited quantitative evidence to back up the usual advice. The results of this study suggest that they need wait no longer.

The present study appears to be the first to provide a direct, quantitative comparison between a statistical summary of risk and one in which the risk is 'placed in context' by means of a risk comparison. Asking subjects to report not their guesses as to how they would expect *others* to respond, but how they would respond themselves, and using the kinds of simplified writing commonly found in media reports, the study finds that the risk comparison is actually associated with an *increase* in opposition.

While any number of explanations could be put forward, the most plausible is that it is time for some of the common, albeit often unstated assumptions of the risk assessment community to be re-examined. The risk comparisons might indeed have proved more persuasive if the opposition were simply a matter of 'misinformation'. Similarly, if the opposition were merely a matter of rationally selfish economic calculations, proposed financial compensation would have been expected to have led to a significant increase in the willingness to allow one's community to host a proposed incinerator. Instead, the financial compensation measure was identified by subjects as the least desirable of six options offered – being singled out for particular criticism by opponents of the proposed incinerator, 58 per cent of whom specifically named this as the worst of the available options, three times as high as the proportion naming any other option.

It would be excessive to interpret this paper's findings as indicating a complete lack of value for risk comparisons; the nature of the potential value, however, needs to be tested explicitly in future research. That research also needs to deal further with the issue of trust. Based on current findings, perhaps the most plausible hypothesis would be that comparisons could prove not only to be useful, but to be appreciated by citizens, in cases where appropriate comparisons are offered by persons or institutions that *do* enjoy high levels of public trust. If spokespersons are perceived as having 'something to sell', however, the nature of the situation may quickly shift towards increased suspicion and distrust, although, to repeat, these possibilities need to be tested explicitly in future research.

Indeed, at a broader level, there is considerable need for explicit social science research, dealing with risk communication as well as a variety of risk-related topics. As noted by Fischhoff et al more than a decade ago,[26] the field of risk analysis displays in a particularly clear way a common, if paradoxical, tendency. Most technical experts are quite cautious about not overstepping the bounds of their own expertise – at least so long as they are discussing questions that involve their own disciplines. Somewhat surprisingly, however, the same caution tends not to be in evidence when discussion turns to matters that lie entirely outside of the same experts' training and expertise – particularly when the questions at issue are ones that involve human behaviour. Unfortunately, it is as true in the social sciences as in the physical or biological sciences that conviction is a poor substitute for evidence. Particularly given that many of the most important issues that need to be faced by the members of the Society for Risk Analysis are ones that revolve fundamentally around human and social factors, those social science issues need to be not the subject of assertion, but the focus for the same kinds of systematic attention and funding that have long been sought for other areas of risk analysis.

References

1   E Roth, M G Morgan, B Fischhoff, L Lave, and A Bostrom. 'What Do We Know About Making Comparisons?' *Risk Analysis* no 10(3), pp375–87 (1990).
2   P Slovic, N Kraus, and V T Covello. 'What Should We Know About Making Risk Comparisons?' *Risk Analysis* no 10(3), pp389–92 (1990).
3   See, eg B J Hance, C Chess, and P M Sandman, *Improving Dialogue with Communities: A Risk Communication Manual For Government* (Rutgers University Environmental Communication Research Programme, New Brunswick, NJ, 1988); National Research Council, *Improving Risk Communication* (National Academy Press, Washington, DC, 1989).
4   Examples include B L Cohen and I Lee, 'A Catalog of Risks,' *Health Phys.* no 36, pp707–722 (1979); R Wilson and E A C Crouch, 'Risk Assessment and Comparisons: An Introduction,' *Science* no 236, pp267–270 (1987); E A C Crouch and R Wilson, 'Inter-risk Comparisons,' in J V Rodricks and R G Tardiff (eds), *Assessment and Management of Chemical Risks* (American Chemical Society, Washington, DC, 1984); E A C Crouch and R Wilson, *Risk/Benefit Anal.* (Ballinger, Cambridge, MA, 1982).
5   V Covello, P M Sandman, and P Slovic, *Risk Communication, Risk Statistics, and Risk Comparisons: A Manual for Plant Managers* (Chemical Manufacturers Association, Washington, DC, 1988).
6   For comparable findings from a study of food irradiation, see S Sapp, 'Food Safety as a Public Policy Decision: The Case of Food Irradiation,' Annual Meeting of Rural Sociological Society, Columbus, OH, Aug (1991).
7   E A Rosa and W R Freudenburg, 'Nuclear Power at the Cross-roads,' in W R Freudenburg and E A Rosa (eds). *Public Reactions to Nuclear Power: Are There Critical Masses?* (American Association for the Advancement of Science/Westview, Boulder, CO, 1984), p27.

8   For more detailed discussions of this point, see, eg W R Freudenburg and R
    Gramling, *Oil in Troubled Waters: Perceptions, Politics, and the Battle Over Off-
    shore Drilling* (State University of New York Press, Albany, 1994); W R Freudenburg
    and E A Rosa (eds), *Public Reactions to Nuclear Power: Are There Critical Masses?*
    (American Association for the Advancement of Science/Westview, Boulder, CO,
    1984).
9   See, eg W P Davison, 'The Third-Person Effect in Communication', *Public Opin Q.*
    no 47, pp1–15 (1983); A. Gunther, 'What We Think Others Think: The Role of
    Cause and Consequence in the Third-Person Effect', *Commun Res* no 18, pp355–
    372 (1991).
10 See, eg N D Weinstein, 'Optimistic Biases About Personal Risks?' *Science* Dec.
    no 8, pp1232–1233 (1989).
11 Unrealistic optimism is also a key feature of 'the disqualification heuristic,' but
    that broader heuristic or judgmental rule of thumb involves the temptation to
    conclude that 'it can't happen at *all.*' See L Clarke, 'The Disqualification Heuris-
    tic: When Do Organizations Misperceive Risk?' *Res. Soc. Problems Public Policy*
    no 5, pp289–312 (1993).
12 See A Mazur, 'Media Influences on Public Attitudes Toward Nuclear Power,' in
    W R Freudenburg and E A Rosa (eds), *Public Reactions to Nuclear Power: Are
    There Critical Masses?* (American Association for the Advancement of Science/
    West-view, Boulder, CO, 1984), pp97–114.
13 US Atomic Energy Commission, *Annual Report to Congress of the Atomic Energy
    Commission for 1967* (US Atomic Energy Commission, Washington, DC, 1968).
14 W R Freudenburg and R K Baxter. 'Host Community Attitudes Toward Nuclear
    Power Plants: A Reassessment,' *Soc. Sci. Q.* no 65. pp1129–1136 (1984); W R
    Freudenburg and R K Baxter, 'Nuclear Reactions: Public Attitudes and Public
    Policies Toward Nuclear Power Plants,' *Policy Stud. Rev.* no 5, pp96–110 (1985).
15 J Flynn, P Slovic, and C K Mertz, 'The Nevada Initiative: A Risk-Communication
    Fiasco,' *Risk Analysis* no 13(5), pp497–502 (1993).
16 W Budd, F Rosenman, and R Rosenman, 'Risk Externalities: Compensation and
    Nuclear Siting in Japan,' *Environ Prof.* no 12, pp208–213 (1990).
17 J T Liu and V K Smith, 'Risk Communication and Attitude Change: Taiwan's
    National Debate Over Nuclear Power.' *J Risk Uncertainty* no 3, pp327–345 (1990).
18 United Press International, 'Islanders Protest Construction of Nuclear Waste Stor-
    age Facility,' United Press International News Wire Story, New York, Nov 8 (1990).
19 See, eg R E Dunlap and M E Olsen, 'Hard-Path Versus Soft-Path Advocates: A
    Study of Energy Activists,' *Policy Stud. J.* no 13, pp413–428 (1984); L C Gould,
    G T Gardner, D R DeLuca, A R Tiemann, L W Doob, and J A J Stolwijk, *Percep-
    tions of Technological Risk and Benefits* (Russell Sage, New York, 1988); R C
    Mitchell, 'Rationality and Irrationality in the Public's Perceptions of Nuclear Power,'
    in W R Freudenburg and E A Rosa (eds), *Public Reactions to Nuclear Power: Are
    There Critical Masses?* (American Association for the Advancement of Science/
    Westview, Boulder, CO, 1984), pp137–179; W R Freudenburg and S K Pastor,
    'Public Responses to Technological Risks: Toward a Sociological Perspective,'
    Sociol Q. no 33(3), pp389–412 (1992). For a thoughtful review, see T Dietz, P C
    Stern, and R W Rycroft, 'Definitions of Conflict and the Legitimation of Resources:
    The Case of Environmental Risk.' *Sociol Forum* no 4, pp47–70 (1989); see also
    B B Johnson and V T Covello (eds), *The Social and Cultural Construction of Risk:
    Essays on Risk Selection and Perception* (Reidel, Dordrecht, Holland, 1987); M
    Kraft and B B Clary, 'Citizen Participation and the NIMBY Syndrome: Public Re-

sponse to Radioactive Waste Disposal,' *West Polit. Q.* no 44, pp299–328 (1991); R E Kasperson 'Six Propositions on Public Participation and Their Relevance for Risk Perception,' *Risk Analysis* no 6, pp275–281 (1986); D J Fiorino 'Technical and Democratic Values in Risk Analysis,' *Risk Analysis* no 9, pp293–299 (1989).

20 M R Fowlkes and P Y Miller, 'Chemicals and Community at Love Canal,' in B B Johnson and V T Covello (eds), *The Social and Cultural Construction of Risk: Essays on Risk Selection and Perception* (D Reidel, Dordrecht, Holland, 1987), pp64, 65. See also P Brown, 'Popular Epidemiology: Community Response to Toxic Waste-Induced Disease in Woburn, Massachusetts,' *Sci. Technol. Hum. Values* no 12, pp78–85 (1987); S R Couch and J S Kroll-Smith, 'Chronic Technical Disaster: Toward a Social Scientific Perspective,' *Soc. Sci. Q.* no 66, pp564–575 (1985); M R Edelstein, *Contaminated Communities: The Social and Psychological Impacts of Residential Toxic Exposure* (Westview, Boulder, CO, 1988); K Finsterbusch 'Community Responses to Exposures to Hazardous Wastes,' in D L Peck (ed), *Psycho-social Effects of Hazardous Toxic Waste Disposal on Communities* (Charles C Thomas, Springfield, IL, 1989); N Freudenberg, 'Citizen Action for Environmental Health: Report on a Survey of Community Organizations,' *Am J Public Health* no 74, pp444–448 (1984); J S Kroll-Smith, S R Couch, and A G Levine, 'Technological Hazards and Disasters,' in R E Dunlap and W Michelson (eds). *Handbook of Environmental Sociology* (Greenwood, Westport, CT, in press); C Krauss, 'Community Struggles and the Shaping of Democratic Consciousness,' *Social Forum* no 4(2), pp227–239 (1989); A G Levine, *Love Canal: Science, Politics, and People* (Lexington, Lexington, MA, 1982).

21 See, eg P Slovic, 'Perceived Risk, Trust, and Democracy,' *Risk Analysis* no 13, pp675–682 (1993); B Barber, *The Logic and Limits of Trust* (Rutgers University Press, New Brunswick, NJ, 1983); D A Bella, 'Organizations and Systematic Distortions of Information,' *J Prof Issues Eng.* no 113, pp117–129 (1988); L Clarke and J F Short, 'Social Organization and Risk: Some Current Controversies,' *Annu. Rev. Sociol.* no 19, pp375–399 (1993); W R Freudenburg and S K Pastor, 'NIMBYs and LULUs: Stalking the Syndromes,' *J Social Issues* no 48, pp39–61 (1992); W R Freudenburg and T I K Youn, 'A New Perspective on Problems and Policy,' *Res. Social Problems Public Policy* no 5, pp1–20 (1993); G Jacob, *Site Unseen: The Politics of Siting a Nuclear Waste Repository* (University ot Pittsburgh Press, Pittsburgh, 1990); A H Mushkatel, K D Pijawka, P Jones, and N Ibitayo, *Governmental Trust and Risk Perceptions Related to the High-Level Nuclear Waste Repository: Analyses of Survey Results and Focus Groups* (Nuclear Waste Policy Office, Carson City, NV, 1992); S Rayner and R Cantor, 'How Fair is Safe Enough? The Cultural Approach to Societal Technology Choice,' *Risk Analysis* no 7, pp3–9 (1987); R S Stoffle, M W Traugott, C L Harshbarger, F V Jensen, M J Evans, and P Drury, 'Risk Perception Shadows: The Superconducting Super Collider in Michigan,' *Pract. Anthropol.* no 10, pp6–7 (1988).

22 W R Freudenburg, 'Risk and Recreancy: Weber, the Division of Labor, and the Rationality of Risk Perceptions,' *Social Forces* no 71, pp909–932 (1993).

23 Ref 22, pp916–917.

24 See, eg the studies listed in Ref 19; see also P Slovic, M Layman, N Kraus, J Flynn, J Chalmers, and G Gesell, 'Perceived Risk, Stigma, and Potential Economic Impacts of a High-Level Nuclear Waste Repository in Nevada,' *Risk Analysis* no 11, pp683–696 (1991).

25 For a discussion and empirical investigation that found such expectations may need to be adjusted in the case of facilities that are seen as posing unacceptable

risks, see H Kunreuther and D Easterling, 'Are Risk-Benefit Tradeoffs Possible in Siting Hazardous Facilities?' *Am. Econ. Assoc. Papers Proc.* no 80, pp252–256 (1990).

26 B Fischhoff, P Slovic, and S Lichtenstein, 'Lay Foibles and Expert Fables in Judgments about Risks,' in T O'Riordan and R K Turner (eds), *Progress in Resource Management and Environmental Planning,* vol 3 (Wiley, New York, 1981), pp 161–202.

How Fair Is Safe Enough? The Cultural Approach to Societal Technology Choice

Steve Rayner[1] and Robin Cantor[1]

Introduction: Redefining Risk

Three notions have dominated discussions of societal risk management since Chauncey Starr's seminal article in 1969. The first of these is that there is a definable (ie measurable) phenomenon called risk. Second is that societal risk management is concerned with minimizing the probability and/or magnitude of undesired consequences without incurring excessive costs. Third is the assumption that the critical question facing risk managers charged with this delicate balancing act is 'How safe is safe enough?'

We want to challenge all three of the dominant assumptions of societal risk management and suggest:

* That we have reified the concept of risk to the extent that we have lost sight of many aspects of this multifaceted phenomenon in pursuit of (a) bettering our own understanding of probabilities, and (b) correcting public misunderstanding about them.
* That while assessments of probabilities and magnitudes of undesired outcomes are essential to making engineering decisions about competing designs or alternative materials, they are largely irrelevant to societal technology choices.
* That the critical question facing societal risk managers is not 'How safe is safe enough?' but 'How fair is safe enough?'

Let us take each of these three dominant assumptions in turn. First is that there is a single, if complex, phenomenon called *Risk*. This is generally defined as:

$$\text{Risk} = \frac{\text{Probability} \times \text{Magnitude}}{\text{Time}}$$

---

1 Energy Division, Oak Ridge National Laboratory, Oak Ridge, Tennessee 37831.

However and wherever it is discussed, it seems that there is a consensus that the essence of risk consists of the probability of an adverse event and the magnitude of its consequences. Other considerations, such as those of societal risk management, may be recognized as important, but are viewed as deriving from this definition. While this definition may be adequate to define risk at the level of engineering-type calculations, it is quite misleading at the broader, more intractable, level of large-scale societal risk management.

Common-sense definitions of risk frequently do not depend on probabilities of loss. They may rest exclusively on magnitude. For example, consider the man who insists that he occasionally likes to bet, but he never gambles. His definition of risk is not dependent on probability of loss, but on the prospect of losing more than he can afford. Rayner[2] has argued that risk may be a polythetic concept, which is composed of a chain of items sharing features with their neighbours on either side, but lacking any single essential feature. In these systems of concept formation, items at one end of the chain need not have any conditions in common with those at the other end. This seems to be the case with risk, where engineering assurances about probability and magnitude of loss often do not satisfy the concerns of public interest groups opposed to risky technology.

Even the most enlightened of our colleagues in sociology, economics, anthropology and psychology have framed the problem of public acceptance of risks in terms of differential perceptions of probabilities. But the choices between those probabilities are incomprehensible to most of the public and, certainly, to a lot of policymakers as well. But most of the public probably does not care about probabilities in choosing between two courses of action when the differences in probability are so small as they are in most of the risk-management decisions that policymakers currently face. These are not situations where the probabilities and magnitudes are indisputably high, but unclear cases involving very low probabilities, such as occupational radiation-exposure levels in medicine and industry or permissible levels of possible carcinogens in food or the environment.

The second assumption that we wish to question is that the challenge of societal risk management is to minimize the probability and/or magnitude of adverse events without incurring excessive costs. Economic rationalists argue that individuals decide to take a risk weighing its potential costs and benefits and then opting for the course of action that they think will maximize the advantages that will accrue. This assumption, popular among professional policymakers and sanctified by the US Supreme Court, is well known as the *utility principle*.

The problems with the utility principle in making public policy are well known. Ken Arrow[3] has shown that collective preferences cannot be derived by aggregating individual choices. Peter Self[4] has illustrated the absurdity of trying to trade off incommensurables by reducing them to dollars or cents. Herbert Simon[5] has shown us how decisions are made under conditions of *bounded rationality*, and Mary Douglas[6] has argued that the bounding of rationality is a cultural phenomenon based on differing experiences of social organization between the various institutions and constituencies that compose a complex industrial society.

The third assumption that we wish to challenge is that the critical question facing risk managers is 'How safe is safe enough?' Contrary to the accepted wisdom of those who criticize the activities of intervenors and consumer advocates, our experience has been that only a tiny minority of the public expects that life ought to be entirely free of involuntary danger. So, what does the vast majority of the policymakers' constituencies care about? Our recent research indicates at least three things:

1   Is the procedure by which collective consent is obtained for a course of action acceptable to those who must bear its consequences?
2   Is the principle that will be used to apportion liabilities for an undesired consequence acceptable to those affected?
3   Are the institutions that make the decisions that manage and regulate the technology worthy of fiduciary trust?

We suggest that when all three of these factors are amenable to the risk-bearing population, it will hardly consider many of the low-probability, high-consequence events that currently obsess us to be worthy of the term 'risk' at all. What is needed is a polythetic definition that encompasses both societal concerns about equity at the risk-management end of the conceptual chain and engineering-type concerns about probability and magnitude at the technical end. Such a definition would truly open new approaches to large-scale technology choice for which the proper question would become not 'How safe is safe enough?' but 'How fair is safe enough?'

This is not merely a linguistic quibble, substituting 'fair' for 'safe', for this would still leave us with a reified concept of risk as a thing 'out there' in nature. Risk is rather a way of classifying a whole series of complex interactions and relationships between people, as well as between man and nature. The point of changing the societal risk management question to 'How fair is safe enough?' is to encourage risk managers to debate technology options on the explicit basis of social conflicts over trust and equity, rather than on rival estimates of the probability and magnitude of unlikely events. Such a change will require a broad interdisciplinary approach to risk management.

A Broad Interdisciplinary Approach to Risk Management

A broad interdisciplinary approach will incorporate ethical, political, legal, cultural and economic comparisons of various constituencies and their liability preferences. For example, these aspects may be integrated within an analytic framework based on the cultural hypothesis of risk perception.[7] This hypothesis states that for different institutional settings, each generates its own characteristic view of the world, variously referred to as a 'cosmology' or 'cultural bias'.[6] In turn, it has been suggested that characteristic attributes of cultural bias, particularly, preferred aesthetics, principles of social justice, and perceived economic interests, will lead members of each type of institution to choose a particular liability distribution.[8]

Consider four ideal kinds of social organization found in the socioeconomic literature. It should be borne in mind that no real constituency could be expected to fit one of these descriptions in every respect. First is an entrepreneurial or market individualism, where restrictions on social behaviour arising from rules or prior claims of others are kept to a minimum, giving rise to a competitive way of life. In contrast, consider the case where formal institutions make increasing demands of incorporation and regulation, control is vested in formal systems of accountability. This is a hierarchical or bureaucratic social environment. Often opposed to both competitive individualism and bureaucratic hierarchy is a third type, the collectivist egalitarian constituency such as that which is maintained within many religious sects, revolutionary political groups, and some segments of the antinuclear energy movement. Finally, there is the constituency of atomized, often alienated, individuals. In competitive organizations there are people who, having no goods or services to exchange, get driven out of the market. In hierarchical systems there are people who are excluded from the established institutions of representation. Very often, these are people who have the fewest or the least socially valued skills in a wider social arena. They tend to be the most vulnerable in any social system.

The relevance of the typology to the problem of liabilities arising from potentially hazardous technologies lies in the fact that the social organization of each type of system makes its members sensitive to different aspects of the problem and leads them to favour characteristically different decision strategies. In particular, it is suggested that the preferred spread of liabilities and benefits will vary between the four different kinds of organizations.

Policymakers in competitive-individualist organizations will favour a *loss-spreading* approach to liability,[9] in which market mechanisms determine who bears losses. When pure market solutions are not available, institutions of this sort will attempt to reproduce what the market would have done if it had not been impeded by high information and/or transaction costs.

To the extent that principles of liability frequently take account of whether consent was obtained from an injured party, it is worth noting that loss spreading would be consistent with a *revealed preference* approach[10] to obtaining consent sometimes called *implicit consent*.[11] This allows market forces to determine planning priorities, the rationale being that people's preferences for one solution or another will be accurately reflected in how they spend their money.

Competitive-individualist risk takers will prefer to invest their confidence in successful individuals to most effectively manage risk. This is an environment wherein the larger-than-life troubleshooter will thrive, whether the risk is technological (eg Red Adair) or economic (eg Lee Iaccoca) in origin.

Members of bureaucratic or hierarchical organizations will favour *redistributive taxation* as a means of apportioning costs. In this way, bureaucracies make use of redistributive mechanisms to apportion liabilities in a way that seems to them to be least disruptive – not to the whole of society perhaps, but certainly to those constituencies whose stability they see as important to the survival of the institution.

Liability principles may be affected here by the preferences of hierarchical or bureaucratic organizations for what is sometimes called 'hypothetical consent'.[12] The citizen is assumed to have entered into a social contract with the decision-making institution, whereby he may be deemed to assent to decisions made through the rational procedures of that institution, even though he may not like the particular outcome.

Bureaucratic organizations have a propensity to trust routine procedures for risk management. They tend, therefore, to have most confidence in long-established institutions that have stood the test of time. The implicit assumption is that those whose routines are not appropriately adapted to cope with the hazards they manage will not survive. The Coast Guard and the American Medical Association are but two examples of long-lived regulators.

Members of egalitarian groups will seek a moral determination of liability for unforeseen costs that appeals to ranked values, rather than the market or distributive approaches to losses favoured by entrepreneurs or bureaucrats. This is a *strict fault system*.[9] The acceptability of potentially hazardous technologies will, therefore, be determined according to criteria that are very different from those invoked by entrepreneurs or bureaucrats. Egalitarians will favour expressed preferences that also appeal lo explicit judgements of ranked values (shared by the group) rather than the revealed preference or hypothetical consent approaches favoured by the other groups.

Egalitarians distrust both individualisis and bureaucracies. The requirement for explicit consent to societal risk taking leads egalitarian groups to trust consensus decision making in participatory institutions such as affinity groups or town meetings.

As a broad generalization about each of these three institutional or social types, it can be said that egalitarians favour a *rights-based* approach, while market cultures tend towards a pragmatic *consequentialism*. Implicitly following the principles enunciated in Rawls' *Theory of Justice*, bureaucrats will equate system maintenance with the *contractualist* principle of justification.

There is less to be said about the preferences of stratified individuals. They tend not to articulate any distinctive theory of distribution or of consent. For them, as Thompson[13] has argued following Mrs Gaskell, 'life is like a lottery'. When it comes to issues of trust and confidence, these people will tend to rely for protection on non human agencies such as luck, providence or, in some cases, the spirit world. Generally, atomized individuals are not decision makers themselves since most of the options for societal choice are monopolized by the other three cultural types. It is likely that these people will express discontent that their consent is seldom, if ever, sought by any means and that they are constantly having to bear the costs of other people's errors.

From the contrast between the four institutional cultures engaged in controversies over technological risk (Table 5.1), it is clear that policymakers within each type of sociocultural framework will have great difficulty in understanding the fears and objections of others – hence, societal conflict. In particular, given the variation of the desired spread of costs, each constituency is likely to encounter problems in designing a liability package that would satisfy another constituency with a different cultural bias. There is no magic solution to this problem. However, both scholarly understanding of the liability issues and democratic conduct of policy debates could be enhanced by making explicit the roots of liability preferences in the cultural biases of different forms of institutional organization.

Table 5.1 *Summary of preferred principles of consent, liability and trust according to type of constituency*

A Competitive/market	B Atomized individual	C Bureaucratic/hierarchical	D Egalitarian group
Liability: loss-spreading	No special principles elaborated for liability or consent	Liability: redistributive	Liability: strict-fault system
Consent: implicit/revealed preference		Consent: hypothetical	Consent: explicit/expressed preference
Trust: successful individuals (Red Adair, Lee Iaccoca)	Trust: non human forces (nature, luck, spirits)	Trust: long-established formal organizations (AMA, USCG, etc)	Trust: participatory information institutions (town meetings, affinity groups, etc)
Justification: consequentialist	No consistent justification	Justification: contractualism	Justification: rights-based
Goal: market success	Goal: survival	Goal: system maintenance	Goal: new social order

A Pilot Study: New Nuclear Technologies

The problem we selected for a pilot study using this approach was the issue of the market acceptability of new nuclear-power reactor technologies with so-called passive safety features. These included, for example, the PIUS and the modular high-temperature gas-cooled reactor. This analysis was part of a larger programme of evaluating these concepts on engineering, economic and regulatory criteria.[14] As only one segment of the programme, we were responsible for the analysis of the market viability of these technologies within the 2000–2010 time period.

Our concept of risk management requires that the analysis explicitly recognize the social issues of trust and equity. Consequently, we focused on questions about the preferred principles different parties hold with respect to obtaining consent from those affected by the risks, distributing the liabilities and justifying trust in the relevant institutions. For the purposes of this pilot study, we limited the scope of the analysis to three constituencies: (1) the utilities, (2) state public utility commissions (PUCs), and (3) public interest groups critical of nuclear power.

Given the focus outlined above, an important aspect of the analytical framework is to recognize explicitly sources and channels of social conflict that arise over the equity and trust issues when societal technology choices are made. The first step in this process is to identify the constituency that provides the occasion for conflict by being the primary user of the technology, in this case, the electric utilities.

We conducted direct interviews with utility executives and systems-planning staff as well as with members of the PUCs and public staffs about their roles in the capacity-choice decision. Of course, the utilities are instigators of the technology choice. The PUC's role in the market place is generally to approve the need, site, technological option and apportionment of financial responsibilities for building a plant. Because of their regulatory powers, these state agencies effectively hold a potential veto over the commercialization of any nuclear technology. Thus, to appreciate their perspective on the trust and equity aspects of risk, PUCs must be thoroughly understood regarding their legislative mandate, regulatory philosophy and procedures, analytical skills and the degree of access of all parties to the state regulatory process.

The role of public interest groups in relation to the construction and operation of nuclear plants was analysed through focus-group discussions which were held in each state. Opinions were sought from members of a variety of environmentalist and antinuclear organizations on matters relating to confidence in institutions associated with nuclear power, the manner in which liabilities from potentially hazardous technologies are distributed within society, and the problems associated with obtaining legitimate societal consent for such technologies.

Examining the perspectives of the major constituencies on the basis of the *technology choice*, and not the *probability of harm*, indicated that their predominant concerns about risks were fundamentally different. For the utilities, the risk from the decision is investment risk (ie the risk that the costs of plants will not be fully recovered from ratepayers). This is not to say that utilities are unconcerned with health and safety risks. However, they view them as part of the technical design which is licensed by regulators. State PUCs are concerned with economic risks that might arise either because costs are incurred that were not anticipated, utilities fail to perform as expected, or demand fails to grow at a rate that warrants new capacity. Their concern for health and safety risks is incorporated into their general concern that, from the public's point of view, a plant's costs will outweigh the benefits.

In contrast, the public interest groups focus almost entirely on health and safety risks, pointing out that because these risks are imposed by one group and inevitably fall unevenly on others, they cannot be treated as acceptable under any circumstances. For them, a risk that threatens an individual's health is a risk that cannot be spread equitably. Such incompatibilities in the type of risk being addressed by each constituency make the search for solutions considerably more difficult.

The analysis of the PUCs and public interest groups reveals that these constituencies conceptualize basic nuclear issues differently. We contend that the ways in which they differ suggest implicit agenda of interest that make it difficult for them to understand the concerns of others. The different ways of conceptualizing problems are indicated in three critical regulatory concerns: (1) the need for the plant, (2) who pays for the plant, and (3) the management of the technology.

With regard to the basic question of the need for the plant, the PUCs frame the issue as primarily a forecasting problem that simply requires the utility to present adequate data and justification that the power will be needed when the plant becomes operational. Many PUCs have also become involved in judging whether the utility has selected the correct technological option to meet the demand forecast. While intervenor groups must contest the issues on these terms, the more important philosophical question in intervenors' minds is the need to secure consent of the parties affected by construction and operation of a nuclear plant. Rather than delegating responsibility to regulatory bodies to decide if the plant is needed, intervenors would prefer to decide, perhaps by popular referendum, if people want the plant.

The second important concern is that of who pays the costs of the plant. PUCs view this concern as primarily a financing one with some overtones of equity frequently intervening in the decision. If the utility can demonstrate that its construction costs were reasonably incurred and not the result of poor management, then costs of the plant will be allowed in the rate base and consumers will pay for the plant. If some construction costs are found by the PUC to be unwarranted, then the normal procedure is to pass those costs along to stockholders rather than ratepayers.

Intervenors tend to view concerns associated with costs of the plant in broader ethical terms. While intervenors will address the issue of paying for the plant on the PUC's terms because the regulatory process requires it, intervenors would prefer to focus on the more basic issue of who bears the various safety, economic, and managerial costs in society resulting from the plant and who enjoys the benefits and how can the costs and benefits be shared equitably.

The last important concern is that of management in the nuclear enterprise. PUCs focus on issues associated with management prudency. Intervenors conceive the management concern to be not merely a judgement of the utility's qualifications but, also a questioning of the regulators' qualifications as well. Ultimately, there is the question of whether nuclear technology can, indeed, be managed safely. Intervenors demonstrate a strong consensus that the technology is simply too complex to oversee and that nothing can be done to alter this inherent flaw. Their view of the regulators is that such agencies are too sympathetic to the industry and are not to be trusted.

Thus, with respect to the concern of managing the nuclear enterprise, PUCs tend to view the issues in narrower terms that allow regulators to address specific management problems, frequently in technical contexts. Intervenors expand the scope of management beyond the utilities to include any institutions that are responsible for nuclear technology. They do not trust these institutions at all because regulators and the technology itself are perceived to be parts of the nuclear problem.

These results support the propositions, regarding implicit agenda, of the cultural model of institutional risk behaviour. We see that process is the domain of the regulators, and their objective is the adherence to that process, regardless of the outcome it produces. This objective suggests an implicit agenda for system maintenance. On the other hand, intervenors are concerned with achieving an outcome that is consistent with their antinuclear goals. Adherence to process is irrelevant. Their concerns are broad and directed at policy level questions for which regulalory environments are not well suited. Their implicit agenda calls for a new social and political order that would make the current distribution of resources more equitable. Indeed, intervenors in a very real sense are fighting legislative battles in regulatory proceedings.

In short, the agenda of each of the constituencies in our pilot study corresponded quite well to one or another of the packages of consent liability and trust principles predicted by the fairness hypothesis. PUCs are clearly adopting bureaucratic values, particularly with respect to hypothetical consent and the institutional redistribution of liabilities, provided that certain standards of prudency are observed by the utility. The utilities are clearly happy for the market for electric power to stand as a surrogate for societal consent, and prefer to spread losses among consumersrather than stockholders. The intervenors expressed clear preferences for direct participation in decision making and favoured stockholder responsibility for managerial decisions. The utilities trust good managers to make decisions. PUCs trust the process, and the intervenors trust only the explicit collective will of the people.

We have presented the design and results of a single pilot study which explores the question 'How fair is safe enough?' The results of this study are intended to help evaluate whether or not this is a meaningful question for risk managers to ask. We believe that the approach uncovers the risk conflicts between constituencies that are rooted in disagreements over principles for consent, liability and trust; and thus provides unique and valuable information to the decision makers.

As our example illustrates, the problem of finding a risk-management solution to satisfy all constituencies is a difficult one. However, both greater understanding of the liability issues and the processes of policy debates could be enhanced by this kind of approach. Further research into the trust and equity-aspects of risk can benefit from using the approach for other examples of societal technology choice and risk management. As examples of relevant problems, we are exploring conservation investments, hazardous waste management, and innovative medical practices.

Research in this area could also provide important contributions to the decision-theoretic approaches of economics and psychology that are often used in problems of risk management. We see these contributions occurring at both the micro- and macro-levels of analyses where models of decision making are applied. At the micro-level, as an alternative to using preferences regarding the probabilistic concept of risk, we suggest using the decision maker's preferences for principles of consent, liability and trust as underlying determinants of derived risk perceptions.

Finally, for a broader level of analysis which must mesh together the preferences of several constituencies, exploring each constituency's preferences for these principles would help risk managers construct meaningful possible solutions to be offered in public forums. Such a practice might enhance the negotiations between constituencies in these open debates by avoiding the insults to strongly held principles that occur because offered solutions fail to reflect these considerations.

References

1   NAS *Risk Assessment in the Federal Governments Managing the Process* (National Academy Press, Washington, DC 1983).
2   Steve Rayner, 'Learning from the Blind Man and the Elephant: or Seeing Things Whole in Risk Management.' (Society for Risk Analysis Annual Meeting. Knoxville, Tennessee, 1984). To be published in V Covello et al (eds), *Uncertainty in Risk Assessment, Risk Management and Decision Making* (Plenum Press, New York, in press).
3   K J Arrow, *Social Choice and Individual Values* (Wiley, New York, 1951).
4   Peter Self *The Econocrats and the Policy Process: The Politics and Philosophy of Cost-Benefit Analysis* (Macmillan, London, 1975).
5   H A Simon, 'A Behavioral Model of Rational Choice,' *Quarterly Journal of Economics* no 69, pp99–118 (1955).
6   Mary Douglas, *Cultural Bias* (Royal Anthropological Institute, Occasional Paper no 35, London, 1978).
7   Mary Douglas and Aaron Wildavsky *Risk and Culture* (University of California Press, Berkeley, California, 1982).
8   Steve Rayner, 'Disagreeing About Risk: The Institutional Cultures of Risk Management and Planning for Future Generations' in S Hadden (ed), *Risk Analysis, Institutions, and Public Policy* (Associated Faculty Press, Port Washington, New York, 1984).
9   Guido Calabresi, *The Cost of Accidents* (Yale University Press, New Haven, Connecticut, 1970).
10 R Thaler and S Rosen, 'The Value of Saving a Life,' in N Terleckyj (ed), *Household Production and Consumption* (National Bureau of Economic Research, New York, 1975).
11 Douglas MacLean, *Values at Risk* (Rowman and Allenheld, Totowa, New Jersey, 1986).
12 John Rawls, *A Theory of Justice* (Belknap Press, Cambridge, Massachusetts, 1971).
13 Michael Thompson, *Among the Energy Tribes: The Anthropology of the Current Energy Debate* (Working Paper pp82–59, International Institute for Applied Systems Analysis, Laxenburg, Austria, (1982)).
14 D Trauger et al, *Nucleur Power Options Viability Study, Vol III, Nuclear Discipline Topics* (ORNL/TM-9780/3, Oak Ridge National Laboratory, Oak Ridge, 1986).

Theories of Risk Perception:
Who Fears What and Why?

Aaron Wildavsky and Karl Dake

In social science rival theories seeking to answer the same questions rarely confront one another. Indeed, a variety of perspectives has been employed in research on public perception of risk, but alternative formulations remain largely untested. Missing most of all is a focused comparison of rival hypotheses.

One could hardly find many subjects that are better known or considered more important to more people nowadays than the controversies over harm to the natural environment and the human body attributed to modern technology, whether this be from chemical carcinogens or nuclear power or noxious products introduced by industry into the land, sea or air, or into water or food supplies. Thus we ask: Why are products and practices once thought to be safe (or safe enough) perceived increasingly as dangerous? Who (what sort of people) views technology as largely benign, and who as mostly dangerous? To what degree are different people equally worried about the same dangers or to what extent do some perceive certain risks as great that others think of as small? And how do concerns across different kinds of risk – war, social deviance, economic troubles as well as technology – vary for given individuals? Only by comparisons across types of danger can we learn whether individuals have a general tendency to be risk averse or risk taking, or whether their perceptions of change depend upon the meaning they give to objects of potential concern. The test we shall put to each theory of risk perception is its ability to predict and explain what kinds of people will perceive which potential hazards to be how dangerous.

The most widely held theory of risk perception we call *the knowledge theory:* the often implicit notion that people perceive technologies (and other things) to be dangerous because they *know* them to be dangerous. In a critical review of *Risk and Culture,*[1] by Mary Douglas and Aaron Wildavsky, for instance, John Holdren's belief that perceivers are merely registering the actual extent of danger to themselves – the of-course-people-are-worried-they-have-lots-to-worry-about thesis – comes out clearly:

> *A much simpler description might suffice: people worry most about the risks that seem most directly to threaten their well being at the moment; environmental concerns predominate only where and when people imag-*

Reprinted by permission of *Dædalus*, Journal of the American Academy of Arts and Sciences.

1 Mary Douglas and Aaron Wildavsky, *Risk and Culture: An Essay on the Selection of Technological and Environmental Dangers* (Berkeley: University of California Press, 1982).

> *ine the risks of violence and economic ruin to be under control.... What is wrong, after all, with the simple idea – paralleling Maslow's stages of wants – that worries about more subtle and complex threats will materialize if, and only if, the most direct and obvious threats are taken care of?[2]*

If Holdren is correct, perception of danger should accord with what individuals know about the risk in question. But do risk perceptions and knowledge coincide?

Another commonly held cause of risk perception follows from *personality theory*. In conversations we frequently hear personality referred to in such a way that individuals seem to be without discrimination in their risk-aversion or risk-taking propensities: some individuals love risk taking so they take many risks, while others are risk averse and seek to avoid as many risks as they can. We will test this common, if extreme, view. We will also examine a more moderate theory of personality: that stable individual differences among persons are systematically correlated with their perceptions of danger. Leaving aside the extraordinary Oblimov-like characters staying in bed all their lives, or Evel Knievels breaking bones on too-daring feats, this version of personality theory suggests that individuals are so constituted as to take or reject risks in an enduring manner.[3] But do traditionally assessed attributes of personality such as intrapsychic dynamics and interpersonal traits relate to risk perceptions and preferences in predictable ways?

The third set of explanations for public perceptions of danger follow two versions of *economic theory*. In one, the rich are more willing to take risks stemming from technology because they benefit more and are somehow shielded from adverse consequences. The poor presumably feel just the opposite. In 'post-materialist' theory, the rationale is reversed, however: precisely because living standards have improved, the new rich are less interested in what they have (affluence) and what got them there (capitalism), than in what they think they used to have (closer social relations) and what they would like to have (better health).[4] Is it true, however, that the newly affluent aspire to post-materialist values, such as interpersonal harmony, and hence fear environmental pollution and chemical contamination?

Other explanations for public reactions to potential hazards are based on *political theory*. These accounts view the controversies over risk as struggles over interests, such as holding office or party advantage. The view of politics as clashing interests connects conflicts to different positions in society. The hope for explanatory power in such approaches to risk perception is thus placed on social and demographic characteristics such as gender, age, social class, liberal–conservative ratings, and/or adherence to political parties.[5]

Viewing individuals as the active organizers of their own perceptions, *cultural theorists* have proposed that individuals choose what to fear (and how much to fear

---

2 John Holdren, 'The Risk Assessors,' *Bulletin of the Atomic Scientists* 39 (1983): quotation 36.

3 K R MacCrimmon and D A Wehrung, *Taking Risks: The Management of Uncertainty* (New York: Free Press, 1986); R G Mitchell Jr, *Mountain Experience: The Psychology and Sociology of Adventure* (Chicago: University of Chicago Press, 1983).

4 Ronald Inglehart, *The Silent Revolution: Changing Values and Political Styles among Western Publics* (Princeton: Princeton University Press, 1977).

5 Stephen Cotgrove, *Catastrophe or Cornucopia: The Environment, Politics and the Future* (Chichester, England: John Wiley & Sons, 1982); Dorothy Nelkin and Michael Pollack, *The Atom Besieged: Antinuclear Movements in France and Germany* (Cambridge: MIT Press, 1981).

it), in order to support their way of life.[6] In this perspective, selective attention to risk and preferences among different types of risk taking (or avoiding) correspond to *cultural biases* – that is, to worldviews or ideologies entailing deeply held values and beliefs defending different patterns of social relations. *Social relations* are defined in cultural theory as a small number of distinctive patterns of interpersonal relationship – hierarchical, egalitarian, or individualist.[7] No causal priority is given to cultural biases or social relations; they are always found together interacting in a mutually reinforcing manner. Thus there are no relationships without cultural biases to justify them, and no biases without relations to uphold them.

Socially viable combinations of cultural biases and social relations are referred to in cultural theory as *ways of life* or as *political cultures*. More specifically, then, hierarchical, egalitarian, and individualist forms of social relations, together with the cultural biases that justify them, are each hypothesized to engender distinctive representations of what constitutes a hazard and what does not. Among all possible risks, those selected for worry or dismissal are functional in the sense that they strengthen one of these ways of life and weaken the others. This sort of explanation is at once more political (there is a political purpose to all of this perceiving – defending a way of life and attacking others) and less obvious (what has risk perception to do with ways of life?).

Since cultural biases are forms of ideology, there should be high correlations between certain biases and corresponding ideologies (eg egalitarianism and political liberalism). When we vary the kinds of possible dangers to which people react, however, we should see that the left–right distinction captures the cultural bias of egalitarianism but fails to distinguish between hierarchy and individualism. Hence we expect the three cultural biases to predict a broad spectrum of risk perceptions better than political ideology does.

According to cultural theory, adherents of hierarchy perceive acts of social deviance to be dangerous because such behaviour may disrupt their preferred (superior/subordinate) form of social relations. By contrast, advocates of greater equality of conditions abhor the role differentiation characteristic of hierarchy because ranked stations signify inequality. Egalitarians reject the prescriptions associated with hierarchy (ie who is allowed to do what and with whom), and thus show much less concern about social deviance.

Individualist cultures support self-regulation, including the freedom to bid and bargain. The labyrinth of normative constraints and controls on behaviour that are valued in hierarchies are perceived as threats to the autonomy of the individualist who prefers to negotiate for himself. Social deviance is a threat to individualist culture only when it limits freedom, or when it is disruptive of market relationships. Our expectation is that individualists should take a stance between hierarchists, to whom social deviance is a major risk, and egalitarians, to whom it is a minor risk at most.

---

6 Mary Douglas, 'Cultural Bias,' Occasional Paper 35 (London: Royal Anthropological Institute, 1978), republished in *In the Active Voice* (London: Routledge & Kegan Paul, 1982), 183–254; 'Passive Voice Theories in Religious Sociology,' *Review of Religious Research* 21 (1979): 51–56; *Essays in the Sociology of Perception* (London: Routledge & Kegan Paul, 1982). See also Douglas and Wildavsky, *Risk and Culture*; Michael Thompson, Richard Ellis, and Aaron Wildavsky, *Cultural Theory, or, Why All that is Permanent is Bias* (Boulder: Westview Press, 1990).

7 Cultural theory delineates two additional cultures: fatalists and hermits; it also makes finer distinctions regarding nature, technology, and risk perception than are discussed here. Were it possible, we would prefer to measure cultural biases in their social context. Instead, we have taken the approach suggested by the survey data at our disposal. We assess cultural biases as worldviews.

Egalitarians claim that nature is 'fragile' in order to justify sharing the earth's limited resources and to discomfort individualists whose life of bidding and bargaining would be impossible if they had to worry too much about disturbing nature. On the contrary, individualists claim that nature is a 'cornucopia', so that if people are released from artificial constraints (like excessive environmental regulations) there will be no limits to the abundance for all, thereby more than compensating for any damage they do. Hierarchists have something in common with individualists: they approve of technological processes and products, provided their experts have given the appropriate safety certifications and the applicable rules and regulations are followed. In hierarchical culture, nature is 'perverse or tolerant'; good will come if you follow their rules and experts, bad if you don't.

People who hold an egalitarian bias (who value strong equality in the sense of diminishing distinctions among people such as wealth, race, gender, authority, etc) would perceive the dangers associated with technology to be great and its attendant benefits to be small. They believe that an inegalitarian society is likely to insult the environment just as it exploits poor people. Those who endorse egalitarianism would also rate the risks of social deviance to be relatively low. What right has an unconscionably inegalitarian system to make demands or to set standards? The perceived risks of war among egalitarians would be low to moderate: they are likely to mistrust the military (a prototypical hierarchy); they also believe that the threat of war abroad is exaggerated by the establishment coalition of hierarchy and individualism in order to justify an inegalitarian system at home.

Cultural theory's predictions for the individualist bias are just the opposite: its adherents perceive the dangers of technology as minimal, in part because they trust that their institutions can control or compensate for the severity of untoward events. These same predictions hold for the cultural bias of hierarchy. How, then, do we distinguish between the worldviews of hierarchists and individualists? By varying the object of concern. A study of technological risks alone would leave these two cultures hopelessly confounded. Both are technologically optimistic, individualists because they see technology as a vehicle for unlimited individual enterprise – to them risk is opportunity – and hierarchists because they believe that technology endorsed by their experts is bound to improve the quality of life.

Due to the emphasis placed on obedience to authority within hierarchy, its supporters scorn deviant behaviour. In contrast, individualists, who prefer to substitute self-regulation for authority, are much more willing to permit behaviour that is the product of agreement. And yet, here too a distinction must be made. If the object of attention is personal behaviour, such as sex between consenting adults, individualists will be against allowing government to intervene. But if the subject is crime or violence against established institutions, they will be more disposed to support a governmental crackdown. In other words, if 'order' signifies support for the stability and legitimacy necessary for market relationships, individualists will support government action towards that end.

Economic troubles represent a different kind of risk from those of technology or social deviance, since almost everyone has a reason to worry about them – egalitarians because lower living standards are especially harmful to the poorest people, and adherents of hierarchy because it weakens the system they wish to defend. We would expect individualists to fear economic failure more than others, however, because the marketplace is the institution most central to their life of negotiated contracts.

To test these rival theories – knowledge, personality, economic, political, and cultural – we drew upon the risk-perception data archives established by Kenneth

H Craik, David Buss and Karl Dake at the University of California's Institute of Personality Assessment and Research.[8] We used the *pro-risk* index of their *Societal Risk Policy* instrument to gauge the extent of an individual's endorsement of risk taking versus risk aversion in regard to technology. This pro-risk index assesses whether risk taking and risk management are viewed as opportunities for advancement or rather as invitations to catastrophe at the societal level.

We assessed perceptions of risk associated with *technology and the environment, war, social deviance* and *economic troubles* by using variables chosen from a list of 36 'concerns that people have about society today'. Following procedures similar to those used in the most important pioneering study of risk perceptions, we selected average ratings of 25 technologies on *risk* and *benefit* for use.[9] These indices enable us to compare public responses to different kinds of dangers. Now we turn to the factors that have been used to explain such responses.

Knowledge One measure of knowledge we have used is the individual's self-report of how much he or she knows about specific technologies. Another measure is self-report of educational level. Self-ratings are the simplest and best way to address some psychological phenomena (who knows better than the individual how much dread a perceived hazard evokes for him?), while with regard to other phenomena they are notoriously poor. To avoid the potential pitfalls of relying only on self-reported knowledge, we developed a measure of perceptual accuracy based on differences between public and expert judgements of annual fatalities associated with eight technologies: contraceptives, nuclear power, diagnostic X-rays, bicycles, lawn mowers, motor vehicles, home appliances and commercial aviation.[10]

Personality In order to explore the correlations among personality characteristics and risk perceptions, we have drawn upon a broad set of traditional personality measures, including the *Adjective Check List* and the *California Psychological Inventory*.[11]

---

8 Intensive assessments of 300 ordinary citizens were conducted, including measures of perceptions of technologies, preferences for societal decision approaches and societal risk policy, confidence in institutions, sociotechnological and political orientations, personal values, environmental dispositions, self-descriptions, personal background, and more.
Two public samples were drawn from cities in the East Bay area of the San Francisco region: Richmond, Oakland, Piedmont, and Alameda. Stratified samples were selected on the basis of an analysis of social trends that provided detailed information regarding the median demographic characteristics of each postal zip code in the sample region. Participants were recruited via telephone directory sampling, letter of invitation, and telephone follow-up. Most, but not all, of the current findings are based on analysis of sample 2 (which had 134 participants), leaving sample 1 (which had 166 participants) available for replication of this study.
9 Participants rated how risky, and how beneficial, they judged each of 25 technologies to be: refrigerators, photocopy machines, contraceptives, suspension bridges, nuclear power, electronic games, diagnostic X-rays, nuclear weapons, computers, vaccinations, water fluoridation, rooftop solar collectors, lasers, tranquilizers, Polaroid photographs, fossil electric power, motor vehicles, movie special effects, pesticides, opiates, food preservatives, open-heart surgery, commercial aviation, genetic engineering, and windmills. See Baruch Fischhoff, Paul Slovic, Sarah Lichtenstein, Stephen Read, and Barbara Coombs, 'How Safe is Safe Enough? A Psychometric Study of Attitudes toward Technological Risks and Benefits,' *Policy Sciences* 9 (1978): 127–152.
10 The measure of perceptual accuracy was motivated by Paul Slovic, Baruch Fischhoff, and Sarah Lichtenstein in 'Facts and Fears: Understanding Perceived Risk,' in R Schwing and W Albers, Jr, *Societal Risk Assessment: How Safe is Safe Enough?* (New York: Plenum, 1980), 181–216.
11 Harrison Gough, *California Psychological Inventory Administrator's Guide* (Palo Alto: Consulting Psychologists Press, 1987); Harrison Gough and Alfred Heilbrun, *The Adjective Check List Manual* (Palo Alto: Consulting Psychologists Press, 1983).

Political orientation To evaluate predictions of risk perceptions based on political variables, we utilize measures of political party membership and liberal–conservative ideology (both self-rated and calculated on the basis of 20 policy issue stances).[12]

Cultural biases To test the relations among perceptions of danger and the world-views justifying *hierarchy, individualism,* and *egalitarianism,* we developed new measures to assess individual endorsement of three cultural biases.

Our hierarchy index embodies support for patriotism ('I'm for my country, right or wrong'), law and order ('The police should have the right to listen in on private telephone conversations when investigating crime'), and strict ethical standards ('I think I am stricter about right and wrong than most people'). It also expresses concern about the lack of discipline in today's youth and supports the notion that centralization is 'one of the things that makes this country great'.[13]

Our index for the cultural bias of individualism expresses support for continued economic growth as the key to quality of life and private profit as the main motive for hard work. It espouses the view that democracy depends fundamentally on the existence of the free market and argues that 'the welfare state tends to destroy individual initiative'. The individualism scale also indicates support for less government regulation of business and endorses private wealth as just rewards for economic endeavour: 'If a man has the vision and ability to acquire property, he ought to be allowed to enjoy it himself'.[14]

Our measure of egalitarianism is based on survey items written to assess attitudes toward equality of conditions. The egalitarianism scale centres on political solutions to inequality: 'Much of the conflict in this world could be eliminated if we had more equal distribution of resources among nations' and 'I support federal efforts to eliminate poverty', and 'I support a tax shift so that the burden falls more heavily on corporations and persons with large incomes'. The egalitarianism index also covers perceived abuses by the other political cultures: 'Misuse of scientific and expert knowledge is a very serious problem...' and 'The human goals of sharing and brotherhood are being hindered by current big institutions....'[15]

There are many theories that might account for the perceptions of risks, from those based on knowledge, personality, or economics, to those based on politics or culture. Our task is to discriminate among these rival theories by comparing their power to predict who fears what and why.

Cultural Biases Best Predict Risk-Perception Findings

If it were true that the more people know about technological risk or about technology in general, the more they worry about it, it should follow that risk perception

---

12 The measure of liberalism-conservatism based on policy preferences follows Edmond Costantini and Kenneth H Craik, 'Personality and Politicians: California Party Leaders, 1960–1976,' *Journal of Personality and Social Psychology* 38 (1980): 641–61.

13 Quotations, in order, are from Leonard Furguson, 'The Isolation and Measurement of Nationalism,' *Journal of Social Psychology* 16 (1942): 224; Hans Eysenck, *Sex and Personality* (London: Open Books, 1976), 153; Gough; David Buss, Kenneth H Craik, and Karl Dake, *The IPAR Risk Perception Data Archives: Assessment II Instruments,* unpublished document, Institute of Personality Assessment and Research (Berkeley: University of California, 1982).

14 Quotations, in order, are from Eysenck, 155, and from Furguson, 224.

15 Quotations concerning a tax shift and the elimination of poverty are from Costantini and Craik; the balance are from Buss, Craik, and Dake, 1982.

goes along with such knowledge. Using the measure of self-rated knowledge about technologies and self-rated education, we see quite the opposite.

Our findings show that those who rate their self-knowledge of technologies highly also tend to perceive greater average benefits associated with technologies than those who are less confident about their knowledge.[16] Those who report higher levels of education tend to perceive less threat from the risk of war. Otherwise, self-rated knowledge and education bear only weak (ie statistically insignificant) relations to preferences for societal-risk taking or to perceived risks associated with technology and the environment, social deviance, and economic troubles.

The more an individual's annual fatality estimates correspond to expert estimates, in addition, the more likely that person is to rate other risks as small – at least compared with those who are less accurate. While on the whole those who are more in accord with expert mortality estimates perceive less risk, they are also less optimistic regarding the benefits of technology. *Overall, the conclusion is compelling that self-rated knowledge and perceptual accuracy have a minimal relationship with risk perception.*

With regard to personality, we find that those who feel our society should definitely take technological risks can be described as patient, forbearing, conciliatory, and orderly (ie the pro-risk measure is positively correlated with the personality traits 'need for order' and 'deference').[17] Advocates of societal risk taking tend not to be aggressive, or autonomous, or exhibitionistic, but are more likely to be cautious and shy and to seek stability rather than change. *This pattern is suggestive of a technologically pro-risk personality which emerges as that of an obedient and dutiful citizen, deferential to authority.* Such a personality structure fits extremely well with the political culture of hierarchy.

By contrast, those citizens who perceive greater risk with regard to technology and the environment tend to turn up positive on exhibitionism, autonomy and the need for change, but negative on the need for order, deference and endurance (ie just the opposite of those who score as favouring societal risk taking). *This technologically risk-averse pattern of personality traits also holds for those who endorse egalitarianism.*

Those who endorse egalitarianism are also more likely to be personally risk taking but societally risk averse, while those who favour hierarchy tend to be personally risk averse but societally pro-risk with respect to technology and the environment. *Thus, we find no evidence for a personality structure that is risk taking or risk averse across the board.* Risk taking and risk aversion are not all of a piece, but depend on how people feel about the object of attention. Cultural theory would predict, for example, that hierarchists would be risk averse when it comes to taking risks with the body politic.

Relative to conservatives, those who rate themselves as liberals tend to be technologically risk averse at the societal level, are more likely to rate the risks of technology and the environment as very great, and are comparatively unconcerned about the risks of social deviance. As the self-rating of liberal increases, the average ratings for the risks of the 25 specific technologies increases, and the average ratings of their benefits decreases.

---

16 We report correlations throughout this essay, not means or mean differences. For sample 1 (134 participants), a correlation must be greater than 0.15 or less than –0.15 to be statistically significant. Nothing about average scores or group comparisons is implied.

17 Gordon Allport, *Pattern and Growth in Personality* (New York: Henry Holt and Company, 1961); see also *Personality: A Psychological Interpretation* (New York: Henry Holt and Company, 1937).

Political party membership is less predictive of risk perceptions and preferences than left–right ideology, especially on the Democratic side (undoubtedly because Democrats are the more heterogeneous party). When we ask what it is about thinking of oneself as a liberal or a conservative that makes such a big difference compared with thinking of oneself as a Democrat or a Republican, the findings are informative. Whether by self-rating or policy designation, *liberals have strong tendencies to endorse egalitarianism* (r = 0.52 and r = 0.50), *and to reject hierarchy* (r = –0.55 and r = –0.51) and *individualism* (t = –0.37 and r = –0.31). Likewise, membership in the Democratic party is correlated with egalitarianism (r = 0.30), but is not predictive of agreement or disagreement with the hierarchical or individualist point of view. *Republicans have a penchant towards individualism* (r = 0.31) *and hierarchical biases* (r = 0.40), *and an equally strong proclivity for rejecting egalitarianism* (r = –0.45). These correlations among political party membership, left–right ideology, and cultural biases are huge by the standards of survey research.

How does cultural theory compare with other approaches to perceived risk? *Cultural biases provide predictions of risk perceptions and risk-taking measures of knowledge and personality and at least as predictive as political orientation.* We find that egalitarianism is strongly related to the perception of technological and environmental risks as grave problems for our society (r = 0.51) and hence to strong risk aversion in this domain (r = –0.42). Egalitarianism is also related positively to the average perceived risks and negatively to the average perceived benefits of 25 technologies. One could hardly paint a worse picture of technology – little benefit, much risk and the risks not worth taking.

Individualist and hierarchist biases, in contrast, are positively related to a preference for technological risk-taking (r = 0.32 and r = 0.43) and to average ratings of technological benefits (r = 0.34 and r = 0.37). Here the image is more sanguine: the benefits are great and the risks small, so society should press on with risk taking to get more of the good that progress brings with it.

Discussion

We have shown that whether measured by cultural biases or by political orientation, perceptions of technology are predictable given the worldview of the perceiver. But one should not conclude that the establishment cultures of individualism and hierarchy always favour risk taking or that egalitarians are always risk averse. *Perception of danger is selective; it varies with the object of attention.* For we find that compared with advocates of egalitarianism, those in greater agreement with individualism perceive greater risk in respect to war (r = 0.15 versus r = 0.40 respectively). Likewise, it is the hierarchical bias that is most highly correlated with perceived threat of social deviance (r = 0.35 compared with r = 0.15 for egalitarianism). Nor is it always the adherents of establishment cultures versus those of egalitarianism. As predicted by cultural theory, *it is not that devotees of individualism and hierarchy perceive no dangers in general, but that they disagree with those who favour egalitarianism about how danger should be ranked; just as technological and environmental risks are most worrisome to egalitarians, social deviance is deemed most dangerous to hierarchists, and the threat of war (which disrupts markets and subjects people to severe controls) is most feared by individualists.*

It is obvious that culture neither causes nor influences demographic character-istics such as gender or age (though it may influence their social meanings). Thus we do not argue that the weak correlations we find between cultural biases and per-sonal attributes like income or social class reveal the influence of political culture on those variables. Whether we look at knowledge, personality, political orientation or demographic variables, however, we find that cultural theory provides the best predictions of a broad range of perceived risks and an interpretive framework in which these findings cohere.

The importance of using a wide range of risks in studying how people perceive potential dangers should now be apparent. Employing only dangers from technol-ogy, while better than nothing, is far less powerful than considering a panoply of dangers from the threat of war to social deviance to economic collapse. Broadening the spectrum of related questions to be considered allows for more discriminating tests of rival theories. With perceived dangers from technology as the only issue, moreover, one cannot tell whether the level of concern registered by an individual comes from aversion to or acceptance of risk in general, or is evoked differentially by various risks. By observing whether there is a variegated pattern of risk percep-tion (now we know there is) and by ascertaining who rates each kind of risk in which way, we may study *patterns of risk perception.* Fitting these patterns to alternative explanations, we believe, is a superior test of competing theories.

Comparing rival theories, not just a single explanation, has similar advantages. Making the rival theories confront each other reduces the temptation to claim easy victories. It is not enough to show respectable correlations; it is also necessary to do better than the alternatives.

Viewed in this light, the cultural theory's greater power than alternative expla-nations is manifest in its ability to *generate* broader and finer predictions of who is likely to fear, not to fear or fear less, different kinds of dangers. Having derived from cultural theory a number of explanations approximated in our findings, the next question is what this tells us about risk perception.

Our findings show that it is not knowledge of a technology that leads people to worry about its dangers. In the current sample, the difference between public and technical estimates of annual fatalities ranges up to several orders of magnitude in size. The enormous variation in these public perceptions is not accounted for by knowledge, leaving considerable room for other explanations. Indeed, if people have little knowledge about technologies and their risks, then public fears can hardly coincide with how dangerous various technologies have proved to be.

Wait a minute! Everyone knows that nuclear radiation and AIDS can kill. We agree. When these subjects become politicized, however, disagreement develops along the fault lines of policy differences, seizing upon whatever cracks of uncertainty now exist: What are the health consequences of prolonged exposure to low levels of ra-diation? Is there such a thing as an amount of radiation so small that exposure causes no harm? Can AIDS be passed along by social contact? Should sufferers from AIDS be quarantined? Should their sexual contacts be traced and informed?

Our findings on personality raise the question of why there are such interest-ing sets of correspondence among traditionally assessed traits and cultural biases. Part of the difficulty in interpreting these findings is that personality entails such a wide set of characteristics – from intrapsychic to interpersonal relations – that virtu-ally no aspect of individual life is left out. Were there theories connecting particular aspects of personality to patterns of risk perception, interpretation would be easier, for then we could test these hypotheses. One possibility is that personal orientations may guide individuals to make commitments consistent with specific political cultures, while at the same time, cultures may select from among individuals those that support their way of life. Since there are no such theories, however, we are left to explore among personality characteristics to see what fits.

Assuming both personality and political culture are operative, which is more powerful in predicting perceptions of danger and preferences for risk taking? Clearly, the closer one gets to asking questions about policy preferences, the better one's predictions of the selective perceptions of danger should be. Since our measures of cultural biases are closer to public policy than traditional measures of personality are, we should expect our measures (other things being equal) to predict better. And they do. But if that were all there were to prediction – proximity of the explanation to the explained – then we would expect assessments of political ideology to predict risk preferences far better than cultural bias does. As we have shown, however, public policy stances and self-rated political orientation do not do as well as cultural biases in predicting risk preferences and perceptions – even though they are the most proximal to risk policy of all the variables we test.

How, then, do cultural biases, which are so remote from the evidence regarding risks, guide people in choosing what to fear? A detailed answer is presented in *Risk and Culture*. Here, we can say only that hierarchists favour technological risk taking because they see this as supporting the institutions that they rely on to make good their promises, to wit: technology can promote a stronger society and a safer future provided that their rules (and stratified social relations) are maintained. Individualists also deem technology to be good. They hold that following market principles (and individually negotiated social relations) will allow technological innovation to triumph, conferring creative human value on otherwise inert resources. They also believe that the enormous benefits of technological innovation will convey their premise that unfettered bidding and bargaining leaves people better off. If they believed that free market institutions are intrinsically ruinous to nature, individualists could no longer defend a life of minimum restraints. By the same token, egalitarians are opposed to taking technological risks because they see them as supporting the inegalitarian markets and coercive hierarchies to which they are opposed.

By this time readers are right to wonder, in view of the assertions we are making, whether other surveys support our claims. A recent one to come to our attention is supportive in many ways. Its subject is the irradiation of food as a preservative process, widely considered safe by scientists, but a topic of considerable worry to concerned consumers. The participants were 195 adult women chosen from Pennsylvania women's groups of various kinds – religious, civic, professional, social and political. The respondents were given a questionnaire to fill out, then were shown different kinds of information about food irradiation, then filled out another questionnaire and finally were engaged in group discussion. The authors, Richard Bord and Robert O'Conner, find, as we do, that knowledge (based on the information given to participants) is inversely related to fear of a technology: 'Having accurate knowledge about the food irradiation process translates into greater acceptance.' They add significantly that:

> *whether respondents received a technical or non-technical communication about the food irradiation process and whether they received a detailed discussion of the major arguments for and against food irradiation had no discernible effect on their judgments.*

It is not knowledge per se, but confidence in institutions and the credibility of information that is at issue:

> *Trust in business and industry in general, the food irradiation industry specifically, government regulators, and science as a provider of valid and useful knowledge is the major predictor of whether the respondent indicates she will or will not try irradiated food.... Learning that others have used food irradiation safely and of its approval by prestigious professional organizations enhanced its acceptability.... People who oppose big government and big business express greater fear of radiation.*
> *[One of the main topics of group discussion] was the respondents' view that complex technology bears a burden of too much uncertainty, too much greed on the part of its sponsors, and too little effective governmental control. The point was frequently made that even if the scientific-technical plan was flawless the people executing the plan and managing the technology would inevitably create serious problems.*[18]

It is not only that 'the facts' cannot by themselves convince doubters, but that behind one set of facts are always others relating to whether business and government can be trusted.

If there are any people to whom knowledge about hazards should make the most difference, it is those who are professionally employed in the analysis and management of risk. Yet a survey of risk professionals drawn from government, industry, environmental groups and universities shows something dramatically different. Thomas Dietz and Robert Rycroft find that self-reported ideology:

> *appears to have the strongest links to environmental attitudes and values of risk professionals.... For example, on the question of whether we are seeing only the tip of the iceberg with regard to technological risk, 88.5 percent of [the] very liberal ... agreed ... as did 74 percent of [the] liberals. Only 25 percent of [the] very conservative and 36.4 percent of [the] conservative respondents agreed.*[19]

The more perceptions of contested subjects are studied, we believe, the more they will reveal the strong influence of cultural biases. In this respect, Paul Sabatier and S Hunter's study of causal perceptions in belief systems is especially useful because, like the present analysis, it focuses on perceptual biases from more than one cultural direction:

> *Environmentalists perceived water clarity to be getting worse, while those in favor of economic growth and property rights simply refused to believe the wealth of documented, and widely diffused, scientific evidence developed by one of the world's leading limnologists demonstrating statistically significant declines in water clarity over the previous 10–15 years.*

18 Richard Bord and Robert O'Conner, 'Risk Communication, Knowledge, and Attitudes: Explaining Reactions to a Technology Perceived as Risky,' (manuscript submitted for publication), quotations 14, 11–12, 14–15. Authors are at Pennsylvania State University.
19 Thomas Dietz and Robert Rycroft, *The Risk Professionals* (New York: Russell Sage Foundation, 1987), quotation 47.

> *This suggests that in high-conflict situations, perceptions on even rela-*
> *tively straightforward technical issues can be heavily influenced by elites'*
> *normative presuppositions.*[20]

This position reaffirming the importance of worldviews is bolstered by the 'risk and benefit perceptions, acceptability judgements, and self-reported actions toward nuclear power' spoken of by Gerald Gardner and his co-authors. Their respondents were taken from environmental groups, blue-collar workers, college students, businesspeople, and technologists (scientists and engineers employed by a utility company). While education, sex, gender, religion and other sociodemographic variables were not related to protests or other personal actions taken on nuclear power, Gardner et al found that liberal–conservative ideology was predictive: 'The most important correlate of reported action and "acceptability" … appeared to represent a "liberal/ public interest group vs. a conservative/private enterprise" dimension'.[21]

The power of the ideological explanation is strengthened further by Stanley Rothman and S Robert Lichter, who analysed questionnaires filled out by a sample of 1203 congressional staff, civil servants, television and print journalists, lawyers, officials of public interest groups, moviemakers, military officers, and energy and nuclear power experts. The results vary widely by group membership, with 98.7 per cent of nuclear energy experts thinking nuclear power plants are safe, compared with only 6.4 per cent of public interest officials and 30.6 per cent of journalists on television networks. Their major finding is that, compared with a variety of demographic, social, and economic variables, political ideology was by far the most powerful predictor. 'We hypothesize,' they conclude, 'that nuclear energy is a surrogate issue for more fundamental criticism of US institutions'.[22] This restates the thesis of *Risk and Culture* for nuclear technology.

Whenever other studies present comparable findings, they reveal that the most powerful factor for predicting risk perceptions is trust in institutions or ideology, which is largely about which institutions can be trusted. *Such findings show that, however conceptualized – whether as political ideology or cultural biases – wordviews best account for patterns of risk perceptions.*

In summary, the great struggles over the perceived dangers of technology in our time are essentially about trust and distrust of societal institutions, that is, about cultural conflict. Once we vary the object of concern, we do indeed discover that egalitarians (who fear social deviance less than hierarchists and individualists) fear technology a great deal – seeing in it, or so the cultural theory claims, the corporate greed they believe leads to inequality. Individualists, who believe in competition, and who are exceedingly loathe to place restraints on what they consider to be mutually profitable relationships, deem technology to be good. In contrast, hierarchists, who fear disorder and erosion of status differences, are more worried about social deviance and less worried about technological dangers than egalitarians.

We have shown that other surveys, with different assumptions, methods and sample populations find, as we do, that risk perceptions and preferences are pre-

---

20 Paul Sabatier and S Hunter, 'The Incorporation of Causal Perceptions into Models of Elite Belief Systems,' *Western Political Quarterly* 42 (1989): quotation 253.
21 Gerald Gardner, Adrian Tiemann, Leroy Gould, Donald Deluca, Leonard Doob, and Jan Stolwijk, 'Risk and Benefit Perceptions, Acceptability Judgments, and Self-reported Actions toward Nuclear Power,' *Journal of Social Psychology* 116 (1982): 116, quotations 194–95.
22 Stanley Rothman and S Robert Lichter, 'Elite Ideology and Risk Perception in Nuclear Energy Policy,' *American Political Science Review* 81 (1987): 81, quotation 395.

dictable, given individual differences in cultural biases. It is the congruence of our analysis with others' that gives us the most confidence in our findings. We would have preferred to ask more subtle and differentiated questions about knowledge; but the other surveys we cite do that, and they also show the importance of cultural biases. Above all, we would have preferred more elaborate statistical analysis than small samples permit.[23]

Knowing what sorts of perceptions come from which kinds of people may allow for practical applications of cultural theory in a variety of policy contexts. Risk communication programmes, for instance, might profitably focus on the underlying causes of risk perception – such as confidence (or lack of trust) in institutions, or the credibility of hazard information – rather than only on 'the facts' regarding possible harms. Since cultural theory generates clues to the propensities of those with various worldviews to underestimate or overestimate specific kinds of risk, in addition, it can be used to tailor educational programs – say cigarette and alcohol warnings – to the plural rationalities represented in the general public.

It has been two decades since Chauncy Starr's seminal essay 'Social Benefit versus Technological Risk' asked how much our society is willing to pay for safety.[24] Since then, a lively and spirited research community has grown up around the issues of technological risks.[25] We hope to have pointed the study of risk perception in the right direction by: (1) expanding the scope of the questions asked to include patterns of risk perception (not only technological hazard, but also war, social deviance, economic decline, etc); and by (2) comparing rival explanations of public fears. As predicted by cultural theory, we find that individuals perceive a variety of risks in a manner that supports their way of life.

---

23 Our findings call for multivariate statistical analysis of the interactions between cultural biases and the other classes of predictors. We are fully aware of the difficulties of regression or path analysis on small samples, so efforts are under way on larger samples. We are also sensitive to the fact that correlations do not necessarily imply causation. Cultural theory makes causal attributions, however, and the correlations we do find are consistent with its predictions.

24 Chauncy Starr, 'Social Benefit versus Technological Risk: What is Our Society Willing to Pay for Safety?' *Science* 165 (1969): 1232–38.

25 National Research Council, Committee on Risk Perception and Communication, *Improving Risk Communication* (Washington, DC: National Academy Press, 1989).

Explaining Risk Perception: An Empirical Evaluation of Cultural Theory

Lennart Sjöberg

Introduction

Perceived risk is of central interest in many current policy discussions and there is much research interest on the topic (Drottz-Sjöberg, 1991). Many studies have shown that the perceived risk level of a technology is a more potent factor in risk acceptability or various political intentions, such as intended voting, than perceived or expected benefits.

If risk perception can be understood, risk communication would profit. To communicate successfully, one needs to understand the basis of the beliefs of the other party (Sjöberg, 1980).

The question naturally arises how level of perceived risk should be explained (Sjöberg, 1996). That is the question to be treated in the present paper. I will mainly utilize work carried out in our own unit for this purpose, since these data are readily available for exposition and reanalysis. I will, of course, also draw upon general work in risk perception but I will not attempt to review it in full; see Sjöberg and Drottz-Sjoberg (1994b) for such a review.

There will be an emphasis on a current approach in this area: cultural theory of risk perception (Douglas and Wildavsky, 1982). Several researchers have claimed that this theory offers a promising approach to understanding risk perception; it was of interest to evaluate these claims. Cultural theory is currently suggested as a partial basis for risk communication (eg Peters and Slovic, 1996; Palmer, 1996).

In addition the social and cultural context of risk perception is obviously of importance (Sjöberg, 1987). Moral notions have, for example, been found to have an influence on risk acceptability (Sjöberg and Winroth, 1986). This does not imply, however, that cultural theory, as specified in the Douglas-Wildavsky tradition, necessarily will be successful in accounting for risk perception. The question is an empirical one and, in the present paper, I will review the empirical and quantitative evidence for the theory.

Cultural Theory

In the discussion of cultural theory it is useful to employ a distinction between distal and proximal variables in accounting for behaviour. Proximal variables are semantically close to the target behaviour to be predicted. Distal variables are more dissimilar in terms of contents.

Proximal variables are usually far more efficient in accounting for behaviour than distal variables. Outside of social sciences people are generally unaware of the tremendous difficulty in accounting for *anything* by means of distal variables. The prime example is the failure of personality variables to predict behaviour (Mischel, 1968) – still widely believed by the public to be strongly related to behaviour. Risk attitudes as discussed in economics also assume generality across domains, an assumption of doubtful validity.

Cultural theory is an attempt to provide a distal explanation of risk perception. The theory has its roots in work by anthropologist Mary Douglas and political scientist Aaron Wildavsky (Douglas, 1992; Douglas and Wildavsky, 1982). For a critical review of the theory, see Boholm (1996).

Social relations are conceptualized by cultural theory in a small number of major distinctive patterns: hierarchy, egalitarian and individualist.[1] These are defined operationally as belief-value structures. Briefly, hierarchy ideology supports the establishment, promotes trust in expertise and abhors social deviance. Individualist ideology, on the other hand, gives priority to individual achievement and stresses that people should have material rewards for their work. Egalitarians, finally, are distrustful of institutions and their experts, which are seen as motivated by selfishness and greed, and as obstacles to a society characterized by brotherhood and equality.

In this model, egalitarians stand out as the most suspicious of technology and hence likely to rate its risks as high while the other two types of ideologies would be associated with a lenient attitude to technology risks, and with fear of social deviance (hierarchists), or war and economic hardship (individualists).

Cultural theory seems to capture an important facet of risk perception, in spite of its unclear and at times ad hoc character. Whether it can in fact explain risk perception is of course another matter. And how much can it add to what is already explained by other models?

Furthermore, is risk perception really such a resilient phenomenon that we are justified in using the terminology of Douglas and Wildavsky and saying that people *choose* which risks to fear? In my view, this terminology is misleading. People do not freely choose what to fear. Indeed, people would like to be free of their fears, when they are seen as irrational, or of the objects of fear, when the fear is seen as rational. Fear is an emotion which is quite predominant in human life. Expectations about the future have been found to be dominated by fears or negative expectations (Sjöberg, 1989). It is hard to believe that fears have merely social functions. The biological function of fear in protecting an organism from danger is quite obvious. We are biological as well as social beings.[2]

A further problem is connected with the concept of social relations. These of course differ, depending on which group membership is considered: work group, family, or leisure. If a person responds to a questionnaire, which role is he or she adopting? The answer may depend on many factors such as the contents of the ques-

---

1 Cultural Theory suggests that there are two more 'cultures': fatalists and hermits. A scale for measuring fatalism is included in the British but not in the US version of the cultural biases scales.

2 The notion that phobias have something to do with reactions to modern technology is far-fetched. The tendency to attach a catchy phrase such as 'radiophobia' to people's fear of radiation is very unfortunate (Drottz-Sjöberg and Persson, 1993) since it is merely a devious way of trying to persuade the listener that the fear in question is irrational (phobias are by definition irrational).

tionnaire, the setting in which it is administered and its stated purpose. This problem badly needs further analysis.

It can still be argued that the framework of cultural theory is persuasive and credible. Few people who are not professional social scientists demand more than such intuitive credibility, and that is probably one reason why the theory is 'successful'. It is sometimes claimed that Douglas and Wildavsky have explained, once and for all, why people perceive risks in different ways. The often cited book by Douglas and Wildavsky (Douglas and Wildavsky, 1982) is, however, a rather strange text, full of assertions which are hard to comprehend and even harder to relate to empirical evidence. Sociological applications of the theory to the study of risk perception, for example Rayner (1990), tend to be qualitative in their orientation. They may be stimulating to read but they do not answer the question about the validity of the theory. However, the matter is open to empirical investigation, and when this approach is taken a different story emerges, as will be demonstrated in the following.

Empirical and Quantitative Investigations of Cultural Theory

In this section I discuss tests of cultural theory using quantitative methods. It is clear that both the theory and the methods are tested simultaneously. Positive results support both, but negative results can be due to inadequacy of methods, theory or both.

The first work on empirical and quantitative testing of cultural theory is Dake's thesis (Dake, 1990), which has subsequently been published in journal articles (Dake, 1991; Wildavsky and Dake, 1990).

What Dake did was essentially the following. He devised attitude scales for measuring the cultural biases, and, using these scales, he observed that they correlated with a set of 36 societal concerns in a pattern predicted by the theory.

Dake reported results based on survey data from two convenience samples. He found that the egalitarian scale correlated positively with ratings of technological risk, the hierarchy scale with risks of social deviance and the individualist scale with war risks. Results were reported only for 19 out of 36 societal concerns; the 17 not reported were not significantly correlated with cultural biases. The highest correlations reported by Dake were in the 0.40s.

Dake's thesis was the first work in which cultural theory was subjected to a quantitative test but it is incomplete in that respect. The samples were rather small (two samples and a total of 300 individuals), there was no information on reliability of the measures used for measuring cultural biases,[3] and the data analysis was not carried very far. No multivariate analyses were reported.

The samples are said to be representative, but the assertion is not convincingly justified. No details about the response scales used for measuring the cultural biases are given in the thesis or the subsequent publications; both replication and interpretation of the results are thereby hampered.

There have been a few more attempts at quantitative study of cultural theory dimensions. Grendstad's thesis is a major attempt (Grendstad, 1990). Based on extensive survey data from ten European countries, he constructed a system for measuring the group/grid dimensions suggested by cultural theory. At least two of the

---

3 Recently, Palmer (1996) reported reliabilities (Cronbach's alpha) around 0.6 for the three most important scales (egalitarianism, individualism, hierarchy).

dependent variables he related to this classification system can be regarded as risk perception variables: that the future is uncertain, and the perceived likelihood of war. The amount of variance explained in these two dimensions varied between 0.002 and 0.093 (uncertain future) and 0.000 and 0.084 (war). On the average, only about 5 per cent of the variance in risk perception within countries was explained.

Slovic and coworkers used a few items to test the cultural theory notions in a survey of Canadian public opinion (Slovic et al, 1992). The study involved an improvement on Dake's work since they used a large and representative sample. However, the correlations between those items and risk ratings were very low. They reported seven correlations between cultural theory items and a pooled risk perception index. The correlations were 0.23, –0.01, 0.05, 0.05, –0.11, 0.19 and –0.01. Although three of these seven correlations were statistically significant, given the very large sample size in this study, it is difficult to regard the findings as strongly supportive of cultural theory.

Renn et al obtained data from small convenience samples of students and also got very weak correlations between cultural theory items and risk ratings (Renn et al, 1992).

A further Norwegian study should also be mentioned. Grendstad and Selle (1994) used eight items, two for each of the four cultural theory dimensions,[4] and correlated them with environmental attitudes. A large random sample of the Norwegian population participated. They also employed a measure of post-materialism (Inglehart, 1977 and 1990), and a scale of radicalism–conservatism as predictors of environmental attitudes. The environmentalist attitude items were factor analysed and a factor of environmental danger was obtained. This is the closest they came to analysing risk perception. I report their results for this dimension only. The correlations with fatalism, individualism, egalitarianism and hierarchy were 0.08, –0.08, 0.23, and –0.13, respectively. Radicalism–conservatism and post-materialism correlated –0.20 and 0.13 with perceived environmental danger. All six predictors together accounted for 9 per cent of the variance of risk perception. Hence, this recent large-scale survey agreed with other work cited here in showing the cultural theory items did not predict risk perception to any noticeable degree.

In a still more ambitious attempt to test cultural theory, the British version of the scales was translated to French and used in a large scale survey of the French population (Brenot et al, 1996). The scale reliabilities were satisfactory, according to the authors. However, correlations with personal risk ratings were only of the order 0.1. Trust in information and general risk ratings were even more weakly related to the scales.

A recent British study, with a smaller convenience sample, reported very weak correlations between cultural theory scales and risk perception data (Marris et al, 1996). The finding that some people seemed to function according to the theory may be interesting, but the data show very clearly that inter-individual differences in risk perception must be explained in other ways.

Peters and Slovic (1996)[5] used some Dake items and a few additional ones to measure cultural biases. They obtained very low reliabilities of two of the scales,[6]

---

4 Of course, reliabilities could not be estimated for scales measured by only two items. However, the factor analysis they reported for these eight items showed that they were not all pure measures of the postulated factors.

5 Results are from a large sample survey study with a rather low response rate. The authors do not state if the respondents were biased with regard to education and income.

6 The reported reliability of 0.42 of the individualist scale is remarkably low.

but argued that these reliabilities would increase if more items were to be added. They even state that 'These alpha coefficients are not necessarily low ...' (p1438, note 6). While it is true that scales with more valid items would be more reliable, provided that such items can be constructed, it does not change the fact that the scales, as they are, are of very low reliability and therefore measure the attitudes only with large random error components.

Peters and Slovic investigated correlations between the scales and various risk judgments and found a number of, mostly very weak, but often statistically significant correlations, which they describe in the text in an optimistic manner. For example, the correlations between the egalitarian subscale and technology concerns were –0.22, –0.10, –0.01 and 0.02, a not very impressive set of correlations. Nonetheless the authors wrote: 'As predicted (Dake, 1991), these data confirm the hypothesis that the Egalitarian factor will be *strongly* related to concerns about technology ...' (Peters and Slovic, 1996, p1439, italics added). With a set of 25 correlations between the Egalitarian scale and risk ratings varying from 0.04 to 0.27, the authors wrote that '... the Egalitarian factor scores correlate *strongly* in a positive direction with almost all the perceived risk items.' (p1443, italics added).

It seems that the authors concluded that they had strong correlations when they had significant correlations. If so, they were in error, especially with such a large sample (N = 1179). A correlation of 0.10 is not 'strong' even it has a p value < 0.01. Indeed, several of the correlations they report are very close to 0 and the findings should be taken as support of the conclusion that cultural theory is not supported, on the whole.

Let us look at how much variance was explained. For concerns, the mean share of variance accounted for by the fatalist/hierarchy, individualist and egalitarian subscales were 0.037, 0.020 and 0.036, respectively. With the scales in the same order, the corresponding values for health risks were 0.005, 0.005 and 0.022. Thus, virtually nothing was explained.[7] It is surprising that Peters and Slovic describe these trivial results as 'strong' relationships. At any rate, their results are quite in line with other studies of cultural theory and risk perception. Only a tiny fraction of the variance of risk perception is explained – but it can of course be demonstrated to be statistically significant with large survey samples.

Some further work by Frewer and colleagues on cultural biases has been oriented towards trust and communication (Frewer et al, 1996; Frewer et al, 1993). Related studies have been reported by Cvetkovich and Earle (Earle and Cvetkovich, 1994). Some interesting results have been obtained – eg that messages compatible with the cultural bias of the recipient are more credible – but this work, while related, is outside the proper scope of the present paper which is devoted to the explanation of risk perception.

Jenkins-Smith (1994) reported an interesting development of Slovic's stigma model and the image association method. He also related image data to a typology based on scales for measuring cultural biases. Significant associations were found, but it is unclear how strong they were.

A small scale study by Palmer (1996), using a group of college students of psychology as subjects, was recently reported. She used Dake's scales and grouped subjects in three worldview categories. Risk ratings by these subjects were regressed

---

7 A number of arguments in defence of Cultural Theory are discussed in the General Discussion, among them the notion that the theory will turn out to be a strong explanation if only measurement error could be eliminated.

on ratings of harm and benefit of 22 activities, according to a model proposed by Holtgrave and Weber (1993). There were some suggestive differences between types of subjects as to the fitted regression coefficients, but risk ratings per se differed significantly only in two of the 22 activities. Strength of relationship was not reported. For health risks, probability and severity of harm were important predictors of risk for all three subject categories and there were some weak signs that hierarchists may also have been considering benefits. This is hardly more than very weak support for cultural theory, in particular since mean risk ratings did not differ between the three groups, except in two cases.

In a preliminary study, I reported results on the full subscales[8] designed by Dake, and related scores on those scales to risk perception data in a sample from Sweden (Sjöberg, 1995). The scales were translated to Swedish and administered to a group of 145 students who applied for admission to the Stockholm School of Economics. The correlations were not impressive. Of 216 correlations, only 24 were significant at the 0.05 level. There was no trend that risks due to technology/industry were more strongly correlated with the egalitarian attitude than other risks.

A replication study of Dake's original work carried out in the USA (Sjöberg, in press a), with procedures as close as possible[9] to Dake's gave very similar results to the Swedish study just mentioned, only a somewhat higher level of explanation (about 10 per cent). In a study of trust and risk perception, the Dake scales were again used (a Swedish sample), and the result was once more a very low level of explained variance of perceived risk (Sjöberg, in press b).

Summing up, little work has shown that cultural theory can explain a large share of risk perception. Yet the theory has many supporters and work is currently published where statistical significance seems to be taken as evidence for explanatory power, much in the manner of Dake's own work. Further investigation and documentation is clearly called for.

It should also be noted that the theory is not investigated in full in this kind of work. In particular, no published work on the basic assumption that cultural biases and ways of life are driven by social relations has been carried out in a quantitative mode (with the possible exception of Grendstad's thesis, discussed above).

Dake considered his results to be very strong indeed,[10] and he also argued that the instrument he devised for measuring cultural biases constituted 'one of the more promising for crosscultural comparisons' (Dake, 1990, p43). This is an important claim, and the present work goes on to test the theory in cross-cultural comparisons using the British version of the Dake items.

I now turn to two more of our own empirical studies which were intended to test the cultural theory approach to risk perception. For a more complete review, the reader is referred to Sjöberg (1995) which also describes some work on cultural comparisons not covered here.

---

8 I am grateful to Karl Dake for providing these scales (the British version).

9 Dake does not describe his procedures in a very detailed manner so an exact replication was not possible.

10 A citation from the thesis: *Cultural biases are related pervasively and strongly with societal concerns* (Dake, 1990, p33).

Teachers in Sweden and Brazil

The results mentioned in the previous section (Swedish student sample) call for further validation. The student sample was rather unrepresentative. The risks were partly different from those investigated by Dake and Wildavsky. Also, problems may have arisen in translating the items to Swedish. A further (remote) possibility is that the level of perceived risk is so low in Sweden that a replication there is of questionable value. For these reasons, I decided to try yet another culture, a very different one, and a culture with a high level of risk: Brazil.

The scale items were translated into Portuguese. Risk perception data were obtained for the same list of risk items as in the original Dake work, and every attempt was made to ensure the comparability of the procedures, with the exception that we obtained ratings of both general and personal risks. Data were obtained from 102 school teachers in São Paulo, sampling from the whole spectrum of disciplines, and from 94 teachers in Stockholm, sampling from comparable stages and disciplines. Most of the teachers were employed by high schools.

Cronbach's alpha in the Brazilian group and for the egalitarian, individualism, hierarchy and fatalistic attitudes were 0.71, 0.74, 0.56 and 0.65 respectively. Corresponding values in the Swedish group were 0.77, 0.62, 0.37 and 0.57.

The mean scores[11] of the Brazilian group, with dimensions in the same order as above, were 4.19 (SD = 0.46), 3.47 (SD = 0.55), 3.42 (SD = 0.64) and 2.40 (SD= 0.55). The corresponding values for the Swedish group were 3.64 (SD = 0.49), 3.21 (SD = 0.44), 3.20 (SD = 0.46) and 2.19 (SD = 0.41). Hence, these subjects were about equally likely to endorse items from the first three dimensions, with some preference for egalitarian items, but tended to reject fatalism as an orientation. The correlations among the four sets of mean risk ratings are given in Table 5.2.

Risk ratings were strongly correlated between the two countries, speaking against a cultural interpretation of risk perception. At the same time, pronounced level differences were obtained, with Brazilian teachers rating most risks as much higher than the Swedish group did. The regression lines show that the difference was roughly constant over the range of risks.

Correlations between subscales and risk ratings were computed. In the case of the Brazilian data, only 53 of the 272 correlations between the cultural theory scales and risk judgements were significant at the 0.05 level; of these, 18 were correlations involving the egalitarian subscale. These relations appear to be mostly random.

The Swedish data (Table 5.3) gave somewhat more positive results. There were more significant correlations than in the corresponding Brazilian data: 81 out of 256. This is probably somewhat more than can be expected from chance alone. Al-

Table 5.2 *Correlations among mean risk ratings, teachers in Brazil and Sweden*

	Brazil, general risks	Brazil, personal risks	Sweden, general risks	Sweden, personal risks
Brazil, general risks	–	–	–	–
Brazil, personal risks	0.930	–	–	–
Sweden, general risks	0.770	0.716	–	–
Sweden, personal risks	0.629	0.614	0.923	–

11 The scores were computed as means of ratings of items which had been responded to.

most half of the significant correlations (31) came from the egalitarian subscale. There was a pattern here: nuclear energy risks were rated higher by egalitarians, risks from social conflicts or economic decline as lower.

The Swedish findings were consistent with the *results* reported by Dake. He investigated 36 societal concerns with three scales of cultural bias, and thus computed 108 correlations. Of these, 73 or 68 per cent were not significant at the 0.05 level, 32 per cent significant.

In the study of the Swedish teachers, 68 per cent of the correlations were not significant, but the sample was only half of the one analysed by Dake. To investigate some further details, the present results and the ones reported by Dake are reproduced in Table 5.4. The Swedish teacher data were selected for comparison because they were most promising.[12] Only results from general risk ratings are given in this table, because that was the only kind of risk studied by Dake.

Corresponding correlations are plotted against each other. Regression lines refer to each of the three sets of correlations, one for each cultural bias scale. It was found that the results were similar, although higher in Dake's data especially for the egalitarian scale. The squared correlations between the two sets of data were 0.60, 0.84 and 0.64 for the egalitarian, individualistic and hierarchy scales respectively. The major difference lies in the conclusions drawn from the results. Dake concluded that he had found very strong relationships, I conclude the opposite. A few correlations around 0.4 are not enough to support a conclusion as strongly formulated as that of Dake's: 'cultural biases are related pervasively and strongly with societal concerns ...' (Dake, 1990, p33).

A more appropriate method to investigate the relationship between perceived risk and cultural biases is to use multiple regression. A model was fitted to each perceived risk, using the three main cultural biases (egalitarianism, individualism and hierarchy) as explanatory variables. Considering the explained variance obtained in the multiple regression analyses, it was found that the average was about 5 per cent.

The weak trends in the direction of the cultural theory predictions found thus far seem to be essentially what Dake also found, only he chose to present his results and to draw conclusions from them as if he had found a powerful explanation of risk perception.

Swedish Cultural Biases and Perceived Risk of Nuclear Waste

The studies mentioned so far were mostly concerned with rather small convenience samples, just as most previous work on cultural theory. To investigate further the generality of the findings it was decided to obtain data from a large, nationally representative sample. This is a manageable task in Sweden because there is access to a data file of the whole population, and we have extensive experience showing the feasibility of using mailed questionnaires in population studies of risk perception.

In this study, six items have been investigated which intended to measure the three major dimensions of cultural theory – namely, the egalitarian, hierarchy and individualistic dimensions. An extensive questionnaire was used to measure risk

---

12 The Swedish data gave a much closer approximation to Dake's results than the Brazilian ones. This finding could not be explained by lower reliability in the Brazilian data; they were quite comparable to the Swedish results.

Table 5.3 *Correlations between societal concerns and cultural biases, Swedish data.*

Item no	General risk				Personal risk			
	Egalitarian	Individualistic	Hierarchic	Fatalistic	Egalitarian	Individualistic	Hierarchic	Fatalistic
1	-0.14	0.08	0.04	-0.09	-0.22	0.30	0.31	-0.13
2	-0.24	0.26	0.31	0.12	-0.33	0.28	0.46	-0.00
3	-0.00	0.25	0.09	-0.00	-0.34	0.40	0.36	0.02
4	-0.07	0.13	0.13	0.24	-0.29	0.32	0.33	0.19
5	-0.20	0.27	0.19	0.07	-0.29	0.36	0.35	-0.06
6	0.33	-0.17	-0.18	0.16	0.14	-0.17	0.00	0.04
7	0.38	-0.18	-0.04	-0.11	0.19	-0.18	-0.01	-0.08
8	0.29	-0.22	-0.12	0.02	0.03	0.03	-0.06	-0.17
9	0.06	-0.05	0.17	0.16	-0.24	0.33	0.19	0.04
10	-0.37	0.26	0.29	-0.02	-0.44	0.33	0.41	-0.13
11	0.39	-0.22	-0.09	0.02	0.22	-0.16	-0.10	-0.02
12	-0.28	0.28	0.41	0.25	-0.36	0.33	0.42	0.22
13	0.16	-0.30	0.15	0.02	0.20	-0.31	-0.04	-0.06
14	-0.18	0.20	0.12	0.11	-0.20	0.19	0.13	-0.05
15	0.12	-0.18	0.12	-0.01	-0.27	0.18	0.43	0.05
16	-0.08	0.07	0.11	-0.11	-0.27	0.26	0.30	-0.02
17	0.42	-0.15	-0.21	0.02	0.03	0.01	-0.01	0.14

Table 5.3 *(continued)*

Item no	General risk				Personal risk			
	Egalitarian	Individualistic	Hierarchic	Fatalistic	Egalitarian	Individualistic	Hierarchic	Fatalistic
18	0.03	0.06	0.11	0.03	-0.23	0.26	0.24	0.14
19	0.03	-0.07	0.06	0.05	-0.11	0.09	0.15	-0.01
20	-0.05	-0.11	0.11	-0.07	-0.04	0.02	0.14	-0.11
21	0.08	-0.20	-0.03	-0.04	0.11	-0.14	-0.10	-0.06
22	-0.14	0.01	0.01	-0.10	-0.27	0.15	-0.01	-0.03
23	0.19	-0.22	-0.15	0.29	0.05	-0.04	-0.03	0.25
24	0.30	-0.24	-0.07	-0.10	0.28	-0.22	-0.06	-0.09
25	0.08	-0.06	-0.09	0.14	0.04	-0.01	-0.09	0.18
26	0.18	-0.26	-0.18	0.07	0.07	-0.14	-0.16	-0.03
27	-0.37	0.21	0.25	0.00	-0.38	0.13	0.12	-0.08
28	0.30	-0.35	-0.18	-0.13	0.20	-0.24	-0.07	-0.04
29	0.11	-0.17	-0.12	-0.02	0.05	-0.14	-0.08	0.04
30	-0.22	-0.02	0.01	-0.08	-0.19	0.04	0.08	-0.04
31	-0.34	0.20	0.19	-0.18	-0.33	0.18	0.23	-0.04
32	0.01	-0.18	0.02	-0.16	-0.02	-0.11	0.05	-0.18
Number of significant correlations	14	16	5	3	17	13	11	2

Table 5.4 Correlations between cultural theory subscales and risk ratings, Swedish school teachers and Dake's (1990) results. Only general risk.

	Egalitarian attitude		Individualistic attitude		Hierarchic attitude	
	Present results	Dake's results	Present results	Dake's results	Present results	Dake's results
1 Decline of national wealth	-0.15	–	0.08	–	-0.04	–
2 Civil disobedience (eg, illegal political acts)	-0.24	0.07	0.27	0.31	-0.15	0.28
3 The lack of stable investment climate	-0.01	0.03	0.25	0.26	0.09	0.09
4 Absence of strong national leadership	-0.07	0.39	0.13	-0.05	0.13	-0.06
5 Economic inflation	-0.20	0.17	0.27	0.25	0.19	0.18
6 Environmental pollution	0.33	0.40	-0.17	-0.14	-0.18	-0.27
7 Middle East conflict	0.38	–	-0.18	–	-0.04	–
8 Poverty and unemployment	0.29	–	-0.22	–	-0.12	–
9 Decline in moral values	0.06	0.33	-0.05	0.05	0.17	0.09
10 Federal over-regulation	-0.37	-0.12	0.26	0.23	0.29	0.19
11 Dangers associated with nuclear energy (eg, nuclear waste)	0.39	0.42	-0.22	-0.12	-0.09	-0.28
12 Loss of respect for authority	-0.29	-0.02	0.28	0.30	0.41	0.27
13 Misuse of scientific and expert knowledge	0.16	–	-0.31	–	0.15	–
14 Excessive permissiveness in society	-0.18	–	0.20	–	0.12	–
15 Decline of public confidence in most major institutions	0.12	–	-0.18	–	0.12	–
16 Increased crime rates	-0.08	–	0.07	–	0.11	–
17 Worldwide overpopulation and starvation	0.42	0.27	-0.16	-0.06	-0.21	-0.10
18 National debt	0.03	0.17	0.06	0.25	0.11	0.18

Table 5.4 (continued)

	Egalitarian attitude		Individualistic attitude		Hierarchic attitude	
	Present results	Dake's results	Present results	Dake's results	Present results	Dake's results
19 Corruption in the political process	0.03	0.29	-0.07	0.02	0.06	-0.04
20 Failure of law and order	-0.05	–	-0.11	–	0.11	–
21 Breakdown in social/interpersonal harmony	0.08	0.32	-0.20	-0.14	-0.03	-0.07
22 Decline in productivity and innovation	-0.14	–	0.01	–	0.01	–
23 Rapid economic growth	0.19	0.32	-0.22	-0.06	-0.15	-0.02
24 Threat of nuclear war and annihilation	0.30	0.46	-0.24	-0.31	0.07	-0.35
25 Concentration of power in 'big' government and industry	0.08	–	-0.06	–	-0.09	–
26 Dangers associated with technology	0.18	0.39	-0.26	-0.23	-0.18	-0.11
27 Strikes and boycotts	-0.37	–	0.21	–	0.25	–
28 Racial injustice	0.30	–	-0.35	–	-0.18	–
29 Breakdown in cooperation and decision making processes	0.11	–	-0.17	–	0.12	–
30 Energy shortage	-0.22	–	-0.02	–	0.01	–
31 Demonstrations and protests	-0.35	0.15	0.20	0.23	0.19	0.30
32 Restriction of civil liberties	0.01	0.31	-0.18	-0.12	0.02	-0.22

perception of nuclear waste and data were obtained from a large and representative sample ($N = 1200$, response rate 64.6 per cent) of the Swedish population. A basic model, using proximal variables, was applied in order to explain perceived nuclear waste risk. This model explained 0.656 and 0.647 of the variance of perceived general and personal risk, respectively (Sjöberg, 1995). The six cultural theory items in isolation explained only 0.049 and 0.042 of the variance in nuclear waste risk perception. When they were added to the basic model, they improved predictability by 0.005 and 0.004. Hence, cultural theory items did very poorly indeed in these analyses.

The six cultural theory items were analysed further. The correlations between individual items and risk perceptions, general and personal, are given in Table 5.5.

The correlations are very weak, but some of them are statistically significant. Mean risk perception scores were computed for each level of the response scales of the six items. According to cultural theory, the hierarchy and individualism items should show decreasing trends (since the risk under study is a technology risk), and the egalitarian items should show increasing trends. Although the picture was somewhat confusing, it is clear that one can easily find some items which appeared to fit the theory rather well. One egalitarian item could indeed be used to give an impression of the power of cultural theory. Other items, for obscure reasons, did not work at all according to theory predictions. Again, however, the explanatory value of all items was very marginal. Conclusions about the theoretical and practical value of the theory would be unwarranted on the basis of analyses of single items such as these; they say little about the predictive value of the items. It is also possible that the fact that some of them appear to 'work' is due to other factors than those postulated by cultural theory.

General Discussion

Why is it that data show such small correlations between perceived risk and cultural biases?

It should first be noted that the present results are not all that different from the ones reported by Dake – see the discussion above of the study of teachers in Sweden and Brazil. The differences are mostly a question of the conclusions drawn, not the data per se.

Table 5.5 *Correlations between individual items and perceptions of individual and general risk of nuclear waste.*

Item	General risk	Personal risk
Hierarchy 1	0.030	−0.013
Hierarchy 2	0.051	0.083*
Individualism 1	−0.040	−0.051
Individualism 2	0.000	0.030
Egalitarian 1	0.165***	0.146***
Egalitarian 2	−0.103**	−0.058

* $p < 0.05$

** $p < 0.01$

*** $p < 0.001$

The most likely explanation of the present results, in my view, is that cultural theory is simply wrong. Cultural biases are *not* major factors in risk perception, but make only a very minor contribution to its explanation. Variability within the general public in a country is probably due to factors other than cultural biases or world views, perhaps to some extent trust (Freudenburg and Pastor, 1992). The tremendous variability that is found when comparing experts and the public is not a matter of cultural biases, but other factors can probably explain it better, eg possibly familiarity and perceived control over a risk. Early socialization of values could also be important (Drottz-Sjöberg and Sjöberg, 1991).

Is there any hope at all to explain risk perception with general value dimensions? In another study, I tried out a number of value scales and related them to risk perception (Sjöberg, 1995). The correlations were found to be very low.

In our department, we have conducted a large-scale study of risk perception of household waste in which we included Schwartz's complete value scale (Schwartz, 1992), with a representative sample of the Swedish population, on the basis of a review of the literature on waste and human behaviour (Pinsky and Andersson, 1993) carried out by our co-workers. Results show that the Schwartz dimensions are only weakly related to risk perception (Andersson, 1994), in agreement with results reported here.

Some researchers, see Marris et al (1996), argue that better world view scales probably would show much stronger relationships, but taking reliability estimates of the current scales into account, the corrected correlations will increase only from 5 to 7 per cent explained variance.

What is the reason that cultural theory attracts so much attention in spite of its poor performance when measured against actual empirical data? There are probably several factors at play, some of which may be mentioned here.

First, the conclusions from studies are often based mostly on statistically significant results; this is, of course, a general trend in the social and behavioural sciences (Schmidt, 1996). It is unfortunate, because researchers have very often ignored how small these effects often are, and they have therefore neglected to search for the really important determining factors. If findings are considered to be important and constituting a sound empirical basis as soon as they are statistically significant, researchers will be engaged in something of a random walk.

Second, there is a pervasive individualistic bias in the approach to theory testing taken in the studies cited here. People are assumed to carry, as it were, the sources of their beliefs in other beliefs, or other psychological processes. There is a holistic bias here which involves the belief that the ultimate cause of anything psychological resides permanently in the structure of the individual mind. But this could be wrong. People may have beliefs because of all sorts of events and processes which they have, directly or indirectly, been exposed to. These events may have left no other traces in their minds than the very beliefs that we study. In this sense the human mind may be fragmentary, or consisting of several layers with little or no relationships. Certainly, the data so far suggest just this. Risk perception can be well explained, but only with proximal variables. When distal variables, such as those postulated by cultural theory, are brought in as explanatory constructs, the result is failure.

Thirdly, cultural theory purports to deal with dimensions which are universally believed to be important, such as social relations, 'ways of life' or 'world views'. As long as the discourse is limited to theory and occasional illustrative case studies, it is very hard to find a counter-argument. How could one argue that 'culture' and 'social relations' are *not* important in risk perception? However, when appropriate empirical data are brought forward, in the present, it becomes clear that the dimensions carry only marginal explanatory power when it comes to risk perception.

The properties of belief structures which account for risk judgements may yet be of great interest, even if they are not well accounted for by cultural theory constructs. Semantically distant contexts may be connected by means of beliefs about causal relationships, such as the belief that homosexuals spread the AIDS disease (Sjöberg, 1991). The question of the direction of causal influence (from attitudes to perceived risk, or vice versa) would be interesting to pursue in this context.

Finally, is cultural theory important for risk communication and, if so, what are the implications of the present results? The theory purports to have a strong explanation of risk perception, and if that claim is valid, it should certainly be of interest to the field of risk communication. Since people are, by the theory, asserted to 'choose' their objects of worry and concern, on the basis of social relations and general world views, it seems that risk communication should not be directed towards the concrete hazards that people say they are concerned about. Other approaches, perhaps more in the line of traditional Public Relations, seem to be called for. At any rate, a rational discourse about concerns would be out of place.

Cognitive biases were at one time believed to be an important cause of 'distorted' risk perceptions (Tversky and Kahneman, 1973; Sjöberg, 1979). Here, the public was seen as uninformed about probabilities and in need of education. The Psychometric Model (Fischhoff et al, 1978; Sjöberg, 1996) also places the public in a rather unflattering position. 'Gut reactions' and such dimensions as new versus old technology are thought to guide risk concerns.

These traditional models paint a picture of the public as emotional, arbitrary and irrational. But since data do not support them, communicators should look elsewhere for a foundation of principles of communication, possibly to a conception of the public as intelligent and honestly concerned about the topics under discussion – not as just having 'chosen' these topics because of quite extraneous reasons.

References

Andersson, L (1994) *Motivating Environmentally Responsible Behavior. An Empirical Study*. Research Report AFR Report 50, Swedish Waste Research Council, Stockholm

Boholm, Å (1996) 'Risk perception and social anthropology: critique of cultural theory,' *Ethnos* 61, pp64–84

Brenot, J, S Bonnefous and C Mays, (1996) 'Cultural theory and risk perception: validity and utility explored in the French context,' – *Radiation Protection Dosimetry* 68, pp239–243

Cvetkovich, G and T C Earle, (1994) 'The construction of justice: a case study of public participation in land management' in *Journal of Social Issues* 50, pp161–178

Dake, K (1990) 'Technology on trial: orienting dispositions toward environmental and health hazards'. PhD thesis, University of California, Berkeley

Dake, K (1991) 'Orienting dispositions in the perception of risk' in *Journal of Cross-Cultural Psychology* 22, pp61–82

Douglas, M and A Wildavsky (1982) *Risk and Culture*, University of California Press, Berkeley CA

Douglas, M (1992) *Risk and Blame. Essays in Cultural Theory* Routledge, London

Drottz-Sjöberg, B-M (1991) *Perception of Risk. Studies of Risk Attitudes, Perceptions and Definitions*, Stockholm School of Economics, Center for Risk Research, Stockholm

Drottz-Sjöberg, B-M and L Sjöberg (1991) 'Attitudes and conceptions of adolescents with regard to nuclear power and radioactive wastes' in *Journal of Applied Social Psychology* 21, pp2007–2035

Drottz-Sjöberg, B-M and L Presson (1993) 'Public reaction to radiation: fear, anxiety or phobia?' in *Health Physics* 64, pp223–231

Earle, T and G Cvetkovich (1994) 'Risk Communication: The Societal Construction of Meaning and Trust', in B Brehmer and N E Sahlin (eds) *Future Risks and Risk Management*, pp141–181, Kluwer, Amsterdam

Fischhoff, B, P Slovic, S Lichtenstein, S Read and B Combs (1978) 'How safe is safe enough? A psychometric study of attitudes towards technological risks and benefits' in *Policy Science* 9, pp127–152

Freudenburg, W R and S K Pastor, (1992) 'Public response to technological risks: toward a sociological perspective', *The Sociological Quarterly* 33, pp389–412

Frewer, L J, D Hedderley, J Wakeling, C Howard and R Shepherd (1998) 'Methodological approaches to assessing risk perceptions associated with food related hazards', *Risk Analysis*, vol 18, no 1, pp95–102

Frewer, L J, C Howard, D Hedderly, and R Shepherd (1996) 'What determines trust in information about food related risks? Underlying psychological constructs', in *Risk Analysis* 16, pp473–485

Frewer, L J, R Shepherd and P Sparks (1993) 'Validation of cultural bias in the context of risk and trust perceptions associated with food-related hazards', in *British Psychological Society Abstracts* 2, p42

Grendstad, G, and P Selle (1994) *Comparing Theories of Political Culture in Explaining Environmental Attitudes*, Norwegian Research Centre in Organization and Management (LOS-senteret), Bergen

Grendstad, G (1990) 'Europe by cultures. An exploration in grid/group analysis', graduate thesis, Department of Comparative Politics, University of Bergen

Holtgrave, D R, and E U Weber (1993) 'Dimensions of risk perception for financial and health risks', in *Risk Analysis* 13, pp553–558

Inglehart, R (1977) *The Silent Revolution: Changing Values and Political Styles Among Western Public*, NJ: Princeton University Press, Princeton

Inglehart, R (1990) *Culture Shift in Advanced Industrial Society*, Princeton University Press, Princeton, NJ

Jenkins-Smith, H C (1994) 'Stigma models: Testing hypotheses of how images of Nevada are acquired and values attached to them', Report, UNM Institute for Public Policy, Department of Political Science, University of New Mexico

Marris, C, J Langford and T O'Riordan (1996) 'Integrating sociological and psychological approaches to public perceptions of environmental risks: detailed results from a questionnaire study', CSERGE Marking Paper No. GEC 96–07, Centre for Social and Economic Research into the Global Environment, Norwich

Mischel, W (1968) *Personality and Assessment*, Wiley, New York

Palmer, C G S (1996) 'Risk perception: an empirical study of the relationship between worldview and the risk construct', in *Risk Analysis* 16, pp717–723

Peters, E and P Slovic (1996) 'The role of affect and worldviews as orienting dispositions in the perception and acceptance of nuclear power', in *Journal of Applied Social Psychology* 26, pp1427–1453

Pinsky, G and L Andersson (1993) *Motivational Factors in Waste-Related Behavior. A Review*. AFR-Report no 24, Swedish Waste Research Council, Stockholm

Rayner, S (1990) 'Management of radiation hazards in hospitals: plural rationalities in a single institution', in *Social Studies of Science* 16, pp573–591

Renn, O, J Kasperson, R Kasperson and S Tuler (1992) 'Cultural Prototypes, Signals, and Qualitative Risk Characteristics: How Do People Judge The Seriousness of Risk?' in *Society for Risk Analysis Annual Meeting*, San Diego, CA

Schwartz, S H (1992) 'Universals in the content and structure of values: Theoretical advances and empirical tests in twenty countries' in *Advances in Experimental Social Psychology* 25, pp1–65

Schmidt, F L (1996) 'Statistical significance testing and cumulative knowledge in psychology: Implications for training of researchers' in *Psychological Methods* no 1, pp115–129

Sjöberg, L (1979) 'Strength of belief and risk' in *Policy Science* no 11, pp39–57

Sjöberg, L (1980) 'The risks of risk analysis?', *Acta Psychologica* no 45, pp301–321

Sjöberg, L (1987) *Risk and Society. Studies in Risk Taking and Risk Generation* Hemel Hempstead, George Allen & Unwin

Sjöberg, L (1989) 'Mood and Expectation' in A F Bennett and K M McConkey (eds) *Cognition in Individual and Social Context* pp337–348, Elsevier, Amsterdam

Sjöberg, L (1991) *AIDS: Riskuppfattning, Attityder Och Kunskaper. En Enkätundersökning av Åldersgrupperna 30–45 år* Rhizikon: Rapport från Centrum för Riskforskning No 1, Center for Risk Research, Stockholm School of Economics, Stockholm

Sjöberg, L (1995) *Explaining Risk Perception: An Empirical and Quantitative Evaluation of Cultural Theory* Rhizikon: Risk Research Reports No 22, Center for Risk Research, Stockholm School of Economics, Stockholm

Sjöberg, L (1996) 'A discussion of the limitations of the psychometric and Cultural Theory approaches to risk perception' in *Radiation Protecting Dosimetry* no 68, pp219–225

Sjöberg, L (In press a) 'World views, political attitudes and risk perception', *Risk Health, Safety and Environment*

Sjöberg, L (In press b) 'Perceived competence and motivation in industry and government as factors in risk perception'

Sjöberg, L and Drottz-Sjöberg, B-M (1994b) 'Risk Perception' in B Lindell, T Malmfors, E Lagerlöf, T Thedéen and G Walinder (eds) *Comprehending radiation risk. A report to the IAEA* pp29–59. International Atomic Energy Agency, Vienna

Sjöberg, L and E Winroth (1986) 'Risk, moral value of actions, and mood', *Scandinavian Journal of Psychology* no 27, pp191–208

Slovic, P, J Flynn, C K Mertz and L Mullican (1992) *Health Risk Perception in Canada*, Decision Research, Eugene, Oregon

Tversky, A and D Kahneman (1973) 'Availability: a heuristic for judging frequency and probability' in *Cognitive Psychology* no 4, pp207–232

Wildavsky, A and K Dake (1990) 'Theories of risk perception: who fears what and why?' *Daedalus* vol 4, no 119, pp41–60

Risk Perception and Communication Unplugged: Twenty Years of Process

Baruch Fischhoff

Introduction

Biology teaches us that 'ontogeny recapitulates phylogeny' – that is, the development of the individual mimics the evolution of the species. For example, a human fetus acquires an increasingly differentiated cellular structure, as did the precursor species to Homo sapiens.

Over the past 20 years or so, risk communication research has undergone its own evolution. At each stage, it has made progress toward acquiring some new skills, only to discover that there were additional, more complicated problems to solve. Every year (or, perhaps, every day), some new industry or institution discovers that it, too, has a risk problem. It can, if it wishes, repeat the learning process that its predecessors have undergone. Or it can attempt to short-circuit that process, and start with its product – namely, the best available approaches to risk communication.

Although learning from the experience of others is appealing in principle, it may be difficult in practice. One possible obstacle is being too isolated to realize that others have faced the same tasks. A second is being too headstrong to admit that help is needed. A third is not having a chance to observe others' learning process. As a result, newcomers may be condemned to repeat it. Few risk communication researchers or practitioners can claim to have got it right the first time. If what they tried first made sense to them at the time, it may also tempt others. Although the ensuing mistakes may be intelligent ones, they are still wasteful if they could have been avoided. Moreover, in risk (or other) communication, the damage can be irreversible – if relations with one's communicants are poisoned. A shadow of a doubt can be difficult to erase. Ask industries or politicians who have tried to rescue tarnished reputations.[1]

This essay offers a brief history of risk communication, organized around the developmental stages listed in Table 6.1. Each stage is characterized by a focal communication strategy which practitioners hope will do the trick – and by the lessons learned about how far that strategy can go. Each stage builds on its predecessors. It does not, however, replace them. Simple skills are often essential to executing sophisticated plans.

Obviously, such an account is quite speculative. No one has systematically documented the history of risk communication. Moreover, even if my interpretation were entirely accurate, capitalizing on the experience that it summarizes would present

Table 6.1 *Developmental stages in risk management*
(ontogeny recapitulates phylogeny)

- All we have to do is get the numbers right
- All we have to do is tell them the numbers
- All we have to do is explain what we mean by the numbers
- All we have to do is show them that they've accepted similar risks in the past
- All we have to do is show them that it's a good deal for them
- All we have to do is treat them nice
- All we have to do is make them partners
- All of the above

a significant challenge. In many areas, complex skills are acquired slowly. And, by many accounts, it is hard to proceed to a new stage until one has mastered its predecessors.[2,3] Thus, aspiring musicians need to attend many concerts and practise many hours before they can benefit from participating in master classes. At any stage, it is important to know the limits to one's abilities. That way, one can avoid commitments that one cannot fulfil, have realistic expectations for what one does try and secure complementary services for the rest.

Continuing the metaphor, there may be value in music appreciation classes long before one is ready to solo. However, those who provide those classes or hortatory talks like this one have an obligation to be candid about the limits to their craft. Describing one's own learning process might be part of such candor – as long as the state of the art is presented as offering a current best guess and not a definitive solution.

First Developmental Stage

All We Have to Do Is Get the Numbers Right

Communication often begins before a word is said. One's very willingness to talk sends a message, which is amplified by one's suppositions about what needs to be said. Often, risk communication gets off on the wrong foot when the potential sources of information have no intent of saying anything. Those sources may have something to hide, either from the public or from competitors. However, they may also just see no need to talk about the risks in their care, as long as those risks are being kept at acceptable levels.

Instead, these risk experts focus on the (arduous and skilled) tasks of trying to master the design, execution and operation of their technology. It seems self-evident to them that they are the best-qualified individuals for these jobs. Moreover, both their professional pride and market forces (eg waste minimization, liability reduction) provide strong incentives to control risks. As a result, there doesn't seem to be much to talk about; the risks are as small as they reasonably could be. In some cases, the experts might be required to back up their claims with quantitative risk analyses. If so, then their job may seem to be over once the numbers come out satisfactorily (perhaps after some design revision).

Indeed, quietly doing diligent technical work will often suffice. The risks of many enterprises attract no attention at all. Unfortunately, if a risk does become an issue, the preceding silence may raise suspicions – of a sort that can complicate the ensuring communication. There may have been good reasons for the risk managers not to have initiated contact on their own (eg 'no one asked', 'no one would listen', 'we reported everything to the government'). The credibility of such excuses may depend on how well the technology bears up under public scrutiny.

Technologies that have relied on risk analyses may have particular difficulty in demonstrating their adequacy. In part, this is because of the unfamiliar, even esoteric qualities of risk analysis. In part, this is because risk analysis is, in fact, hard to perform adequately. Diligent analysts do the best work they can, gathering observational data, adapting it to novel cases with expert judgement, and tying the pieces together with some model. None the less, even the most sophisticated analyses are still exercises in disciplined guesswork.[4-8]1

Those who work within a discipline accustom themselves to its limitations. They learn to live with the reality of critical unsolved problems (eg how to model operator behaviour, how to extrapolate from animal data). They are vulnerable, though, if living in the world of analysis makes them too comfortable with its limits. Further vulnerability arises from treating an applied intellectual technology as a scientific pursuit. Like other pursuits (such as much survey research and cost-benefit analysis), risk analysis may seek the rights of science without assuming its full responsibility (eg independent peer review, data archiving, credentialing processes). Although understandable, adopting such a narrow view may compound public suspicions. It means, in effect, that the analysts are assuming more responsibility for risk management than they can deliver. Conceivably, talking to others might have been a useful antidote to hubris.

Second Developmental Stage

All We Have to Do Is Tell Them the Numbers

When risk managers discover that they have not been trusted to do their work in private, a natural response is to hand over the numbers. How good a story those numbers have to tell depends on how well the first developmental stage has been mastered. How successfully they tell that story depends on how well the numbers speak for themselves. Frequently the answer is 'not very well'. None the less, numbers are often delivered to the public in something close to the form in which they are produced. This may occur in corporate reports, public briefings, press statements or computerized data bases.

There is something touching and forthright about such a straightforward delivery. However, it is likely to be seen, perhaps accurately, as reflecting the distance between the analysts and their audience – in so far as the experts clearly do not realize how poorly they are communicating. Being seen as out of touch is a good way to undermine one's credibility. Further erosion will follow if the numbers make no sense, especially if that is seen as the result of deliberate obfuscation, rather than inadvertent obscurity.

---

1 It will be interesting to see what effect, if any, is achieved by the current fad of relabelling probabilistic risk analysis as probabilistic safety analysis. The change could put a happier face on the process or be seen as a disingenuous diversion.

Confused recipients of such raw materials may add some of their own uncertainty to that expressed by the analysts. Suspicious recipients may adjust risk estimates upward or downward to accommodate (what they see as) likely biases. Both responses should frustrate those analysts who have tried to do conscientious work and report it as they saw it. They are, in effect, being treated as too different from ordinary folk to be trusted to appraise events occurring in the real world. Attention may settle on those few technical issues that prove readily accessible. Perhaps there is some local expertise, perhaps an activist group has summarized the relevant research, perhaps citizens have independent perspectives (eg on the validity of evacuation plans or operator behaviour models). Technical experts may find this as unduly narrow. Citizens may treat the focal issues as representative of the impenetrable whole. If there is some truth to their suspicions, then citizens may not trust the numbers any more than their producers should.[7,9]

Clarifying the uncertainty surrounding quantitative risk estimates means admitting one kind of subjectivity. That admission is gradually gaining acceptance in professional circles.[2] There is slower growth in awareness of a second kind of subjectivity, the extent to which risk estimates reflect ethical values. Risk analysts have fought hard to create a clear distinction between the facts and values of risk management.[11,12] Doing so, to the maximum extent possible, is a matter of good intellectual hygiene. However, there is a limit to how far it can be done. Values are inherent in risk assessment. They influence, for example, the allocation of resources to studying specific risks or risks in general – and, thereby, produce the data needed to motivate action or quiet concerns. Values are also reflected in how risks are characterized.[13-15] For example, hazards may be ranked differently if their risks are assessed in terms of the probability of premature fatalities or in lost life expectancy (which puts a premium on deaths among the young).

One of the earliest results in risk perception research was the discovery that experts and lay people might agree about the fatalities that a technology produces in an average year, but still disagree about its degree of 'risk'. These disagreements seem to reflect differences in how 'risk' is defined. One possible difference is that lay people place greater weight on catastrophic potential. The size of that potential is a topic for scientific research (although one where hard estimates are particularly hard to come by). However, the weight to be given to that potential is a matter of public policy.[16,17]

Risk analysts often seem unaware of such issues, or at least uncomfortable with them. Their assigned job is to produce estimates, not determine social values. However, where the choice of definition affects the estimated riskiness of technologies, they cannot escape some responsibility – any more than cost–benefit analysts can escape the analogous responsibility when they work the other side of the ledger.[18] Unless these assumptions are made explicit, the risk numbers will not speak for themselves.

---

2 It is, I believe, advocated in Vice-President Gore's (10) *Reinventing government.*

Third Developmental Stage

All We Have to Do Is Explain What We Mean By the Numbers

When the numbers do not speak for themselves, explaining them is an obvious next step. Those who attempt such full disclosure face significant technical problems, including a largely unprepared audience. For example, individuals who have only heard confident-sounding experts might misinterpret an explicit expression of uncertainty as evasiveness or equivocation. They might get the impression that scientists are completely confused or that one scientist's guess is as good as any other's. The controversy over climate change sometimes seems to be interpreted in this way. There is considerable overlap in the probability distributions of those scientists who are most and least concerned about greenhouse warming, yet the debate is sometimes interpreted as though 'anything goes'.

Thus, those who initially introduce a perspective may take some heat for it, as though they were needlessly obscuring or complicating the issue. This realization may account for the reluctance of many sources, including journalists, to use numbers at all, much less probability distributions – or more nuanced expressions of uncertainty.[6] Indeed, the very idea of analysis may be foreign, even offensive.[19,20] As a result, those communicators who first 'come clean' may get a mixed reception. Thus, there is a learning process for the public paralleling that for the experts. Those who start on that process will face a messy transition period.

One way to smooth that transition is to pick one's fights carefully. Clearly communicating any number is a complicated task. Therefore, one should focus on those numbers that really matter. All too often, however, communications about risk involve a gush of issues, with little selection. Even widely disseminated communications (eg the Surgeon General's AIDS brochure) may fail the test of 'why are they telling me this?' Even when an outpouring of information is mandated (eg toxic release inventories), it has to be possible to focus attention on those facts that matter the most to their recipients. Telling much more than people need to know can be (and be seen as) deliberately unhelpful.

Communications should tell people things that they need to know. Doing so requires thinking, in detail, about recipients' circumstances. That is a natural part of everyday conversations with specific individuals. It becomes much more difficult with distant and diverse audiences. Merz[21,22] approached the problem of selecting decision-relevant information by creating explicit models of people's decisions. Then he evaluated the impact of learning about various risks on the expected utility of the ensuing choices, assuming that people were rational decision makers. Applied to a medical procedure, carotid endarterechtomy, his procedure showed that only a few of the many possible side effects made any practical difference. Thus, while physicians should hide nothing, their primary obligation should be ensuring that those few critical facts are understood.

Merz's approach assumes that recipients (a) know nothing to begin with and (b) can stop learning once they have mastered a few quantitative estimates. The former assumption often holds with medical procedures. The latter assumption would hold for people who have well-formulated decision problems; and are waiting for a few inputs in order to run the numbers. At times, though, people aren't particularly interested in parameter estimates. Rather, they just want to know how a risky process works. They may need to know how to operate a piece of equipment, or want to monitor activities at a local industrial facility, or hope to follow the public debate over a technology. They may even feel that they can get a better feel for the degree of risk in a process from seeing how it operates than from hearing about some esoteric numbers.

We have attempted to address this need with what we call the 'mental models' approach. It begins by creating an influence diagram,[3] showing the factors involved in creating and controlling a hazardous process – as those are understood by science. Individuals' beliefs are elicited using a mixture of open-ended and structured procedures. Those beliefs, or 'mental model', are then characterized in terms of the influence diagram, or 'expert model'. Communications can be crafted to fill gaps, reinforce correct beliefs and correct misconceptions – with some assurance that the messages are to the point and can be comprehended by recipients.

Fourth Developmental Stage

All We Have to Do Is Show Them That They've Accepted Similar Risks in The Past

While systematic analyses of people's decisions are rare, more casual analyses are quite common. They often take the form of risk comparisons, in which an unfamiliar risk is contrasted with a more common one. Individuals are invited to use their response to the familiar situation as a guide to action in the new one. Certainly, it is legitimate to seek consistency in one's actions. However, little follows directly from most comparisons. Risk decisions are not about risks alone. One can accept large risks if they bring large benefits and reject small risks if they bring no good.

Even within these constraints, risk comparisons could still be mildly informative. Unfortunately, the specific comparisons often are chosen with rhetorical purpose. Their canonical form then becomes something like, 'the risks of Technology X [which we promote] are no greater than those of Activity Y which you do already [so why not accept X?]'. The anecdotal experience of many risk communicators is that such comparisons are as unpopular in practice as they are disinguous in principle. In their well-known guide to risk comparisons, Sandman, Covello and Slovic[24] repeatedly warn that 'USE OF DATA IN THIS TABLE FOR RISK COMPARISON PURPOSES CAN SEVERELY DAMAGE YOUR CREDIBILITY' (capitals in the original). Risk comparisons can backfire even when they are created in good faith – by people who find them eminently sensible. Such individuals need to pass through this developmental stage themselves before they can create useful messages for others.

A common corollary of this perspective is to believe that people must want zero risk, if they won't accept a small risk. That observation is often accompanied by homilies regarding how important it is for people to realize that everything has risks.[25] It is, of course, convenient to have ad hominem arguments against people who oppose one's plans. However, the systematic evidence supporting this claim is thin.[26] Moreover, there is no reason to accept any avoidable risks, unless there are com-

---

3 This is a form of directed graph. It is formally related to the decision-tree representation of a choice. That relationship helps to ensure the decision-relevance of the material included in an influence diagram. These properties are not, however, exploited fully in this work (23).

pensating benefits. It is altogether possible that people sometimes neglect the small benefit that they receive from technologies that create small risk.[27] Misperceiving benefits is, however, different from having unreasonable aversion to any risk.

Fifth Developmental Stage

All We Have to Do Is to Show Them That It's a Good Deal for Them

People need information about both the risks and the benefits of any activity that might affect them. This realization requires changes in more than just the formatting of messages. Within an organization, it means adding the skills of analysts capable of estimating benefits (both economists and specialists in consequences that cannot be readily monetized). Externally, it means acknowledging the public's right to compensation for risk. That compensation might include reductions in other risks, as well as more conventional payments (eg tax abatements, jobs).

Thinking seriously about benefits raises issues analogous to those confronted when estimating risks. For example, analyses can be specified in different ways, with alternative specifications representing different ethical positions – belying their ostensible objectivity.[18,28] Whatever specification is chosen, the uncertainty surrounding its results will have to be assessed and expressed. That uncertainty will include disagreements about parameter estimates and disagreements about fundamental theories.

Together, risk and benefit estimates tell a story that neither does alone. Their juxtaposition alone may prompt changes in risk management – such as redesigning industrial processes so that they provide an acceptable trade-off for each person exposed to their risks. If that case cannot be made, then the message will be a disheartening and, perhaps, embarrassing one.

Whatever tale there is in the numbers, it will have to be told. We have rather less experience and research regarding the communication of benefits, trade-offs and deals. However, the basic research literature suggests some special problems. One class of those problems is 'framing effect', in which formally equivalent representations of the same trade-offs evoke inconsistent evaluations.[29-32] For example, a payment may seem less attractive than a losing gamble when labelled a 'sure loss', but more attractive when labelled an 'insurance premium'. A health programme may seem more attractive when described in terms of the lives that it will save, rather than the lives that will still be lost. Explicitly showing the cumulative benefits of a protective measure may enhance its attractiveness, even though they can be inferred directly from its short-term benefits. The relative and absolute increase in risk that a technology causes may seem to demand rather different compensation (eg a doubling of risk – from .000001 to .000002).

These effects mean that the attractiveness of an action may depend on how it is presented. That can lead to instability in preferences, as frames vary over time. It can lead to suspicions of manipulation, in the choice of frame. As with risk comparisons, the choice of frame need not reflect malicious intent. People may just present the perspective that makes sense to them. If that perspective led to the choice that served their interests, there would be little natural incentive to think hard about alternative perspectives.

It is, of course, also possible to influence perceptions with alternative representations that are not formally equivalent. For example, genetic counsellors (and other medical professionals) have found surprising (to them) gaps in patients' understanding of medical conditions (and, hence, the risks and benefits of treatment). As a result, they have focused on what consequences really mean (eg what it is like to live with cystic fibrosis).[33] In such cases, fuller descriptions are actually different descriptions. Or, some technical analysts have moved on from comparing risks to comparing options, computing the reductions in risk that are possible with a given investment in competing risk-reduction strategies.[34,35] These comparisons are, however, more rhetorical than meaningful if the funds are not fundable (ie if they cannot be moved to take advantage of the best buys in risk reduction). As before, choosing a presentation that favours a particular option may be intentional or inadvertent.

Sixth Developmental Stage

All We Have to Do Is Treat Them Nice

Thus, getting the content of a communication right requires a significant analytical and empirical effort. It means summarizing the relevant science, analysing recipients' decisions, assessing their current beliefs, drafting messages, evaluating their impact and iterating the process as needed. Accomplishing these tasks can significantly reduce the chances of producing messages that patently violate the norms of communication.

However, even perfect messages need not be perceived as such. It can take recipients a while to analyse the adequacy of a message carefully. Preceding or replacing that effort, recipients may look for more general cues. In particular, they may ask how trustworthy the communication and communicator seem to be. If that first impression is bad, they may look no further or discount some of what they do find. Even with a perfect message, an inappropriate delivery can exact a toll. People want to be treated respectfully, in addition to being levelled with. That desire is, in part, a matter of taste and, in part, a matter of power. People fear that those who disrespect them are also disenfranchising them. In risk debates, charges of incompetence are a (perhaps the) classic path to brushing aside pesky citizens.[36]

The need for a suitable demeanour is increasingly being recognized, whether as a public right or a practical necessity. A popular response to this challenge is training in communication skills. There are enough subtleties to the mechanics of communication that most people can use some help (and not just with risk issues). Some problems with the mechanics of communication are neatly preserved in many published messages. For example, these messages may lack an overview and summary, even though both are known to aid learning. They may impose no obvious logical order on their material. They may use language that is needlessly condescending or technical. Their displays may be cluttered and poorly labeled.[37] Even if these are just 'mechanical' oversights, they still can undermine relationships. It takes a sophisticated recipient to forgive a communicator for failing to get professional help. It may have been ignorance or oversight, but still looks like neglect.

In-person communication offers additional pitfalls and opportunities. Blank looks and hostile expressions can quickly show when messages need refinement; ad lib responses may make matters better or worse. Non-verbal cues can support or undermine an overt message. Nervousness over the act of public speaking can be mis-construed as discomfort over what is being said. As a result, training in presentation skills per se make may a real and legitimate difference by eliminating unwarranted suspicions. A smooth delivery could, of course, compound problems if the content of the message is inadequate, so that smoothness is seen as a substitute for sub-stance. The ignorant smiles of PR types are a good tool for digging oneself into a hole.

Seventh Developmental Stage

All We Have to Do Is Make Them Partners

Dispensing niceness is an element of essential decency. It may, however, repel recipi-ents if it seems as though the experts are doing the public a favour, or attempting to cool it out, by pre-emptively softening opposition. Doing so respects the public's ability to prevent solutions, but not to create them. The only responses of interest are, in effect, 'I don't understand you' and 'I don't believe you'. Often, though, mem-bers of the public want, and can fill, a more active and constructive role. At times, they have information to consider. At other times, they may just want a seat at the table. These are components of being partners in risk management.[38]

Anthropologists often use 'indigenous technical knowledge' to describe non-spe-cialists' unique understanding of how their world works.[39] Risk knowledge might be divided into exposure, toxicity, and mitigation information. Laypeople could, in prin-ciple, have privileged knowledge about each component.[40] For example, whatever the source of a risk, exposure to it is the result of human activities. Although their knowledge may not be organized in a systematic way, people should have some in-sight into where they go, how deeply they breathe, what they eat and drink, how long they shower, when they wash their hands, and so on. Careful study may estimate and reduce biases in their perceptions (eg self-serving exaggeration of positive ac-tivities, overestimating how recently unusual events have occurred).

Analogous arguments surround the strengths and weaknesses of lay beliefs re-garding other components of risk. For example, what does it mean when they per-ceive health effects that science has not established? Or how should one treat their scepticism about an elaborate official evacuation or inspection or training plan? Might they know something about what motivates people like themselves? Do they have an independent perspective on what motivates technical experts, possibly clouding their professional judgement?

Unless their every suggestion is to be rejected out of hand, it pays to ask. Just asking redefines a relationship, in ways that recognize the public's reality and com-petence. The sooner one asks, the greater the impact that public concerns will have on the analytical process. Other things being equal, risk data should be collected, vetted and presented in ways that suit the audience that they are meant to convince. If the experts see things differently, then a mutually respectful relationship will pro-vide a forum for making their case. Or better, it might allow for bringing lay mem-bers up to speed on that kernel of technical information needed to make policy-rel-evant judgements.[41]

One of the miracles of democratic life is the ability of lay people, often with little formal education, to master technical material when sufficiently motivated (eg by the siting of a hazardous facility). Unfortunately for risk managers, the motivation for this self-education often comes from a feeling of having been wronged. If passions become inflamed in the process, then this learning may produce more heat than light. All sides will be tempted to focus on data supporting their prejudices. Each will master the radical scepticism needed to assail any study having inconvenient conclusions.

Yet some comprehensive knowledge is a necessary condition for stable beliefs, immune from buffeting by each new result and rumour. Ideally, the more people know about a technology, the more they will like or dislike it – as its true colours emerge.[42] Attracting the interest of people whose minds are still open will require special efforts. Some seemingly successful efforts involve active outreach. For example, the neighbours of an industrial facility might be invited to learn about its activities and, perhaps, join a standing advisory committee.

Such invitations run the risk of revealing problems that people had never imagined. However, they can also show the safety measures taken in recognition of those risks. Moreover, this kind of communication fulfils other conditions of a partnership. It shows an interest in the public without its having to cause trouble or even raise suspicions. It can also reduce experts' fear of the public by offering direct contact, in regulated settings conducive to creating human relations. Those fears can colour perceptions, if they create the impression that the experts have something to hide or just dislike the public. Recognizing that they are people, too, with foibles and emotions, is a part of experts' developmental process.

Partnerships are essential to creating the human relations needed to damp the social amplification of minor risks – as well as to generate concern where it is warranted.[23,43] Often controversies over risk are surrogates for concern over process. People feel that they have been treated shabbily. However, they discover that being disgruntled does not have legal standing, while complaining about risks does. After some period of complaint and friction, the ensuing controversies over risk can take on a life of their own.

Conclusion

Developmental psychologists distinguish between capacity and performance – that is, between having the ability to execute a task and exploiting that potential. Individuals (and organizations) who have gone through a developmental process may still not use what they have learned. That may reflect sloppiness or unwillingness to make the effort.

On purely practical grounds, deciding how much effort to make requires a comparison of the costs and benefits of perfunctory communications. In some ways, communication is like an insurance policy. It is a fixed cost that can prevent larger damage. In evaluating a particular policy, one needs to decide how complete the coverage is, how much protection one can afford, and how much the attendant peace of mind is worth. Like other protective behaviours, it is most easily justified when there is the threat of catastrophic damage.

In making these estimates, the descriptive literature on risk communication can help predict which issues will get out of hand or escape needed attention – in the absence of deliberate competent communications.[46] It can also show something about the ability of communications to help recipients focus their risk-related efforts. In both cases, the evidentiary record is less full than one would like. Moreover, some issues are inherently hard to study, like cases where proactive communication has helped risk issues to play out constructively.

In addition to addressing these pecuniary concerns, effective risk communication can fulfil part of the social contract between those who create risks (as a byproduct of other activities) and those who bear them (perhaps along with the benefits of those activities). That should, of course, be an end in itself. If additional encouragement is needed to make the extra effort, one might invoke the value of preserving a civil society. A complex network of mutually respectful relationships may offer the best hope of reaching agreements, when they are there to be had.

It must, however, be recognized that avoiding all conflict is not a realistic, or even a legitimate, goal for risk communication. It should not and, in an open society, often cannot paper over situations where people are getting a bad deal. The best-case scenario for risk communication (and, indeed, risk management) is having fewer but better conflicts. Some conflicts would be avoided by preventing needless misunderstandings, others by forestalling (or redesigning) unacceptable projects. Those that remain would be better focused on real issues.

For any of this potential to be realized, risk communication has to be taken seriously. One cannot rely on undisciplined speculation about the beliefs or motivations of other people. One cannot expect to quiet a raging controversy with a few hastily prepared messages. One cannot assume that expensively produced communications will work without technically competent evaluations. Those who ignore these issues may be the problem, as much as the risk is. The price of their ignorance is borne by everyone concerned. The public is demeaned by the experts as being hysterical, while the experts are vilified as being evil.

Ideally, risk management should be guided by the facts. Those facts concern not just the sizes of the risks and benefits involved, but also the changes in political and social status that arise from the risk-management process. A few people make their living from provoking or stifling controversies. Most, however, just want to get on with their lives. As a result, there should be a market for social settings within which the facts matter. However, creating them requires considerable attention to detail. It also requires realistic expectations, tempered by knowledge of how far we have progressed in this developmental sequence, and how much we will invest in applying what we know.

References

1   Chess, C, K L Salomon & B J Hance (1994), 'Managing risk communication agency reality: Research priorities.' *this volume*
2   Polanyi, M (1962). *Personal knowledge.* Routledge and Kegan Paul, London
3   Rasmussen, J (1986). *Information processing and human machine interaction.* North Holland, Amsterdam
4   Fischhoff, B (1977). 'Cost-benefit analysis and the art of motorcycle maintenance.' *Policy Sciences*, no 8, pp177–202
5   Fischhoff, B (1989). 'Eliciting knowledge for analytical representation.' *IEEE Transactions on Systems, Man and Cybernetic*, no 13, pp448–461
6   Funtowicz, S O & J R Ravetz (1990). *Uncertainty and quality in science for policy.* Kluwer, Boston

7   Morgan, M G & M Henrion (1990). *Uncertainty: A guide to dealing with uncertainty in quantitative risk and policy analysis.* Cambridge University Press, New York

8   Reason, J (1990). *Human error.* Cambridge University Press, New York

9   Shlyakhter, A I & D M Kammen (1993). 'Uncertainties in modeling low probability/high consequence events: Application to population projections and models of sea-level rise.' *Second International Symposium on Uncertainty Modeling and Analysis* (pp246–253). IEEE Computer Society Press, Washington, DC

10   Gore, A (1993). *Reinventing government.* US Government Printing Office, Washington, DC

11   Hammond, K R & L Adelman (1976). 'Science, values and human judgment.' *Science*, no 194, pp389–396

12   National Research Council. (1983). *Risk assessment in the federal government: Managing the process.* National Academy Press, Washington, DC

13   Crouch, E A C & R Wilson (1981). *Risk/benefit analysis.* Ballinger, Cambridge, MA

14   Fischhoff, B, S Lichtenstein, P Slovic, S L Derby & R L Keeney (1981). *Acceptable risk.* Cambridge University Press, New York

15   Fischhoff, B, S Watson & C Hope (1984) 'Defining risk.' *Policy Sciences*, no 17, pp123–139

16   Slovic, P, B Fischhoff & S Lichtenstein (1979) 'Rating the risks.' *Environment*, no 21(4), pp14–20,36–39

17   Slovic, P, B Fischhoff & S Lichtenstein (1984). 'Modeling the societal impact of fatal accidents.' *Management Science*, no 30, pp464–474

18   Fischhoff, B & L A Cox, Jr (1985). 'Conceptual framework for regulatory benefit assessment' in J D Bentkover, V T Covello and J Mumpower (Eds), *Benefits assessment: The state of the art* (pp51–84). D Reidel, Dordrecht, The Netherlands

19   O'Brien, M (1993). *A proposal to address, rather than rank environmental problems* Institute for Environmental Studies, University of Montana, Missoula: MT

20   Tribe, L H (1972). 'Policy science: Analysis or ideology?' *Philosophy and Public Affairs*, no 2, pp66–110

21   Merz, J F (1991). *Toward a standard of disclosure for medical informed consent: Development and demonstration of a decision-analytic methodology.* Ph D dissertation, Carnegie Mellon University

22   Merz, J F, B Fischhoff, D J Mazur & P S Fischbeck (1993), 'A decision-analytic approach to developing standards of disclosure for medical informed consent'. *Journal of Products and Toxics Liabilities*, no 15, pp191–215

23   Burns W & R Clemen (1993). 'Covariance structure models and influence diagrams.' *Management Science*, no 39, pp816–834

24   Sandman, P, V Covello & P Slovic (1988). *Risk communication, risk statistics, and risk comparisons: A manual for plant managers.* Chemical Manufacturers Association, Washington, DC

25   Freudenberg, W R & S K Pastor (1992). 'NIMBYs and LULUs: Stalking the syndromes,' *Journal of Social Issues*, no 48(4), pp39–62

26   Zentner, R D (1979). 'Hazards in the chemical industry.' *Chemical and Engineering News*, no 54(45), pp25–27

27   Fischhoff, B (1994). 'Acceptable risk: A conceptual proposal,' *Risk: Health, Safety & Environment*, no 1, pp1–28

28   Campen, J T (1988). *Benefit, cost and beyond,* South End Press, Boston

29   Fischhoff, B (1991). 'Value elicitation: Is there anything in there?' *American Psychologist*, no 46, pp835–847

30 Fischhoff, B, P Slovic, S Lichtenstein (1980). 'Knowing what you want: Measuring labile values,' in T Wallsten (Ed), *Cognitive processes in choice and decision behavior* (pp117–141), Erlbaum, Hillsdale, NJ

31 Hogarth, R (Ed) (1982). *New directions for methodology of social and behavioral science: Question framing and response consistency.* Jossey-Bass, San Francisco

32 Kahneman, D & A Tversky (1984). 'Choices, values, and frames.' *American Psychologist*, no 39, pp341–350

33 Holtzman, N A (1989). *Proceed with caution: Predicting genetic risks in the recombinant DNA era.* Johns Hopkins University Press, Baltimore

34 Graham, J D & J B Wiener (ed), *Risk roulette*, Harvard University Press, Cambridge, MA

35 Zeckhauser, R J & W K Viscusi (1991), 'Risk within reason,' *Science*, no 238, pp559–564

36 Fischhoff, M (1993). *Ordinary housewives: Women activists in the grassroots toxic movement.* Unpublished honors thesis, Department of Social Studies, Harvard University.

37 Schriver, K A (1989) 'Evaluating text quality.' *IEEE Transactions Professional Communication*, no 32, pp238–255

38 Hallman, W K & A Wandersman (1992) 'Attribution of responsibility and individual and collective coping with environmental threats,' *Journal of Social Issues*, no 48,(4), pp101–118

39 Brokensha, D W, D M Warren & O Werner (1980). *Indigenous knowledge: Systems and development.* University Press of America, Lanham, MD

40 Johnson, B (1993) 'Advancing understanding of knowledge's role in lay risk perception,' *Risk*, no 3, pp189–212

41 Maharik, M & B Fischhoff (1993b), 'Public views of using nuclear energy sources in space missions.' *Space Policy*, no 9, pp99–108

42 Maharik, M & B Fischhoff (1993).'Contrasting perceptions of risks of using nuclear energy sources in space,' *Journal of Environmental Psychology*, no 13, pp243–250

43 Kasperson, R E, O Renn, P Slovic, H S Brown, J Emel, R Goble, J S Kasperson & S Ratick (1988). 'Social amplification of risk: A conceptual framework' *Risk Analysis*, no 8, pp177–187

44 Furby, L, P Slovic, B Fischhoff & R Gregory (1988). 'Public perceptions of electric power transmission lines,' *Journal of Environmental Psychology*, no 8, pp19–43

45 Krimsky, S & A Plough (1988), *Environmental hazard: Communicating risks as a social process.* Auburn House, Dover, MA

46 Slovic, P (1987), 'Perception of risk'. *Science*, no 236, pp280–285

Part Three

Outcomes of Risk Communication Studies: Conceptual Angles

The Social Amplification of Risk: A Conceptual Framework

Roger E Kasperson, Ortwin Renn, Paul Slovic, Halina S Brown,
Jacque Emel, Robert Goble, Jeanne X Kasperson, and Samuel Ratick

Risk in Modern Society

The investigation of risks is at once a scientific activity and an expression of culture. During the 20th century, massive governmental programmes and bureaucracies aimed at assessing and managing risk have emerged in advanced industrial societies. Despite the expenditure of billions of dollars and steady improvements in health, safety and longevity of life, people view themselves as more rather than less vulnerable to the dangers posed by technology. Particularly perplexing is that even risk events with minor physical consequences often elicit strong public concern and produce extraordinarily severe social impacts, at levels unanticipated by conventional risk analysis. Several difficult issues require attention:

- The technical concept of risk focuses narrowly on the *probability* of events and the *magnitude* of specific consequences. Risk is usually defined by multiplication of the two terms, assuming that society should be indifferent towards a low-consequence/high-probability risk and a high-consequence/low-probability risk with identical expected values. Studies of risk perception have revealed clearly, however, that most persons have a much more comprehensive conception of risk. Clearly, other aspects of the risk such as voluntariness, personal ability to influence the risk, familiarity with the hazard and the catastrophic potential, shape public response.[1,2] As a result, whereas the technical assessment of risk is essential to decisions about competing designs or materials, it often fails to inform societal choices regarding technology.[3]
- Cognitive psychologists and decision researchers have investigated the underlying patterns of individual perception of risk and identified a series of heuristics and biases that govern risk perception.[4,5] Whereas some of these patterns of perception contrast with the results of formal reasoning, others involve legitimate concern about risk characteristics that are omitted, neglected or underestimated by the technical concept of risk. In addition, equity issues, the circumstances surrounding the process of generating risk and the timeliness of

management response are considerations, important to people, that are insufficiently addressed by formal probabilistic risk analysis.[6,7]

- Risk is a bellweather in social decisions about technologies. Since the resolution of social conflict requires the use of factual evidence for assessing the validity and fairness of rival claims, the quantity and quality of risk are major points of contention among participating social groups. As risk analysis incorporates a variety of methods to identify and evaluate risks, various groups present competing evidence based upon their own perceptions and social agenda. The scientific aura surrounding risk analysis promotes the allocation of substantial effort to convincing official decision makers and the public that the risk assessment performed by one group is superior in quality and scientific validity to that of others. Controversy and debate exacerbate divergences between expert and public assessment and often erode confidence in the risk decision process.[8,9]

In short, the technical concept of risk is too narrow and ambiguous to serve as the crucial yardstick for policy making.

Public perceptions, however, are the product of intuitive biases and economic interests and reflect cultural values more generally. The overriding dilemma for society is, therefore, the need to use risk analysis to design public policies on the one hand and the inability of the current risk concepts to anticipate and explain the nature of public response to risk on the other. After a decade of research on the public experience of risk, no comprehensive theory exists to explain why apparently minor risk or risk events,* as assessed by technical experts, sometimes produce massive public reactions, accompanied by substantial social and economic impacts and sometimes even by subsequently increased physical risks. Explaining this phenomenon and making the practice of risk analysis more sensitive to it, is one of the most challenging tasks confronting the societal management of risk. This paper takes up that challenge.

The explanations that have emerged, while affording important insights, have been partial and often conflicting. The past decade has witnessed debates between the 'objectivist and subjectivist' schools of thought, between structuralistic and individualistic approaches, between physical/life scientists and social scientists. Even within the social sciences, psychologists see the roots of explanation in individual cognitive behaviour,[10] a claim extensively qualified by anthropologists, who insist that social context and culture shape perceptions and cognition,[11,12] and by analysts of technological controversies, who see 'stakeholder' interaction and competing values as the keys.[13] The assumption underlying these debates is that the interpretations are mutually invalidating. In fact, we shall argue, the competing perspectives illuminate different facets of the public experience of risk.

A comprehensive theory is needed that is capable of integrating the technical analysis of risk and the cultural, social and individual response structures that shape the public experience of risk. The main thesis of this article is that risk events interact with psychological, social and cultural processes in ways that can heighten or attenuate public perceptions of risk and related risk behaviour. Behavioural patterns, in turn, generate secondary social or economic consequences but may act

---

* In this article, the term 'risk event' refers to occurrences that are manifestations of the risk and that initiate signals pertaining to the risk. Risk events thus include routine or unexpected releases, accidents (large and small), discoveries of pollution incidents, reports of exposures, or adverse consequences. Usually such risk events are specific to particular times and locations.

also to increase or decrease the physical risk itself. Secondary effects trigger demands for additional institutional responses and protective actions or, conversely (in the case of risk attenuation), impede needed protective actions. The social structures and processes of risk experience, the resulting repercussions on individual and group perceptions, and the effects of these responses on community, society and economy compose a general phenomenon that we term *the social amplification of risk*. This article sets forth an initial conceptualization of the elements, structure and processes that make up this phenomenon.

Background

The technical assessment of risk typically models the impacts of an event or human activity in terms of direct harms, including death, injuries, disease and environmental damages. Over time, the practice of characterizing risk by probability and magnitude of harm has drawn fire for neglecting equity issues in relation to time (future generations), space (the so-called LULU or NIMBY issue), or social groups (the proletariat, the highly vulnerable, export of hazard to developing countries). It also has become apparent that the consequences of risk events extend far beyond direct harms to include significant indirect impacts (eg liability, insurance costs, loss of confidence in institutions or alienation from community affairs).[14] The situation becomes even more complex when the analysis also addresses the decision-making and risk-management process. Frequently, indirect impacts appear to be dependent less on the direct outcomes (ie injury or death) of the risk event than on judgements of the adequacy of institutional arrangements to control or manage the risk, the possibility of assigning blame to one of the major participants, and the perceived fairness of the risk-management process.

The accident at the Three Mile Island (TMI) nuclear reactor in 1979 demonstrated dramatically that factors besides injury, death and property damage can impose serious costs andsocial repercussions. No one is likely to die from the release of radioactivity at TMI, but few accidents in US history have wrought such costly societal impacts. The accident devastated the utility that owned and operated the plant and imposed enormous costs – in the form of stricter regulations, reduced operation of reactors worldwide, greater public opposition to nuclear power and a less viable role for one of the major long-term energy sources – on the entire nuclear industry and on society as a whole.[15] This mishap at a nuclear power plant may even · have increased public concerns about other complex technologies, such as chemical manufacturing and genetic engineering.

The point is that traditional cost–benefit and risk analyses neglect these higher-order impacts and thus greatly underestimate the variety of adverse effects attendant on certain risk events (and thereby underestimate the overall risk from the event). In this sense, social amplification provides a corrective mechanism by which society acts to bring the technical assessment of risk more in line with a fuller determination of risk. At the other end of the spectrum, the relatively low levels of interest by the public in the risks presented by such well-documented and significant hazards as indoor radon, smoking, driving without seat belts or highly carcinogenic aflatoxins in peanut butter serve as examples of the social attenuation of risk. Whereas attenuation of risk is indispensable in that it allows individuals to cope with the multitude of risks and risk events encountered daily, it also may lead to potentially serious adverse consequences from underestimation and underresponse. Thus both social amplification and attenuation, through serious disjunctures between expert and public assessments of risk and varying responses among different publics, confound conventional risk analysis.

In some cases, the societal context may, through its effects on the risk assessor, alter the focus and scope of risk assessment. A case in point is the series of actions taken in 1984 by the Environmental Protection Agency with regard to a soil and grain fumigant, ethylene dibromide (EDB).[16] An atmosphere charged with intense societal concern about protecting the nation's food and groundwater supplies from chemical contaminants prompted the Agency to focus primarily on these two pathways of population exposure to EDB, although it was well aware that emissions of EDB from leaded gasoline were a significant source of population exposure. Consequently, the first-line receivers of the risk information – the risk managers, the mass media, the politicians, and the general public – heard from the start about cancer risks from tainted water and food, but not from ambient air. This example illustrates how the filtering of information about hazards may start as early as in the risk assessment itself and may profoundly alter the form and content of the risk information produced and conveyed by technical experts.[16]

Other researchers have noted that risk sources create a complex network of direct and indirect effects that are susceptible to change through social responses.[9,17] But because of the complexity and the transdisciplinary nature of the problem, an adequate conceptual framework for a theoretically based and empirically operational analysis is still missing. The lack of an integrative theory that provides guidelines on how to model and measure the complex relationships among risk, risk analysis, social response and socioeconomic effects has resulted in a reaffirmation of technical risk assessment, which at least provides definite answers (however narrow or misleading) to urgent risk problems.

The concept of social amplification of risk can, in principle, provide the needed theoretical base for a more comprehensive and powerful analysis of risk and risk management in modern societies. At this point, we do not offer a fully developed theory of social amplification of risk, but we do propose a fledgling conceptual framework that may serve to guide ongoing efforts to develop, test and apply such a theory to a broad array of pressing risk problems. Since the metaphor of amplification draws upon notions in communications theory, we begin with a brief examination of its use in that context.

Signal Amplification in Communications Theory

In communications theory, amplification denotes the process of intensifying or attenuating signals during the transmission of information from an information source, to intermediate transmitters, and finally to a receiver.[18] An information source sends out a cluster of signals (which form a message) to a transmitter or directly to the receiver. The signals are decoded by the transmitter or receiver so that the message can be understood. Each transmitter alters the original message by intensifying or attenuating some incoming signals, adding or deleting others, and sending a new cluster of signals on to the next transmitter or the final receiver where the next stage of decoding occurs.

The process of transmitting is more complex than the electronic metaphor implies. Messages have a meaning for the receiver only within a sociocultural context. Sources and signals are not independent entities but are perceived as a unit by the receiver who links the signal to the sources or transmitters and draws inferences about the relationship between the two. In spite of the problems of the source–receiver model, the metaphor is still powerful enough to serve as a heuristic framework for analysing communication processes. In a recent literature review of 31 mass-communication textbooks, the source–receiver metaphor was, along with the concept of symbolic meaning, the predominant theoretical framework.[19]

Each message may contain factual, inferential, value-related and symbolic meanings.[20] The factual information refers to the content of the message (eg the emission of an air pollutant is X mg per day) as well as the source of the message (eg EPA conducted the measurement). The inferential message refers to the conclusions that can be drawn from the presented evidence (eg the emission poses a serious health threat). Then those conclusions may undergo evaluation according to specific criteria (eg the emission exceeds the allowable level). In addition, cultural symbols may be attached that evoke specific images (eg 'big business', 'the military–industrial complex', 'high technology', etc) that carry strong value implications.

Communication studies have demonstrated that the symbols present in messages are key factors in triggering the attention of potential receivers and in shaping their decoding processes.[21] If, for example, the communication source is described as an independent scientist or a group of Nobel laureates, the content of the message may well command public attention. Messages from such sources may successfully pass through the selection filters of the transmitters or receivers and be viewed as credible. A press release by the nuclear industry, by contrast, may command much less credibility unless other aspects of the message compensate for doubts about the impartiality of the source.

Transmitters of signals may detect amplification arising from each message component.[22] A factual statement repeated several times, especially if by different sources, tends to elicit greater belief in the accuracy of the information. An elaborate description of the inference process may distract attention from the accuracy of the underlying assumptions. Reference to a highly appreciated social value may increase the receiver's tolerance for weak evidence. And, of course, a prestigious communication source can (at least in the short run) compensate for trivial factual messages. But adding or deleting symbols may well be the most powerful single means to amplify or attenuate the original message.

Amplification of signals occurs during both transmission and reception. The transmitter structures the messages that go to a receiver. The receiver, in turn, interprets, assimilates and evaluates the messages. But a transmitter, it should be noted, is also a new information source – one that transcribes the original message from the source into a new message and sends it on to the receiver, according to institutional rules, role requirements and anticipated receiver interests. Signals passing through a transmitter may, therefore, be amplified twice – during the reception of information and in recoding.

Signal amplification in communications, then, occupies a useful niche in the overall structure of the social amplification of risk. A discussion of the proposed conceptional framework takes up the next section of this paper.

Roger E Kasperson, Ortwin Renn, Paul Slovic, Halina S Brown et al

A Structural Description of the Social Amplification of Risk

Social amplification of risk denotes the phenomenon by which information processes, institutional structures, social-group behaviour and individual responses shape the social experience of risk, thereby contributing to risk consequences (Figure 7.1). The interaction between risk events and social processes makes clear that, as used in this framework, risk has meaning only to the extent that it treats how people think about the world and its relationships. Thus there is no such thing as 'true' (absolute) and 'distorted' (socially determined) risk. Rather the information system and characteristics of public response that compose social amplification are essential elements in determining the nature and magnitude of risk. We begin with the information system.

Like a stereo receiver, the information system may amplify risk events in two ways:

- By intensifying or weakening signals that are part of the information that individuals and social groups receive about the risk.
- By filtering the multitude of signals with respect to the attributes of the risk and their importance.

Signals arise through direct personal experience with a risk object or through the receipt of information about the risk object.[18] These signals are processed by social, as well as individual, amplification 'stations', which include the following:

- The scientist who conducts and communicates the technical assessment of risk.
- The risk-management institution.
- The news media.
- Activist social organization.
- Opinion leaders within social groups.
- Personal networks of peer and reference groups.
- Public agencies.

Social amplification stations generate and transmit information via communications channels (media, letters, telephones, direct conversations). In addition, each recipient *also* engages in amplification (and attenuation) processes, thereby acting as an amplification station for risk-related information. We hypothesize that the key amplification steps consist of the following:

- Filtering of signals (eg only a fraction of all incoming information is actually processed).
- Decoding of the signal.
- Processing of risk information (eg the use of cognitive heuristics for drawing inferences).
- Attaching social values to the information in order to draw implications for management and policy.
- Interacting with one's cultural and peer groups to interpret and validate signals.
- Formulating behavioural intentions to tolerate the risk or to take actions against the risk or risk manager.

- Engaging in group or individual actions to accept, ignore, tolerate, or change the risk.

A full-fledged theory of the social amplification of risk should ultimately explain why specific risks and risk events undergo more or less amplification or attenuation. Whether such a theory will carry the power to predict the specific kinds of public responses and the anatomy of social controversy that will follow the introduction of new risks must await the test of time. It may prove possible to identify and classify attributes of the risk source and of the social arena that heighten or attenuate the public response to risk.

Social amplifications of risk will spawn behavioural responses which, in turn, will result in *secondary impacts*. Secondary impacts include such effects as the following:

- Enduring mental perceptions, images and attitudes (eg antitechnology attitudes, alienation from the physical environment, social apathy, stigmatization of an environment or risk manager).
- Local impacts on business sales, residential property values and economic activity.
- Political and social pressure (eg political demands, changes in political climate and culture).
- Changes in the physical nature of the risk (eg feedback mechanisms that enlarge or lower the risk).
- Changes in training, education or required qualifications of operating and emergency-response personnel.
- Social disorder (eg protesting, rioting, sabotage, terrorism).
- Changes in risk monitoring and regulation.
- Increased liability and insurance costs.
- Repercussions on other technologies (eg lower levels of public acceptance) and on social institutions (eg erosion of public trust).

Secondary impacts are, in turn, perceived by social groups and individuals so that another stage of amplification may occur to produce third-order impacts. The impacts thereby may spread or 'ripple' to other parties, distant locations or future generations. Each order of impact will not only disseminate social and political impacts but may also trigger (in risk amplification) or hinder (in risk attenuation) positive changes for risk reduction. The concept of social amplification of risk is hence dynamic, tak-

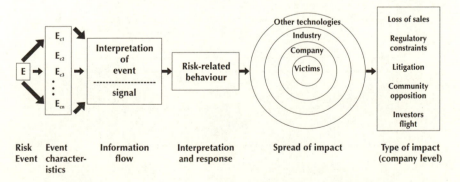

Figure 7.1 *Highly simplified representation of the social amplification of risk and potential impacts on a corporation*

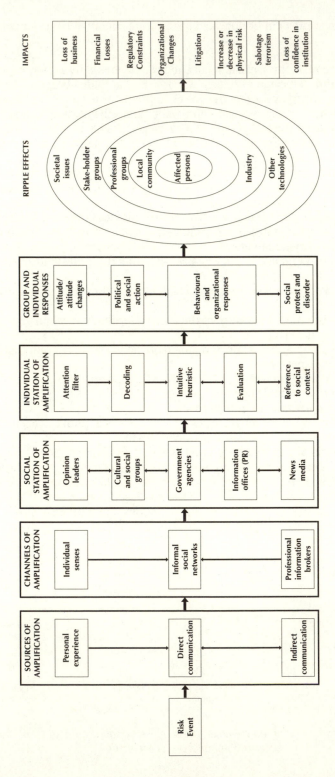

Figure 7.2 *Detailed conceptual framework of social amplification of risk.*

ing into account the learning and social interactions resulting from experience with risk.

The analogy of dropping a stone into a pond (see Fig 7.1) serves to illustrate the spread of the higher-order impacts associated with the social amplification of risk. The ripples spread outward, first encompassing the directly affected victims or the first group to be notified, then touching the next higher institutional level (a company or an agency) and, in more extreme cases, reaching other parts of the industry or other social arenas with similar problems. This rippling of impacts is an important element of risk amplification since it suggests that amplification can introduce substantial temporal and geographical extension of impacts. The same graphic representation demonstrates the possibility that social amplification may, quantitatively and qualitatively, increase the direct impacts. In this case the inner circle changes its shape with each new round of ripples. Figure 7.2 depicts in greater detail the hypothesized stages of social amplification of risk and its associated impacts for a hypothetical corporation.

Several examples illustrate the ripple effect of risk events. Following the Three Mile Island accident, nuclear plants worldwide were shut down and restarted more frequently for safety checks, although these phases of operations (as with aircraft take-offs and landings) are by far the riskiest operational stages. In a more recent case of risk amplification, Switzerland recalled and ordered the incineration of 200 tons of its prestigious Vacherin Mont d'Or cheese because of bacterial contamination. Rival French cheesemakers at first celebrated their good fortune until it became apparent that public concern over the event had caused worldwide consumption of the cheese, from all producers, to plummet by over 25 per cent. An entire industry, in short, suffered economic reversal from a specific risk event.[23]

Social amplification of risk, in our current conceptualization, involves two major stages (or amplifiers) – the transfer of information about the risk or risk event, and the response mechanisms of society.

Informational Mechanisms of Social Amplification

The roots of social amplification lie in the social experience of risk, both in direct personal experience and in indirect, or secondary, experience, through information received about the risk, risk events and management systems. Direct experience with risky activities or events can be either reassuring (as with automobile driving) or alarming (as with tornadoes or floods). Generally, experience with dramatic accidents or risk events increases the memorability and imaginability of the hazard, thereby heightening the perception of risk.[24] But direct experience can also provide feedback on the nature, extent and manageability of the hazard, affording better perspective and enhanced capability for avoiding risks. Thus, whereas direct personal experience can serve as a risk amplifier, it can also act to attenuate risk. Understanding this interaction for different risks, for different social experiences and for different cultural groups is an important research need.

But many risks are not experienced directly. When direct personal experience is lacking or minimal, individuals learn about risk from other persons and from the media. Information flow becomes a key ingredient in public response and acts as a major agent of amplification. Attributes of information that may influence the social amplification are *volume*, the degree to which information is *disputed*, the extent of *dramatization* and the *symbolic connotations* of the information.

Independent of the accuracy and particular content of information, large volume of information flow may serve as a risk amplifier. In an analysis of media coverage of Love Canal and Three Mile Island, Mazur argued that the massive quantity of media coverage not only reported the events but defined and shaped the issues.[25] Repeated stories, of course, direct public attention towards particular risk problems and away from competing sources of attention. Moreover, the news media tend to become battlegrounds where various participants vie for advantage. However balanced the coverage, it is unclear that reassuring claims can effectively counter the effects of fear-arousing messages.[26] In Alvin Weinberg's metaphor, it is much harder to 'unscare' people than to scare them.[27] High volumes of information also mobilize latent fears about a particular risk and enhance the recollection of previous accidents or management failures or enlarge the extent to which particular failures, events or consequences can be imagined. In this way, technologies or activities may come to be viewed as more dangerous.[2,28]

The second attribute of information is the degree to which individuals or groups dispute factual information or inferences regarded as credible by interested members of the public. Debates among experts are apt to heighten public uncertainty about what the facts really are, increase doubts about whether the hazards are really understood and decrease the credibility of official spokespersons.[29] If the risks are already feared by the public, then increased concern is the likely result.

Dramatization, a third attribute, is undoubtedly a powerful source of risk amplification. The report during the Three Mile Island accident that a hydrogen bubble inside the reactor could explode within the next two days, blow the head off the reactor, and release radioactive material into the atmosphere certainly increased public fears near the nuclear plant (and around the world). Sensational headlines ('Thousands Dead!') following the Chernobyl accident increased the memorability of that accident and the perceived catastrophic potential of nuclear power. If erroneous information sources find ready access to the mass media without effective antidotes, then large social impacts, even for minor events, become entirely possible.

The channels of information are also important. Information about risks and risk events flows through two major communication networks – the news media and more informal personal networks. The news media as risk articulators have received the bulk of scientific attention for their critical role in public opinion formation and community agenda setting.[29,30] Since the media tend to accord disproportionate coverage to rare or dramatic risks, or risk events, it is not surprising that people's estimates of the principal causes of death are related to the amount of media coverage they receive.[31]

Informal communication networks involve the linkages that exist among friends, neighbours and co-workers, and within social groups more generally. Although relatively little is known about such networks, it is undoubtedly the case that people do not consider risk issues in isolation from other social issues or from the views of their peers. Since one's friends or co-workers provide reference points for validating perceptions but are also likely to share a more general cultural view or bias, the potential exists for both amplifying and attenuating information. If the risk is feared, rumour may be a significant element in the formation of public perceptions and attitudes. Within social group interaction, these interpretations of risks will tend to be integrated into larger frames of values and analysis and to become resistant to new, conflicting information. It should be expected, therefore, that interpersonal networks will lead to divergent risk perceptions, management preferences and levels of concern. Since experts also exhibit cultural biases in their selections of theories, methods and data, these variable public perceptions will also often differ as a group from those of experts.

Finally, specific terms or concepts used in risk information may have quite different meanings for varying social and cultural groups. They may also trigger associations independent of those intended.[32] Such symbolic connotations may entail 'mushroom clouds' for nuclear energy, 'dumps' for waste disposal facilities or feelings of 'warmth and comfort' for solar power technologies.

Response Mechanisms of Social Amplification

The interpretation and response to information flow form the second major stage of social amplification of risk. These mechanisms involve the social, institutional and cultural contexts in which the risk information is interpreted, its meaning diagnosed and values attached. We hypothesize four major pathways to initiate response mechanisms:

- *Heuristics and values*
  Individuals cannot deal with the full complexity of risk and the multitude of risks involved in daily life. Thus people use simplifying mechanisms to evaluate risk and to shape responses. These processes, while permitting individuals to cope with a risky world, may sometimes introduce biases that cause distortions and errors.[28] Similarly, the application of individual and group values will also determine which risks are deemed important or minor and what actions, if any, should be taken.
- *Social group relationships*
  Risk issues enter into the political agenda of social and political groups. The nature of these groups will influence member responses and the types of rationality brought to risk issues.[3] To the extent that risk becomes a central issue in a political campaign or in a conflict among social groups, it will be vigorously brought to more general public attention, often coupled with ideological interpretations of technology or the risk-management process.[11,12] Polarization of views and escalation of rhetoric by partisans typically occur and new recruits are drawn into the conflicts.[29] These social alignments tend to become anchors for subsequent interpretations of risk management and may become quite firm in the face of conflicting information.
- *Signal value*
  An important concept that has emerged from research on risk perception is that the seriousness and higher-order impacts of a risk event are determined, in part, by what that event signals or portends.[4] The informativeness or 'signal value' of an event appears to be systematically related to the characteristics of the event and the hazard it reflects. High-signal events suggest that a new risk has appeared or that the risk is different and more serious than previously understood (see Table 7.1). Thus an accident that takes many lives may produce relatively little social disturbance (beyond that experienced by the victims' families and friends) if it occurs as part of a familiar and well-understood system (such as a train wreck). A small accident in an unfamiliar system (or one perceived as poorly

Table 7.1 *Risk events with potentially high signal value*

Events	Messages
Report that chlorofluorocarbon releases are depleting the ozone layer	A new and possibly catastrophic risk has emerged
Resignation of regulators or corporate officials in 'conscience'	The managers are concealing the risks: they cannot be trusted
News report of off-site migration at a hazardous waste site	The risk managers are not in control of the hazard
Scientific dispute over the validity of an epidemiological study	The experts do not understand the risks
Statement by regulators that the levels of a particular contaminant in the water supply involve only very low risks as compared with other risks	The managers do not care about the people who will be harmed; they do not understand long-term cumulative effects of chemicals

understood), such as a nuclear reactor or a recombinant-DNA laboratory, however, may elicit great public concern if it is interpreted to mean that the risk is not well understood, not controllable or not competently managed, thus implying that further (and possibly worse) mishaps are likely. In sum, signals about a risk event initiate a process whereby the significance of the event is examined. If found to be ominous, these implications are likely to trigger higher-order social and economic impacts.

- *Stigmatization*
Stigma refers to the negative imagery associated with undesirable social groups or individuals.[33] But environments with heavy pollution, waste accumulation or hazardous technology may also come to be associated with negative images. Love Canal, the Valley of the Thousand Drums, Times Beach and the Nevada Test Site evoke vivid images of waste and pollution. Since the typical response to stigmatized persons or environments is avoidance, it is reasonable to assume that risk-induced stigma may have significant social and policy consequences.[34] Research is needed to define the role of risk in creating stigma, the extent of aversion that results and how durable such stigma become.

In addition to these four mechanisms, *positive feedback to the physical risk itself* can occur due to social processes. If a transportation accident with hazardous materials were to occur close to a waste-disposal site, for example, protests and attempted blockage of the transportation route could result. Such actions could themselves become initiating or co-accident events, thereby increasing the probabilities of future accidents or enlarging the consequences should an accident occur. Or, alternatively, an accident in waste handling at the facility could lead opponents, or a disgruntled worker, to replicate the event through sabotage. Especially where strong public concern exists over a technology or facility, a wide variety of mechanisms is present by which health and safely risks may be enlarged through social processes.[35]

Next Steps

Only partial models or paradigms exist for characterizing the phenomenon we describe as the social amplification of risk. Understanding this phenomenon is a prerequisite essential for assessing the potential impacts of projects and technologies, for establishing priorities in risk management, and for setting health and environmental standards. We put forth this conceptual framework to begin the building of a comprehensive theory that explains why seemingly minor risks or risk events often produce extraordinary public concern and social and economic impacts, with rippling effects across time, space and social institutions. The conceptualization needs scrutiny, elaboration and competing views. Empirical studies, now beginning, should provide important tests and insights for the next stage of theory construction.

References

1   P Slovic, B Fischhoff and S Lichtenstein (1982) 'Why Study Risk Perception?' in *Risk Analysis* no 2, pp83–94
2   O Renn (1986) 'Risk Perception: A Systematic Review of Concepts and Research Results,' in *Avoiding and Managing Environmental Damage from Major Industrial Accidents*, Proceedings of ihe Air Pollution Control Association International Conference in Vancouver, Canada, November 1985 (The Association, Pittsburgh, 1986), pp377–408
3   S Rayner and R Cantor (1987) 'How Fair is Safe Enough? The cultural Approach to Societal Technology Choice,' in *Risk Analysis* no 7, pp3–13
4   P Slovic (1987) 'Perception of Risk' in *Science* no 236, pp280–290
5   C A Vlek and P J M Stallen (1981) 'Judging Risks and Benefits in the Small and the Large' in *Organizational Behavior and Human Performance* no 28, pp235–271
6   J M Doderlein (1983) 'Understanding Risk Management,' in *Risk Analysis* no 3, pp17–21
7   R E Kasperson (ed) (1983) *Equity Issues in Radioactive Waste Management* Oelgeschlager, Gunn and Hain, Cambridge
8   H J Otway and D von Winterfeldt (1982) 'Beyond Acceptable Risk: On the Social Acceptability of Technologies' in *Policy Science* no 14, pp247–256
9   B Wynne, 'Public Perceptions of Risk' in J Surrey (ed) *The Urban Transportation of Irradiated Fuel*, Macmillan, London 1984, pp246–259
10   B Fischhoff, P Slovic, S Lichtenstein, S Read and B Combs (1978) 'How Safe is Safe Enough?: A Psychometric Study of Attitudes Towards Technological Risks and Benefits' in *Policy Sciences* no 8, pp127–152
11   M Douglas and A Wildavsky (1982) *Risk and Culture: An Essay on the Selection of Technological and Environmental Dangers* University of California Press, Berkeley
12   B Johnson and V Covello (eds) (1987) *Social and Cultural Construction of Risk* Reidel, Boston
13   D von Winterfeldt and W Edwards (1984) *Understanding Public Disputes about Risky Technologies* technical report, Social Science Research Council, New York
14   M T Katzman (1985) *Chemical Catastrophes: Regulating Environmental Risk Through Pollution Liability Insurance* R D Irwin, Springfield, Illinois

15 C D Heising and V P George (1986) 'Nuclear Financial Risk: Economy Wide Cost of Reactor Accidents' in *Energy Policy* no 14, pp45–52

16 H I Sharlin (1985) *EDB: A Case Study in the Communication of Health Risk* Office of Policy Analysis, Environmental Protection Agency, Washington, DC

17 I Hoos (1980) 'Risk Assessment in Social Perspective' in *Perceptions of Risk* National Council on Radiation Protection and Measurement, Washington, DC, pp37–85

18 M L DeFleur (1966) *Theories of Mass Communication* D McKay, New York

19 P J Shoemaker (1987) 'Mass Communication by the Book; A Review of 31 Texts' in *Journal of Communication* no 37, vol 3, pp109–131

20 H D Lasswell (1948) 'The Structure and Function of Communication in Society' in L Bryson (ed) *The Communication of ideas: A Series of Addresses* Cooper Square Publishers, New York, pp32–35

21 C J Hovland (1948) 'Social Communication' in Proceedings of the American Philosophical Society no 92, pp371–375

22 J H Sorensen and D S Mileti 'Decision-Making Uncertainties in Emergency Warning System Organizations' in *International Journal of Mass Emergencies and Disasters*

23 S Grunhouse (1988) 'French and Swiss Fight about Tainted Cheese' in *New York Times*, January, p2

24 P Slovic (1986) 'Informing and Educating the Public about Risk' in *Risk Analysis* no 6, pp403–415

25 A Mazur (1984) 'The Journalist and Technology: Reporting about Love Canal and Three Mile Island' in *Minerva* no 22, pp45–66

26 J Sorensen et al (1987) *Impacts of Hazardous Technology: The Psycho-Social Effects of Restarting TMI* State University of New York Press, Albany

27 A Weinberg (1977) 'Is Nuclear Energy Acceptable?' in *Bulletin of the Atomic Scientists* no 33, vol 4, pp54–60

28 D Kahneman, P Slovic and A Tversky (eds) (1982) *Judgment under Uncertainty: Heuristics and Biases* Cambridge University Press, New York

29 A Mazur (1981) *The Dynamics of Technical Controversy* Communication Press, Washington, DC

30 National Research Council (1980) *Disasters and the Mass Media* National Academy of Sciences Press, Washington, DC

31 B Combs and P Slovic (1979) 'Newspaper Coverage of Causes of Death' in *Journalism Quarterly* no 56, pp837–843, 849

32 H Blumer (1969) *Symbolic Interactionism: Perspective and Method* Prentice Hall, Englewood Cliffs, NJ

33 E Goffman (1963) *Stigma* Prentice Hall, Englewood Cliffs, NJ

34 P Slovic (1987) 'Forecasting the Adverse Economic Effects of a Nuclear Waste Repository' in R G Post (ed) *Waste Management '87* Arizona Board of Regents, University of Arizona, Tucson

35 R E Kasperson, J Emel, R Goble, C Hohenemser, J X Kasperson and O Renn (1987) 'Radioactive wastes and the Social Amplification of Risk' in R G Post (ed), *Waste Management '87* Arizona Board of Regents, University of Arizona, Tucson

Incorporating Structural Models into Research on the Social Amplification of Risk: Implications for Theory Construction and Decision Making

William J Burns, Paul Slovic, Roger E Kasperson, Jeanne X Kasperson, Ortwin Renn and Srinivas Emani

Introduction

Risk research in the social sciences has developed along two important but distinct paths. Behavioural scientists have sought to describe how people and institutions perceive and respond to risk, while management scientists have attempted to develop methods that prescribe appropriate actions for managers to take. Despite significant progress in these separate areas, there is still no comprehensive approach that integrates our understanding of how a society experiences risk with formal methods of decision-making (eg cost–benefit analysis and decision analysis). Managers continue, for example, to be surprised and dismayed when 'minor events', as assessed by experts, spark great alarm and subsequent societal disruption.

A comprehensive approach to managing risk must draw upon the descriptive insights of the behavioural sciences and the prescriptive strengths of the management sciences. Formal analytic methods, for example, typically have assessed the impact of accidents or other adverse events in terms of expected loss of life or property damage. The contribution of these methods has been to provide risk managers with explicit guidance, using criteria that are well defined. A nice illustration of these methods can be seen in Keeney,[1] who develops a utility model for evaluating potential fatalities and associated uncertainties of occurrence. The effect of fatalities on the public is evaluated in terms of the direct personal impacts of suffering and economic hardship and the indirect societal impacts of possible political and economic turmoil. Keeney's disaggregation of impacts into personal and societal is insightful, and his approach leads to clear recommendations for action. However, focusing on fatalities or related criteria may not adequately anticipate public concerns as perceptions of threat and social response appear less a matter of physical outcomes than of attitudes, social influences and cultural identity.[2]

Research from multiple disciplines may help broaden the criteria considered by prescriptive methods. Psychometric research,[3] for instance, has identified numerous factors that appear related to perception and acceptance of risk, such as voluntary exposure, controllability, familiarity and perceived catastrophic potential. Sociological analysis has examined social and organizational factors that influence risk experiences,[4,5] the capability of risk management institutions to cope with large-scale risks,[6,7] and perceived equity in the distribution of risks and benefits.[8,9]

Providing managers with a better understanding of how society perceives and responds to risk will help managers make more informed decisions. Likewise, developing better prescriptive strategies will also contribute to improved risk decisions even if these strategies largely ignore societal perceptions. The challenge, however, is to draw on the knowledge, theories and methodological tools of each perspective to provide risk managers with comprehensive and well-formulated recommendations. Our paper discusses methodological and theoretical developments in the social sciences that may contribute to a more comprehensive approach to risk management. It also describes, briefly, how these developments can be combined with more formal methods of risk analysis.

Modelling the Social Amplification of Risk: An Examination of a Hazard Data Base Using Structural Models

Description of Theory and Relationships Among Model Constructs

Aiming to link the technical assessment of risk with psychological and cultural perspectives on risk-related behaviour, Kasperson et al[10] proposed a theoretical framework labelled 'the social amplification of risk'. According to the social amplification model, the effects of an adverse event such as an accident sometimes extend far beyond the direct damages to victims, property and environment and may result in massive indirect impacts. The theory postulates that the social and economic impacts of an adverse event are determined not only by the direct biological and physical consequences of the event, but by the interaction of powerful psychological, cultural, social and institutional processes that amplify or attenuate public response to the event. When an event occurs, information regarding the event flows through various channels to the public and its many cultural and social groups. This information is interpreted largely on the basis of its interaction with the above processes which, in turn, triggers risk-related behaviour. Such behaviour, together with the influence of the media and special interest groups, generates secondary social and economic consequences that eventually call for additional institutional responses and protective actions (or, in the case of risk attenuation, eventually impede protective actions).

In the present study, we investigate the social amplification theory by developing structural models based on factors assumed to contribute to an event's impact. The theoretical models are tested using judgements obtained from samples of lay persons and experts. The factors in the models include the event's physical consequences, associated risk perception characteristics, media coverage and ability to stimulate public response. The hypothesized relationships among these factors are depicted in Figure 7.3.

In Figure 7.3, *public response* (degree to which the public becomes involved with reducing a hazard's risk) and *media coverage* (volume of news coverage) are assumed to have a strong, positive and direct effect on an event's impact. The nature of these effects is illustrated by the single-headed arrows connecting these two factors with *societal impact*. For example, the media and public may put pressure on policy-makers to increase regulation of a hazard as a result of some mishap. This could result in substantial costs to a particular firm or industry.

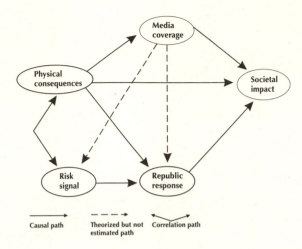

Figure 7.3 *Proposed model prior to interaction with data (all constructs have multiple measures)*

The *physical consequences* of an event (number of people and amount of property directly exposed to risk or actually harmed by the event) may also have a direct and positive effect on its impact. However, according to the theory, an event's physical consequences will have their primary influence by stimulating media coverage and public reaction. Examples of this phenomenon are events in which large numbers of people are exposed to risk, though few are actually harmed. Perceived exposure to risk may stimulate media and public attention and thus have a large indirect impact without having much direct impact.

Finally, it is hypothesized that an event's *risk signal* (degree to which an event leads the public to believe that a new risk has appeared or that the risk is different and more serious than previously thought) will have a strong, positive, and direct effect on *public response*.[3] It is further hypothesized, however, that *risk signal* will influence an event's *societal impact* only indirectly through its ability to incite *public response*. It is expected that adverse events inspiring dread, or believed to be managed incompetently, or perceived to pose future danger to others will be viewed as high signal events and will elicit strong public reaction that in turn may affect a firm or an industry. For example, events surrounding nuclear power generally have high signal value,[11] and this helps explain the public's reaction to the accident at Three Mile Island and to other, lesser, problems in the nuclear industry. The theory also suggests that the amount of media coverage should influence how the public perceives and responds to a hazard event. This contention is portrayed by the dashed arrows in Figure 7.3. However, this influence path cannot be examined in this study because the respondents providing information on these variables were not differentially exposed to media coverage. For many respondents this survey may have represented their only exposure to an event regardless of how much media coverage it received.

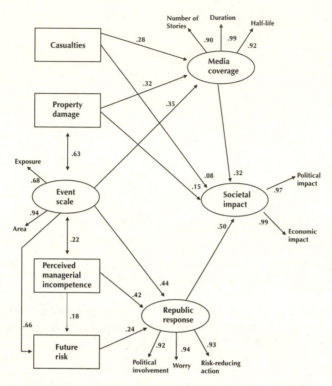

Figure 7.4 *Covariance structure model for sample 1*

Operationalizing the Model

In Figure 7.3 we provided the general intuition behind the social amplification process and specified the expected relationships among its constructs. However, estimation and theory testing require that these abstract constructs be tied to measurable phenomena. Hence, we now describe how each construct was measured and we provide a brief discussion of the structural model investigated.

The model used to estimate the relations depicted in Figure 7.3 is shown in Figure 7.4, and its measured variables are discussed in Table 7.2. For purposes of estimation, we represent an event's physical consequences by three constructs describing the size of the event (*event scale*), the number of people harmed (*casualties*) and the amount of property damaged (*property damaged*). Likewise, we capture *risk signal* by *perceived managerial incompetence* and *future risk*. Variables depicted with ovals are latent constructs and are represented by multiple measures. For example, *societal impact* is measured by an assessment of the political and economic impacts of each event. Some constructs, such as *casualties*, have only one measure and are depicted with squares. Single-headed arrows imply causality, while double-headed arrows imply only correlation. Some causal paths such as from *casualties* to *public response* do not appear because they were statistically insignificant and so were removed from our proposed model. The same is true for a number of correlational paths. The findings from this estimation will be discussed in a later section.

Description and Selection of the Adverse Events Data Base

The adverse events selected for this study included routine as well as unexpected events and included mishaps as well as reports of potential dangers. Almost all events occurred in North America during the ten-year period between 1976 and 1987. A comprehensive set of events was selected with guidance from a taxonomy of hazards suggested by Hohenemser et al.[12] Their taxonomy characterizes hazard events

Table 7.2 *Description of model variables for each construct*

EVENT SCALE[a]	
Exposure[b]	The number of people exposed to harm from a hazard
Area[b]	The amount of area exposed to harm from a hazard
CASUALTIES	
Casualties[b]	The number of people injured or killed by a hazard
PROPERTY DAMAGE	
Property Damage[b]	The amount of monetary damage to property from a hazard
MEDIA COVERAGE	
Nstories[c]	The number of follow-up news stories reporting on a hazard
Duration[c]	The number of days between the first and last news stories
Half-life[c]	The number of days until half the news stories appeared
RISK SIGNAL	
Future Risk[d]	Degree to which other people are at risk of experiencing harm from future hazards of this type
Perceived Managerial Incompetence[e]	Degree to which the public believes that a hazard implies that similar risks are being managed incompetently
PUBLIC RESPONSE	
Political Involvement	Degree to which the public is willing to become politically involved to reduce future risks posed by a hazard
Worry[e]	Degree to which the public worries about the risks posed by a hazard
Risk-Reducing Action[e]	Degree to which the public is willing to become actively involved (eg, joining an action-oriented group) to reduce future risks posed by a hazard
SOCIETAL IMPACT	
Political Impact[f]	Degree to which a hazard generates political attention by public officials
Economic Impact[f]	Degree to which a hazard generates economic impacts (eg, loss of sales, increased costs due to regulation)

[a] Constructs are given in capital letters.
[b] Assessed by risk experts at Clark University on a scale of 1–9.
[c] Data generated from Nexis data base.
[d] Rated by University of Oregon students on a scale of 1–7 (during phase I) and 0–8 (during phase II).
[e] Rated by University of Oregon students on a scale of 0–8.
[f] Assessed by a Delphi panel of professionals on a scale of 0–10.

as belonging to five classes: Biocidal (eg vaccines), Persistent/Delayed effects (eg mercury release), Rare Catastrophes (eg airplane crashes), Threats to Life (eg smoking) and Global/Diffuse Hazards (eg CO_2 release). Radiological Hazards (eg nuclear accidents) were also included.

Events representing each of the classes were identified through a search of the *New York Times Index*. Using this *Index* as a list from which to sample, events were chosen to represent a wide range of consequences pertaining to people and the environment. Within each class, effort was made to balance the distribution of recent and less recent events. Each class had approximately the same number of events. Data were collected on 108 events and these events provided the stimuli upon which expert and public assessment was based.

Respondents received a brief news clipping for each event or report. A group of risk experts received a synopsis of the actual news story, while the non-experts received an even briefer version of the story, omitting names and extraneous details. For example, one particular news story covering the side effects of a vaccination read 'Joshua Reed received his third DPT shot in Hallstead, PA. He had seizures and suffered brain damage.' The modified version read 'Child suffers brain damage from routine vaccination.'

Data Collection and Variable Description

Physical Consequences

The physical consequences of an event were initially divided into two categories: consequences affecting human systems and consequences affecting non-human systems. Human systems consequences were measured by the number of people exposed to harm (*exposure*) as well as by the severity of the harm (*casualties*). Non-human systems were measured by the estimated area of impact (*area*) and the estimated dollar amounts of damage (*property damage*).

All four physical consequence variables were measured on a scale ranging from 1–9, where the scale values were defined according to the guidelines given in Hohenemser et al.[12] Ratings of each event on all four variables were obtained through a consensus on the part of three experts (a physicist, chemist and geographer) from the Hazard Assessment Group at Clark University. Where specific references to the extent of a mishap were not reported, the experts inferred the magnitude of the consequences.

Media Coverage

Identification of suitable news stories relied upon a manual search of *The New York Times Index* for coverage of events representative of categories in the seven-class taxonomy mentioned previously. The search provided index entries for all 108 hazard events. Once these stories were identified, information from their index entries was used to investigate follow-up coverage in NEWS, which is a group file in the Nexis data base. From this search, abstracts were obtained with information pertaining to the number of follow-up stories covering or mentioning the event (*num-*

ber of stories), the duration of coverage for the event (*duration*), and the number of days until half of the total stories on the event had appeared (*half-life*).

Risk Perceptions and Public Response

Data pertaining to people's perceptions of risk and their likely response to an adverse event were obtained using students at the University of Oregon. Scales mea-

Table 7.3 *Examples of measures of risk signal and public response*

Perceived managerial incompetence (risk signal)

In this question I'm interested in *to what extent you think that those people in charge of these events or hazards are doing an adequate or competent job.* Some events or types of hazards are more difficult to manage than others. Likewise, some hazards pose greater threats to general safety or well-being if not managed properly. Considering these factors, ask yourself whether this type of event or hazard is being managed competently by those in charge. Some events, all things considered, may lead you to believe that risks of this type are being managed well. While other events may lead you to believe that risks of this type are not being managed very well.

To what extent does the event or hazard referred to in this story imply that the risks of this type are being managed properly by those in charge?

It implies risks   It implies risks of this type
of this type   *are not being managed*
are being   *properly*
managed properly   0 1 2 3 4 5 6 7 8

Future risk (risk signal)

To what extent are other people at risk of experiencing harm from future events of this kind?

Not at risk   0 1 2 3 4 5 6 7 8   At very great risk

Political involvement (public response)

Some events concern us to the point of being willing to support political activity that would reduce future risks posed by a particular event. This involvement might take the form of signing a petition or writing letters to public officials. It could also mean donating money to or joining a political action group. While some events, though they may concern us, do not seem to have this effect on us.

To what extent would this event cause you to become politically involved with reducing the future risks posed by this hazard?

This event   This event *would cause* me
would not   to get very involved
cause me to
get very involved   0 1 2 3 4 5 6 7 8

---

suring *future risk* and *perceived managerial incompetence* were investigated to assess the domain of risk signal. To understand better how risk perceptions translate into political and economic impacts, information was sought pertaining to people's behavioural reaction to a hazard. However, it was not feasible to observe how the public would actually react, so information on their behavioural intentions was used as a proxy. Scales such as *political involvement* and *risk-reducing action* were used instead to represent the public's response to hazard events. Respondents were asked to rate all 108 adverse events on a nine-point scale, for each of the risk perception and public response variables. Ratings for each event on each variable were then averaged across respondents to yield an aggregate score for each adverse event on a particular variable. Examples of some of these scales are provided in Table 7.3.

Societal Impact

The amount of sociopolitical attention (*political impact*) and socioeconomic impact (*economic impact*) were both assessed by a Delphi panel consisting of 12 experts from the fields of risk analysis, journalism, law and politics. The Delphi procedure consisted of three rounds of discussion and assessment in which three experts were randomly assigned to one of four groups for each of the rounds. Each group was asked to rate each event in terms of both *political impact* and *economic impact* on a scale of 0–10. The scores obtained from these three rounds were averaged to provide a single score on both variables for each event.

Model Estimation Using Covariance Structure and Partial Least-Squares Modelling

Covariance structure and partial least squares (PLS) modelling were used to investigate the social amplification of risk framework as modelled in Figure 7.4. Both these modelling tools are general multivariate procedures that allow a researcher to investigate the relationships among variables (latent or observed) of theoretical interest. These procedures augment exploratory methods such as factor analysis, multidimensional scaling, cluster analysis and regression analysis that have been used to understand and predict public reaction to hazardous events.

Covariance structure analysis and PLS represent complementary approaches to structural equation modelling with the former being better suited for theory testing and the latter for prediction.[13] Covariance structure modelling typically uses a full information (eg maximum-likelihood or generalized least-squares) estimation approach. This full information approach potentially yields very efficient parameter estimates but also requires relatively large samples and the assumption of multivariate normality. PLS uses a very different estimation approach, relying on iterative minimization of residual variance with respect to a subset of the parameters (given either fixed-point constraints or final estimates of other model parameters).[14] This approach has the advantage of requiring neither large samples nor specific distributional assumptions if parametric statistical tests are not desired (non-parametric procedures can be used to generate standard errors and assess model adequacy), but yields less efficient estimates than maximum likelihood.

Covariance structure and PLS models possess a number of advantages for development of comprehensive theory in risk management. For example, they both are capable of incorporating an ever-expanding theoretical and empirical knowledge about how society experiences risk. This capability allows insights from many disciplines to be explicitly considered by risk managers. Likewise, these two approaches allow examination of the structural relationships among risk constructs that have emerged from exploratory procedures. They also permit an assessment of how well these constructs have been measured. Additionally, covariance structure and PLS modelling give unambiguous expression to the relative contribution of each model variable (directly or indirectly) to a dependent construct such as hazard impact. Thus, they are helpful in the construction of prescriptive models that seek to properly formulate risk decisions and estimate the probabilities of impact-related costs.[15]

Results*

Description of Extreme Events

A description of events scoring in the top or bottom 5 per cent is given in Table 7.4 for a selected number of model variables. These examples suggest that an event's newsworthiness, ability to stimulate public reaction and eventual impact may have less to do with injuries or fatalities than with perceived potential to do harm. Observe, for *risk-reducing action*, that respondents indicated they would take little action to prevent fatalities resulting from an auto accident like the kind described in Table 7.3 but said they would be highly motivated to reduce the risk of a pesticide in food products. Similarly, for *perceived managerial incompetence* the two events showed both represent serious hazards. However, the event depicting a voluntary effort to correct the risk falls in the lowest 5 per cent, while the other event falls in the highest 5 per cent. In this case, respondents viewed the former as demonstrating competent management. Perceptions that a firm is managing a hazard properly signal less need to worry for the future and hence less felt need to take risk-reducing action.

Correlations Among Variables

The correlations between model variables are provided in Table 7.5. Notice that variables measuring the same construct (enclosed), with one exception, are more correlated with each other than with other model variables. This is one indication that construct measures are performing as they should. As predicted, indicators of media coverage and public response are more related to event impact than are other model variables. Somewhat surprising is that the number of casualties has little correlation with measures of public perceptions or response. This may again suggest that indications of injuries or fatalities alone do not trigger public reaction to a hazard event.

---

* A preliminary analysis of this data set has been presented by O Renn, W J Burns, J X Kasperson, R E Kasperson and P Slovic (1992) in *Journal of Social Issues* No 8, pp137–160

Table 7.4 *Examples of events scoring in highest or lowest 5 per cent on a subset of model variables*

Variable	Event score
1. Exposure (range: 1–9, mean: 3.85)	
a. *Low* Tractor trailer carrying 246 containers of low-level radioactive waste through Long Island City, Queens, splits open as it passes below elevated subway track. No material leaked or spilled.	1
b. *High* New tests and surveys suggest that potentially harmful levels of radon gas may be contaminating homes in New York, New Jersey and Pennsylvania well beyond Reading Prong information; radon is believed to cause from 5000 to 20,000 of 100,000 lung-cancer deaths each year in the US; New York State Health Commissioner, Dr David Axelrod, sees 'very significant public health threat'.	9
2. Casualties (range: 1–6, mean: 1.71)	
a. *Low* Uranium-processing plant north of Cincinnati, Ohio, leaked a small cloud of radioactive uranium hexafluoride gas from cracked metal cylinder, no workers injured.	1
b. *High* Delta Airlines L–1011 Jumbo Jet with 161 people aboard crashes and explodes in violent thunderstorm as it tries to land at Dallas-Fort Worth Airport. 137 die, 24 survivors.	4
3. Property damage (range: 1–9, mean: 4.66)	
a. *Low* Three elderly individuals went to the same health clinic in Pittsburgh to receive influenza shots. All three died within 6 hours of being inoculated.	1
b. *High* First state-wide study of New Jersey shows that average acidity of rain, sleet and snow to be at least 30 times greater than normal. The most highly acidic rain comes from storms that contain winds coming from the north-west section of the country, where much SO_2 is emitted.	9
4. Number of stories (range: 0–2064, mean: 94.58)	
a. *Low* Chartered bus carrying homeless men from several cities in East and Middle West to Rajneesh religious commune in Oregon collides with car. One person dies and 31 are injured in Notus, Idaho, accident.	0
b. *High* Huge discharge of toxic chemicals into Rhine River confronts Europe with worst ecological disaster in recent years. 1000 tons of chemicals (including 8 tons of mercury) spill into Rhine after fire in chemical storage warehouse in Basel, Switzerland.	551
5. Risk-reducing action (range: .5–6.69, mean: 3.32)	
a. *Low* A van and a pickup truck collide. Five people are killed, and four are injured.	1.15
b. *High* High levels of the cancer-causing pesticide EDB have been found in flour, pancake mixes and other widely used food products.	5.08
6. Perceived managerial incompetence (range: 1.84–7.24, mean: 5.02)	
a. *Low* Manufacturer announces a voluntary candy-bar recall after tests show salmonella bacteria in several batches.	2.96
b. *High* High levels of the cancer-causing pesticide EDB have been found in flour, pancake mixes and other widely used food products.	6.60
7. Future risk (range: 2.38–6.43, mean: 4.45)	
a. *Low* A major dam collapses. The water released kills 14 and devastates ½ million acres of land.	2.96
b. *High* Three hazardous waste and dump sites were recently added to four already known to exist around the same harbour and dangerous chemicals have been found to be leaking into the groundwater.	6.01
8. Economic impact (range: 0–8.5; mean: 2.12)	
a. *Low* Chartered bus carrying homeless men from several cities in East and Middle West to Rajneesh religious commune in Oregon collides with car. One person dies and 31 are injured in Notus, Idaho, accident.	.5
b. *High* Times Beach, Missouri, resident Lane Jumper says soil tests by Envirodyne engineers have found high concentrations of dioxin and other hazardous chemicals.	7.0

Covariance Structure Modelling

The covariance structure model in Figure 7.4 (its path coefficients and fit statistics are also provided in Table 7.5) was estimated using a generalized least-squares procedure provided in a statistical package known as EQS.[16]

To improve estimation, the distributions of all model variables were examined for normality and variables were transformed where necessary. For example, the measures of *societal impact* and *media coverage* were re-expressed using the natural log. Multivariate normality was then assessed using Mardia's coefficient, a statistic provided by the output of EQS. Mardia's coefficient suggested the assumption of multivariate normality was plausible.

All path estimates have been standardized; as a result, causal links (one-way arrows) are represented by standardized regression coefficients and covariance links (two-way arrows) are represented by correlation coefficients. For example, the standardized path coefficient linking *media coverage* with *societal impact* is .32. This means that events that are one standard deviation above the mean for *media coverage* tend, on average, to be .32 standard deviations above the mean for *societal-impact*. Likewise, the coefficients associated with paths connecting constructs with their measurement indicators (ie measurement coefficients) are correlations and hence provide evidence of the relation between a construct and each of its measures. For instance, the measurement coefficients for *public response* range from .92 to .94,

Table 7.5 *Correlations among model variables from phase I*

	Exposure	Area	Casualties	Property damage	Perceived managerial incompetence	Future risk	Number of stories	Duration	Half-life	Political involvement	Worry	Risk-reducing action	Political impact	Economic impact
Exposure	—													
Area	.48	—												
Casualties	.19	-.11	—											
Property damage	.23	.58	.07	—										
Perceived managerial incompetence	.25	.16	.06	-.01	—									
Future risk	.35	.61	-.10	.41	.31	—								
Number of stories	.37	.33	.36	.47	.17	.35	—							
Duration	.42	.43	.22	.46	.17	.39	.87	—						
Half-life	.37	.39	.17	.44	.12	.40	.80	.89	—					
Political involvement	.49	.47	.05	.23	.54	.55	.33	.35	.32	—				
Worry	.42	.56	-.04	.27	.56	.64	.34	.38	.37	.84	—			
Risk-reducing action	.46	.55	-.05	.30	.56	.58	.41	.44	.42	.83	.84	—		
Political impact	.46	.34	.30	.39	.40	.41	.65	.63	.51	.57	.54	.59	—	
Economic impact	.48	.33	.36	.41	.39	.37	.67	.61	.53	.59	.53	.62	.95	—

indicating that they are highly correlated with the construct they are intended to measure.

The overall fit for the model in Figure 7.4 was assessed by examining the χ^2 statistic and the Bentler-Bonnet Normed Fit Index (NFI). The χ^2 statistic ($\chi^2 = 90.22$, $df = 67$, $P = .03$) indicated that the model fit the data only marginally well (a $P > .05$ typically is considered acceptable). However, when correlations among observed variables are high (see Table 7.5), the χ^2 test will tend to indicate a lack of fit even for models that fit the data well. The NFI, which compares the fit of the model to that of a model that claims there is no underlying correlational structure, was .99. The maximum value of the NFI is 1.00 and values over .9 are typically considered acceptable. Hence, taken together, these two indices suggest the model is reasonably consistent with the data.

The quality of measurement was investigated by examining both the size of the measurement coefficients and the tendency of measurement indicators to load on constructs other than the one they are supposed to measure. All indicators except *exposure* have coefficients of .90 or above, suggesting they are highly related to their underlying constructs. There was little evidence to suggest that substantial improvements in model fit could be obtained by allowing measures, where plausible, to load on more than one construct. Hence, the model constructs appear to be measured well.

After one model revision in which insignificant paths were removed, all path coefficients in Figure 7.4 are statistically significant with the exception of the coefficients for paths linking *casualties* and *property damage* with *societal impact*. The marginal direct influence of these two constructs on *societal impact* is important in light of the prominent role these two variables play in risk analysis. Hence, these paths were retained despite their small effect size. As anticipated, *media coverage* and *public response* exert a strong direct influence on *societal impact*. Together, these four factors (*casualties*, *property damage*, *media coverage* and *public response*) combined explain about 62 per cent of the variance of *societal impact*. *Event scale*, *casualties* and *property damage* directly affect *media coverage* but explain only about 45 per cent of its variance. *Future risk*, *perceived managerial incompetence*, and *event scale* appear to directly influence *public response* and explain 71 per cent of its variance. Noteworthy is the finding that *casualties* and *property damage* did not appear to directly influence *public response*. Finally, *event scale* and *perceived managerial incompetence* directly influence *future risk* and explain 53 per cent of its variance. All five exogenous constructs (constructs that are not causally dependent on other model variables) exert an indirect effect on *societal impact* because of their direct influence on either *media coverage* or *public response*.

To illustrate how 'downstream' constructs are influenced by 'upstream' constructs, the effects of predictor variables from the model in Figure 7.4 were decomposed into total, direct and indirect effects and are shown in Table 7.7. Based on the size of the total effects, *media coverage* and *public response* are major contributors to *societal impact*. *Event scale* also contributes a great deal to *societal impact* but does so through these two factors as well as through *future risk*. For example, the total effect of *event scale* on *societal impact* is comprised of its indirect effects through *media coverage*, *public response* and *future risk*. The total effect was calculated as follows:

$$(.35)(.32) + (.44)(.50) + (.66)(.24)(.50) = .41$$

Observe that *perceived managerial incompetence* has a larger influence on *societal impact* than does *casualties*; however, it operates through its indirect effects.

Corroboration Using PLS

To corroborate the findings of the previous model, a PLS model was estimated using the same input variables. Its path coefficients are shown in Table 7.6. As noted

Table 7.6 *Model comparisons across samples using covariance structure and PLS analysis*

	Phase 1		Phase 2		Combined
	Covariance	PLS	Covariance	PLS	Covariance
Structural paths[a]					
ES → FR[b]	.66[c]	.54	.60	.54	.62
PMI → FR	.18	.19	.24	.28	.24
C → MC	.28	.24	.13	.24	.24
PD → MC	.32	.31	.33	.32	.38
ES → MC	.35	.31	.25	.31	.25
ES → PR	.44	.35	.13	.10	.26
PMI → PR	.42	.41	.60	.51	.52
FR → PR	.24	.29	.40	.45	.34
C → SI	.08	.24	.25	.36	.13
PD → SI	.15	.09	.15	.19	.15
MC → SI	.32	.35	.39	.29	.39
PR → SI	.50	.45	.43	.38	.48
Measurement paths					
Exposure	.68	.82	.58	.83	.66
Area	.94	.90	.96	.89	.94
No. of stories	.90	.94	.89	.94	.89
Duration	.99	.97	.97	.97	.98
Half-life	.92	.94	.89	.94	.89
Political involvement	.92	.94	.98	.96	.98
Worry	.94	.95	.83	.91	.92
Risk-reducing action	.93	.94	.89	.94	.95
Political impact	.97	.99	.97	.95	.96
Economic impact	.99	.99	.81	.95	.95
Correlational paths					
ES ↔ PD[d]	.63	.49	.60	.49	.62
ES ↔ PMI	.22	.23	.31	.41	.28
Fit indices					
X^2	90.20	None	84.70	None	84.10
df	67.00		67.00		67.00
P	.03		.07		.08
NFI	.99		.99		.99

[a] Structural path abbreviations: ES: event scale; PMI: perceived managerial incompetence; C: casualties; PD: property damage; FR: future risk; PR: public response; MC: media coverage; SI: societal impact.

[b] →, Causality.

[c] All estimates have been standardized.

[d] ↔, Correlation.

Table 7.7 *Effect decomposition for the combined model*

Constructs	Total[a]	Direct[b]	Indirect[c]
SOCIETAL IMPACT[d]			
Casualties	.17[e]	.08	.09
Property damage	.25	.15	.10
Event scale	.41	.00	.41
Perceived managerial incompetence	.23	.00	.23
Future risk	.12	.00	.12
Media coverage	.32	.32	.00
Public response	.50	.50	.00
MEDIA COVERAGE			
Casualties	.28	.28	.00
Property damage	.32	.32	.00
Event scale	.35	.35	.00
PUBLIC RESPONSE			
Event scale	.60	.44	.16
Perceived managerial incompetence	.46	.42	.04
Future risk	.24	.24	.00
FUTURE RISK			
Perceived managerial incompetence	.18	.18	.00
Event scale	.66	.66	.00

[a] Total effect is the sum of the direct effect and the indirect effect.
[b] Direct effect is the effect due only to the predictor variable of interest.
[c] Indirect effect is the effect due to the predictor's influence on intervening variables which in turn influence the dependent variable of interest. These effects are multiplicative.
[d] Dependent constructs are shown with capital letters.
[e] Standardized effects.

previously, in situations where sample size is small and multivariate normality is violated, PLS is more robust with respect to small sample size and violations of multivariate normality than the generalized least squares procedure used in the previous model. The PLS model does not have an overall measure of fit. However, the significance of the structural and measurement paths in the PLS model was evaluated non-parametrically by computing the ratio of the jack-knifed path estimates to jack-knifed standard errors. All such ratios were found to be extremely large, suggesting the viability of these paths. The measurement coefficients appear to be slightly larger than their counterparts in Figure 7.2 while the structural coefficients appear in most cases smaller. Based on the evaluation criteria used under each estimation procedure and the similarity of their findings, it appears that the structure depicted in the covariance structure and PLS models works reasonably well.

To examine the statistical replicability of the covariance structure and PLS models, 12 new Delphi panelists were chosen and information was again obtained regarding the political and economic impact of a hazard. In addition, a new group of students was asked to provide information regarding risk perceptions and public response.

Covariance structure and PLS models were estimated using this new data and the results are shown in Table 7.5. The evidence gathered from the across-sample and across-estimation method comparisons suggests that the model structure shown in Figure 7.4 works reasonably well. The comparisons across samples indicate that while the substantive conclusions of the model appear to be upheld, the path estimates are in many cases different. This could be due in part to an instability of some measures of *event scale, public response* and *societal impact* construct measures.

To increase the reliability of the measures, the two samples were combined. Combining these samples appeared reasonable because both were drawn from the University of Oregon student population only seven months apart. Model coefficients and fit statistics are once again shown in Table 7.5. The χ^2 statistic and the NFI for the model based on the combined sample indicate a good fit.

Discussion

Summary

Our paper has emphasized the need for an integrated approach to risk management that combines research emerging from both the behavioural and management sciences. Addressing this need, we described two structural modelling approaches that are able to bring diverse types of risk information into a single model and that should be helpful in the construction of prescriptive models that seek to properly formulate risk decisions.

We also investigated a number of predictions implied by the social amplification of risk framework. Our findings support the contention that the behaviour of the media and the public play crucial roles in determining the impact of a hazardous event. Each of these factors contributes significantly to an event's impact even when controlling for the event's scale and for harm to people and property. The physical consequences of an event also strongly influence societal impact but do so primarily through intervening variables. For example, the scale of the event exerts a strong effect on event impact but operates through its ability to stimulate media and public behaviour. Likewise, the number of casualties moderately affects media behaviour but has only a weak direct influence on societal impact. Perceptions of managerial incompetence influence the public's response to a hazard to a degree approaching the scale of the event. Further, public judgement about managerial competence affects societal impact to a greater extent than does the number of casualties and to a similar extent as does the amount of property damage. These findings also support the claim that risk signal, depicted as perceptions of managerial incompetence and future risk, operates through its ability to stimulate public behaviour and does not directly cause event impact.

The implications of our findings suggest that focusing solely on the probability and magnitude of physical consequences may greatly underestimate the actual impact of an event. Misjudging event impact can occur, for example, by either failing to consider important exogenous variables (eg risk signal) or by failing to understand the paths through which these exogenous factors operate (eg ignoring intervening variables like media coverage). For instance, model estimates suggest that the public's assessment of how competently a hazard is being managed plays a more important role than number of casualties in predicting event impact. Thus, by concentrating only on the number of casualties it is possible to underestimate the impact of an event that causes few injuries but is perceived to represent gross managerial incompetence. Likewise, though the total effect of scale, casualties and property damage on event impact is substantial, the direct effect of each is much smaller. Hence, ignoring intervening factors like media coverage and public response may cause forecasts of event impact to be inaccurate.

Understanding how people perceive different types of hazards may not only improve predictions of impact but may mitigate long-term consequences by fostering communication between risk managers and the public. The theory of risk amplification predicts that the societal cost of a hazardous event is determined, to a large extent, by what the event signals or portends. The findings of this study support the conclusion that when an event implies that the hazard is improperly managed or that the future risk is great, the public and its representatives will act to reduce this threat. The public in a sense examines the significance of the event while formulating behavioural intentions to tolerate the risk or take actions against the risk and perhaps against those in charge of the risk. Lack of evidence linking the number of casualties and the amount of property damage to public response suggests the public does not use this information alone as a cue to action. However, the public does seem sensitive to the scale of the event, particularly events affecting large areas. The scale of an event may, in the public's mind, be more diagnostic of personal risk than reports of the number of casualties. The Tylenol poisonings represent a potent example of public reaction to an event that is perceived as exposing large numbers of people to danger despite the fact that relatively few people were banned. Mitchell[17] examined the effect of these poisonings on the stock prices of Johnson & Johnson, Inc. and estimated a loss of $2.11 billion to shareholders. He placed the losses realized by other over-the-counter drug companies at about $4.06 billion.

Study Limitations

The risk events in this study were not selected randomly but were chosen in accord with the taxonomy suggested by Hohenemser et al.[12] As a result, we cannot rely on sampling theory to assess how close the sample covariance matrix conforms to some population matrix. However, the Hohenemser taxonomy is a reasonable representation of the world of hazards, and the model variables were approximately normally distributed across the chosen events. Even so, generalizations beyond this sample must be made cautiously and model estimates should be treated as more descriptive of sample characteristics than inferential of population parameters.

While this study has examined variables indicative of risk signal – namely, perceptions of managerial incompetence and future risk – inclusion of other variables such as dread or familiarity may lead to a fuller portrayal of risk signal. Perceptions of managerial incompetence and threat from future risk are powerful motifs but may represent higher-order concerns relative to signals such as dread.

Public response has been measured in this study by variables representing behavioural intentions. According to Ajzen and Fishbein,[18] the immediate antecedent of any behaviour is the intention to perform the behaviour in question. However, more research is needed to determine how well intentions predict public response to risk.

Similarly, the behavioural intentions university students display towards a hazardous event may be different from those of the general population.

The amplification of risk framework depicts the media as a potential amplification source and hence the media is predicted to exert a strong influence on people's perception of risk and their likely response. However, we were unable to examine this assertion because our survey may have been the only exposure respondents had to many of these events. Failure to capture these important influences undoubtedly affected our path estimates. The most likely effect was to overestimate the direct influence of media coverage on event impact. Event impact itself was only assessed by means of Delphi judgements. Better modelling and analysis of impact is needed.

Prescriptive Implications

Understanding factors that contribute to the impact of a hazardous event and marshalling this insight to promote sound decision strategies will become increasingly important for risk managers. We have restricted our attention to structural models; however, Burns and Clemen[15] have shown how to convert a causal model to a decision analytic technique known as a Gaussian influence diagram.[19] Influence diagrams provide a vehicle for incorporating decision and criterion variables into a structural model, thus allowing the decision maker to move from a purely descriptive portrayal of the environment to a prescriptive analysis of the decision situation. In addition, the decision-analysis perspective can be of value in the early stages of developing the structural model by helping the researcher to identify and focus on issues important to decision makers. Hence, structural models and influence diagrams can be used in tandem to provide a more comprehensive approach to the management of risk.

References

1   R Keeney (1980) 'Evaluating Alternatives Involving Potential Fatalities', in *Operations Research* no 28, pp188–205
2   S Krimsky and D Golding (1992) *Theories of Social Risk* Praeger-Greenwood, Westport, CT
3   P Slovic (1987) 'Perception of Risk,' Science no 236, pp280–285
4   L Clarke (1989) *Acceptable Risk: Making Decisions in a Toxic Environment*, University of California Press, Berkeley, California
5   B Wynne (1992) 'Misunderstood Understanding: Social Identities and Public Uptake of Science' in *Public Understanding of Science*, no 1, pp281–304
6   C Perrow (1984) *Normal Accidents: Living with High Risk Technologies* Basic Books, New York
7   W Freudenburg (1989) *The Organizational Attenuation of Risk Estimate* paper presented at the Society for Risk Analysis Meeting, San Francisco, October/November
8   R Kasperson and J Kasperson (1983) 'Determining the Acceptability of Risk: Ethical and Policy Issues' in J Rogers and D Bates (eds), *Assessment and Perception of Human Health* Royal Society of Canada, Ottawa, pp135–155

9   S Rayner and R Cantor (1987) 'How Fair Is Safe Enough? The Cultural Approach to Societal Technology Choice' in *Risk Analysis* no 7, pp3–9

10 R E Kasperson, O Renn, P Slovic, H S Brown, J Emel, R Goble, J X Kasperson and S Ratick (1988) 'The Social Amplification of Risk: A Conceptual Flamework' in *Risk Analysis* no 8, pp177–187

11 P Slovic (1990) 'Perception of Risk from Radiation', in W K Sinclair (ed), *Prceedings of the Twenty-fifth Annual Meeting of the National Council on Radiation Protection and Measurements, Vol 11: Radiation Protection Today: The NCRP at Sixty Years* NCRP, Bethesda, Maryland, pp73–97

12 C Hohenemser, R W Kates and P Slovic (1983) 'The Nature of Technological Hazard', *Science* no 220, pp378–384

13 J C Anderson and D W Gerbing (1988) 'Structural Equation Modeling in Practice: A Review and Recommended Two-Step Approach', in *Psychological Bulletin* no 103, pp411–423

14 C Fornell, 'A Second Generation of Multivariate Analysis: Classification of Methods and Implications for Marketing Research', (1987) in M J Houston (ed) *The Review of Marketing 87: Section 6* American Marketing Association, Chicago, pp407–450

15 W J Burns and R T Clemen (1993) 'Covariance Structure Models and Influence Diagrams', in *Management Science* no 39, pp816–834

16 P Bentler (1989) *EQS Structural Equations Program Manual,* Version 3.0, BMDP Statistical Software, Los Angeles, CA

17 M L Mitchell (1989) 'The Impact of External Parties on Brand-Name Capital: The Tylenol Poisonings and Subsequent Cases', in *Economic Inquiry* no 27, pp601–618

18 I Ajzen and P Fishbein (1980) *Understanding Attitudes and Predicting Social Behavior* Prentice Hall, Englewood Cliffs, NJ

19 R Shachter and C Kenley (1989) 'Gaussian Influence Diagrams', in *Management Science* no 35, pp527–550

Perceived Risk, Trust and Democracy

Paul Slovic

Introduction

My objective in this paper is to examine the interplay between several remarkable trends within our society pertaining to the perception and management of risk.

The first of these trends is the fact that during a 20-year period during which American society has grown healthier and safer on average and spent billions of dollars and immense effort to become so, the American public has become more – rather than less – concerned about risk. We have come to perceive ourselves as increasingly vulnerable to life's hazards and to believe that our land, air and water are more contaminated by toxic substances than ever before.

A second dramatic trend – that I believe is closely related to the first – is the fact that risk assessment and risk management (like many other facets of our society) have become much more contentious. Polarized views, controversy and overt conflict have become pervasive. Frustrated scientists and industrialists castigate the public for behaviours they judge to be based on irrationality or ignorance. Members of the public feel similarly antagonistic toward industry and government. A desperate search for salvation through risk-communication efforts began in the mid-1980s – yet, despite some localized successes, this effort has not stemmed the major conflicts or reduced much of the dissatisfaction with risk management.

Early studies of risk perception demonstrated that the public's concerns could not simply be blamed on ignorance or irrationality. Instead, research showed that many of the public's reactions to risk could be attributed to a sensitivity to technical, social and psychological qualities of hazards that were not well-modelled in technical risk assessments (eg qualities such as uncertainty in risk assessments, perceived inequity in the distribution of risks and benefits, and aversion to being exposed to risks that were involuntary, not under one's control, or dreaded). The important role of social values in risk perception and risk acceptance thus became apparent.[1]

More recently, another important aspect of the risk–perception problem has come to be recognized. This is the role of trust. In recent years there have been numerous articles and surveys pointing out the importance of trust in risk management and documenting the extreme distrust we now have in many of the individuals, industries and institutions responsible for risk management. This pervasive distrust has also been shown to be strongly linked to risk perception and to political activism to reduce risk.[2-6]

In this paper I shall look beyond current perceptions of risk and distrust and attempt to explain how they came to be this way. My explanation begins with the idiosyncrasies of individual human minds, befitting my background as a psychologist. However, individual psychology is not fully adequate to account for risk perception and conflict. A broader perspective is necessary, one that includes the complex mix of scientific, social, political, legal, institutional and psychological factors operating within our society's risk-management system.

The Importance of Trust

Everyone knows intuitively that trust is important for all forms of human social interaction. Perhaps because it is such a familiar concept, its importance in risk management has not been adequately appreciated. However, numerous recent studies clearly point to *lack of trust* as a critical factor underlying the divisive controversies that surround the management of technological hazards.[7-21]

To appreciate the importance of trust, it is instructive to compare those risks that we fear and avoid with those we casually accept. Starr[22] has pointed to the public's lack of concern about the risks from tigers in urban zoos as evidence that acceptance of risks is strongly dependent on confidence in risk management. Similarly, risk–perception research[23] documents that people view medical technologies based on use of radiation and chemicals (ie X-rays and prescription drugs) as high in benefit, low in risk and clearly acceptable. However, they view *industrial* technologies involving radiation and chemicals (ie nuclear power, pesticides, industrial chemicals) as high in risk, low in benefit and unacceptable. Although X-rays and medicines pose significant risks, our relatively high degree of trust in the physicians who manage these devices makes them acceptable. Numerous polls have shown that the government and industry officials who oversee the management of nuclear power and non-medical chemicals are not highly trusted.[3,6,18,24]

During the past several decades, the field of risk assessment has developed to impart rationality to the management of technological hazards. Risk assessment has its roots in epidemiology, toxicology, systems analysis, reliability theory and many other disciplines. Probably more than $1 billion has been spent to conduct innumerable animal bioassays and epidemiological studies to assess the human health consequences of exposure to radiation and chemicals and to develop probabilistic risk analyses for nuclear reactors, dams, hazardous waste treatment and other engineered facilities. The Environmental Protection Agency, the Nuclear Regulatory Commission and numerous other government agencies have made risk assessment the centrepiece of their regulatory efforts.[25-27]

It is now evident that public perceptions and acceptance of risk from nuclear and chemical technologies are not much influenced by technical risk assessments. Nowhere is this phenomenon more dramatically illustrated than in the unsuccessful struggle, across many years, to dispose of the accumulating volume of spent fuel from the nation's commercial nuclear reactors. The Department of Energy's programme to establish a national repository has been stymied by overwhelming public opposition, fuelled by public perceptions that the risks are immense and unacceptable.[6] These perceptions stand in stark contrast to the prevailing view of the technical community, whose risk assessments assert that nuclear wastes can be disposed of safely in an underground repository (see Table 8.1). Public fears and opposition to nuclear-waste disposal plans can be seen as a 'crisis in confidence', a profound breakdown of trust in the scientific, governmentaly and industrial managers of nuclear technologies. It is clear that the Department of Energy and the US Congress have not adequately appreciated the importance of (dis)trust in the failure of the nuclear-waste programme, nor have they recognized the implications of this situation.[6,21] Analogous crises of confidence can be demonstrated in numerous controver sies surrounding exposures to chemicals. Again, risk assessment, in these situations based primarily on toxicology, is often impotent when it comes to resolving conflict about chemical risks.[28]

Because it is impossible to exclude the public in our uniquely participatory democracy, the response of industry and government to this crisis of confidence has been to turn to the young and still primitive field of risk communication in search of methods to bring experts and lay people into alignment and make conflicts over technological decisions easier to resolve (see, eg William Ruckelshaus' stirring speeches on this topic,[26,29] the National Academy of Sciences report on risk communication[30] and the Chemical Manufacturers' Association communication manual for plant managers[31]). Although attention to communication can prevent blunders that exacerbate conflict, there is rather little evidence that risk communication has made any significant contribution to reducing the gap between technical risk assessments and public perceptions or to facilitating decisions about nuclear waste or other major sources of risk conflict. The limited effectiveness of risk-communication efforts can be attributed to the lack of trust. If you trust the risk manager, communication is

Table 8.1

The following comments reflect expert viewpoints on the risks from nuclear-waste disposal and the public's perceptions of these risks.

'Several years ago... I talked with Sir John Hill, ...chairman of the United Kingdom's Atomic Energy Authority. "I've never come across any industry where the public perception of the problem is so totally different from the problems as seen by those of us in the industry...," Hill told me. In Hill's view, the problem of radioactive waste disposal was, in a technical sense, comparatively easy.' L J Carter (1987) *Nuclear Imperatives and Public Trust.* Resources for the Future, Inc., Washington, DC, p9

'Nuclear wastes can be sequestered with essentially no chance of any member of the public receiving a non-stochastic dose of radiation. ...Why is the public's perception of the nuclear waste issue at such odds with the experts' perception?' A M Weinberg (1989) *Public Perceptions of Hazardous Technologies and Democratic Political Institutions* paper presented at Waste Management '89, Tucson, Arizona, pp1–2

'The fourth major reason for public misunderstanding of nuclear power is a grossly unjustified fear of the hazards from radioactive waste...there is general agreement among those scientists involved with waste management that radioactive waste disposal is a rather trivial technical problem.' B L Cohen (1989) *Before It's Too Late: A Scientist's Case for Nuclear Energy* Plenum, New York, p119

'The risk is as negligible as it is possible to imagine...It is embarrassingly easy to solve the technical problems, yet impossible to solve the political ones.' W W Lewis (1990) *Technological Risk* W W Norton, New York, pp245–246

---

relatively easy. If trust is lacking, no form or process of communication will be satisfactory.[32] Thus, trust is more fundamental to conflict resolution than is risk communication.

Creation and Destruction of Trust

One of the most fundamental qualities of trust has been known for ages. Trust is fragile. It is typically created rather slowly, but it can be destroyed in an instant – by a single mishap or mistake. Thus, once trust is lost, it may take a long time to rebuild it to its former state. In some instances, lost trust may never be regained. Abraham Lincoln understood this quality. In a letter to Alexander McClure he observed: 'If you *once* forfeit the confidence of your fellow citizens, you can *never* regain their respect and esteem' (italics added).

The asymmetry between the difficulty of creating trust and the ease of destroying it has been studied by social psychologists within the domain of interpersonal perception. For example, Rothbart and Park[33] had people rate 150 descriptive traits (adventurous, gentle, lazy, trustworthy, etc) in terms of the number of relevant behavioural instances necessary to establish or disconfirm the trait. Favourable traits (like trustworthiness) were judged to be hard to acquire (many behavioural instances needed) and easy to lose. Unfavourable traits were judged to be easier to acquire and harder to lose. The number of behavioural instances required to disconfirm a negative quality (eg dishonesty) was greater than the number required to disconfirm a positive trait. As Abraham Lincoln might have predicted, trustworthiness stood out among the 150 traits as requiring a relatively large number of confirming instances to establish the trait and a relatively small number of relevant instances to disconfirm it. (Note that data here were judgements of the number of instances that would be required as opposed to data documenting the number of instances that actually confirmed or disconfirmed a trait.)

The fact that trust is easier to destroy than to create reflects certain fundamental mechanisms of human psychology that I shall call 'the asymmetry principle'. When it comes to winning trust, the playing field is not level. It is tilled towards distrust, for each of the following reasons:

1. Negative (trust-destroying) events are more visible or noticeable than positive (trust-building) events. Negative events often take the form of specific, well-defined incidents such as accidents, lies, discoveries of errors or other mismanagement. Positive events, while sometimes visible, more often are fuzzy or indistinct. For example, how many positive events are represented by the safe operation of a nuclear power plant for one day? Is this one event? Dozens of events? Hundreds? There is no precise answer. When events are invisible or poorly defined, they carry little or no weight in shaping our attitudes and opinions.

2. When events do come to our attention, negative (trust-destroying) events carry much greater weight than positive events. This important psychological tendency is illustrated by a study in which my colleagues and I asked 103 college students to rate the impact on trust of 45 hypothetical news events pertaining to the management of a large nuclear power plant in their connmunity.[34] Some of these events were designed to be trust increasing, such as:

• There have been no reported safety problems at the plant during the past year.

- There is careful selection and training of employees at the plant.
- Plant managers live nearby the plant.
- The county medical examiner reports that the health of people living near the plant is *better* than the average for the region.

Other events were designed to be trust decreasing, such as:

- A potential safety problem was found to have been covered up by plant officials.
- Plant safety inspections are delayed in order to meet the electricity production quota for the month.
- A nuclear power plant in another state has a serious accident.
- The county medical examiner reports that the health of people living near the plant is *worse* than the average for the region.

The respondents were asked to indicate, for each event, whether their trust in the management of the plant would be increased or decreased upon learning of that event. After doing this, they rated how strongly their trust would be affected by the

Figure 8.1 *Differential impact of trust-increasing and trust-decreasing event.*
Note: Only percentages of Category 7 ratings (very powerful impact) are shown here.

185

event on a scale ranging from 1 (very small impact on trust) to 7 (very powerful impact on trust).

The percentages of Category 7 ratings, shown in Figure 8.1, dramatically demonstrate that negative events are seen as far more likely to have a powerful effect on trust than are positive events. The data shown in Table 8.2 are typical. The negative event, reporting plant neighbours' health as *worse* than average, was rated 6 or 7 on the impact scale by 50.0 per cent of the respondents. A matched event, reporting neighbours' health to be *better* than average was rated 6 or 7 by only 18.3 per cent of the respondents.

There was only one event perceived to have any substantial impact on increasing trust. This event stated that: 'An advisory board of local citizens and environmentalists is established to monitor the plant and is given legal authority to shut the plant down if they believe it to be unsafe.'

This strong delegation of authority to the local public was rated 6 or 7 on the impact scale by 38.4 per cent of the respondents. Although this was a far stronger showing than for any other positive event, it would have been a rather average performance in the distribution of impacts for negative events.

The reasons for the greater impact of trust-destroying incidents are complex, and I shall not discuss them here except to note that the importance of an event is at least in part related to its frequency (or rarity). An accident in a nuclear plant is more informative with regard to risk than is a day (or even a large number of days) without an accident. Thus, in systems where we are concerned about low-probability/high-consequence events, problematic events will increase our perceptions of risk to a much greater degree than favourable events will decrease them.

3. Adding fuel to the fire of asymmetry is yet another idiosyncracy of human psychology – sources of bad (trust-destroying) news tend to be seen as more credible than sources of good news. For example, in several studies of what we call 'intuitive toxicology',[35] we have examined people's confidence in the ability of animal studies to predict human health effects from chemicals. In general, confidence in the validity of animal studies is not particularly high. However, when told that a study has found that a chemical is carcinogenic in animals, people express consid-

Table 8.2 *Judged impact of a trust-increasing event and a similar trust-decreasing event[a]*

	Impact on trust						
	Very small						Very powerful
	1	2	3	4	5	6	7
Trust-increasing event The county medical examiner reports that the health of people living near the plant is *better* than average	21.5	14.0	10.8	18.3	17.2	16.1	2.2
Trust-decreasing event The county medical examiner reports that the health of people living near the plant is *worse* than average	3.0	8.0	2.0	16.0	21.0	26.0	24.0

[a] Cell entries indicate the percentage of respondents in each impact rating category.

erable confidence in the validity of this study for predicting health effects in humans. Regulators respond like the public. Positive (bad news) evidence from animal bioassays is presumptive evidence of risk to humans; negative evidence (eg the chemical was not found to be harmful) carries little weight.[36]

4. Another important psychological tendency is that distrust, once initiated, tends to reinforce and perpetuate distrust. This occurs in two ways. First, distrust tends to inhibit the kinds of personal contacts and experiences that are necessary to overcome distrust. By avoiding others whose motives or actions we distrust, we never get to see if these people are competent, well-meaning and trustworthy. Second, initial trust or distrust colours our interpretation of events, thus reinforcing our prior beliefs. Persons who trusted the nuclear power industry saw the events at Three Mile Island as demonstrating the soundness of the 'defence in depth' principle, noting that the multiple safety systems shut the plant down and contained most of its radiation. Persons who distrusted nuclear power prior to the accident took an entirely different message from the same events, perceiving that those in charge did not understand what was wrong or how to fix it and that catastrophe was averted only by sheer luck.

The System Destroys Trust

Thus far, I have been discussing the psychological tendencies that create and reinforce distrust in situations of risk. Appreciation of those psychological principles leads us toward a new perspective on risk perception, trust and conflict. Conflicts and controversies surrounding risk management are not due to public irrationality or ignorance but, instead, can be seen as expected side effects of these psychological tendencies, interacting with our remarkable form of participatory democratic government, and amplified by certain powerful technological and social changes in our society. The technological change has given the electronic and print media the capability (effectively utilized) of informing us of news from all over the world – often right as it happens. Moreover, just as individuals give greater weight and attention to negative events, so do the news media. Much of what the media reports is bad (trust-destroying) news.[37] This is convincingly demonstrated by Koren and Klein,[38] who compared the rates of newspaper reporting of two studies, one providing bad news and one good news, published back to back in the 20 March 1991 issue of the *Journal of the American Medical Association.* Both studies examined the link between radiation exposure and cancer. The bad news study showed an increased risk of leukaemia in white men working at the Oak Ridge National Laboratory. The good news study failed to show an increased risk of cancer in people residing near nuclear facilities. Koren and Klein found that subsequent newspaper coverage was far greater for the study showing increased risk.

The second important change, a social phenomenon, is the rise of powerful special interest groups – well-funded (by a fearful public) and sophisticated in using their own experts and the media to communicate their concerns and their distrust to the public in order to influence risk policy debates and decisions.[39] The social problem is compounded by the fact that we tend to manage our risks within an adversarial legal system that pits expert vs expert, contradicting each other's risk assessments and further destroying the public trust.

The young science of risk assessment is too fragile, too indirect, to prevail in such a hostile atmosphere. Scientific analysis of risks cannot allay our fears of low-probability catastrophes or delayed cancers unless we trust the system. In the absence of trust, science (and risk assessment) can only feed distrust, by uncovering more bad news. A single study demonstrating an association between exposure to chemicals or radiation and some adverse health effect cannot easily be offset by numerous studies failing to find such an association. Thus, for example, the more studies that are conducted looking for effects of electric and magnetic fields or other difficult-to-evaluate hazards, the more likely it is that these studies will increase public concerns, even if the majority of these studies fail to find any association with ill health.[40,41] In short, such risk-assessment studies tend to increase perceived risk.

Where Next? Risk and Democracy

Although the study of risk perception and trust has not yet led to a solution to our risk-management problems, it appears to be leading to a more adequate diagnosis of the root causes of risk concerns and risk conflicts. As we begin to understand the complexity of risk conflicts, we recognize the need for new approaches to risk management. The road branches in two very different directions.[42] One direction leads toward less public participation and more centralized control. One might call this the French model. France leads the world in the percentage of electricity generated by nuclear power (73 per cent in 1991, compared to 21 per cent for the US). France, like the US, was rocked by strong antinuclear protests during the late 1970s, but the state acted forcefully to repress these protests and the antinuclear movement never gained favour with the political parties in power. Today, surprisingly, the perception of risk from nuclear power remains extremely high in France – as high as in the US according to national surveys my colleagues and I recently conducted in both countries. However, French citizens, while recognizing that they have little control over risks to their health and safety, have a high degree of trust in their government and in the experts who design and operate nuclear power plants. Americans, in contrast, combine their similarly high degree of perceived risk with a distrust of government, science and industry, and a belief that they do have some ability to control risks. In fact, the American system does provide individual citizens and citizen groups considerable freedom to intervene in administrative proceedings, to question expert judgements of government agencies and to force changes in policy through litigation.[43]

Political scientists have recognized that, in a climate of strong distrust, the French approach, in which policy formation and implementation is not accessible to public intervention, is expedient.[44] Campbell,[45] for example, argues that formal democratic institutions providing political access to nuclear critics may be fundamentally incompatible with commercial success of nuclear power.

What works in France, however, is unlikely to be achievable in the US. The French nuclear power programme is run by the state, not private industry. Electricité de France has long had a strong reputation for being competent and putting service above profits. The French have a tradition of looking to a scientific elite for guidance in policy matters. Jasper,[46] noting that the word as well as the image of a 'technocrat' arose in France, observed that 'Perhaps no other political system provides as large a role for people to exercise power on the basis of technical training and certification' (p83).

America, since Thomas Jefferson, has had a different approach to democracy, and it is not surprising that attempts to restrict citizens' rights to intervene directly in national risk-management policies have been vigorously opposed. A recent example is the unsuccessful attempt in Congress to strip the state of Nevada of its rights to issue environmental and safety permits for nuclear waste studies at Yucca Mountain.[47]

Given that the French approach is not likely to be acceptable in the US, restoration of trust may require a degree of openness and involvement with the public that goes far beyond public relations and 'two-way communication' to encompass levels of power sharing and public participation in decision making that have rarely been attempted.[48–50] Even this, however, is no guarantee of success.[51,52] In many situations, we may have to recognize that relationships are so poisoned that trust and conflict resolution cannot realistically be achieved in the short run. The bitter conflict over the proposed nuclear waste repository in Nevada is a prime example of such a situation. To preserve the form of democracy we value so highly, we will need to develop ways to work constructively in situations where we cannot assume that trust is attainable.[15]

We have a long way to go in improving our risk–management processes. Although we have expended massive amounts of time, money and resources on scientific studies designed to identify and quantify risks, we have failed to expend the effort needed to learn how to manage the hazards that science is so good at identifying. Gerald Jacob[53] frames the challenge well in the context of nuclear waste disposal, and his words are also relevant to many other risk problems:

> *While everyone can appreciate that a complex, highly sophisticated engineering is required to safely store nuclear materials for thousands of years, few have appreciated the political requirements necessary to design and implement such a solution. While vast resources have been expended on developing complex and sophisticated technologies, the equally sophisticated political processes and institutions required to develop a credible and legitimate strategy for nuclear waste management have not been developed. The history of high-level radioactive waste management describes repeated failure to recognize the need for institutional reform and reconstruction (p164).*

Some may view the analysis in this paper as a depressing one. I do not. Understanding the root causes of social conflict and recognizing the need to create better risk-management processes are essential first steps toward improving the situation. It is far more depressing, in my view, to fail to understand the complex psychological, social, cultural and political forces that dictate the successes and failures of risk management.

References

1   P Slovic (1987) 'Perception of Risk' in *Science* no 236, pp280–285
2   R J Bord and R E O'Connor (1990) 'Risk Communication, Knowledge, and Attitudes: Explaining Reactions to a Technology Perceived as Risky' in *Risk Analysis*, no 10, pp499–506

3   J Flynn, W Burns, C K Mertz and P Slovic (1992) 'Trust as a Determinant of Op-
    position to a High-Level Radioactive Waste Repository: Analysis of a Structural
    Model' in *Risk Analysis* no 12, pp417–430
4   H C Jenkins-Smith (1992) *'Culture, Trust, Ideology and Perceptions of the Risks
    of Nuclear Wastes: A Causal Analysis'* paper prepared for the Annual Meeting
    of the Society for Risk Analysis, San Diego, California, 6–9 December
5   A H Mushkatel and K D Pijawka (1992) *Institutional Trust, Information, and Risk
    Perceptions: Report of Findings of the Las Vegas Metropolitan Area Survey, 29 June–
    1 July 1992* (NWPO-SE-055-92) Nevada Nuclear Waste Project Office, Carson
    City, Nevada
6   P Slovic, J Flynn and M Layman (1991) 'Perceived Risk, Trust, and the Politics
    of Nuclear Waste' in *Science* no 254, pp1603–1607
7   D A Bella (1987) 'Engineering and Erosion of Trust' in *Journal of Professional
    Issues in Engineering* no 113, pp117–129
8   D A Bella, C D Mosher and S N Calvo (1988) 'Establishing Trust: Nuclear Waste
    Disposal' in *Journal of Professional Issues in Engineering* no 114, pp40–50
9   D A Bella, C D Mosher and S N Calvo (1988) 'Technocracy and Trust: Nuclear
    Waste Controversy' *Journal of Professional Issues in Engineering* no 114,
    pp27–39
10 G Cvetkovich and T C Earle (1992) *Social Trust and Value Similarity: New Inter-
    pretations of Risk Communication in Hazard Management* paper presented for
    the Annual Meeting of the Society for Risk Analysis, San Diego, California, 6–9
    December
11 M R English (1992) S*iting Low-Level Radioactive Waste Disposal Facilities: The
    Public Policy Dilemma* Quorum, New York
12 J Flynn and P Slovic (1993) 'Nuclear Wastes and Public Trust' in *Forum for Ap-
    plied Research and Public Policy* no 8, pp92–100
13 W Freudenburg, *Risk and Recreancy: Weber, the Division of Labor, and the Ratio-
    nality of Risk Perceptions* (1991) unpublished manuscript, Department of Ru-
    ral Sociology, University of Wisconsin, Madison
14 B B Johnson *Trust in Theory: Many Questions, Few Answers* (1992) paper pre-
    sented for the Annual Meeting of the Society for Risk Analysis, San Diego, Cali-
    fornia, 6–9 December
15 R Kasperson, D Golding and S Tuler (1992) 'Social Distrust as a Factor in Sit-
    ing Hazardous Facilities and Communicating Risks' in *Journal of Social Issues*
    no 48, pp161–187
16 F N Laird (1989) 'The Decline of Deference: The Political Context of Risk Com-
    munication' in *Risk Analysis* no 9, pp543–550
17 J V Mitchell (1992) 'Perception of Risk and Credibility at Toxic Sites' in *Risk Analy-
    sis* no 12, pp19–26
18 K D Pijawka and A H Mushkatel (1992) 'Public Opposition to the Siting of the
    High-Level Nuclear Waste Repository: The Importance of Trust' in *Policy Stud-
    ies Review* no 10, pp180–194
19 S Rayner and R Cantor (1987) 'How Fair Is Safe Enough? The Cultural Approach
    to Societal Technology Choice' in *Risk Analysis* no 7, pp3–9
20 O Renn and D Levine (1991) 'Credibility and Trust in Risk Communication' in
    R E Kasperson and P J M Stallen (eds) *Communicating Risks to the Public* Kluwer
    Academic, Dordrecht, pp175–218
21 US Department of Energy (1992) *Draft Final Report of the Secretary of Energy Ad-
    visory Board Task Force on Radioactive Waste Management* Washington, DC

22 C Starr (1985) 'Risk Management, Assessment, and Acceptability' in *Risk Analysis* no 5, pp97–102
23 P Slovic (1990) 'Perception of Risk from Radiation' in W K Sinclair (ed), *Proceedings of the Twenty-Fifth Annual Meeting of the National Council on Radiation Protection and Measurements. Vol 11: Radiation Protection Today: The NCRP at Sixty Years* NCRP, Bethesda, Maryland, pp73–97
24 D V McCallum, S L Hammond, L A Morris and V T Coveilo (1990) *'Public Knowledge and Perceptions of Chemical Risks in Six Communities'* Report no 230-01-90-074, US Environmental Protection Agency, Washington, DC
25 S Levin (1984) 'Probabilistic Risk Assessment: Identifying the Real Risks of Nuclear Power' in *Technology Review* no 87, pp40–44
26 V D Ruckelshaus (1983) 'Science, Risk, and Public Policy' in *Science* no 221, pp1026–1028
27 US Nuclear Regulatory Commission (1983) *Safety Goals for Nuclear Power Plant Operation* USNRC Report NUREG-0880, Washington, DC
28 J D Graham, L C Green and M J Roberts (1988) *In Search of Safety: Chemicals and Cancer Risk* Harvard, Cambridge, Massachusetts
29 W D Ruckelshaus (1984) 'Risk in a Free Society' in *Risk Analysis* no 4, pp157–162
30 National Research Council (1989), *Improving Risk Communication* National Academy Press, Washington, DC
31 V T Covello, P M Sandman and P Slovic (1988) *Risk Communication, Risk Statistics, and Risk Comparisons: A Manual for Plant Managers* Chemical Manufacturers Association, Washington, DC
32 J Fessendon-Raden, J M Fitchen and J S Heath (1987) 'Providing Risk Information in Communities: Factors Influencing What Is Heard and Accepted' in *Science Technology and Human Values* no 12, pp94–101
33 N Rothbart and B Park (1986) 'On the Confirmability and Disconfirmability of Trait Concepts' in *Journal of Personality and Social Psychology* no 50, pp131–142
34 P Slovic, J Flynn, S Johnson and C K Mertz (1993) *'The Dynamics of Trust in Situations of Risk'* report no 93-2, Decision Research, Eugene, Oregon
35 N Kraus, T Malmfors and P Slovic (1992) 'Intuitive Toxicology: Expert and Lay Judgments of Chemical Risk' in *Risk Analysis* no 12, pp215–232
36 E Efron (1984) *The Apocalyptics* Simon & Schuster, New York
37 J Lichtenberg and D MacLean (1992) 'Is Good News No News?' *The Geneva Papers on Risk and Insurance* no 17, pp362–365
38 G Koren and N Klein (1991) 'Bias Against Negative Studies in Newspaper Reports of Medical Research' in *Journal of the American Medical Association* no 266, pp1824–1826
39 *Wall Street Journal* (1989) 'How a PR Firm Executed the Alar Scare' ppAl–A3, 3 October
40 D MacGregor, P Slovic and M G Morgan (1992) *Perception of Risks from Electromagnetic Fields: A Psychometric Evaluation of a Risk-Communication Approach* report no 92-6, Decision Research, Eugene, Oregon
41 M G Morgan, P Slovic, I Nair, D Geisler, D MacGregor, B Fischhoff, D Lincoln, and K Florig (1985) 'Powerline Frequency Electric and Magnetic Fields: A Pilot Study of Risk Perception' in *Risk Analysis* no 5, pp139–149
42 D Fiorino (1989) 'Technical and Democratic Values in Risk Analysis' in *Risk Analysis* no 9, pp293–299
43 S Jasanoff (1986) *Risk Management and Political Culture* Russell Sage Foundation, New York

44 J F Morone and E J Woodhouse (1989) *The Demise of Nuclear Energy? Lessons for a Democratic Control of Technology* Yale University, New Haven, CT

45 J L Campbell, *Collapse of an Industry: Nuclear Power and the Contradictions of U.S. Policy* Cornell University Press, Ithaca, New York

46 T M Jasper (1990) *Nuclear Politics: Energy and the State in the United States, Sweden, and France* University Press, Princeton, NJ

47 T Batt (1992) 'Nevada Claims Victory in Yucca Deal' in *Las Vegas Review-Journal* 23 July, pp1A–3A

48 H Flynn, R Kasperson, H Kunreuther, and P Slovic (1992) Time to Rethink Nuclear Waste Storage', *Issues in Science and Technology* no 8, pp42–48

49 H Kunreuther, T D Aarts and K Fitzgerald (1993) 'Siting Noxious Facilities: A Test of the Faculty Siting Credo' in *Risk Analysis* no13, pp301–318

50 D H Leroy and T S Nadler (1993) 'Negotiate Way Out of Siting Dilemmas' in *Forum for Applied Research and Public Policy* no 8, pp102–107

51 R J Bord (1988) 'The Low-Level Radioactive Waste Crisis: Is More Citizen Participation the Answer?' in M A Burns (ed), *Low-Level Radioactive Waste Regulation: Science, Politics, and Fear* Lewis, Chelsea, Michigan, pp193–213

52 D Nelkin and M Pollak (1979) 'Public Participation in Technological Decisions: Reality or Grand Illusion?' in *Technology Review*, pp55–64 August/September

53 G Jacob (1990) *Site Unseen: The Politics of Siting a Nuclear Waste Repository* University of Pittsburgh, Pittsburgh, Pennsylvania

What Determines Trust in Information About Food-Related Risks? Underlying Psychological Constructs

L J Frewer, C Howard, D Hedderley and R Shepherd

Introduction

There is much current debate in the literature about the most effective way in which to convey information about hazards and their associated risks to the public.[1,2] Of great concern is the conveyance of information about food-related hazards, as there is potential for members of the public to alter lifestyle behaviours (eg, in the reduction of fat consumption in the diet) or to accept or reject the consumer products of particular technologies (eg, genetic engineering as applied to food production). People are unlikely to change their behaviour or attitudes if they do not trust the source of risk information. However, to date, little research has been conducted into this particular area of risk communication. The aim of this research was to determine the reasons why some information sources about food-related hazards are trusted and others are not.

Trust in risk information about food-related hazards may be as important a determinant of consumer reactions as the content of the risk information. The risk perception and risk communication literatures have identified the role of trust as being of critical importance.[3] In the case of many technological hazards the responsibility for risk management is considered to be at the level of society.[4] However, public concern with environmental effects resulting from the application of technology has been paralleled by a decline in trust of technology and government regulation of the technology.[5] There has been relatively little empirical research to date which has either examined the effects of trust and distrust, or examined why some sources are trusted while others are not.

One of the central questions addressed by the risk communication literature is *why* some individuals and organizations are trusted as sources of risk information and others are not. For example, government officials are perceived as being insensitive to the information needs and concerns of the public.[6] To be trusted, information must be provided by sources which are not seen as biased or self-serving.[7] If the public believe governments work closely with industry, which may be seen as possessing a vested interest in putting forward a particular point of view, trust in regulation and legislative controls may be reduced.[8]

Social distrust has been cited as one of the most important factors in predicting the public acceptability of siting hazardous facilities and effectively communicating risks about the hazard to the public.[9,10] Disagreement between sections of the public and scientists over the relative risks associated with particular technologies has been interpreted as reflections of underlying public distrust of scientific institutions.[11] The best predictors of perceived risk are the degree to which people trust science, and business and governmental ability to manage danger.[12] Professional risk managers and the general public strongly disagree about the seriousness of many risks.[13] However, it is argued that the conflicts and controversies surrounding risk management are not due to public ignorance or irrationality but are the result of the technological and social changes which systematically destroy trust in the sources of control and providers of risk messages.[14] For example, the decline in public trust in authority has resulted in the resentment and rejection of 'involuntary' risks.[15] Distrust in risk 'managers' has been linked to political activism to reduce risk.[16]

The importance of 'source characteristics' has long been recognized in social psychological models of communication and attitude change.[17] One approach to the study of trustworthiness of information sources in terms of underlying source characteristics is the factor-analytic approach,[18,19] where two major dimensions have emerged as being important in determining trust – that of 'competence', the expertise held by the communicator and the extent to which they are able to pass on information about a particular subject area, and 'trustworthiness', the degree to which the communicator will be truthful in the information communicated. Criticism of this approach has focused on the way in which scales are selected on a predetermined basis, the absence of a context within which communicators are to be rated by respondents, and the interpretation of factor labels across different situations.[20] Typically, respondents make ratings on experimenter-generated characteristics rather than on those which they generate themselves, and refer to ratings of trust removed from the context of a particular hazard type, which may influence ratings.

The first aim of this research was to identify the underlying dimensions of trust in information sources about food-related hazards in order to understand differences in public perceptions of trust in these sources, within a specific hazard domain. We aimed to develop understanding of these underlying dimensions which define trust in information sources from descriptors produced by the respondents themselves, utilizing two methods to ensure that important constructs were not omitted from the analysis. These were the semi-structured interview and the repertory grid method. Second, the results of these two studies were combined and were validated in a larger representative survey, to enable the generalizability of the findings to be assessed and to determine how the underlying factor structure reflected previous research findings.

Study 1: Semi-Structured Interview

Procedures

Fifteen male and 20 female respondents (mean age 39.8 ± 14.7 years) were recruited from a range of occupations. A series of open-ended questions designed to elicit important determinants of trust in different information sources was used to elicit constructs about trust in information sources (Table 8.3). Open-ended questions were used to enable respondents to describe their reasons for trusting or distrusting different sources in their own words, thus avoiding the use of experimenter-generated characteristics to examine the underlying constructs which determine trust. In addition, the use of open-ended interview methodology permitted direct comparison of the results to be made with study 2, which also used respondent-generated characteristics. Respondents were questioned in their own homes by one of three interviewers. In addition, quantitative data were collected to examine the question of whether trust in information about different kinds of food-related issues varied according to information source (Table 8.3). Each respondent completed a quantitative questionnaire following completion of the open-ended questions. The structure of the questionnaire is described in Table 8.3.

Table 8.3 *Questions used in the interview study*

---

a.   Open-ended interview questions
   1. Information about food-related hazards can come from many different sources. Can you name three such sources?
   2. Which of the sources listed in your answer to question 1 would you trust the most to provide information about food-related hazards?
   3. Please state why you gave this answer.
   4. Which of the sources listed in your answer to question 1 would you trust the least to provide information about food-related hazards?
   5. Please state why you gave this answer.
   6. In general, why do you trust information sources?
   7. In general, why do you distrust an information source?
   8. What would cause you to gain trust in an information source?
   9. What would cause you to lose trust in an information source?
b.   Structure of quantitative questionnaire
   'Each of the following sources[a] has provided information about the potential risks associated with alcohol use.[b] Please indicate to what extent you would trust that information should it become available to you.' Ratings were made on 100-mm line scales anchored at one pole by 'trust completely' and the other by 'distrust completely'.

---

[a] Sources included a consumer organization, an environmental pressure group, the food industry, friends, a government minister, a government ministry, a government scientist, a medical doctor, a member of parliament, a supermarket information leaflet, a tabloid newspaper, a television documentary, a television news broadcast, and a university scientist.
[b] Or food irradiation or food poisoning or genetic engineering applied to food production or a high fat diet or microwave ovens or natural toxins or pesticide residues.

Results

Information Sources

The number of respondents who named the media as one of their three primary sources of food-hazard information was as follows: 29 respondents named television, 26 named newspapers, eight named magazines, and five named radio. As many respondents did not specify types of media (eg, stating television rather than television news versus television documentary, or newspaper rather than tabloid newspaper versus quality newspaper), these were not further classified in the analysis. Ten

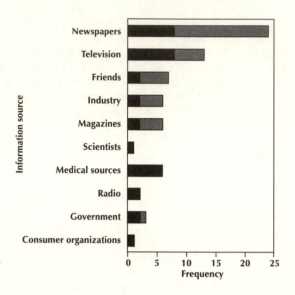

Figure 8.2 *Results from the interview study (study 1). Trusted and distrusted sources of food-related information sources are in the order of frequency mentioned by respondents as being a source of information about food-related hazards.*
■ = *Trusted sources;* ▨ = *Distrusted sources.*

respondents named friends, nine industry (a definition which includes supermarket information and manufacturers' labels on the packets). Scientific sources were named by six respondents, medical sources by six respondents, government sources by four respondents and consumer organizations by two respondents.

The most important and frequently cited source of information about food-related information was therefore the media, with 65 per cent of all named sources being media-related.

The frequency of naming most trusted and least trusted sources of information is given in Figure 8.2.

Previous research has indicated that television current affairs programmes and quality newspapers are among the most trusted sources of information about food-related hazards, whereas the tabloid press and government sources the least trusted.[21] More respondents stated that they distrusted government sources than trusted newspapers. Similarly, a substantial minority named television as a distrusted source. As respondents did not differentiate between different types of newspaper or television programme, these results are not inconsistent with previous research.

Scientists, medical sources, radio and consumer organizations were all named as trusted, but not distrusted, sources. However, they were infrequently named by respondents as important sources of food-related information.

Reasons for Trusting or Distrusting Information

Qualitative data were independently analysed by two independent researchers using a predetermined category system. This category system was subsequently modi-

Table 8.4 *Reasons for trusting or distrusting information – responses from interview study*[a]

Trust (categories)	Trust in information (questions 3 and 6)	Gaining trust (question 8)	Distrust (categories)	Distrust in information (questions 5 and 7)	Losing trust (question 9)
Accountable	1	1	**Amplification**[b]	**16**	2
Expert	**12**	2	**Biased**	**16**	4
Factual	**12**	1	**Lack of knowledge**	7	4
Knowledgable	**12**	3	Not accountable	1	0
No vested interest	**9**	5	**Not factual**	**9**	4
Proactive	2	5	Out of date	0	1
Proven right	11	14	**Proven wrong**	8	**15**
Responsible[c]	**8**	1	**Vested interest**	**14**	3
Truthfulness	**6**	0	What you want to hear	2	0
Unbiased	**13**	**8**	Withholding information	1	3
Other	0	3	Other	2	2

[a] Response categories which have been mentioned by at least five respondents are indicated in bold. These items were later included in the validation study. See Table 8.3 for question numbers.

[b] Defined as the 'source sensationalizing the information, this process increasing chronologically at various stages of information transmission in various stages of information transmission'.

[c] Defined as the 'source feels a responsibility to the public to provide accurate food-related information'.

fied if responses did not fit into a predetermined category. Thus, some new categories were created during the course of analysis, while others were eventually not used at all. In cases of disagreement between the two observers, final categorization was determined by discussion between the two observers until agreement was reached (Table 8.4).

Table 8.4 incorporates both reasons why a particular source, or information sources in general, are trusted or distrusted. The table summarizes the number of respondents out of the total who gave a particular response. The stated reasons why respondents gain or lose trust in information sources are also given.

The most important determinant of gain or loss of trust in a source is whether the information is subsequently proven right or wrong. In the case of gaining trust, an important determinant of trust is that the source is subsequently demonstrated to be unbiased.

Quantitative Data

(a) Differences in Trust Within Sources for Different Hazards.
Analysis of variance was used to test for differences in rated distrust for the different information sources as assessed by the quantitative questionnaire. A significant effect was found ($F_{14,13}$ = 9.84, p < 0.005, Figure 8.3). The pattern of results confirmed the findings of previous research.[19] A similar analysis was applied to test for differences in distrust in information concerning different hazards ($F_{7,20}$ = 2.51, p < 0.05, Figure 8.4). Information about natural toxins, genetic engineering and pesticide residues was most distrusted, and information about high-fat diets, microwave ovens, food poisoning, food irradiation and alcohol use more trusted. One interpretation is that this effect reflects the degree of familiarity people have with the different hazards, such that information about non-familiar hazards is more likely to be

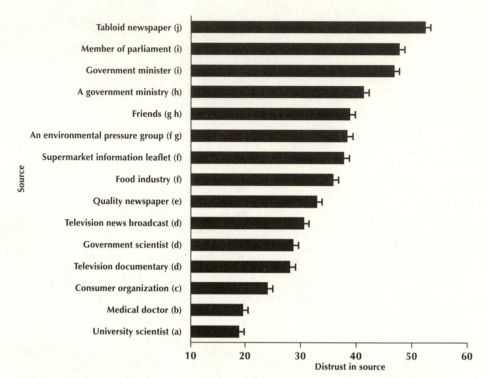

Figure 8.3 *Results from the interview study (study 1). Distrust in different informa-tion sources. Rated distrust for the different information sources used in the semi-structured interview study. Sources identified with the same letters were not significantly different from each other.*

distrusted, as people have no prior knowledge against which to assess new informa-tion. However, further analysis indicated that these effects may be source dependent.

(b) Differences in Trust Ratings

Analysis of variance was used to test for differences in trust ratings between differ-ent hazards within each information source category. Differences in trust in infor-mation about different types of hazard were observed for the information sources 'Friends' ($F_{7,27}$ = 2.97, $p < 0.02$), 'Industry' ($F_{7,28}$ = 3,76, $p < 0.05$), 'Medical Sources' ($F_{7,28}$ = 4.90, $p < 0.001$), and 'Supermarket Information Leaflet' ($F_{7,26}$ = 4.15, $p < 0.003$). Examination of the means (Table 8.5) indicates that, within source categories, dif-ferences in distrust for different hazards appear to be dependent on the perceived characteristics of the source itself.

In the source category 'friends', distrust tended to be greater for 'technological' hazards (genetic engineering of food, pesticide residues, and food irradiation) and 'technical' hazards (natural toxins) compared to 'lifestyle' hazards (high-fat diet, food poisoning, microwave ovens).[4] It is possible that this perceived effect is related to perceived knowledge about the hazards, distrust increasing with decreased source knowledge. The hazard which was an exception to this trend was alcohol use, which, although categorized as a lifestyle hazard, has other associations related to its psy-chotropic and addictive properties. It is possible that information from friends is seen as 'biased' towards a particular viewpoint.

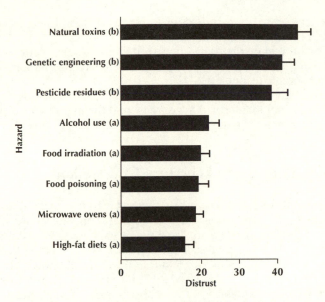

Figure 8.4 *Results from the interview study (study 1). Trust ratings for different food-related hazards. Sources identified with the same letters were not significantly different from each other.*

Similarly, greatest distrust in information provided by industry was associated with 'technological' hazards and alcohol use, whereas greatest trust was associated with 'lifestyle' hazards, microwave ovens and natural toxins. This may again be associated with the perceived knowledge base that industry has about the hazards. Alternatively, increased distrust may be associated with vested interest in the promotion of particular technologies (or, in the case of alcohol, a particular product).

Medical sources are likely to be viewed as 'expert' in medically related areas, less so in technological risk assessment, as this is the nature of their knowledge base.

Table 8.5 *Mean distrust ratings for sources where there were differences by hazard type[a]*

	Information source			
Hazard	*Friends*	*Industry*	*Medical doctor*	*Supermarket information*
Alcohol use	40.6 (3.2) c,d	37.9 (3.4) c,d	16.4 (2.9) b	36.0 (3.3) a
Food irradiation	40.1 (3.5) b,c,d	41.8 (3.4) d	22.6 (2.9) c,d	45.5 (3.5) b
Food poisoning	37.0 (3.4) b	33.1 (3.8) a,b,c	15.2 (2.5) a,b	35.2 (3.7) a
Genetic engineering	41.2 (3.2) d	37.4 (3.6) b,c,d	21.6 (2.8) c	34.2 (3.0) a
High-fat diet	32.1 (3.0) a	32.9 (3.8) a,b	11.6 (1.9) a	36.9 (3.3) a
Microwave ovens	37.1 (2.9) b,c	31.2 (3.5) a	26.3 (3.1) d	37.4 (3.0) a
Natural toxins	42.2 (3.4) d	33.8 (3.7) a,b,c	21.0 (2.7) c	34.4 (3.7) a
Pesticide residues	40.2 (3.3) c,d	38.5 (4.1) d	21.6 (2.8) c,d	42.3 (3.8) a

[a] Means which are not significantly different are identified by the same letters (least significant differences test, $p < 0.05$) within information sources. The standard error is given in parentheses.

Thus, they are trusted to a greater extent in the provision of information about 'lifestyle' hazards than technological hazards.

Supermarkets are more distrusted to provide information about food irradiation. It is again suggested that this is likely to reflect a perceived 'vested interest' in the promotion of specific technologies.

The results of study 1 clearly demonstrate that different psychological constructs are associated with trust in information sources, and the importance of further investigating these constructs in any study of trustworthiness is indicated.

Study 2: The Repertory Grid Method

The advantage of applying the repertory grid method is that individual respondents can determine their own, highly individual, range of descriptions for associated constructs. The resulting data are then analysed using generalized Procrustes analysis (GPA).[22] This methodology and analysis has been successfully applied to free choice profiling in sensory evaluation studies[23-25] and in the study of public perceptions of the risks associated with chemicals in food.[26] Unlike other multivariate techniques, respondents do not use a common set of variables to make ratings, and no assumptions are made regarding the underlying determinants of attitudes at the outset of the experiment. One advantage of the technique is that respondents describe their attitudes toward the stimulus in their own words and are not led to make ratings on items which are not relevant to them as individuals. The second advantage (when comparing the technique to traditional interviewing) is that maps of consensus agreement linking stimuli to the different constructs are provided, which have explanatory value. There is recognition of agreement or disagreement between respondents and the most important constructs can be identified. Thus, the advantage over factor analytic techniques is that there is no reliance on what questions respondents are asked initially where a given item cannot load on a factor unless data are specifically collected on that item at the outset of the experiment. Thus, the resulting factor structure is dependent on what is considered relevant at the outset and is not determined by novel responses generated by respondents.

The application of GPA results in a representation of a stimulus (in this case, an information source) in several dimensions, each new dimension comprising psychological constructs from all the individuals. The most highly correlated are deemed to be the most important dimensions in the resultant model, accounting for a greater proportion of the factor structure.

GPA is of particular utility for information about how individuals differ and to what extent they agree in their perceptions of the same stimulus.[27] The technique allows for individual differences in perception to be incorporated into the subsequent analysis.[28]

Method

Thirty-five respondents were recruited from the Reading area, nine males and 26 females (mean age 39.9 years, ± 18.4 years). Upon completion of both parts of the experiment, respondents were paid £10 (approximately US $15). All respondents attended the Institute of Food Research Laboratory at Reading, UK. Initial interviews took between 30 and 45 minutes. The second part of the experiment was conducted after one week and took between 30 minutes and an hour.

Respondents were asked about the reasons that they trust or distrust 15 possible sources of risk information associated with food-related hazards (Table 8.6). The repertory grid method[29] was divided into two phases. The first entailed the elicitation of constructs describing trust in information sources, the second the rating of each source on each construct.

Table 8.6 *Different information sources used in the repertory grid study*

Consumer organization
Environmental pressure group
Food industry
Friends
Government minister
Government ministry
Government scientist
Medical sources
Member of parliament
Quality newspaper
Supermarket information leaflet
Tabloid newspaper
Television news broadcast
Television documentary
University scientist

Each respondent was presented with a questionnaire[30] with the sources of information presented in groups of three on separate pages, in fully randomized order. Each source was presented twice within the questionnaire, to give ten triadic combinations in total. Respondents were asked 'which of following sources of information do you trust the most, and why?' for each triadic presentation. Similarly, respondents were also asked 'Which of following sources of information do you distrust the most, and why?' Different orders of presentation were used between respondents. The respondents thus listed reasons, attributes or constructs which they used to distinguish between the different sources of information. For example, a respondent might identify that one source is distrusted more than another because the distrusted source has been 'proven wrong in the past', or because the source 'does not know what it is talking about'. Responses were written down on the questionnaire by the respondents themselves. Interobserver reliability techniques (involving agreement between two different researchers) were used to identify key constructs. From these data, a personalized questionnaire was produced for each respondent.

Respondents returned after one week to complete their personalized questionnaires. The respondent then rated each of the sources of information for each construct on unstructured line scales with personalized labelled endpoints contingent on constructs elicited in part 1 of the experiment.

Data Analysis

The data were submitted to generalized Procrustes analysis (all data being scaled using the method described by Dijsterhuis and Gower).[25] The analysis was conducted using the GENPROC procedure[31] under the GENSTAT statistical package.[32] A consensus perceptual space was obtained, illustrating the relative positions of the applications.

To interpret the main perceptual dimensions of the spaces, the correlations between each construct and each principal axis for each individual were examined.[33] These correlations provide a weighting for each attribute on a principal axis from which it can then be decided which attributes are important. The procedure used here was to select those attributes which correlate significantly at the 5 per cent level (ie 0.51 per cent or greater) (Table 8.7).

Results

A taxonomic classification system for constructs was developed at the outset of the experiment using the NUD*IST qualitative analysis package,[34] although this was subsequently modified and new categories created if appropriate during classification. The final construct classes are listed in alphabetical order (Table 8.7). The mean number of constructs elicited from each respondent was 17.5, (±7.5). The final construct classification consisted of 27 classes, agreement as to classification being reached by two independent researchers. In cases where disagreement occurred, the classification was discussed until agreement was reached. Figure 8.5 describes how the different applications were commonly perceived in relation to the constructs elicited from the respondents. The first two principal axes of the consensus configuration together account for 70 per cent of the variation in the data. Principal axis 3 accounted for 10 per cent, principal axis 4 accounted for 6 per cent, and subsequent principal axes less than 6 per cent. Interpretation was therefore confined to the first two principal axes. Table 8.7 lists the number of constructs that have high correlations with the first two principal axes. This table leads directly to the interpretation of Figure 8.5. Only those construct classes that occur more than six times are considered important – ie, approximately one-sixth or more of the sample indicated that they represented important psychological constructs underlying trust, which represents a reasonable percentage of responses. When construct classes with equal numbers of occurrences on a particular axis appear, the total number of times the construct class is mentioned is taken into account. The construct class is considered more important when the proportion of the total is larger.

The first principal axis explains 45 per cent of the data variation. The terms used to describe trust in information sources on the positive side of principal axis 1 are 'responsible', 'trustworthy', 'accountable', 'accurate' and 'good track record'. The negative side of principal axis 1 was described by the term 'distortion' (Figure 8.5). The positive side of principal axis 2 was described by the construct 'amplification', the negative side was described by 'self-protection'. The constructs 'knowledgeable', 'factual', 'expert', 'vested interest' and 'concern with public welfare' describe both the positive direction of principal axis 1 and the negative direction of principal axis 2. The construct 'vested interest' described the negative ends of both principal axis 1 and principal axis 2, while 'exaggeration' described the negative aspect of principal axis 1 and the positive aspect of principal axis 2.

Table 8.7 *Total number of constructs in each construct class and number of constructs with a high correlation on the first two principal axes*[a]

Construct	Total	PA1 45%		PA2 25%	
		+	−	+	−
Accountable	13	7	1	0	5
Accurate	12	7	1	0	4
Amplification	17	0	3	**14**	0
Biased	35	**16**[g]	**14**	1	4
Changeable	4	0	3	1	0
Distortion	23	0	**20**	2	1
Exaggeration	19	1	6	**12**	0
Expert	24	7	0	0	**17**
Factual	33	**21**	2	3	7
Freedom	15	**6**[g]	**6**	0	3
Good reasons[b]	4	4	0	0	0
Hearsay	9	0	3	5	1
Hidden	8	4	1	1	2
Inaccurate	13	5	3	0	5
Knowledge	52	**20**	1	2	**29**
Public welfare	24	**16**	1	0	7
Responsible	26	**15**	5	2	4
Self-protection[c]	11	1	4	0	**6**
Track record	9	**6**	1	0	2
Trustworthy	9	**7**	0	1	1
Truthful	32	**20**[g]	8	0	4
Understanding[d]	10	4	2	0	4
Up to date	1	0	0	0	1
Vested interest	46	2	**30**	0	**14**
Want to know[e]	1	1	0	0	0
Withholding information[f]	44	**15**[g]	17	3	**9**
Worthless	5	0	5	0	0

Numbers in bold refer to constructs mentioned by enough respondents to be included in Figure 8.5

[a] Constructs with a correlation of ≤ –0.51 or ≥ 0.51 ($P < 0.05$%) on the first two principal axes have been included. A construct can correlate highly on more than one axis.

[b] Defined as the source 'providing information for the right reasons, however these are defined by the respondent'.

[c] Defined as the source 'providing accurate information for reasons of self-protection, or to maintain a positive public image'.

[d] Defined as whether the 'source understands the information which is being transmitted'.

[e] Defined as the 'source providing information that it thinks the public wants to know'.

[f] Defined as whether the 'source actively hides information from the public'.

[g] Constructs which did not polarize on either Principal Axis 1 or Principal Axis 2.

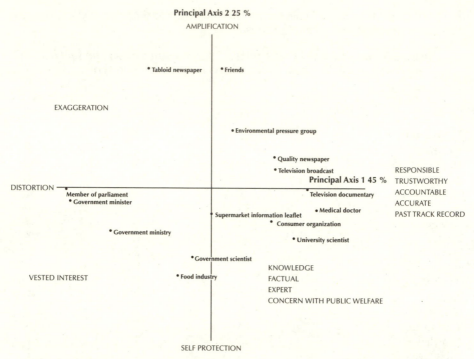

Figure 8.5 *Results from the repertory grid study (study 2). Plot of the different information sources in the plane defined by the first and second principal axes of the consensus configuration.*

Some constructs failed to differentiate different information sources. 'Biased', 'truthful' and 'withholding information' described both the negative and positive direction of principal axis 1, although it is clearly an important construct in the determination of trust. It is possible that these particular items are contingent on individual differences in the population sampled.[35] Different people in the sample may have used these terms differently and hence the pattern of response is not clear. While these constructs are not included in Figure 8.5, they were included in study 3, as there is potential for them to differentiate between sources in larger samples where average scores are used.

The results are consistent with previous research[36] where 'quality' media sources, medical sources and university scientists are seen as more trustworthy than those which are linked with political or government interests. Whilst amplification is associated with the tabloid press and friends, exaggeration is also associated with political actors in the risk debate.

The results of studies 1 and 2 appear to complement each other, insomuch as those sources which were rated as highly distrusted or trusted in study 1 were also highly differentiated in terms of trust or distrust in study two (Figure 8.5). However, while comparisons of the results of the interview study largely confirm the findings of the GPA study, the latter offers the advantage of having greater explanatory value – eg, amplification of information appears to be uniquely associated with tabloid newspapers and friends.

A potential problem of using repertory grids with GPA analysis is that an attitudinal construct which applies equally to all of the stimuli is not likely to be differentiated by the use of the repertory grid method. In cases where the purpose of the experiment is to determine what factors differentiate different stimuli (for example, information sources), this is irrelevant. However, in eliciting concerns about technological hazards within a particular hazard domain (eg, genetic engineering), a concern which is common to all stimuli will not be differentiated. For example, in a study of concerns associated with different applications of genetic engineering, it has been found that control of the technology was not identified as important by the application of the repertory grid technique,[37] although it has been shown to be an important concern relating to the technology overall.[38]

To summarize the results of the two studies, it would appear from these data that reasons for trust and distrust in information are closely linked to specific information sources. Trust in information is also likely to be closely linked to the perceived risk characteristics of the hazard itself and this dimension cannot be ignored.

Study 4: Validation

The results of studies 2 and 3 were validated in a large questionnaire survey, to examine average responses within a more representative population sample. Principal components analysis was used. Thus, a similar methodology to previous studies where experimenter-generated characteristics was applied, with the difference that respondent-generated characteristics were used, enabling comparisons in the underlying attitudinal structure to be assessed.

Design

The combined results of studies 1 and 2 were used to design the self-administered questionnaire. Four thousand questionnaires were mailed to quota sampled individuals whose addresses had been obtained through a mailing list purchased through a market research company. Quota sampling was performed on the basis of gender, age and socioeconomic group, with geographical sampling by region throughout the UK. Potential respondents were informed that they would receive a small 'free gift' (an attractive pen) if they returned the completed questionnaire.

The questionnaire included instructions and questions on demographic information (age, gender, occupation or previous occupation if not currently employed) and educational qualifications obtained. Respondents were also asked to rate each of the information sources used in study 2 (Table 8.6) on the characteristics which were found to be important in determining trust in information sources in both studies 1 and 2 (Table 8.8). The constructs 'exaggeration' and 'amplification' were joined into one item, 'sensationalization', as pilot work indicated that respondents did not differentiate between these two constructs in the questionnaire. Questions are listed in Table 8.8. All responses were rated on 7-point labelled scales (1 = 'not at all' to 7 = 'extremely'). In addition, attitudes to each of the different information sources was rated on a 7-point labelled scale, (1 = not favourable; 7 = extremely favourable).

Table 8.8 *Questions used in the survey (study 3). Attitude characteristics rated in the survey studies (7-point scale and points are indicate in parentheses)*

1. To what extent do you think information about food-related hazards from each of the following sources is *trustworthy?* (not trustworthy to completely trustworthy).
2. To what extent do you think information about food-related hazards from each of the following sources is *accurate?* (not accurate to extremely accurate).
3. To what extent do you think information about food-related hazards from each of the following sources *is factual?* (not factual to extremely factual).
4. To what extent do you think the following sources are likely to *withhold* information about food-related issues from the public? (do not withhold information to withhold a great deal of information).
5. To what extent do you think information about food-related hazards from each of the following sources is *distorted?* (not distorted to extremely distorted).
6. To what extent do you think information about food-related hazards from each of the following sources is *truthful?* (not truthful to extremely truthful).
7. To what extent do you think information about food-related hazards from each of the following sources is *biased?* (not biased to extremely biased).
8. To what extent do you think the following sources have *the freedom* to provide information to the public about food-related hazards (no freedom to complete freedom).
9. To what extent do you think the following sources of information have a *vested interest* in promoting a particular view about food-related hazards? (no vested interest to extremely vested interest).
10. To what extent do you think information about food-related hazards from each of the following sources has been *proven wrong* in the past? (not proven wrong to always proven wrong).
11. To what extent do you think each of the following sources of information is *knowledgable* about food-related hazards (not knowledgable to extremely knowledgeable).
12. To what extent do you think each of the following sources feels a *responsibility* to provide good food-related information to the public? (no responsibility to extremely great responsibility).
13. To what extent do you think each of the following sources of information is *expert* in the area of food-related hazards (not expert to extremely expert).
14. To what extent do you think each of the following sources provide *sensationalized* information about food-related hazards? (not sensationalized to extremely sensationalized).
15. To what extent do you think each of the following sources have a *good track record* of providing information about food-related hazards? (not good to extremely good).
16. To what extent do you think each of the following sources provide accurate information about food-related hazards only *to protect themselves and their own interests?* (not self-protective to extremely self-protective).
17. To what extent do you think each of the sources is *accountable to others (for example, regulatory bodies)* if mistakes are made in the food-related information provided? (not accountable to extremely accountable).
18. To what extent do you think each of the following sources of information about food-related hazards are *concerned about public welfare?* (not concerned at all to extremely concerned).
19. To what extent are you personally *in favour* of using each of the following sources to obtain information about food-related hazards? (not in favour to extremely in favour).

Data Analysis and Results

The response rate was 23 per cent, of which 44 per cent were male. The mean age of the sample was 44 years (SD ± 12.2 years). The characteristic ratings from the questionnaire of each information source on the above characteristics were submitted to principal components analysis, carried out using SPSS.[39] A principal components analysis of the mean scores of each attitude characteristic in relation to each information source indicated a two component solution (unrotated) accounting for 89 per cent of the variance. The first component accounted for 64 per cent of the

Table 8.9 *Loadings from the principal components analysis*

	Component 1	Component 2
Accountable	0.20	**0.92**
Accurate	**0.97**	0.16
Biased	**−0.85**	0.44
Distorted	**−0.97**	0.14[a]
Expert	**0.73**	**0.61**
Factual	**0.96**	0.21
Favour	**0.97**	0.18
Freedom	**0.62**	**−0.63**[a]
Good track record	**0.98**	0.07
Knowledgeable	**0.79**	0.55
Proven wrong in the past	**−0.97**	0.14
Public welfare	**0.93**	0.10
Responsible	**0.80**	0.49
Self-protection	−0.53	**0.84**
Sensationalization	−0.19	**−0.60**
Trustworthy	**0.98**	0.03
Truthful	**0.98**	0.17
Vested interest	−0.21	**0.84**
Withholding information	**−0.70**	**0.69**[a]

Primary factor loadings are indicated in bold under the appropriate component.
[a] Items which did not differentially load on discrete factors.

variance). Variables loading heavily on this component were, on the positive pole, 'truthful', 'good track record', 'trustworthy', 'favour', 'accurate', 'factual', 'concern about public welfare', 'responsible' and 'knowledgeable', and on the negative pole, 'distorted', 'proven wrong in the past' and 'biased'. 'In favour of use' loaded heavily on the positive axis of component 1. The second component accounted for 25 per cent of the variance. 'Accountability', 'protecting themselves and their own interests' and 'vested interest' loaded on the positive pole and 'sensationalization' loaded on the negative pole of this component. 'Freedom' loaded positively on component 1 and negatively on component 2. 'Withholding information' loaded negatively on component 1 and positively on component 2. 'Expert' loaded positively on both principal components 1 and 2 *and thus cannot be interpreted in terms of specific dimensions.* The third component accounted for less than 6 per cent of the variance, and was not considered further. Component loadings are shown in Table 8.9. A representation of the component space for the first two components is provided in Figure 8.6.

Discussion

To some extent, principal component 1 reflects the 'knowledge bias' reported in previous research.[17] These results, however, suggest that knowledge is also linked with other characteristics, such as 'truthfulness', 'trustworthiness', 'having a good track record', 'being concerned witn public welfare', 'responsibility', 'accuracy' and 'factual'. It is suggested that sources which are trusted are also seen as knowledgeable

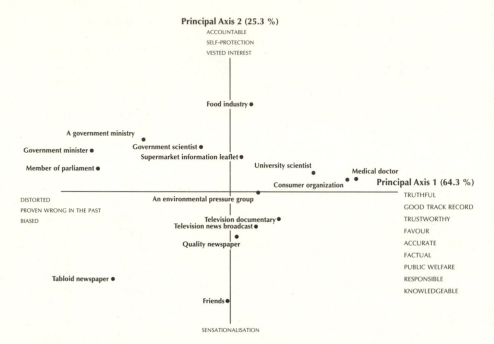

Figure 8.6 *Results from the survey study (study 3). Location of different information sources within the two-component space.*

or at least as providing well-researched information. This may represent a type of 'halo' effect, such that highly trusted sources are associated with multiple positive attributes. Similarly, distrust is associated with inaccurate information (ie, information which is 'distorted', 'proven wrong in the past' and 'biased'). Freedom in itself does not lead to increased trust or distrust.

Increased 'independence' does not lead to increased trust in information. Rather, most trust is likely to be placed in those sources who have moderate degrees of accountability. Too much accountability may be associated with dishonesty and are therefore distrusted. Highly trusted sources tend to fall in the middle of principal component 2. For example, they are seen to be moderately accountable to others, to have a partial vested interest in promoting a particular view and to be reasonably self-protective. Total absence of such characteristics allows for sensationalization of information. For example, a member of the medical profession may have a vested interest in promoting public health, a characteristic which is linked to concern with public welfare.

These results do not support the results of previous factor analytic studies (see Introduction, p193). This may be because the generation of trust characteristics was derived from constructs obtained from respondents rather than experimenter-generated characteristic or because of the nature of the hazard domain itself. Freedom and expertise do not, in themselves, lead to trust in information, but must be associated with other factors linked to trustworthiness. It is possible that perceptions of withholding information are likely to lead to distrust, even if this is because the information source is restricted for reasons of confidentiality, rather than to protect a vested interest in promoting a particular view.

General Discussion

Trust (and distrust) is clearly multidimensional, and cannot be predicted by single items or psychological constructs. What has been shown by these results is that different information sources are associated with different characteristics which differentiate the extent to which they are trusted by the public. Trust appears to be linked with perceptions of accuracy, knowledge and concern with public welfare. Expertise and freedom do not lead to trust unless accompanied by other characteristics. Distrust is associated with perceptions of deliberate distortion of the information by the source and a history of providing erroneous information.

It has been argued that increased scientific literacy in the general public will help decrease perceived risk associated with science and technology and, by implication, the products of those technologies. Against this, the level of scientific literacy required is so high that it is difficult to attain and difficult to motivate the public to attain it.[40] In addition, the amount of scientific information, combined with increased technical complexity, is likely to act as a further barrier to public understanding. The public must therefore rely on independent and trustworthy advisory groups who can filter and disseminate risk (and other relevant) information in an understandable way. Who is responsible for such dissemination? These data would indicate that government sources are, in general, not trusted. If government sources and risk regulators are seen to be proactive in their interactions with the media and with other trusted sources such as consumer organizations, this may positively influence the way in which risk information is reported, as well as increasing trust in government regulation.

Trust in information provided by industry appears to be facilitated by industry's need to protect itself from economic losses. To provide the public with misleading information may result in long-term economic losses to the industry because of negative consumer reactions. Thus, information is moderately trusted, but because the public believes the source is protecting its own interests rather than providing good information out of concern for public welfare.

Even within the scientific community, there are differences in the extent to which technological risks are perceived as risky.[41] This could be an important factor in determining what sources are believed by the public. Admitting to uncertainty, or facilitating public understanding of science as a 'process', could increase communicator trustworthiness.[42]

In relation to technologies involved in food production, it has been suggested that the importance of trust in decision-makers and information sources is likely to be all the more apparent where consumer understanding of those technologies is lacking.[43] People seem to be adverse to ambiguous risks.[44] Trust is all the more likely to be important where there is a perception that accurate estimates of risk are not available,[45] such as in the case of genetic engineering as applied to food production.[46]

References

1   B Fischhoff, A Bostrom, L Lave and C J Atman (1992) 'Communicating risk to the public' in *Environment, Science and Technology*, no 26(11), pp2048–2056

2   V Covello, D Von Winterfeldt and P Slovic (1987) 'Communicating risk informa-
    tion to the public' in J C Davies, V Covello and F Alien (eds) in *Risk Communi-
    cation* The Conservation Foundation, Washington, DC

3   P Slovic (1992) 'Perceptions of risk: Reflections on the psychometric paradigm'
    in S Krimsky and D Golding (eds) *Social Theories of Risk* Praeger, Westport, Con-
    necticut, pp117–152

4   L J Frewer, R Shepherd and P Sparks (1994) 'The role of perceived knowledge
    and perceived control in risk perceptions associated with a range of food-related
    hazards' in *Food Safety* no 14,pp19–40

5   J Flynn, W Burns, C K Mertz and P Slovic (1992) 'Trust as a determinant of op-
    position to a high-level radioactive waste depository: Analysis of a structural
    model' in *Risk Analysis* no 12(3), pp417–429

6   B Fischhoff (1995) 'Managing risk perception' in *Issues in Science Technology* no
    2, pp83–96

7   M H Shamos (1991) 'Scientific literacy: Can it decrease public anxiety about sci-
    ence and technology' in D J Roy, B E Wynne and R W Old (eds), *Bioscience So-
    ciety* Wiley, London

8   R Macfarlane (1993) 'The consumer voice in food safety' *FNA/ANA* nos 8/9,
    pp17–23

9   R E Kasperson, D Golding and S Tuler (1992) 'Social distrust as a factor in siting
    hazardous facilities and communicating risks' in *Journal of Social Issues*, no 48,
    pp161–187

10 J Flynn and P Slovic (1993) 'Nuclear wastes and public trust' *Forum for Applied
    Research into Public Policy* Spring, pp92–101

11 G Turner and B Wynne (1992) 'Risk communication: A literature review and some
    implications for biotechnology', in J Durant (ed), *Biotechnology in Public: A Re-
    view of Recent Research* Science Museum for the European Federation of Bio-
    technology, The Science Museum, London

12 W R Freudenburg (1993) 'Risk and recreancy: Weber, the division of labour, and
    the rationality of risk perceptions', *Social Forces* no 71, pp909–932

13 O Renn (1992) 'Risk communication: Towards a rational discourse with the pub-
    lic' in *Journal of Hazardous Materials* no 29, pp465–519

14 P Slovic, J Flynn, S Johnson and C K Mertz (1993) *The Dynamics of Trust in Situ-
    ations of Risk*, Report no 93-2 Oregon Decision Research, Eugene

15 H I Sharlin (1989) 'Risk perception: Changing the terms of the debate' in *Jour-
    nal of Hazardous Materials* no 21, pp261–272

16 P Slovic (1993) 'Perceived risk, trust and democracy' in *Risk Analysis*, no 13,
    pp675–682

17 W J McGuire (1985) 'Attitudes and attitude change', in G Lindzey and E Aronson
    (eds), *The Handbook of Social Psychology*, vol 2, 3rd ed, Random House, New
    York, pp233–346

18 E S Baudin and M K Davis (1972) 'Scales for the measurement of ethos: An-
    other attempt' in *Speech Monogr.*, no 39, pp296–301

19 R L Falcione (1974) 'The factor structure of source credibility scales for imme-
    diate superiors in the organizational context', in *Central States Speech Journal*,
    no 25, pp63–66

20 D J O'Keefe (1990) 'Persuasion: Theory and research, Chapter 8, source factors'
    in *Curr Commun Adv Text Series*, no 2, pp130–157

21 L J Frewer and R Shepherd (1995) 'Attributing information to different sources:
    Effects on the perceived qualities of information, on the perceived relevance of

information and effects on attitude formation' in *Public Understanding Science*, no 3, pp385–401

22 J C Gower (1975) 'Generalised Procrustes analysis', in *Psychometrica*, no 40, pp33–51

23 N Gains and M H Thompson (1990) 'Sensory profiling of canned lager beers using consumers in their own homes', in *Food Quality Pref* no 2, pp39–47

24 C Guy, J R Piggott and S Marie (1989) 'Consumer profiling of Scotch whisky' in *Food Quality Pref* no 1, pp69–73

25 M M Raats and R Shepherd (1991/1992) 'An evaluation of the use and perceived appropriateness of milk using the repertory grid method and the "item by use" appropriateness method' in *Food Quality Pref* no 3, pp89–100

26 M M Raats and R Shepherd (1996) 'Developing a subject derived terminology to describe perceptions of chemicals in food' in *Risk Analysis*, vol 16, pp133–136

27 G B Dijksterhuis and J C Gower (1991) *The Interpretation of Generalised Procrustes Analysis and Allied Methods*, Research Report RR–91–08, Department of Data Theory, University of Leiden, Leiden

28 G M Arnold and A A Williams (1986) 'The use of generalised Procrustes techniques in sensory analysis' in J R Piggott (ed), *Statistical Procedures for Food Research* Elsevier Applied Science, London

29 G A Kelly (1955) *The Psychology of Personal Constructs: A Theory of Personality* Norton, New York

30 M M Raats, P Sparks and S Grugeon (1994) *Risk Perception and the Psychometric Paradigm: In Search of New Methods*, Proceedings, Society for Risk Analysis Annual Conference, Baltimore, 4–7 December, p48

31 G M Arnold and R W Payne (1989) 'Procedure GENPROC' in R W Payne and G M Arnold (eds), *Genstat Procedure Library Manual: Release 1.3 (2)* Numerical Algorithms Group, Oxford

32 *GENSTAT Statistical Package* (1991) Numerical Algorithms Group Ltd, Oxford

33 A A Williams and G M Arnold (1985) 'A comparison of the aromas of six coffees characterised by conventional profiling, free choice profiling and similarity scaling methods' in *Journal of Sci Food Agric* no 36, pp204–214

34 *Nud*ist, Qualitative Data Analysis Solutions for Research Professionals* (1993) Qualitative Solutions and Research, La Trobe, Australia

35 L J Frewer, D Hedderley, C Howard and R Shepherd 'Methodological approaches to assessing risk perceptions associated with food-related hazards' in *Risk Analysis*, vol 18, no 1, pp95–102

36 L J Frewer, M M Raats and R Shepherd (1993/1994) 'Modelling the media: The transmission of risk information in the British press' in *IMA J Math Appl Bus Ind* no 5, pp235–224

37 L J Frewer, C Howard and R Shepherd 'Public concerns about general and specific applications of genetic engineering: Risk, benefit and ethics' in *Science, Technology and Human Values*, vol 22, pp98–124

38 L J Frewer and R Shepherd (1995) 'Ethical concerns and risk perceptions associated with different applications of genetic engineering: Interrelationships with the perceived need for regulation of the technology' in *Agric Hum Values* no 12, pp48–57

39 *SPSS, Statistical Package for the Social Sciences* (1990) SPSS, Chicago

40 M H Shamos (1991) 'Scientific literacy: Can it decrease public anxiety about science and technology' in D J Roy, B E Wynne and R W Old (eds) *Bioscience Society* Wiley, London

41   R P Barke and H C Jenkins-Smith (1993) 'Politics and scientific expertise: Scientists, risk perception, and nuclear waste policy' in *Risk Analysis,* no 13, pp425–439
42   V T Covello, P Slovic and D Von Winterfeldt (1987) *Risk Communication: A Review of the Literature* National Science Foundation, Washington, DC
43   P B Thompson (1987) 'Agricultural biotechnology and the rhetoric of risk: Some conceptual issues' in *Environ. Prof.* no 9, pp316–326
44   D Ellsberg (1961) 'Risk, ambiguity, and the savage axioms' in *Quart. J. Econ.* no 75, pp643–669
45   P Sparks and R Shepherd (1994) 'Public perceptions of the hazards associated with food production and food consumption: An empirical study' in *Risk Analysis,* no 14, pp79–86
46   P Sparks, R Shepherd and L J Frewer (1995) 'Assessing and structuring attitudes towards the use of gene technology in food production: The role of perceived ethical obligation' in *Basic Appl Soc Psychol* no 16(3), pp267–285

Mental Models in Risk Assessment: Informing People About Drugs

Helmut Jungermann, Holger Schütz, and Manfred Thüring

Introduction

Pharmaceutical drugs have become common in everyday life, having advantages and disadvantages. Almost everybody uses drugs at one time or another, seeking the benefits and accepting the risks. There is little disagreement that people need information about the drugs they use, at least about proper dosage and important interactions (eg with alcohol). Less consensus exists, however, on whether and how users should be educated about the risks involved in taking a drug. Should patients obtain information only about contraindications or also about side effects? Should they be told the likelihoods of effect in numbers or with verbal phrases? Should they receive information about actions to take to protect against inefficacy or overdosage? And should they receive information from their physician exclusively or should additional information be offered through a package insert? Informing about drugs and instructing regarding their usage have been left in most countries to the physician. But in a number of countries information and instructions are also provided via patient package inserts (PPI).

There are a number of empirical studies on whether and how people use PPI. But there exists no theoretical perspective to understand this type of informing and communicating about risks. The mental model approach offers a perspective useful for this type and also for other types of risk analysis that have to take human cognition into account. This approach has become a major topic of research recently in cognitive psychology (see eg, Refs 1–3). It can be traced to Craik, who wrote (in 1943):

> If the organism carries a small-scale model of external reality and of its own possible actions within its head, it is able to try out various alternatives, conclude which is the best of them, react to future situations before they arise, utilize the knowledge of past events in dealing with the present and the future, and in every way to react in a much fuller, safer, and more competent manner to the emergencies which face it.[4]

Generally speaking, a mental model is a mapping from a domain into a mental representation that contains the main characteristics of the domain; a model can be 'run' to generate explanations and expectations, with respect to potential states. Mental models have been proposed in particular as the kind of knowledge structures that people use to understand a specific domain, like, for example, the functioning or a pocket calculator or of electricity,[5] but the concept is being increasingly applied to a much wider category of domains.[2]

The following paper applies the mental model approach to informing people about pharmaceutical drugs with PPI. In the first part we review the major findings of empirical studies on the use of PPI. In the second part we describe the basic features of the mental model approach as it might be applied to this domain. We conclude that this approach provides a useful theoretical basis for studying a number of other phenomena risk analysts are concerned about in addition to drug risks.

Evidence from Empirical Studies

A number of survey studies in the US have investigated the problems of communicating about drugs and examined, among others, the following questions: Are people interested in risk information on drugs? How extensive should risk information be from the users' point of view? Do lay people undestand risk information correctly? Does risk information influence attitudes and behaviour?

Are People Interested in Risk Information on Drugs?

Information on the risks of drugs is widely held to be important; users want to know why they should take a drug and what the risk are in taking it. From 1973 to 1978, the percentage of the US population who believed that detailed information about drugs was important increased from 49 per cent to 64 per cent.[6] In a survey of 137 patients, Joubert and Lasagna[7] found that

> *most of them (93%) wanted to know the reasons for the drugs they were using, the common risks involved (89%), the risk of over dosage (86%), the possibility of rare side effects occuring (81%), the risk of taking too little medication (80%), the risks of not using the drug (79%), and other important uses of the drug (75%) (ref 3, p2).*

Marketing and advertising research has found that, although people might express interest in risk information, they actually make little use of risk information.[18] According to other research, people seem to read PPIs quite extensively. In a study by Eraker, Becker, Jepson and De Tullio[9] 80 per cent of the patients who had received a PPI read it and about 90 per cent still had it available after two weeks. Similar results were reported by Kanouse, Berry, Hayes-Roth, Rogers and Winkler.[10] About 70 per cent of their subjects had read the PPI, between 45 per cent and 56 per cent said they had kept it, and between 22 per cent and 32 per cent had read it more than once. Both studies report a reliable increase in patients' knowledge about drugs and patients' satisfaction with their level of knowledge. These findings indicate that people are seriously interested in risk information on drugs and that 'PPIs appear to be an effective vehicle for getting more information to more people' (ref 10, p3).

How Extensive Should Risk Information Be?

The findings of Joubert and Lasagna[7] indicate that a majority of patients want broad information about risks associated with the drugs they take. It is uncertain, however, whether patients can actually become educated about all possible contraindications and side effects; in fact, it might be questioned whether they should. In particular, what should be done about the serious though rare and the less serious but frequent side effects? When physicians see patients personally, they can consider their specific situation, their knowledge and feelings, and then decide if they want to give particular information or not. A PPI, on the other hand, presents one set of information for all potential users. What information should be presented?

Keown et al[6] found considerable differences between the attitudes of physicians, pharmacists and lay people concerning the number of side effects that should be listed on a PPI. They found that health professionals

> *tended to believe that serious side effects should be listed even when they occur rarely but that minor side effects should be listed only when they happen quite often. In contrast, lay people were much more prone to the general view that all side effects should be listed, no matter how rarely they occur or how minor they are (ref 11, p21).*

The same picture appeared when people were confronted with specific side effects and their probabilities: for lay people and pharmacists, a frequency in the range of 1 in 10,000 to 1 in 100,000 was sufficient for mentioning an effect, while physicians considered a range of 1 in 1,000 to 1 in 10,000 as appropriate. And although lay people and health professionals generally agreed in their ordering of side effects with respect to their seriousness, lay people 'tended to judge most side effects as more serious than did health profesionals' (ref 11, p20).

The request of lay people for full information about the risks associated with the drugs they are using, however minor or rare they might be, may have different roots. People may want to gain some cognitive control over what is happening to them, they may want to feel more on an equal basis with the physician, they may distrust the health professionals or the pharmaceutical industry, and/or they may have become sensitive to all possible dangers in their environment. Whether it is reasonable to provide all available information on a PPI, however, is a different matter. For instance, many people may not be able to understand the information provided on the PPI properly and draw unjustified inferences, generating inadequately optimistic or pessimistic thoughts and feelings, possibly resulting in detrimental actions.

Do Lay people Understand Risk Information Correctly?

Several studies indicate that reading a PPI leads to reliable gains in knowledge about the drug. Eraker et al,[9] for example, found significantly increased knowledge concerning drug-taking conditions, contraindications, possible drug interactions, and side effects. Kanouse et al[10] also found increased knowledge on how the drug works, on contraindications and on food-drug interactions. However, providing additional information about why a drug works or why not to take the drug under certain conditions did not enhance patients' comprehension and retention. Further, emphasizing risks (ie dangers, precautions) did not increase the amount of information remembered. Even basic information on side effects did not increase subjects' knowledge very much but only generated 'a general impression that they occur' (ref 10, p17).

The complexity of the writing seemed to have little effect on patients' understanding, while the visual layout appeared to be important: information presented in an outline format was judged easier to read but also more alarming than information given in a text format. The alarming effects of this format were not, however, interpreted as resulting from increased patients' understanding of the drug's risks.[10] Cognitive research on risk perception[12] further supports the notion that people often have considerable problems in processing information on risks.

Contraindications and side effects represent the types of information on risk given in a PPI. The contraindication of a drug describes the conditions under which the drug should not be taken (eg 'high blood presure'). Readers usually understand that adverse effects can be expected if they take the drug under those conditions. Side effects are more difficult to interpret, particularly since they are usually expressed in terms of frequencies or probabilities (eg sometimes, likely); also, a number of quite different side effects are often listed whose causal interrelations are completely opaque. How do people understand, interpret, and judge information on side effects?

Keown et al found in their survey of students and physicians that 'students appear to weigh the number of side effects too highly, relative to the low relative frequency of occurrence, in evaluating the risk of a prescription drug when compared to physicians' (ref 6, p120). One can question, of course, whether physicians are the appropriate standard of comparison since experts too have been found to be prone to biases in risk judgement (see, for example, refs 12–14).

It further seems that the judged risk of a drug increases with the number of side effects mentioned, independent of their associated probabilities. It remains open whether people do not use the information about probabilities at all or whether they use it incorrectly.

But Keown[8] also found evidence that people try to discriminate in their use of a drug. His subjects tended to reject a drug with a potentially serious side effect (blood clot) for treating minor problems like loss of weight or skin rash. However, they were willing to accept the same drug for treating serious health problems like lung cancer or high blood pressure. People seem to base their decision on a kind of mental risk–benefit analysis.

The general problem, however, has not yet been investigated: does the content and the format of risk information match the individual user's situation? First, can one kind of information representation be expected to match the variety of cognitive and emotional states of the many potential users? Secondly, how can users relate the statistical information (eg probability of side effect X is 1 in 10,000) to their personal state of health (ie whether they have to fear the side effect or not?). Thirdly, what conclusions should patients draw if some side effect (eg destruction of white blood corpuscles) is described in the PPI as 'rare but serious' (ie should they consider the information as relevant for their behaviour?).

Does Risk Information Influence Attitudes and Behaviour?

Strangely enough, the producers of drugs seem to care little about the effect of their PPIs: little effort is spent in industry on optimizing the communication with respect to the potential reader's comprehension and utilization of the information. The reason might be that PPIs are primarily written to protect the producer against lawsuits, not to guarantee understanding and proper use by the patient. But considering the empirical findings reported above, we might expect that the information provided through a PPI will actually affect the readers' attitudes towards a drug and possibly their drug-using behaviour. However the findings on this issue do not give a clear picture.

Keown[8] reports a high correlation ($r = 0.92$) between subjects' assessment of risk and their intention to take a drug. 76 per cent of his student subjects were concerned about the side effects listed and most of them tended to reject using a drug if they were to experience a side effect. In their study with hypersensitive patients, Eraker et al[9] came to a somewhat different result. Information on side effects had no effect on patients' self-reported level of concern about side effects and, in contrast to studies suggesting that information on side effects increases reports of such effects, their patients reported fewer side effects than a control group who received the same drug without a PPI. Moreover, if side effects occured they did not reduce medication compliance. Kanouse et al[10] also found no evidence that drug information affects the attitudes towards a drug, nor did it increase the number of reported side effects and other health problems. However, leaflets in an outline format and leaflets with either specific instructions or additional explanations did increase the number of reported health problems. The inconsistency in these results may be due to the different subject groups: while the subjects in the study by Keown et al simply had to imagine using the drug, the subjects in the studies by Eraker et al as well as Kanouse et al were patients who actually had to use the drug.

As to the actual drug-taking behaviour, Kanouse et al observed 'that PPIs are unlikely to dissuade large numbers of patients from taking the drug' (ref 10, p19). The frequency of patient–physician contacts as well as patients' satisfaction with the drug information obtained from the physician seems to remain unaffected by the information provided with a PPI. Some evidence was found that PPIs can induce people to a discussion with their physician on drug safety and side effects.

From the few available studies it seems that attitudes are indeed affected by risk information via PPI, though depending on its framing. Drug-taking behaviour, on the other hand, is little, if at all, affected by PPI information. However, the empirical basis for these conclusions is still rather weak.

Summarizing the surveys reviewed above, the following picture emerges: people desire information about drugs they are using and they are willing to take this information into account in their usage of drugs. They seem generally motivated to engage in a conscious examination of the problems involved in drugs taking. This is an important result because studies from other areas have found such motivation to be a necessary condition for a successful communication of risk.[15] In order to be influential with respect to drug-taking behaviour, however, additional motivational factors must be present, such as, for example, a personal dependency on the drug.

Mental Models of Drug Effects

A theoretical basis would certainly be useful for interpreting the empirical data on the use of PPI and for guiding further research in this area. More specifically, an approach is needed for analyzing the knowledge and beliefs that different readers of inserts and users of drugs might apply. A better understanding of the cognitive structures and process that characterize people's knowledge and beliefs is an important condition for a successful risk communication, especially when it is a one-way communication as with inserts.

We propose here a theoretical specification and extension of the mental model approach. It is based on earlier treatments of this approach[16,17] and uses ideas from Anderson's unitary theory of the mind.[18] The core of the proposed approach is the assumption that a PPI reader needs two kinds of knowledge: first, (declarative) conceptual knowledge about the important components and their properties and, secondly, (procedural) simulation knowledge about the functional relations among the concepts.

Conceptual Knowledge

We assume that a person has gained through experience some general knowledge C about the domain D ('drugs'). $C(D)$ includes in particular concepts like the drug itself, indication, contraindication, interacting substances, main effect and side effects, but also concepts like symptoms of interactions with other substances as well as symptoms of contraindications. In a formal sense, these concepts are variable with sets of possible realizations (eg 'drug' may be replaced by any specific drug name and 'main effect' may be replaced by 'reduction of pain'). Connected to the conceptual variables are properties that can take different values (eg connected to 'drug' might be 'frequency of use' and 'dosage'). The possible values of a property can be represented as vectors. Property vectors may either be empty as, eg the vector 'intensity' which is connected with 'side effects' and can only be filled when information about a specific drug is provided. Or they may have default values as, eg the vector 'dosage' which is connected with 'drug' and may include the values '1', '2', '3' (daily).

We further assume that the general conceptual knowledge $C(D)$ guides the cognitive processing of information presented in a PPI. When a person reads the PPI accompanying a particular drug D' (eg 'lagretal', a hypohetical drug to alleviate pain), specific knowledge $C(D')$ about this drug is generated. In $C(D')$, the non-specific concepts of $C(D)$ (eg side effects) are substituted by specific concepts (eg 'stomach trouble', 'allergic reactions') and the property vectors are filled (eg the property 'intensity' of side effect takes the value 'weak') or their default values are replaced (eg the proper 'dosage' takes the value '3 daily').

Note that only those concepts and properties can be substituted for which the PPI provides specific information. For example, if nothing is said in the PPI about symptoms of contraindications or the intensity of side effects, the respective concept and property remain unspecified or take the default value. However, specific information in the PPI about some concept or property is only a necessary but not a sufficient condition for the specification in the mental model; for example, a PPI might provide some specific information but the reader might not understand it and therefore not be able or willing to use it for substitution.

Simulation Knowledge

To 'run' the model requires in addition knowledge about the functional dynamic relations among the conceptual variables – ie how a variable X can or will change if some other variable Y changes. A trivial example for this simulation knowledge is that a person usually knows that the major effects can or will occur if a drug is taken; another example is that, if a particular drug is taken for a long time, stomach trouble can occur as a side effect.

We make a similar distinction between general and specific knowledge as before: general simulation knowledge $S(D)$ is associated with $C(D)$ and includes the knowledge about the general conditional and causal relations among the variables (eg 'taking a drug causes a major effect'). Specific simulation knowledge $S(D')$ is substituted for $S(D)$ when a PPI is read and it thus includes the knowledge about the specific functional relations of the drug in question (eg 'taking Lagretal for more than a month can cause serious stomach trouble').

Simulation knowledge can be described in a similar way as productions.[3,18,19] In cognitive science, a production consists of a statement of conditions to be satisfied and action to be taken when and if the conditions are satisfied. In analogy, the knowledge about the relation between two variables may be described by conditional statements. A few examples from $S(D)$ describing relations between the drug, interacting substances, and symptoms of interactions are given below.

> If you take 'a drug'
> And you take 'interacting substances'
> then 'symptoms of interactions' will occur
> If 'symptoms of interactions' occur
> then you have taken 'a drug'
> and you have taken 'interacting substances'
> If you take 'a drug'
> then do not take 'interacting substances'

Examples from $S(D')$ would be more specific, such as, for example,

> If you take 'Lagretal'
> and you take 'alcohol'
> then 'reduction of responsiveness' will occur
> If 'reduction of responsiveness' occurs
> then you have taken 'Lagretal'
> and you have taken 'alcohol'.

Constitution of Mental Models

Conceptual and simulation knowledge constitute a mental model M. $C(D)$ and $S(D)$ form the general mental model $M(D)$ that people have acquired over years by, eg listening to parents, talking to friends, watching television or reading PPIs. A hypothetical general model representing the major concepts and their major conditional causal relations is given in Figure 9.1. $C(D')$ and $S(D')$, on the other hand, form a specific mental model $M(D')$ concerning a particular drug, usually acquired through

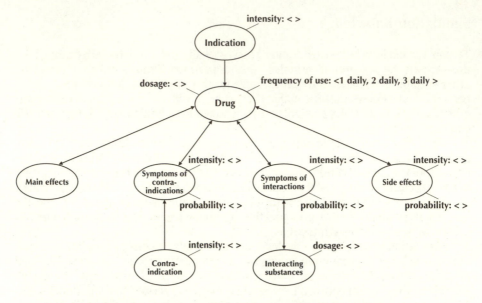

Figure 9.1 *A hypothetical general model of drug effects.*

reading the respective PPI. A hypothetical model of the functioning of the drug, 'Lagretal' is given in Figure 9.2.

Conceptual knowledge and simulation knowledge are both needed for mentally investigating possible states of the model, (ie for posing and answering questions like the following: What would happen with *X* if *Y* would occur? If action *A* were taken, what would be the effect on *B*? Which cause *M*, *N* or *B* would be most probable if P had changed in a specific direction?). From a decision theoretic perspective, the simu-

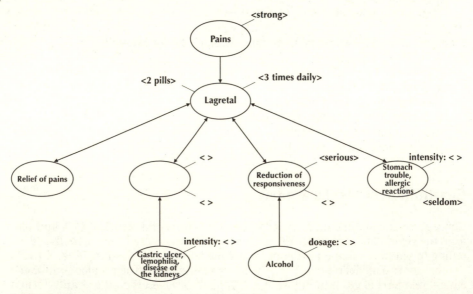

Figure 9.2 *A hypothetical model of the functioning of a specific drug ('Lagretal')*

lation of a mental model generates the cognitive representation of a situation or of a problem: possible consequences of actions and events can be anticipated, and possible preconditions of anticipated consequences can be identified.

For example, assume that the question arises whether taking Lagretal can result in headaches: according to the approach proposed, this question will activate the variable 'Lagretal' in *C(D')* and Lagretal will be used as an input parameter for running the model, (ie for computing the outcomes on other variables as specified in the simulation knowledge). The simulation provides a set of symptoms resulting from taking Lagretal. As 'headaches' are not part of the knowledge, the answer to the question will be 'no' (or 'I don't know'). If we had asked instead whether Lagretal can lead to a reduction of responsiveness, the answer would have been 'yes, if you drink alcohol' because such an effect can result from the interaction between Lagretal and alcohol.

The mental model approach allows for analyses of communication problems related to PPIs. For example, we assume that experts (eg physicians) have a more comprehensive, differentiated and correct knowledge about variables, properties, relation and potential results of simulations than lay people (eg patients). This difference might be one source of communication problems: The conceptual knowledge and the simulation knowledge of the average reader migh not be sufficient to encode and integrate the information provided by the PPI written by an expert (ie to constitute a mental model appropriate for understanding the effects of a drug).

If the PPI lacks some information needed for the constitution and simulation of an appropriate mental model, inadequate or faulty expectations and explanations of effects may result from the use of the fragmentary model. German PPIs, for example, rarely specify which conditions support or inhibit side effects: mostly one has to assume from the text that these effects are equally probable for all users of a drug. This may prevent some people from taking the drug although they have no side effects to fear, while others may erroneously underestimate the risk of side effects and take the drug.

Faulty explanations may result if no specific precautions against such inferences are taken in the PPI. Suppose a PPI says nothing about the time period within which the effects of some specific drug are to be expected. Readers may then transfer their experiences with other drugs (ie use previously stored information as default values). If the main eftects of the drug do not occur within the time period defined by the default value, he or she may attribute the absence of the effects to the dosage. Assume that the simulation knowledge includes the following statement:

> If the 'main effects' do not occur
> then increase the 'dosage' of the 'drug'.

A run of the mental model might then cause the person to increase the dosage too early or too strongly.

Identification of Mental Models

A major topic of research is presently the development and testing of methods for identifying mental models. Rouse and Morris[2] distinguish and discuss four methods: (1) inferring characteristics via empirical study (ie using experimental methods to test assumptions regarding the characteristics of models; (2) empirical modelling (ie algorithmically identifying the relation between a person's observation and subsequent actions); (3) analytical modelling (ie using available theory and data to formulate assumptions about the form, structure and parameters of mental models for particular tasks); (4) verbal/written reports (ie simply asking people about their mental models and letting them 'think aloud'). Each method has, as Rouse and Morris state, substantial advantages for some types of task, but also important weaknesses. The use of multiple approaches can possibly compensate for some of the difficulties. For example, Lugtenburg[20] has developed an interactive computer program that asks the user to define for the domain of interest (eg risks of drugs) the concept (eg dosage, side effects, etc) as well as a relation (eg influences) and to provide judgements for each pair of concepts regarding the kind of relation (eg unidirectional, bidirectional); the program then draws a model based on the user's statements. These data can be used as an input for analytical modelling as well as a basis for empirical studies. Even with multiple approaches the possibility of totally capturing a mental model might be rather remote, but, as Rouse and Morris concede, this may be partly due to the great likelihood that a mental model is not a static entity having only a single form. Furthermore, for many areas of research one might not need to set the goal so high but use the approach more pragmatically as a heuristic approach for interpreting data and generating research perspectives.

Conclusions

In many countries, people are informed about drugs not only by their physician but also through package inserts. There are no studies on how the information provided on inserts is interpreted by users or how inserts should be designed. However, in various countries laws with respect to inserts either have existed for a long time, have recently been passed or are currently being considered.

Studies in the US have found people interested in being informed about drugs and wanting full disclosure of associated risks. Whereas such information seems to have an effect on attitudes towards drugs, sometimes revealing considerable differences between lay people and experts, it is unclear whether the information influences actual drug-taking behaviour. The mental model approach provides a theoretical perspective for analysing the way in which people process information on drugs and derive expectations of and explanations for drug effects. Empirical research could investigate whether the information on package inserts is presented so that people can constitute a mental model and run it to produce correct inferences (ie adequate judgemental and behavioural consequences). Depending on the results of such research, the next task could be to design inserts such that inadequate judgements or behaviours are minimized.

The mental model approach was here applied to informing people about drugs via package inserts. However, this approach should prove quite useful for other types of risk assessment and risk communication as well. Whenever one has to rely on human judgement and decision making, the approach could be used for explaining and predicting behaviour as well as for guiding and improving behaviour towards risks. First of all, the approach probably can be generalized to all attempts to inform and communicate about health and environmental risks like, for instance, smoking, drinking, eating, running, etc.[21] It might also be applied, for example, to problems of threat diagnosis (eg identifying mental models of potential airplane highjackers) or of human reliability analysis (eg identifying mental models of operators in power plants). Rouse and Morris[2] describe a number of other applications (eg regarding supervisory control, manual control, comprehension of computer programs, system design and maintenance. In these and similar applications, the mental model concept might be used for analysis as well as for communication, instruction or task and system design.

References

1   D Gentner and A L Stevens (eds) (1983) *Mental Models* Lawrence Erlbaum Associates, Hillsdale, NJ

2   W B Rouse and N M Morris (1986) 'On Looking into the Black Box: Prospects and Limits in the Search for Mental Models' in *Psychological Bulletin* no 100, pp349–363

3   J H Holland, K J Holyoak, R E Nisbett and P R Thagard (1986) *Induction* MIT Press, Cambridge, Massachusetts

4   K Craik (1983) *The Nature of Explanation* Cambridge University Press, Cambridge

5   D Gentner and A L Stevens (1983) *Mental Models* Lawrence Erlbaum Associates, Hillsdale, NJ

6   C Keown, P Slovic and S Lichtenstein (1984) 'Influence of Information about Side Effect on Perceived Risk of Prescription Drugs' in *Health Marketing Quarterly* no 1, pp111–123

7   P Joubert and L L Lasagna (1975) 'Patient Package Inserts. I: Nature, Notions and Needs', in *Clinical Pharmacology and Therapeutics* no 18, pp507–513

8   C Keown (1982) 'Risk, Judgments and Intention Measures after Reading about Prescription Drug Side Effects in the Format of a Patient Package Insert', unpublished manuscript, University of Hawaii, Honululu

9   St A Eraker, M H Becker, C Jepson and P L De Tullio (1984) 'Patient Attitudes, Knowledge and Compliance after Receipt of Medication Instructions', unpublished manuscript

10 D E Kanouse, S H Berry, B Hayer-Roth, W H Rogers and J D Winkler (1981) 'Informing Patients about Drugs' Rand Publication Series 8

11 C Keown, P Slovic and S Lichtenstein (1981) 'Attitudes of Physicians, Pharmacists, and Laypersons toward Seriousness and Need for Disclosure of Prescription Drug Side Effects' in *Health Psychology* no 3, 1–11, p21

12 P Slovic, B Fischhoff and S Lichtenstein (1982) 'Facts versus Fears: Understanding Perceived Risk' in D Kahneman, P Slovic and A Tversky (eds) *Judgement under Uncertainty, Heuristics and Biases* Cambridge University Press, Cambridge

13 J J J Christensen-Szalanski, D E Beck, C M Christensen-Szalanski and T D Koepsell (1983) 'Effects of Expertise and Experience on Risk Judgments' in *Journal of Applied Psychology* no 68, pp278–284

14 J H Einhorn and R M Hogarth (1978) 'Confidence in Judgment Persistence in the Illusion of Validity' in *Psychological Review* no 85, pp395–416

15 T C Earle and G Cvetkovich 'Failure and Success in Public Risk Communication' (1986) in Air Pollution Control Association (eds) *Avoiding and Managing Environmental Damage from Major Industrial Accidents* APCA, Pittsburgh, Pennsylvania

16 M Thüring and H Jungermann (1986) 'Constructing and Running Mental Models for Inferences about the Future' in B Brehmer, H Jungermann, P Lourens

and G Sevon (eds) *New Directions in Research on Decision Making* North-Holland, Amsterdam

17 H Jungermann and M Thüring (1987) 'The Use of Mental Models for Generating Scenarios' in G Wright and P Ayton (eds) *Judgemental Forecasting* Wiley, New York

18 J R Anderson (1983) *The Architecture of Cognition* Harvard University Press, Cambridge, Massachusetts

19 A Newell and H Simon (1972) *Human Problem Solving* Prentice Hall, Englewood Cliffs, NJ

20 M Lugtenburg (1986) 'GETMO. Ein interaktives Programm zur firheburg mentaler Modelle', technical report, Institut für Psychologie, Technische Universitat, Berlin

21 V T Covello, D V Winterfeldt and P Slovic (1986) 'Communicating Scientific Information about Health and Environmental Risks: Problems and Opportunities from a Social and Behavioral Perspective' in V Covello, A Moghissi and V R R Uppuluri (eds), *Uncertainties in Risk Assessment and Risk Management* Plenum Press, New York

Characterizing Mental Models of Hazardous Processes: A Methodology and an Application to Radon

Ann Bostrom, Baruch Fischhoff and M Granger Morgan

People today face a steady stream of decisions about environmental hazards. Some of those decisions might involve immediate personal behaviour, such as whether to throw out apple juice after hearing that it might be contaminated with Alar (which might be a carcinogen), what to do when the emergency siren sounds at a local chemical plant and how to dispose of used motor oil. Other decisions might involve long-term public actions, such as whether to oppose a hazardous waste incinerator, whether to vote for a candidate who proposes a carbon emissions tax, and what to tell children about the environment that they will inherit.

In some cases, people may have translated these choices into well-formulated decision problems, of the form favoured by decision analysts, with explicit options, outcomes and uncertainties about the chances of experiencing those outcomes (von Winterfeldt and Edwards, 1986; Watson and Buede, 1987; Yates, 1990). When that happens, people need quantitative estimates of the critical parameters in their decision-making models. Typically, these estimates will include measures of how big the hazard is and how much it can be reduced at various prices. For example, a home owner deciding whether to test for radon needs to know how much testing costs, how accurate tests are and how much remediation will cost if a radon problem is discovered (Fischhoff, Svenson and Slovic, 1987).

In such cases, the first task of risk communicators is to determine what lay people currently believe about these parameters. It should then be conceptually straightforward to identify those bits of potentially available information whose provision would have the greatest impact on recipients' ability to make decisions in their own best interest (Fischhoff, 1985; Raiffa, 1968). To that end, many studies have examined the gaps in people's knowledge, even though the question of which gaps are worth filling seldom seems to have been approached analytically. These studies have elicited lay estimates of the size of a wide variety of risks, from nuclear power to communicable diseases, to pregnancy, to natural hazards (Burton, Kates and White, 1978; Environmental Protection Agency, 1990; Freudenburg and Rosa, 1984; Kunreuther et al, 1978; Lichtenstein et al, 1978; Magat, Viscusi and Huber, 1988; National center for Health Statistics, 1987; National Research Council, 1989; Paikoff and Brooks-Gunn, in press). The present study focuses on the problems of conveying information. Three sources of commentary on the social context of risk communication are Fischhoff (1990), Krimsky and Plough (1988) and National Research Council (1989).

In many cases, however, what people need to know most is not summary estimates, but substantive knowledge of what a hazard is and how it works. Such knowledge is essential for following public discussions about a hazard, for assessing one's competence to deal with it, and indeed, for formulating the options that might serve as the focus for decision making. Furthermore, people often have no access to scientific estimates of risk, meaning that they must generate their own estimates on the basis of whatever they know about the nature of a hazard.

Determining what people know – and need to know – about these substantive processes requires quite different research strategies from studying their summary estimates. A straightforward approach is to make a list of 'first things that one needs to know' about the risk. Risk communications could then focus on those first facts that people do not know already.

Some of the problems with this strategy are suggested by a mildly despairing comment made in the Institute of Medicine's (1986) important report, *Confronting AIDS*. It noted that, despite the extensive publicity given to the disease, only 41 per cent of the respondents to a national survey agreed with the (correct) statement that AIDS was caused by a virus. Such ignorance shows a clear gap between expert and lay beliefs. Yet, one must ask, is it an important gap? That is, are there any decisions or substantive inferences that hinge on this knowledge? If not, then alarm over this display of ignorance could be doubly damaging. On the one hand, it would unnecessarily erode experts' respect for lay people (why fault them for ignorance of things that do not matter in the decisions that they face?). On the other hand, it would waste the public's valuable attention by focusing communications on irrelevancies, perhaps eroding public respect for experts (why are they telling us this?).

It is hard to think of a practical decision that would be directly influenced by the fact that 'AIDS is caused by a virus'. Yet that need not mean that this fact is irrelevant to understanding AIDS as a phenomenon. A more systematic approach is needed for circumscribing the set of relevant information.

An Approach Using Influence Diagrams

Figure 9.3 presents one possible approach, illustrated with the risks of radon. It is an *influence diagram*. In it, each node-link-node combination portrays an 'influence' in the sense that the value of the concept at the beginning of an arrow affects the value of the concept at the arrow's point. For example, 'wind velocity and direction' influences the value of 'indoor–outdoor pressure difference'. When completely specified, an influence would be defined in terms of conditional probabilities, where *a influences b* if the probability distribution of *b* conditioned on *a* is different from the unconditioned distribution of *b* (Howard and Matheson, 1984).

As can be seen, this influence diagram has a hierarchical structure. In places, there are up to five levels of detail in the concepts whose values could influence the state of some higher level concept. Those higher level concepts are the primary influences on the risks of radon. In principle, each influence could represent an opportunity to reduce (or increase) those risks – although, of course, there may be no known or feasible way of doing so. Thus, an influence diagram should capture the relationships needed to structure a decision, as well as to estimate its parameters.

As mentioned, a fully specified decision would contain complete conditional probability distributions for all influences. Obviously, this is a considerable challenge

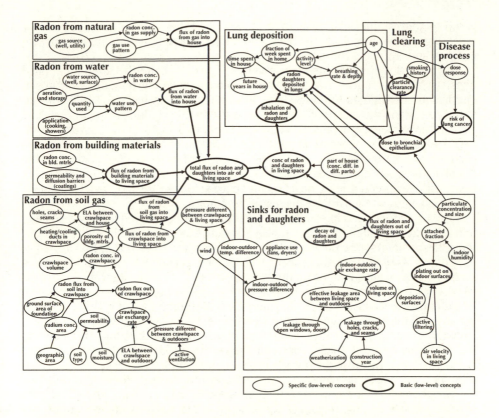

Figure 9.3 *Expert influence diagram for radon risk in house with crawl space.*

even for the technical experts most knowledgeable about an environmental hazard. One could hardly expect lay people to be so well informed. A more modest expectation would be that they understand the directions (and, perhaps, rough magnitudes) of the influences in the diagram. More modest still would be their knowing just the important concepts. Even more modest would be their having no beliefs that are not in the diagram – ie neither misunderstanding the influences that are there nor having erroneous beliefs not even suggested in the diagram.

If people's beliefs could be characterized in terms of deviations from this model, that could provide an orderly basis for determining the content of risk communications. Such messages could try to fill in the gaps and correct the misconceptions. The problems of making such additional information comprehensible would remain. However, those efforts would at least focus on transmitting the relevant information – and correcting misunderstandings that might cause that information to be misinterpreted. If lay people's mental models were organized along the lines of the expert model (or could be structured along those lines through instruction), then communications embodying the structure of the influence diagram might be relatively easy to understand (Atman, 1990).

Pursuing this strategy requires the following steps: *(a)* create an expert influence diagram, *(b)* elicit lay people's relevant beliefs, *(c)* map those beliefs into the diagram, and *(d)* identify gaps and misconceptions. Once risk communications have been composed to address these lacunae, their impact should be evaluated empirically by repeating steps *b* through *d*. The remainder of the article demonstrates a set of procedures implementing this approach.

Figure 9.3 represents step *a*. It was developed by Dr Keith Florig, an applied physicist, through successive iterations with our research group, drawing on scientific sources such as National Council for Radiation Protection (19S5) and National Research Council (1988), and beginning with descriptions of radon decisions such as those offered by Evans, Hawkins and Graham (1988) and Svenson and Fischhoff (1985). Further research about the development of expert influence diagrams can be found in Howard (1989). (In our own work, we have developed analogous diagrams for a variety of hazards, including Lyme disease, skin cancer from exposure to the sun, lead, and nuclear reactors on space vehicles. They are available on request. Responses to most have been studied empirically.)

The procedure used in step *b* begins with a very open-ended interview so as to minimize the imposition of the scientific perspective on respondents' conceptualizations. Respondents are asked to elaborate on all comments that they had made initially as well as to say something about each major aspect of risk: exposure processes (how people come in contact with the hazard), effects processes (how the hazard affects people) and risk management (how the risk can be controlled or reduced). The intent of this procedure is to provide more directive prompts, but without suggesting any unfamiliar concepts. The interview concludes by asking respondents what, if anything, each of a set of diverse photographs has to do with radon. This step was intended to increase the chances of evoking as yet untapped beliefs, but with a greater risk of reactivity. In subsequent work, more easily administered closed-ended questionnaires have been developed, based on these initial results (Bostrom, 1990).

Steps *c* and *d* follow fairly directly from these initial steps, although the details of transcription, coding, reliability checking and data analysis are moderately arduous. We believe they complete a generally applicable and revealing set of procedures.

Method

Respondents

Twenty-four interviews were conducted in the Pittsburgh area by a single interviewer, a registered nurse with experience in communicating occupational hazards. Respondents were recruited from several civic groups, which received a monetary contribution in return for their members' participation, or through signs posted at local libraries, in which case payment was direct. Respondents were divided equally between males and females. Two-thirds were employed; about half of these were professional and half in service/sales/clerical jobs. Three (13 per cent) were students. Fifteen were between 20 and 40 years old, with the remainder divided between the 40–60 and over-60 age brackets. Three-quarters were home owners. Thus, they were a diverse set of adults, although no claim is made about their representativeness.

Procedure

Respondents were interviewed individually, with the typical interview lasting 45 minutes. The first, *non-directive* stage of the interview began by asking respondents to describe everything that they knew about radon and its risks, in what was intended to be a non-evaluative tone (ie 'we want to know what people know so that we can design helpful communications'). Once their spontaneous responses appeared exhausted, respondents were asked to elaborate on each comment that they had made. They were then asked what they knew about each major aspect of radon risk. These follow-up requests were constructed to avoid introducing new physical concepts or problem framings. In the second, *directive* stage of the interview, respondents sorted 36 black-and-white photographs according to whether each had something to do with radon. As respondents worked, they were asked to describe each photograph (to be sure that they saw in it what we had seen) and the reasons for their choice. The photos covered various topics such as a diagram of a lung, a person dusting a bookshelf, and a frozen-food section at a grocery store. As we interpreted them, about one half dealt with radon-related topics, covering the major nodes in the influence diagram.

Coding

All interviews were taped and transcribed. After being checked for accuracy by the interviewer, the transcripts were coded into the expert influence diagram (see Fig 9.3). Concepts that did not fit into the diagram were listed separately, sorted into five types: (a) *misconceptions;* (b) *peripheral beliefs,* correct, but not particularly relevant; (c) *indiscriminate beliefs,* correct as far as they went but imprecise (eg 'radon makes people ill', without specifying the illness); (d) *background beliefs,* such as 'radon is a gas' and 'radon is radioactive'; (e) *valuations,* such as 'radon is dangerous'. Even with only 24 interviews, the final few interviews that were coded added very few new concepts. When respondents mentioned a mitigation procedure explicitly, it was coded according to the underlying concept.

The coding scheme was developed by a pair of researchers, both familiar with the expert diagram but with limited technical knowledge of radon. Coders were given the expert vocabulary and added the lay topics. After reaching agreement on two initial interviews, they, along with a third researcher, coded two additional interviews independently. All three coders agreed about 75 per cent of the time, depending on the interview and concept category. This seems like reasonably good agreement for such a fine-grained coding scheme. The influence diagram contained 14 first-level concepts (ie more important or influential ones – 10 exposure, 4 effects) and 48 more specific concepts (42 exposure, 6 effects). In addition, respondents contributed 6 background concepts, 6 peripheral concepts, 20 indiscriminate concepts, 16 erroneous concepts and 4 valuation concepts, for a total of 114 different concepts. (See Table 9.3 for a complete list of these concepts.)

Results

Statistical Summaries

On average, respondents produced 14.0 concepts in the non-directive portion of the interview and 15.0 concepts in the directive portion. Of the second group, 37 per cent were restatements of concepts mentioned in the first half. The mean number of misconceptions was, however, larger in the second portion of the interview (.67 vs 2.52; $p < .001$; Wilcoxon test), as was the average number of mitigation measures mentioned (.96 vs 1.52; $p < .10$).

Three statistical measures of the extent of respondents' knowledge about radon were defined: completeness, accuracy and specificity. They measured, respectively, how much respondents knew, what proportion of their beliefs were correct, and how detailed (or general) those beliefs were. See Table 9.1 for results on these measures.

Table 9.1 *Mean proportions obtained by respondents on various measures of performance*

	Non-directive phase			Directive phase		
Measures	*All concepts*	*Exposure concepts*	*Effects concepts*	*All concepts*	*Exposure concepts*	*Effects concepts*
Completeness[a]						
All levels	.11	.12	.05	.11	.12	.10
Level 1	.18	.21	.08	.22	.24	.17
Accuracy[b]						
All levels	.06	.09	.03	.06	.09	.04
Level 1	.03	.16	.05	.05	.16	.06

[a] Average proportion of expert concepts that were mentioned by a respondent.
[b] Product of completeness and concurrence (the proportion of a respondent's concepts appearing in the expert influence diagram).

Completeness was computed as the percentage of the concepts in the expert model that a given lay model included. On average, respondents produced 11 per cent of the total expert model in each portion of the interview. As might be expected, the level of completeness was much higher for the (more important) first-level concepts (18 per cent and 22 per cent, for the two halves of the interview, respectively). Perhaps less predictable was the higher level of completeness for exposure concepts than for effects concepts, even though there were many more of the former than the latter. This disparity was considerably larger in the first half (12 per cent vs 5 per cent) than in the second half (12 per cent vs 10 per cent), suggesting that the (more directive) photos managed to elicit some latent knowledge of effects.

There are several possible ways to measure the accuracy of those concepts that respondents did mention. One, called *concurrence,* is the percentage of the concepts in a respondent's model that appeared in the expert influence diagram. This measure was 45 per cent and 44 per cent for the two halves, respectively. Thus, a majority of respondents' concepts were wrong, peripheral, etc. A somewhat more comprehensive measure, called *accuracy,* appears in Table 9.1. It multiplies concurrence by completeness in order to give credit to respondents who not only said primarily right things, but also said many of them. It turned out that completeness and concurrence were strongly correlated in both halves (r = .89, .77, respectively, using Spearman rank-order correlations). For a sample of this size (N = 24), the following significance levels hold: r = 0.45 (p < .05), 0.55 (p < .01), and 0.65 (p < .001). Respondents were equally accurate in both halves, more accurate about the important, first-level concepts, and more accurate about exposure concepts than effects concepts.

There was only a modest positive correlation between respondents' concurrence scores and the number of concepts that they produced (r = .51,. 32, for the two halves). Thus, respondents who said more were somewhat more likely to give a higher percentage of correct information.

Specificity was calculated as the ratio of specific (lower level, levels 2 and below) concepts to more important, general concepts (level 1) in each respondent's data, divided by the comparable ratio for the expert model. Thus, a ratio larger than 1 meant that the respondent had a higher proportion of specific concepts than did the expert diagram. This calculation considered only concepts that were in the expert model, because others did not necessarily fit in the expert hierarchy. The mean ratios were .51 and .40 for the two halves of the interview. Thus, respondents were much more general than the experts (consistent with their higher completeness scores for level 1 than overall). Respondents who provided more concepts were only slightly more specific (r = .29), meaning that saying more was nearly as likely to increase the breadth of coverage as its depth or specificity. Providing more concepts was associated with providing somewhat more wrong concepts in the second half of the interview but not in the first half (r = −.17, .43), suggesting that the photos encouraged some counterproductive groping for concepts.

Substantive Beliefs

Table 9.2 shows the frequency with which each concept in the expert influence diagram was mentioned by respondents. Consistent with the greater completeness at the more general level, respondents mentioned individual general concepts more frequently. Indeed, every general concept (except 'radon from gas supply') was mentioned by at least one of these 24 respondents, whereas many specific concepts were never mentioned at all.

Most respondents mentioned that radon flows into living spaces and concentrates there, two exposure concepts that typically arose in both sections of the interview. Fewer respondents (11) mentioned that radon also flows out of living spaces and most of these respondents did so only in response to one of the photos. Relatively few respondents mentioned the basic sources of radon: water (7), soil gas (6) and building materials (3). Almost none (2) mentioned the fact that radon decays (reducing exposure, as long as no additional radon is added). Radon has a half life of 3.8 days, so that once influx stops, the risk quickly vanishes.

Although most specific exposure concepts were never mentioned at all, a few seemed to be common knowledge. Specifically, most respondents mentioned the influence of the part of the house (17), the geographic area (17), the influx of radon into basements or crawl spaces (14), and the role of pipes and ducts (16) and of holes, cracks and seams (14) in that influx – although they needed the prompts provided by the pictures to think of the latter comments. Smaller numbers of respondents

Table 9.2 *Frequency of mention of expert concepts by 24 respondents*

| Concept | Number of respondents mentioning concept | | | Proportion of respondents mentioning at least once |
	Non-directive phase only	Directive phase only	Both	
Exposure level 1				
Concentration of radon in living space	1	0	21	.92
Total flux of radon into living space	4	2	12	.75
Efflux of radon from living space	2	9	0	.46
Radon from water	0	5	2	.29
Radon from soil gas	2	1	3	.25
Exposure level 2				
Part of house (concentration differs in different parts of house)	11	0	6	.71
Geographic area	15	1	1	.71
Pipes/ducts going into house from the ground/foundation	2	10	4	.67
Holes, cracks, and seams (in foundation, basement floor)	1	7	6	.58
Radon influx to basement/crawl space	4	2	8	.58
Leakage through open windows/doors	2	7	2	.46
Indoor–outdoor air exchange rate	1	0	6	.29
Appliance use (fans, dryers)	0	5	1	.25
Construction of building	3	2	1	.25
Effects level 1				
Inhalation of radon	1	9	3	.54
Lung cancer	1	1	3	.21
Effects level 2				
Smoking history	1	3	1	.21

Note: Concepts mentioned by fewer than five subjects:

Exposure level 1: Building materials contain radon, decay of radon over time.

Exposure level 1: Weatherization; flux of radon from crawl space/basement to living space; effective leakage area between foundation and living space; radon concentration next to foundation/barrier (in basement); radium concentration in soil; radon efflux from basement/crawl space to outdoors; leakage through holes, cracks, seams; soil type; active ventilation of crawl space/basement; radon concentration in water; soil permeability; effective leakage area between living space and outdoors; surface area of foundation/barrier.

Effects level 1: None.

Effects level 2: Time spent in house; age; dose response; breathing depth and rate; habits.

mentioned various methods of air exchange, consistent with the smaller number mentioning the general concept of radon outflow.

As previously seen in the summary statistics, respondents showed much less awareness of effects concepts. The most frequently cited expert concept (the inhalation of radon) was mentioned by only 13 respondents, most of them only after seeing the photographs (which included a diagram of a lung). Although 15 respondents mentioned cancer, only five noted that it was lung cancer, leaving them with (in our terms) indiscriminate beliefs, which are reported in Table 9.3. Indeed, the tables show that expert effects concepts were far outnumbered by incorrect or imprecise ones. There were few mentions of factors that enhance the effects of radon, like smoking and breathing deeply.

Table 9.3 shows the frequency with which the different kinds of non-expert concepts were mentioned. For instance, most respondents reported the background facts that radon is a gas (21) and is detectable with a test kit (23). In addition to 'radon causes cancer', the set of indiscriminate concepts included the facts that radon comes from underground (20), that fans affect radon exposure (10), and that radon causes lung problems (11), illness and death (6), and contamination (6). There is, obviously, some degree of discretion in deciding whether respondents' concepts are sufficiently precise to show that they really know what they are talking about.

Table 9.3 *Frequency of mention of non-expert concepts by 24 respondents*

Concept	Number of respondents mentioning concept			Proportion of respondents mentioning at least once
	Non-directive phase only	Directive phase only	Both	
Background				
Radon is detectable with a test kit	19	0	4	.96
Radon is a gas	4	3	14	.88
Radon is radioactive	1	0	7	.33
Peripheral				
Mining/radon from mines	3	6	1	.42
Affects animals	0	8	0	.33
Indiscriminate				
Radon from underground	4	1	15	.83
Radon attaches to dust	0	7	0	.29
Radon in environment	2	3	0	.21
Fans (ventilation)	0	7	3	.42
More lower in house (correct, but reasons often incorrect)	7	0	3	.42
Cancer	6	3	6	.63
Lung problems	0	10	1	.46
Illness and death	4	2	0	.25
Radon contaminates	0	6	0	.25
Erroneous				
Affects plants	1	13	0	.58
Breast cancer	0	7	0	.29
Contaminates water	0	5	0	.21
Contaminates blood	0	9	0	.38
Radon from garbage	1	4	0	.21
Valuation				
Radon is risky, dangerous	4	3	6	.54

Note: Concepts mentioned by fewer than five subjects:

Background: Radon occurs naturally; radon is undetectable with senses; radon comes from uranium.

Peripheral: Radon in industrial waste; radon in radioactive waste; absorption through skin; radon comes from fossilized materials.

Indiscriminate: Porosity of building materials; health problems; genetic mutation; physiology; health; radon is poisonous; radon is an element; radon is extracted from soil; radon is a form of energy; radon is heavy (a heavy gas); radon is not volatile.

Erroneous: Radon from tank leaks; more higher in house; elevation of land; lead or concrete foundation/barrier (impermeable to radioactivity); leukaemia; contaminates food; corrosion; inhibits growth (in children); skin lesions; radon is manufactured; radon has an odour.

Valuation: Radon is harmful; radon is scary; radon is costly to society.

If one decided, for example, that the 15 respondents who said that 'radon causes cancer' knew what kind of cancer it was (or that such general knowledge was adequate), then there would be an increase in completeness and accuracy scores, along with a decrease in specificity. However, because some respondents explicitly mentioned types of cancer not caused by radon, this inference seemed overly generous to us.

The most common misconception about exposure processes (offered by five respondents) was that radon comes from garbage. This idea might represent confusion between radioactive decay and organic decay. Such a misconception should be easy to correct, and it might merit attention if 20 per cent of a general population shared it. Quite a few respondents mentioned the peripheral facts that radon comes from mining (10) and from industrial waste (3). If respondents believed these were the primary sources of radon, then these responses might better have been treated as misconceptions. If left unchallenged, such beliefs could blunt the effectiveness of risk communications.

The situation with effects processes was quite different. Very few were mentioned in the non-directive segment (except 'radon causes cancer'). The photos, however, evoked a variety of peripheral and erroneous concepts. These include the beliefs that radon affects plants (14) and animals (8), that it causes breast cancer (7) and contaminates blood (9), water (5), and food (4). Quite a few respondents described radon as dangerous (13), harmful (4), etc. Thus, people seem to know that radon is bad for them, but not to have much idea why.

Discussion

This study offered a general method for studying risk perceptions, as a precursor to developing risk communications. The method's usefulness depends on completing several procedures, each with its own criteria for success. The first such procedure is producing an accurate, coherent and encompassing influence diagram. As an example, Figure 9.3 has been reviewed by various individuals and is offered here for readers' scrutiny.

The second procedure is a way to elicit people's beliefs that neither puts new concepts in their minds nor leaves existing ones unstated. The method attempts to balance these somewhat conflicting goals by segmenting the interview into two parts, non-directive and directive. The non-directive approach is able to reveal much more diverse perspectives than the directive interview, which is designed to tap only ignorance and knowledge of expert facts. The risks of omission in the non-directive approach can be seen in the many concepts that appeared only in the second segment. The risks of commission in the directive approach can be seen in the many misconceptions that it evoked. The photographs that were used might be viewed as a sort of cognitive entrapment, suggesting 'relevant' topics that might not have occurred to people otherwise (although that could not have happened if the respondents had understood radon well).

The third procedure is to analyse people's responses. With an open-ended procedure, that means coding responses into a common set of categories. Here, the categories were provided by the influence diagram, supplemented by respondents' non-expert concepts. Despite the large number of categories, coding proved fairly reliable.

This coding scheme produced statistical summaries not only for the frequency of specific beliefs, but also for several aggregate properties of responses – namely their completeness, accuracy and specificity. These statistics showed that respondents here knew relatively few of the facts in the influence diagram, with the known facts concentrated at the highest level of generality and combined with a substantial admixture of non-expert concepts (some wrong, some imprecise and some irrelevant). These results suggest that people like these respondents have a good deal to learn (and to unlearn) before they would understand the basic structure of the radon problem (at the level defined in Figure 9.3).

If overall performance statistics such as these seem to warrant a communication programme, then the belief-specific results could direct its substantive contents. For example, people need to know about the short half-lives of radon's critical decay products. Thinking that all radioactive materials, including radon, will contaminate a home indefinitely might vitiate people's accurate beliefs (eg why test if nothing can be done?). As it happens, this fact was so basic to understanding radon that we did not even include it explicitly in the expert influence diagram (just as we omitted some background facts that respondents did know, such as 'radon is a gas'). This one vital gap notwithstanding, respondents seemed much better informed about exposure processes than about effects processes.

Thus, this set of methods seems to have produced results that are potentially useful for deciding whether to produce risk messages and, if so, what to include in them. As next steps, in addition to replication with broader samples, these results require testing through converging operations. For example, in other studies, we are examining (a) the applicability of these methods to other hazards, (b) the knowledge (and ignorance) shown in responses to closed-ended questionnaires tapping the same domain, and (c) the impact of risk messages designed to fill the gaps identified here (and structured around the influence diagram).

Our choice of method was determined, in part, by our applied focus. Thus, we have emphasized the match between respondents' beliefs and expert knowledge, because deviations indicate opportunities for providing information. We focused on individual pieces of qualitative knowledge because one cannot expect lay people to intuit how much radon their house holds or how various interventions would affect that level. If we were interested in people's quantitative inferences, then a problem-solving task would have been appropriate, such as asking respondents how radon concentrations would change, say, when windows are opened or when ambient temperatures increase. Choosing problem-specific procedures for eliciting and representing beliefs seems an accepted practice in studies of thinking in complex domains (eg Gentner and Stevens, 1983; Johnson-Laird, 1983; Jungermann, Schutz and Thuring, 1988; Rouse and Morris, 1986).

Judging by the results obtained here, people's understanding of the radon problem seems not only incomplete but also incoherent, in the sense of containing scattered and inconsistent items. If they were required to solve particular problems, such people might be expected to access and combine these beliefs quite unreliably. Thus, the process-tracing procedures that have been so useful in describing thinking in better structured domains (Ericsson and Simon, 1984; Montgomery and Svenson, 1989) might reveal a fairly messy situation here. They might also show people's inferences to be quite sensitive to the precise way in which problems are posed (Hogarth, 1982; Poulton, 1989).

Open-ended procedures such as those used here are very labour intensive. Moreover, they take one into the theoretically challenging domain of how people choose and apply propositions at different levels of specificity to rich, life-like situations (Collins and Gentner, 1987). However, they seem the only way to discover pertinent misconceptions (such as 'radon is radioactive indefinitely'). As mentioned above, these misconceptions can blunt the effect of accurate beliefs. However, they will go unchecked if risk messages, as typically happens, are focused solely on the facts that some experts think are worth knowing (Bonneville Power Administration, 1987; Environmental Protection Agency, 1986; University of Maine, 1983; Yuhnke, Silbergeld and Caswell, 1987).

References

Atman, C (1990) *Network structures as a foundation for risk communication* unpublished doctoral dissertation, Department of Engineering and Public Policy, Carnegie Mellon University

Bonneville Power Administration (1987) *Understanding indoor radon* Portland

Bostrom, A (1990) *A mental models approach to exploring perceptions of hazardous processes* unpublished doctoral dissertation, School of Urban and Public Affairs, Carnegie Mellon University

Burton, I, R Kates and G White (1978). *The environment as hazard*, Oxford University Press, New York

Collins, A and D Gentner (1987) 'How people construct mental models' in D Holland and N Quinn (eds), *Cultural models in language and thought* Cambridge University Press, Cambridge

Environmental Protection Agency (1990) *Public knowledge and perceptions of chemical risks in six communities: Analysis of a baseline survey* Washington, DC

Environmental Protection Agency and US Department of Health and Human Services (1986) *A citizen's guide to radon* (OPA-86-004) US Government Printing Office, Washington DC

Ericsson, K A and H A Simon (1984). *Verbal protocols as data.* MIT Press, Cambridge, MA

Evans, J S, N C Hawkins and J D Graham (1988) 'The value of monitoring for radon in the home: A decision analysis' in *Journal of the Air Pollution Control Association* no 38, pp1380–1385

Fischhoff, B (1985) 'Cognitive and institutional barriers to "informed consent"' in M Gibson (ed), *To breathe freely: Risk, consent, and air* (pp169–185). Rowman & Littlefield, Totowa, NJ

Fischhoff, B (1990) 'Psychology: Tool or tool maker?' *American Psychologist* no 45, pp647–653

Fischhoff, B, O Svenson and P Slovic (1987) 'Active responses to environmental hazards' in D Stokols and I Altman (eds) *Handbook of environmental psychology* (pp1089–1133). Wiley, New York

Freudenburg, W R and E A Rosa (eds) (1984) *Public reaction to nuclear power: Are there critical masses?* Westview, Boulder, CO

Gentner, D and A L Stevens (eds) (1983) *Mental models* Erlbaum, Hillsdale, NJ

Hogarth, R (1982) *New directions for methodology of social and behavioral science: Question framing and response consistency* Jossey-Bass, San Francisco

Hovard, R A (1989) 'Knowledge maps' in *Management Science* no 35, pp903–922

Hovard, R A and J E Matheson (1984) 'Influence diagrams' in *Readings on the principles and applications of decision analysis*, vol 2, pp719–762 Professional Collection, Strategic Decision Group, Palo Alto, CA

Institute of Medicine (1986) *Confronting AIDS* Washington, DC

Johnson-Laird, P (1983) *Mental models* Oxford University Press, New York

Jungermann, H, H Schutz and M Thuring (1988) 'Mental models in risk assessment: Informing people about drugs' in *Risk Analysis* no 8, pp147–155

Krimsky, S and A Plough (1988) *Environmental hazards: Communicating risks as a social process* Auburn House, Dover, MA

Kunreuther, H, R Ginsberg, L Miller, P Sagi, P Slovic, B Borkin and N Katz (1978) *Disaster insurance protection* Wiley, New York

Lichtenstein, S, P Slovic, B Fischhoff, M Layman and B Combs (1978) 'Judged frequency of lethal events' in *Journal of Experimental Psychology: Human Learning and Memory* no 4, pp551–578

Magat, W A, W K Viscusi and J Huber (1988) 'Consumer processing of hazard warning information' in *Journal of Risk Uncertainty* no 1, pp201–232

Montgomery, H and O Svenson (eds) (1989) *Process tracing methods for decision making* Wiley, London

National Center for Health Statistics (1987) 'Knowledge and attitudes about AIDS', data from the National Health Interview Survey, August 10–30, 1987. *Advance Data*, no 146

National Council for Radiation Protection (1985) *Evaluation of occupational and environmental exposures to radon and radon daughters in the United States* Report no 78, Washington, DC

National Research Council (1988) *Health risks of radon and other internally deposited alphaemitters: BEIR IV* Washington, DC

National Research Council (1989) *Improving risk communication* Washington, DC

Paikoff, R and J Brook-Gunn (in press) 'Taking fewer chances: Teenage pregnancy prevention programs' in *American Psychologist*

Poulton, E C (1989) *Bias in quantitative estimates* Erlbaum, London

Raiffa, H (1968) *Decision analysis* Addison-Wesley, Reading, MA

Rouse, W B and N M Morris (1986) 'On looking into the black box: Prospects and limits in the search for mental models' *Psychological Bulletin* no 100, pp349–363

Svenson, O and B Fischhoff (1985) 'Levels of environmental decisions' in *Journal of Environmental Psychology* no 5, pp55–68

University of Maine (1983) *Radon in water and air: Health risks and control measures* Land and Resources Center, Oronco

von Winterfeldt, D and W Edwards (1986) *Decision analysis and behavioral research* Cambridge University Press, New York

Watson, S and D Buede (1987) *Decision synthesis* Cambridge University Press, New York

Yates, J F (1990) *Judgment and decision making* Wiley, New York

Yuhnke, R E, E K Silbergeld and J E Caswell (1987) *Radon: The citizens' guide* Environmental Defense Fund, Washington, DC

Optimistic Biases About Personal Risks

Neil D Weinstein

The fact that the public overestimates the harm caused by some problems, such as toxic waste, yet underestimates the number of people harmed by other hazards, such as asthma, is now well recognized.[1] Less familiar is the consistent, optimistic bias that exists concerning personal risks. When asked about their own chances, people claim that they are less likely to be affected than their peers.[2-7]

This optimistic bias in 'self-other' risk comparisons is easy to demonstrate. If these comparisons are not biased, claims of below-average risk will be balanced by admissions of above-average risk. In a representative sample, the mean response will be 'average', Research shows, however, that the mean is usually shifted in the 'below-average' direction. A random sample of New Jersey adults,[2] for instance, yielded the following ratios of 'below-average' to 'above-average' responses: asthma, 9:1; drug addiction, 8:1; food poisoning, 7:1; influenza, 3:1; lung cancer, 2:1; and pneumonia, 5:1. A significant optimistic bias was found for 25 of 32 hazards in this study.

This bias in comparative risk judgements is robust and widespread. It appears with diverse hazards and samples and with different questions used to elicit the personal risk ratings.[2-7] Optimistic biases also appear for positive events: people regard themselves as more likely than others to experience financial success, career advancement and long life.[6] Pessimistic biases[8] are rare.

Some biases occur when people compare themselves with an incorrect norm. The risk of becoming addicted to drugs really is small for most of the population, but it seems that people conclude incorrectly that their risk is far below average by comparing themselves to drug users – a salient high-risk group – rather than to people like themselves who are far more numerous.

Optimism may also arise when ambiguous risk factors are interpreted in a biased manner. People who have not tested their homes for radon gas assert that they are less likely to have problems than their neighbours.[5] Their most frequent explanation is that their houses are well ventilated. Although high air-exchange rates do decrease radon levels, it is hard to consider these explanations unbiased when individuals claiming high ventilation rates outnumber those acknowledging low ventilation rates by a ratio of 26 to 1.

There are also times when people are clearly in high-risk groups but downplay the risk or refer to risk-countering practices of little value. When Bauman and Siegel[8]

Reprinted with permission from *Science* 246, 8 December 1989, pp1232–1233. Copyright © 1989 American Association for the Advancement of Science.

asked gay men to rate the riskiness of their behaviour for contracting AIDS, few who engaged in high-risk sex rated their own risk as high. They justified their beliefs by referring to their relatively low number of sex partners or to ineffective precautions, such as inspecting their partners for lesions or showering after sex.

In general, optimism is greatest for hazards with which subjects have little personal experience, for hazards rated low in probability, and for hazards judged to be controllable by personal action.[2] Optimism is also strong if people think that signs of vulnerability appear early (as they think is true of diabetes, alcoholism and asthma), so that an absence of present signs means they are exempt from future risk.[2]

Predicting when optimism occurs does not tell us why it occurs. One idea is that optimistic biases represent attempts to shield ourselves from the fear of being harmed. Most data do not, however, support this view: life-threatening hazards elicit no greater optimism than minor illnesses.[2,6]

A second proposal focuses on our desire to be better than other people. Admitting that peers are less susceptible to harm can threaten our feelings of competence and self-worth.[9] Threats to self-esteem should be particularly strong for hazards like suicide and alcoholism that are thought to be controllable; victimization in such situations is often regarded as personal weakness. This reasoning is consistent with the strong optimism-controllability correlation that exists.[2]

A third proposal is that optimistic biases are produced by simple cognitive errors. For example, if prevention campaigns create a stereotype of a high-risk individual, people may use this as a standard and conclude incorrectly that their own risk is below average. Excessive extrapolation from the present to the future can also be viewed as erroneous reasoning. Even the association with controllability could be cognitive in origin, because we are more likely to be aware of our own efforts to control risks than others' efforts.

Still, cognitive errors do not provide an adequate explanation for optimistic biases because they do not explain why pessimistic biases almost never appear. The notion that optimistic predictions are actively constructed, rather than arising from simple mental errors, is supported by instances where reasoning is distorted to yield self-serving predictions. For example, people who think they are particularly intelligent rate intelligence as very important to career success, whereas those who think they have a good sense of humour rate this attribute as more important.[10]

Optimistic biases in personal risk perceptions are important because they may seriously hinder efforts to promote risk-reducing behaviours. If people believe they are not susceptible to AIDS, or less susceptible than others, it may be more difficult to convince them to adopt prudent precautions. There are many positive correlations in the literature between beliefs of personal vulnerability and protective behaviour,[11,12] but there are also situations where greater perceived susceptibility does not lead to greater action.[4,12,13] There has been little research on these differences.

Although we usually think of biases as maladaptive, several authors have emphasized the benefits of illusions.[14,15] Optimism about personal risks is associated with less depression.[16] Optimism about successful performance leads people to try harder on difficult tasks, so that they really do succeed more often.[14] A general tendency to be optimistic may even have positive consequences for physical health.[17]

The benefits of illusions, though, surely depend on the nature of the illusion and the nature of the hazard. Overly optimistic expectations about the value of low-cholesterol diets and exercise may help a heart attack victim sustain these life-style changes and be happier and more productive. But a failure to admit that our smoking, driving while intoxicated or unprotected sex puts us at risk may keep us from making changes, and this could prove disastrous.

References

1   B B Johnson and V T Covello (eds) (1987) *The Social and Cultural Construction of Risk* Reidel, Dordrecht; W R Freudenberg (1998) in *Science*, no 242, p44; P Slovic (1987) in *Science* no 236, p280
2   N D Weinstein (1987) *Journal of Behav Med*, no 10, p481
3   L J Bauman and K Siegel (1987) *Journal of Applied Social Psychology*, no 17, p329
4   J G Joseph et al (1987) *Journal of Applied Social Psychology*, no 17, p231
5   N D Weinstein, M L Klotz and P M Sandman (1988) in *American Journal of Public Health*, no 78, p796
6   N D Weinstein (1980) in *Journal of Personal Social Psychology*, no 39, p806
7   W D Hansen and C K Malotte (1986) *Prev Med*, no 15, p363; B C Leigh (1987) *Journal of Stud Alcohol* no 48, p467; J P Kirscht, D P Haefner, F S Kegeles and I M Rosenstock (1966) *Journal of Health and Human Behaviour*, no 7, p248; J A Kulick and H I M Mahler (1987) *Health Psychology*, no 6, p15; L S Perloff and B K Fetzer (1986) *Journal of Personal Social Psychology*, no 50, p1986; N D Weinstein (1982) *Journal of Behav Med*, no 5, p441; V M Mays, G W Albee and S Schneider (eds) (   ) *Health Psychology*, no 3, p431 in *Psychological Approaches to the Primary Prevention of Acquired Immune Deficiency Syndrome* Sage, Beverly Hills CA; D Zakay (1983) *Acta Psychology*, no 53, p271
8   D Dolinski, W Gromski and E Zawisza (1987) *Journal of Social Psychology*, no 127, p511
9   A G Greenwalk, (1980) *American Psychology* no 35, p603; J V Wood, S E Taylor and R R Lichtman (1985) *Journal of Personal Social Psychology*, no 49, p1169; T A Wills (1981) *Psychology Bulletin*, no 90, p245
10 C S Weinstein (1989) *Journal of Teacher Education*, no 40, p53
11 N K Janz and M H Becker (1984) *Health Education Quarterly*, no 11, p1
12 J P Kirscht (1988) in *Health Behaviour: Emerging Research Perspectives* D G Gochman (ed) Plenum, New York, pp27–41
13 H Leventhal (1970) in *Advances in Experimental Social Psychology* L Berkowitz (ed), Academic Press, New York, vol 5, pp119–186
14 S E Taylor and J D Brown (1988) *Psychology Bulletin*, no 103, p193
15 R E Baumeister, paper presented at American Psychological Association Convention, Atlanta, GA, August 1988; R Janoff-Bulman, ibid
16 L B Alloy and A H Ahrens (1987) in *Journal of Personal Social Psychology*, no 52, p366
17 M F Scheier et al (1987) *Journal of Personal Social Psychology*, no 55, p169

Part Four

How Can Social Scientists Contribute to Risk Management?

The Brent Spar Controversy: An Example of Risk Communication Gone Wrong

Ragnar E Löfstedt and Ortwin Renn

Introduction

It is hard to remember an environmental controversy that has received as much media attention as the proposed sinking of the Brent Spar oil storage platform jointly owned by Shell and Exxon on the North Atlantic sea-bed. The episode caused a great deal of embarrassment for Shell, who applied for deep-sea disposal, as well as for John Major and the British Government who defended Shell's decision as the best practicable environmental option (BPEO). Greenpeace, in particular their activists in Germany, mounted a massive campaign against the sinking of the Brent Spar which eventually prompted the German, Danish and Swedish governments to deplore its dumping. The arguments about how the Brent Spar buoy should be disposed of were many, but the environmental reality of the options played little part as the controversy reached the boiling point.

What makes the Brent Spar controversy interesting is that it was an environmental 'non-issue' until the abandoned oil-storage buoy was occupied by Greenpeace activists at the end of April 1995. In this paper, we first report on the case history and then shed light on it with regard to the ideas and conclusions put forward in the risk communication literature. In conclusion, we draw some general conclusions with respect to risk communication.

Case History

In early 1994, two oil giants. Shell and Exxon, had a problem with the disposal of the oil storage buoy named Brent Spar. Although the platform was jointly owned, Shell had operational control of the platform and was thereby in charge of decommissioning procedure. The buoy, originally commissioned in 1976, had been non-operational for five years and was now seen as redundant. Disposing of Brent Spar posed a conundrum as the owners were not required by law to dispose of the buoy on land: the buoy was located in deep water (more than 75 meters) and as it weighed more than 4000 tons (actual weight was 14,500 tons), the International Maritime

Organisation's guidelines stipulate that sinking of the structure in the ocean is an acceptable option. As a result, Shell commissioned no less than 30 separate studies to consider the technical, safety and environmental implications of its disposal. Shell came up with four different options:

* Disposal on land
* Sinking the buoy at its current location
* Decomposition of the buoy on the spot
* Deep sea dumping (but within UK waters)

After thorough examination of these options, Shell decided to implement the fourth option, mainly due to its fairly low cost with little environmental impact (BPEO). The second most realistic option, that of horizontal dismantlement on land, was seen to be four times more expensive and high risk for workers (six times higher) and low but measurable risk of pollution of inshore water in the case of an accidental break-up during transport.[1,2] The other options were seen to be either unfeasible or environmentally harmful.

On the basis of the results of the consulting studies, Shell asked the UK Department of Trade and Industry (DTI) for permission to dump the buoy in the deep sea, as this was in their opinion the BPEO. In December 1994, DTI approved the strategy. Under the guidelines of the new convention on the marine environment (the Oslo–Paris Convention), the UK Government notified other European nations on 16 February of Shell's plan to sink the platform. As no country responded within the 60-day deadline for objections imposed by the Convention (ie by 16 April), the UK Government issued Shell the disposal licence in the first week of May. However, before the licence was issued Greenpeace occupied Brent Spar on 16 April.

Following this initial occupation, the crisis began to unfold. After the Greenpeace occupation, the Brent Spar controversy hit the media with pictures of Greenpeace activists braving the water cannons of Shell's tugboats. On 9 May, the German Environmental and Agricultural Ministries protested to the UK Government that land disposal had not been significantly investigated. As the protest came in after the deadline the UK Government rejected it. Throughout May, Brent Spar remained high on the media agenda. In the period of 20–30 May, for instance, Greenpeace mobilized politicians against deep-sea sinking by collecting signatures and, on 26 May, conservative groups joined Green action groups in asking for a consumer boycott of Shell gasoline stations. The boycott was effective in Germany, Holland and parts of Scandinavia. On 23 May, however, after several attempts, Shell was finally able to remove the Greenpeace activists from the platform. On 1 June, after much campaigning against Shell, the results of a poll in Germany suggested that 74 per cent of the population were willing to boycott Shell gas stations (the survey was financed by Greenpeace).

The controversy, however, did not die down with the protesters removed from the platform. On 5 June, the North Sea Protection Conference look place in Esbjerg, Denmark, and was attended by the Environmental Ministers from the countries surrounding the North Sea and by the EU Environmental Commissioner, Ritt Bjerregaard. At the opening of the conference, virtually all the official delegates (except the UK and Norway) condemned the sinking of the platform and the UK Environmental Minister, John Gummer, was singled out for a large amount of critique which was widely reported in the press. On 6 June, the German Environmental Minister, Angela Merkel, demanded a complete halt of deep-ocean disposal, including oil platforms. At the same time at the G7 summit in Canada, Helmut Kohl informed John Major that stopping the sea dumping of Brent Spar was 'not the looniness of a few greens but a Europewide, worldwide trend for the protection of our seas'.

On 16 June, the platform was again occupied by Greenpeace activists. At this time, Greenpeace made claims that there were large quantities of heavy metals and other highly toxic organic material in the tanks that had not been declared by Shell. On the same day, protesters moved in on Shell headquarters in the Netherlands.

Throughout the crisis, Shell UK received little support. The UK Government was active in trying to persuade its European allies that the deep-sea sinking of the Brent Spar was in fact the BPEO, but these arguments fell on deaf ears. Additionally, Shell UK's position was becoming increasingly untenable due to pressure from Shell Germany and the Netherlands. The company was receiving very negative PR in these two countries. For instance, at Shell's 1728 stations in Germany, gasoline sales were 20 per cent below average, 200 stations were threatened with attacks, 50 stations were vandalized, two stations were firebombed and shots were fired at another. In addition, due to the Greenpeace campaign, Germans were writing letters to the UK DTI and enclosing money to help to pay for on-shore disposal and German women were sending pictures of their children to Shell UK urging its chairman, Dr Chris Fay, to stop the planned sinking for the benefit of future generations. During this period, Shell Germany received over 11,000 letters complaining about the disposal.

In the face of this level of opposition, Shell announced on the 20 June that it had called off plans to sink the Brent Spar, only hours before it was due to be sunk. It cited economic problems due to the boycott. The UK Government felt betrayed and the Energy Minister, Tim Eggar, stated that Shell should have gone through with the deep-sea dumping as it is the BPEO. Following Shell's reversal on the sinking, Greenpeace issued a statement applauding the action and announced that it would help Shell to find an acceptable environmental solution. A poll in Germany indicated that 82 per cent of those interviewed supported boycotts such as the one against Shell as a means for consumers to fight environmentally harmful practices.

However, the fall-out continued. The UK Government felt that they had been unfairly treated by their European colleagues, views which were shared by some of the UK press.

On 27 June, Shell started a damage limitation exercise aimed at German and Danish consumers. In Germany, they took out a one-page advertisement in 100 national and local newspapers with the title 'We will change'. In these, Shell admitted to mistakes and ill-advised Brent Spar policies, but maintained that the decision to dump at sea was correct on technical and environmental grounds. In Denmark, Shell sent letters to 250,000 credit card holders explaining their policies. In July 1995, Shell asked the Norwegian company Det Norske Veritas to investigate the accusations made by Greenpeace about the contents of Brent Spar's empty storage tanks (particularly the statement that they still contained 5000 tons of crude oil). This independent inventory of Brent Spar's contents was published in the autumn of 1995, broadly confirming the figures provided by Shell.[3] A few weeks prior to the report of these findings, Greenpeace admitted that it had made a mistake about the quantity of the remaining pollutants, but maintained that the sinking of Brent Spar would have been wrong.

The Risks of Deep-Ocean Disposal

According to Shell's commissioned studies, the risks posed by the sinking of Brent Spar were quantified: occupational risk was highest with land dismantling and lowest with on-the-spot sinking. Environmental risks were also low for deep-sea disposal. According to these studies, sinking Brent Spar in the deep sea did not pose any significant environmental problems. The total inventory of the hazardous materials within the buoy were minimal: several thousand tons of oil and oily sand, slightly radioactive scale, some oil remnants and other chemicals. In all, the total quantity was less than 1 per cent of the amounts discharged by boats in the North Sea in the course of one year. However, there was a fear of local environmental contamination in the deep sea where Brent Spar would have been dumped which had not been thoroughly researched, although overall experts maintained that the impact was minute relative to existing levels of ocean pollution.

The UK Select Committee on Science and Technology confirmed the low risk situation and expressed approval of the deep-sea disposal option.[4] In May 1996, the Government's Scientific Group on Decommissioning (commonly referred to as the Shepherd Commission), composed of an independent group of scientists set up specifically to consider the scientific environmental aspects of the deep-sea disposal of Brent Spar, also broadly confirmed the scientific assessment of Shell's analysis, but did conclude that: more open procedures were needed, greater mobilization of scientific expertise, international discussions on these types of topics were needed and that public perceptions needed to be accounted for.[5]

So what went wrong? Why did Shell lose its credibility? Why was the public protest so overwhelming? Why was the boycott so successful? We feel that it has a great deal to do with Shell/and the UK Government implementing the wrong risk communication strategy.

Reasons Why Shell's Risk Communication Programme Failed

One issue was the attribution of blame to two actors, Shell in the first instance for taking the policy decision that deep-sea disposal was the BPEO and the UK Government in the second for standing by Shell. Related to this, Shell was seen as a big business, being a transnational corporation, and its defeat at the hands of the public and Greenpeace was described by one UK newspaper as a 'victory for democracy' (which, of course, raises further questions about the presence of democratic procedure with Greenpeace itself). Finally, there was the so-called David and Goliath effect. Greenpeace – David – with its brave activists who occupied the platform, 'slew' the big villain, Shell – Goliath – and the media loved it.

Second, Shell was seen to be greedy. Shell had the necessary capital to choose a more environmentally benign (land disposal) option. In this instance, Shell lost credibility, as the public saw that it was no coincidence that the BPEO was also the cheapest option.

Third, Shell was seen as an easy target to boycott (most motorists are unaware of Shell's large holdings in the chemical sector). It is not a company such as Philip Morris, who has many brand names and is diversified in food and tobacco. A boycott of Shell simply involves driving to another gas station. People experienced the 'feel good factor', as they felt that they had acted in an 'environmentally correct' way without any discomfort or change of habit.

Fourth, politicians (with the exception of those in the UK and Norway) were heavily engaged in condemning Shell as it was an easy way of attracting green votes. Germany, Denmark and Sweden, the nations most opposed to deep-sea dumping, do not have any oil reserves of their own, so supporting the public protest of Shell did not affect them economically. Rather, it gave a chance for the politicians to exercise their green credentials, without any financial or political costs.

Finally, there was a moral issue, that of the sanctity of the deep ocean. One should not dump in it as it supposedly has not been dumped in before. It should remain pristine and untouched.

The Promoters of the Crisis

There were many factors that ensured that Brent Spar remained on the media agenda.

First, there were good pictures, largely provided by Greenpeace (eg pictures of activists on the platform being sprayed by Shell's tugboats).

Second, there were a series of negative factors attached to the proponents of Brent Spar. Shell, as a transnational corporation, is seen to have low public trust as does the UK Government.[6,7] During the Brent Spar crisis, Shell's actions did little to instil greater trust among the public. The company was non-univocal, the messages it relayed were at times confusing and at others arrogant. The UK Government was portrayed by the media as siding with industry, and being both arrogant and stubborn which did not help its public image of trustworthiness.

Third, the controversy came to dominate international meetings. As we described above, it featured heavily in the North Sea Conference held in Denmark. It also arose at the G7 meeting in Canada. The reasons why Brent Spar was highlighted in this way were: due to the confusion of where exactly the dump site was located, it enabled Greenpeace to spread the message that the North Sea was at risk. Second, there was the 'free ride' effect for politicians, as most of the nations opposing the deep-sea dumping do not have oil reserves of their own.

The Failure of the Counter-Information

If there were factors ensuring Brent Spar stayed on the media agenda, one wonders why Shell and/or the UK Government did not launch their own more positive risk communication strategy.

There were several weaknesses with the communication strategies of both Shell and the UK Government. They both adopted a top-down approach rather than a dialogue approach, the latter strongly supported by risk communication research.[8-11] In so doing, they alienated the public immediately and came across as arrogant and unmovable. Once the amplification process was at full speed, time was running out to launch such a dialogue approach.

Second, Shell was not seen as trustworthy, while Greenpeace was. Results from past research shows that in general the public, at least in the UK and Germany, trust NGOs more than they do industry or government.[6,7] Shell was unable to reduce the public's distrust of them due to a confusing mix of information on the Brent

Spar from Shell's offices in the UK and Germany. In other words, Shell did not have one voice, but Greenpeace did, which strengthened their argument.

Third, Shell could not counter the symbolic meaning of dumping in the deep sea. It is difficult to counter a 'gut reaction' that deep-sea dumping is morally wrong. As John Shepherd, chairman of the Scientific Group on Decommissioning, recently said, 'If people have an emotional response to pristine areas such like Antarctica or the deep sea, and want them to remain unpolluted, it is not up to scientists to say this is irrational.' (as cited in ref 12, p14).

Fourth, as the Shepherd report states, the scientists who really knew something about the deep sea and the consequences of dumping Brent Spar were not consulted. In other words, Shell did not use the scientific expertise available to counter the claims made by Greenpeace.[13]

Finally, the media coverage was largely dominated by footage provided by Greenpeace and sent to the major television networks. Greenpeace had taken the initiative and produced highly visible actions, while Shell was forced to react and defend themselves.

Discussion – Lessons for Risk Communication

Could a controversy such as Brent Spar have been avoided once the buoy was occupied by Greenpeace? There is no clear answer to this. Unlike other environmental protests in 1995, such as the attempts by Greenpeace to highlight the inactions of environmental policymakers in reducing CO_2 emissions at the Berlin Climate Conference in April 1995, the Brent Spar had a series of factors stacked against it as identified above: it was an environmental issue associated with the oil industry which everybody loves to hate; it was a problem in which blame could easily be assigned (unlike CO_2 emissions to which we all contribute); the oil storage buoy was an easy symbol to identify with environmental waste; there was the moral issue of dumping in virgin environmental areas; and Shell and the UK Government acted arrogantly throughout the entire process without considering dialogue as a possibility.

There are several lessons that can be learned from the Brent Spar controversy that might help to ensure that future crises of this type are minimized.

Most obviously, a company such as Shell should have adopted a dialogue approach before escalation of the cause. That is to say, it is essential to have a reciprocal strategy where attempts are made to promote dialogue between the public, special interest groups and 'experts' in order to derive solutions acceptable to everyone.[10] The top-down approach used by Shell is not a viable option as research suggests that 'experts' themselves can be biased (or at least motivated by interest and values like everybody else), and that most participants in the risk debate 'have fundamentally different values and priorities which shape their definitions and judgements of risk and acceptability' (ref 9, p54), be they lay citizens or experts.[14,15] Dialogic approaches help to see the logic and rationale of cognitive frames that affect one's own frame. Apparently, this is something that Shell is now trying to do.[2]

Industry needs to develop better and more flexible communication strategies to address criticisms from hostile groups. For example, there could be an independent peer review of any actions carried out by Shell or any other industry for that matter that may mobilize public opposition. These reviews should be published before actions are taken. This ensures that critical marks focus on the issue itself rather than on the organization as a whole. Additionally, some of the most critical representatives should be on the decision-making board in order to ensure openness and empowerment, something that was also briefly mentioned in the Shepherd report[13] and which has already occurred in Sweden concerning an international controversy surrounding the Barsebäck nuclear power station.[16]

Advice concerning how best to deal with these types of crisis should be sought from non-involved social scientists or media counsellors. In the Brent Spar case, such advice was sought only after the controversy was well established.

Companies should also organize panels or focus groups in different countries to account for differences in public perceptions among affected nations. As has been described in this paper, the Germans, for instance, had very different views of Brent Spar from the UK public. Related to this, there is a need to improve consultation and communication with political agencies in other countries. Of particular importance is to test their agreement or approval if new methods are introduced or public outcry is likely to occur. The international dimension was also mentioned in two specific contexts by the Shepherd report. Specifically, some of the best dumping sites may be in international waters and, second, there is no such thing as total containment in the sea – (ie contaminants dumped in one country's territory will not necessarily stay there). The elimination of the so-called 'surprise' factor is a necessity in order to reduce conflicts similar to Brent Spar.

Industry would benefit from a greater understanding of the underlying concerns and fears of the public. It is a strategy that Greenpeace has employed successfully, enabling them to identify which environmental issues have the greatest resonance for the public (eg whaling) and launch campaigns around these issues.

Industry, especially multinationals, should have uniform and unambiguous communication strategies both internally and between different countries. Mixed messages do not help industry's communication efforts. This was clearly seen in the Brent Spar case, where Shell UK was issuing different and often contradictory statements to Shell Germany.

Government licensing agencies should at all times claim independence of special interests. Solidarity with the proposer is not necessary even if the agency in fact agrees with the proposer, as this may be seen in a bad light. This was clearly depicted in the Brent Spar case where foreign publics saw Shell and the UK government working together. Rather, licensing agencies should emphasize control and accountability.

Finally, industries and NGOs alike should strive to form alliances with well-respected allies. With Brent Spar, Shell was only supported by the UK government, while Greenpeace received the support of several European governments, the European Union and a large number of the European public.

References

1   Aberdeen University Research and Industrial Services (1995) 'Brent Spar: Decommissioning Study', in *CEMP News* no 1, p1
2   E Faulds (1996) 'Why is Brent Spar Unique?' speech given at the Institute of Petroleum Conference, 22 February

3   A Rice (1996) 'Does Science Have a Role in Risk Analysis? The Case of Brent Spar and Other Cautionary Tales', paper presented at the Society for Risk Analysis-Europe Conference, June

4   House of Lords Select Committee on Science and Technology (1996) *Decommissioning of Oil and Gas Installations* HMSO, London

5   Natural Research Council (1996) *Scientific Group of the Decommissioning of Offshore Structures. First Report, April 1996* Natural Research Council, Swindon

6   H Peters (1990) 'Risiko-Kommunikation: Kernenegie' in H Jungermann, B Rohrmann and P M Widemann (eds) *Risiko-Konzepte, Risiko-Konflikte, Risiko-Kommunikation – Monographen des Forschungszentrums Julich Band 3* Forschungszentrum Julich, Julich

7   R M Worcester (1995) *Assessing the Public Opinion on the Environment: The Predictable Shock of Brent Spar* National Society for Clean Air and Environmental Protection, Brighton

8   B Fischhoff (1995) 'Risk Perception and Communication Unplugged: Twenty Years of Progress' in *Risk Analysis* no 15, pp137–145

9   L C Gould, G T Gardner, D R DeLuca, A R Tiemann, L W Doob and J A J Stolwijk (1988) *Perceptions of Technological Risks and Benefits* Russell Sage Foundation, New York

10   National Research Council (1989) *Improving Risk Communicaton* National Academy Press, Washington DC

11   P C Stern (1991) 'Learning Through Conflict: A Realistic Strategy for Risk Communication', in *Policy Science* no 24, pp99–119

12   A Abbott (1996) 'Brent Spar: When Science Is Not to Blame' in *Nature* no 380, pp13–14

13   Natural Research Council (1996) *Scientific Group of the Decommissioning of Offshore Structures: First Report, April 1996* Natural Research Council, Swindon

14   W Freudenburg (1988) 'Perceived Risk, Real Risk: Social Science and the Art of Probabilistic Risk Assessment', in *Science* no 242, pp44–49

15   C Hohenemser, R E Kasperson and R Kates (1977) 'The Distrust of Nuclear Power', in *Science* no 196, pp25–34

16   R E Löfstedt 'Risk Communication: The Barsebäck Nuclear Plant Case' in *Energy Policy* no 24, pp689–696

Procedural and Substantive Fairness in Landfill Siting: A Swiss Case Study

Ortwin Renn, Thomas Webler and Hans Kastenholz

Introduction

Modern democratic societies with pluralistic value systems tend to emphasize procedural justice over substantive fairness since the various actors in society disagree about what is a just and fair solution and what ratio of pay-offs and risks is regarded as acceptable.[1] Because disagreement is difficult or even impossible to resolve by abstract reasoning, the minimum requirement for a fair solution is procedural equity.[2] The process of legitimizing decisions by procedure rather than substance, however, faces two major problems: first, regardless of the type of procedure selected, its content relies on the discussion of substantive issues that will surface as part of the discussion or debate within the selected procedure. Even an acceptably fair risk discourse might produce unacceptable risk sharing.[3] For this reason, we believe that procedural fairness in risk decision making must be supplemented with competence. Competence in this sense means that the outcomes will lead to results that people expected when the decision was made. Competence can be evaluated only after the fact but must be assured during deliberations (ie it must be based on the best available judgement at the time). For this reason, it is important that the 'state of the art' in assessing outcomes and consequences and exploring their distributional effects is incorporated in the process. As Kristen Shrader-Frechette points out, knowledge about inequities and subjective perceptions of those who will bear risks need to be combined with the best scientific risk estimate.[4]

Second, procedural solutions of fairness are faced with the plurality of substantive fairness concepts within the discourse of the participants. Substantive fairness is not easy to define: Young[5] distinguishes three basic principles of substantive fairness: equal distribution of resources among all constituents (egalitarianism); distribution of resources according to each person's merits or input (proportionality to contribution); distribution of resources according to some priority principle such as each person's needs (distribution rule). Economists have complemented this list of principles with one significant addition: envy-free distributions. A distribution meets this principle if none of the individuals involved would like to change its share with any other person's share.[6] The question of which principle ought to be selected depends on personal or cultural preferences and social context.

To resolve competing claims with respect to substantive fairness, one needs rules of how to specify which of these claims will eventually prevail.[7] A procedure that does not include rules for evaluating and selecting competing claims and arguments misses its point. It either confines decision making to voting (ie an approximation

of a collective utility maximization strategy – in this way taking sides for one principle of fairness) or it leaves the process to random variations hoping that the lifeworld experiences of the participants will provide sufficient reasoning for finding a
solution that fits all needs.[8] Providing a platform for affected parties does not resolve
the conflicts about the substantive nature of fair distributions unless rules for making validity claims and the selection of default options or reference points are clearly
defined and adopted. These rules may be jointly established by all participants; without such rules, however, any discourse procedure becomes an unpredictable game
of strategic manoeuvring and privileges the strategically superior and rhetorically
skilled actors.

In our attempt to design discourse procedures in which the affected groups are
given the opportunity to be equally represented (as demanded by the egalitarian
interpretation of procedural equity), we deliberately postulated a set of rules regarding substantive issues. These rules do not presuppose the dominance of one philosophical school of fairness and social justice over another school but is oriented
towards a pragmatic procedure that gives all schools of thought an equal chance of
being considered for evaluating the fairness of a decision option. These rules refer
to the following two principles:

- If all affected parties have equal access to the benefits and risks of a proposed
  solution (ie nobody is losing compared to other actors) the situation is called
  'equitable' by default and does not need any further justification. This means
  that we select the egalitarian principle as the starting point of discussion, not
  necessarily the endpoint. Depending on the distribution context, equality may
  refer to chances or to outcomes or both.
- If one affected party benefits more from one solution than any other party or one
  party is asked to take a lager share of the risk than any other party, this solution warrants justification. Such situations may still be judged fair if the privi-
  lege of one party and the surplus risk of another party can be justified by arguments to which both parties agree (such as merits, needs, priority, or envy-free
  solutions). Such arguments can only be sustained if the inequitable solution provides additional benefits to which both parties can ascribe. All participants need
  to agree that the additional benefits coming from an inequitable solution must
  overcompensate the disbenefits associated with the inequalities stemming from
  this particular solution.

These major rules are derived from the meta-principle that all humans are created
equal and should have an equal share of the world's resources in the absence of
good reasons. This is congruent with most equality principles, including Aristotle's
or Rawl's Maximin principle, although his reliance on contracts alone does not legiti-
mize inequitable solutions.[9] Beyond voluntary agreements, the situation in which
the agreement is prepared needs to be free of coercion and should be unrelated to
the status quo.

Here we present the empirical results from one attempt to design and implement a discourse to site an incinerated municipal solid waste landfill. The process
may be seen as a practical implementation of the ideal procedural equity expressed
in discourse ethic philosophy[10] but is structured to include checks to competence
and substantive fairness.

Background of the Case

The topic for this case study is public participation in a decision-making process about siting a municipal waste disposal facility (landfill) in the eastern region of Aargau Canton. Figure 11.1 illustrates the location and the size of the Canton together with

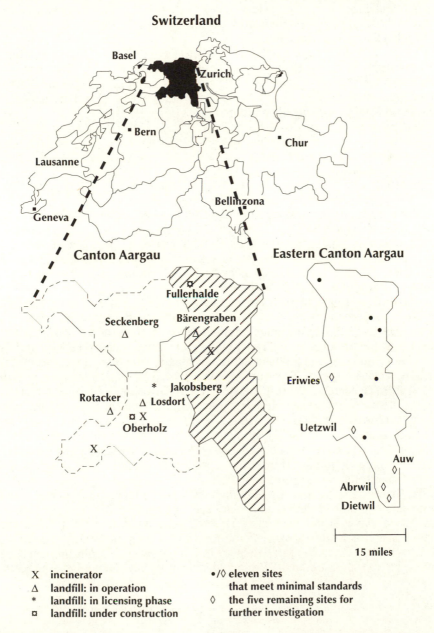

Figure 11.1 *Information about the Canton Aargau and location of solid waste facilities*

255

Table 11.1 *The four phases of site evaluation and decision making*

Evaluation Phase I	Evaluation Phase II	Evaluation Phase III	Getting a permit
Exclusion of non-suitable areas for siting a landfill	8 citizens 1 from each potential site community	Detailed geological surveys	Environmental impact Analysis
Rough analysis for 32 potential sites: selection of 13 eligible sites	Geological surveys Recommendation of a priority list of three sites by the panels	Selection of sites by panels in each of the remaining towns	Public hearing Vote by State Parliament

1991	1992	1993	1994	Time

sites for existing and planned landfills. The Building Department (Baudepartement) in Aargau is charged with responsibility to design the canton's solid waste-disposal plan, but the municipalities are responsible for implementing the plan.* In fact, however, communities have neither the resources nor the inclination to initiate or implement such planning. Instead, they officially ask the Canton to assume the responsibility of design and siting. This was the case in Aargau.

The Building Department's plan for the eastern region included the siting of at least one, but perhaps as many as three new landfills. Before our involvement in the project, the Building Department characterized the need for new disposal facilities and chose potential sites through a mapping-elimination process. Federal and cantonal laws restrict siting landfills in parks, wetlands, inhabited areas, geologically unsound areas and so on. These areas were removed from the map, leaving 32 potential sites. To narrow the list to 13 sites, the Department developed a set of 'preference criteria' and rated each site. Six categories of criteria were used: geology, hydrogeology, utility requirements, settlement–recreation, land and nature protection, and existing use value of land. These steps were done without consultation with the communities. We entered the process just as the results of the mapping elimination process were made public. The selection of 13 potential sites was the product of Phase 1 of selection.

In Phase 2, the main task was to limit the choice to three to five eligible sites. These sites should be selected and prioritized as a result of the geological surveys and the discourse recommendations. This was accomplished in 1993. The present Phase 3 includes detailed geological investigations in conjunction with citizen panels in each site. After one to three sites are finally chosen, the legally binding licensing procedure will be initiated. This includes a formal environmental impact state-

---

* Aargau has an official policy to incinerate 100 per cent of its solid municipal waste. This is accompanied by mandatory recycling of compostable waste, batteries, appliances and metal; and voluntary recycling of newspaper (curbside pick-up by volunteers), glass, tin cans and PET plastic containers (at local self-service bins located near residential areas, usually quite accessible even without a car).

ment, a public hearing and a final vote by the State parliament (Phase 4). All four phases are illustrated in Table 11.1.

Our mandate was to organize a participatory decision process for Phase 2. The objectives were to: develop criteria for comparing the different sites, evaluate the geological data that were collected during that period, eliminate the sites that should not be further considered and to prioritize the remaining sites with respect to suitability to host a landfill. We managed to meet these objectives between November 1992 and September 1993.

Applying the Cooperative Discourse Model for the Swiss Case Study

In line with our understanding of fairness, we convinced the cantonal government that the default option for our process should be a solution in which each community would take care of its own waste. If our efforts to find a common solution failed, each community should be responsible for managing its own waste. This fall-back position was difficult to justify since most waste for the proposed landfill would come from an incinerator rather than from private households in each community. It was feasible, however, to distribute the bottom and fly ash from the two operating incinerators to each community according to the share of waste that they contributed. The default option was explained to the citizens of the four panels. The cantonal government announced it would hand the authority back to each community in the case that no common solution could be accomplished.

Once the default option was defined, we structured the process of decision making in accordance with our model of cooperative discourse that we have developed for resolving environmental problems over the last 12 years.[11] Our model of participatory decision making is an attempt to develop procedural rules for organizing and structuring a discourse that is based on the communication model advocated by Critical Theory.[12] Discourses in Critical Theory serve the purpose of finding common solutions on cognitive, intentional, affective and normative problems. To emphasize fairness, the structure of the discourse has to be based on the following characteristics:[13]

- egalitarian position of each party within the discourse (all parties have equal rights and obligations);
- each party has the right to make claims of all kinds (cognitive, normative, intentional, etc);
- each party has the same right to demand the redemption of claims and ask for justification;
- all parties jointly create or confirm rules for redeeming claims.

In our model of decision making, these rules are adopted by all participants in the beginning of the process and confirmed throughout the process. Different sets of rules are proposed for cognitive (instrumental rationality), intentional (promises and practices) and normative debates (social rationality). These rules need to be adopted by unanimous vote.

Our model of cooperative discourse reflects these basic discourse requirements and offers a structure to make them operational in a given policy context. The main features of the model are: first, we insist that all parties affected by a decision should

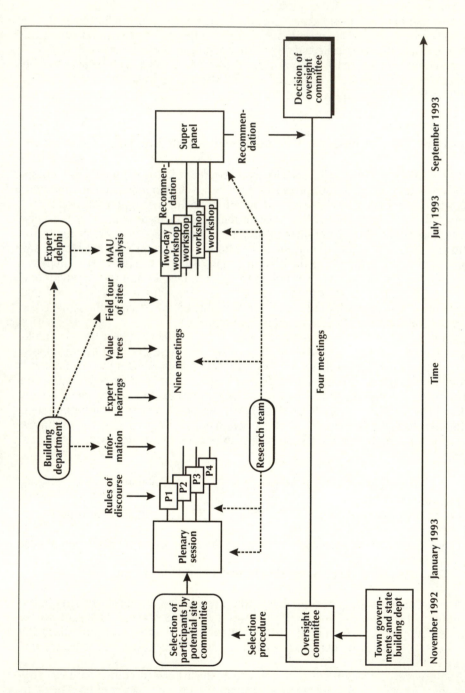

Figure 11.2 *Decision and participation to prioritize landfill sites*

have an equal opportunity to participate in the decision-making process; second, each party participating in the discourse has equal rights and duties and is obliged to provide evidence for its claims; third, we require that the best available knowledge is integrated into the decision process to ensure competency; last, we suggest a rational procedure of decision making which is basically derived from formal decision analysis,[14] but oriented toward a multi-actor, multi-value and multi-interest situation.

To integrate these multi-dimensional aspects of decision making into a practical procedure the model assigns specific tasks to different groups in society. These groups represent three forms of knowledge:

- knowledge based on common sense and personal experience;
- knowledge based on technical expertise;
- knowledge derived from social interests and advocacy.

These three forms of knowledge are integrated into a sequential procedure in which different actors of society are given specific tasks that correspond to their specific knowledge potentials. The model entails three consecutive steps: the first step in policy or decision making is often the identification of objectives or goals that the process should serve once a problem is identified or a political programme is established.[15] The identification of concerns and objectives is best accomplished by asking all relevant stakeholder groups (ie socially organized groups that are or perceive themselves as being affected by the decision) to reveal their values and criteria for judging different options. This can be done by using a process called value-tree-analysis.[17] The evaluative criteria derived from the value-trees are then operationalized and transformed into indicators by the research team or an external expert group. With different policy options and criteria available, experts representing varying academic disciplines and viewpoints about the issue in question are asked to judge the performance of each option on each indicator. For this purpose, we have developed a special method called the group delphi.[17] It is similar to the original delphi exercise but based on group interactions instead of individual written responses.

The last step is the evaluation of each option profile by a group or several groups of randomly selected citizens. This procedure has been developed by Peter Dienel[18] in Germany and – with a slightly different emphasis – by Ned Crosby in the US.[19] We refer to these panels as 'Citizen Panels for Policy Evaluation and Recommendation'. The objective is to provide citizens an opportunity to learn about technical and political facets of policy options and to enable them to discuss and evaluate these options and their likely consequences according to their own set of values and preferences. The idea is to conduct a process loosely analogous to a jury trial with experts and stakeholders as witnesses and advisers on procedure as 'professional' judges. For meaningful and productive discourse, the number of participants is limited to about 25. Discourse proceeds in citizen panels with the research team as discussion leaders who guide the group through structured sessions of information, personal self-reflection and consensus building.

Figure 11.2 is a schematic illustration of the cooperative discourse process as organized for the siting decision in Aargau.

In late October 1992, the town councils (Gemeinderäte) of the communities in which the potential sites were located were invited to send one member of the town council to serve on an oversight committee (Behördendelegation). The oversight committee consisted of one member of each town council and the Director of the Build-

ing Department. Sites located near boundaries were represented by two communities. All but one community opted to send a member of the council to the committee. The one town that did not participate also abstained from selecting representatives for the citizen panels. The oversight committee had the legitimate right to
make the final recommendation to the Building Department. In addition, they were
asked to inform the public about the site selection process, to review and critique
the participation process, and to select the representatives from each of their communities for the citizen panels.

The selection of representatives for the citizen panels differed from our theoretical approach. Rather than use random selection, we gave the oversight committee
the task to recruit and select citizen participants. The sponsoring agency was concerned about the legitimacy of the recommendations issued by the panels and felt
that random selection would not be seen as a legitimate way of choosing representatives. Using lotteries as a political means of achieving equity is alien to the Swiss
political culture. In substitution we proposed that either a town meeting or the community government nominate the representatives, with some assistance by the research team to encourage consideration of all relevant social and political viewpoints.
We asked each community to select eight representatives.

Once representatives were chosen, all were asked to attend a first general meeting in January 1993. The Director of the Building Department outlined the selection task; one of the authors, Ortwin Renn, introduced the procedure and rules of
discourse. Then four panels were formed, each consisting of two representatives
from each potential site community, and each was given identical tasks:

* review the past mapping – elimination process;
* review and interpret the technical feasibility analyses that were undertaken by
  engineering companies parallel to the deliberation period;
* consider social, political, ecological and economic impacts and equity issues
  including benefit sharing packages;
* develop criteria for evaluating sites;
* make a suggestion for three to five eligible sites;
* develop a priority list of sites for further investigation.

The Building Department was also interested to have the panels recommend a set
of criteria suitable for evaluating future landfill sites.

Results of the Discourse Process

Each panel met for three hours on one weekday evening, every two or three weeks
over a period of six months. In the first meeting of each panel, Renn discussed the
rules of discourse, the desired procedure for making final decisions and the moderation process. All four panels unanimously adopted the suggested rules and asked
the research team to moderate each session (among the moderators were Renn and
Hans Kastenholz, another author). Although we proposed consensus, to our surprise, the panels rejected it as a decision rule for placing communities on the priority list, arguing that consensus was politically impractical. Panellists also felt it
would place too much pressure on the representatives of selected sites to vote with
all the others once the group had come to a convincing conclusion. All panels voted

unanimously that they wanted a voting procedure based on some kind of qualified majority vote. Yet, interestingly, all four panels reached consensus in their final verdict in spite of initial scepticism.

Between January and June 1993, the panels met seven to nine times before they attended a two-day workshop to come up with the final decision. With the exception of one community, every town sent eight people to the panels. Not a single one of these dropped out. During the first half of the process, most emphasis was placed on informing the citizens about the problem of waste disposal and educating them about potential risks and problems a landfill can cause. They received a brochure in question-and-answer format prepared by a member of the research team and validated by a team of technical experts. Several experts were invited to talk about technical or economic issues, and the results of geological surveys were conveyed to the panellists by the principal investigators of the engineering companies who made the surveys. In June of 1993, the research team conducted a group delphi with ten experts on landfills and asked the group to provide best scientific estimates on all those indicators that demand physical measurements or highly professional judgements. The results of this group delphi were given to the panellists.

Before making final assessments of each site on each criterion, panellists had the opportunity to visit each site, talk to geologists at the site and ask questions of local representatives. During and after this process of obtaining information, each panel was instructed to come up with their own value tree and to compute a single quantitative assessment of each site. For this purpose, participants weighted each branch of the tree and evaluated each site on each indicator. The procedure is taken from MAU analysis as described in Watson[20] or von Winterfeldt and Edwards.[21] This task was quite substantial. One panel's tree had 50 indicators. Each of the nine potential sites was evaluated on each indicator, making for as many as 450 evaluations. The result was a numerical characterization of each potential site. Since each panel adopted the same construction principle for their value trees (main criteria were: impacts to humans, impacts to nature, impacts to society and economic costs), it is possible to directly compare the results of the four panels as in Figure 11.3.

Each panel accepted the priority list that the MAU procedure suggested and articulated a consensual recommendation. Although all four panels recommended the same first priority site, they had differences in the order of the remaining priorities. To resolve this conflict, each panel appointed five representatives to a super panel that met in September 1993 and issued a consensual list of five sites, two adjacent to each other. This list was later approved by the oversight committee and forwarded to the Building Department.

In December 1993, the result of the participation process was made public and the Canton's government entered Phase 3 of the process by initiating further tests at the selected sites. Unfortunately the Canton did not honour the order of the remaining sites but started a new characterization process giving all five sites equal weight. As a result the inhabitants of the site with the lowest ranking announced fierce opposition against this procedure, while the other towns allowed further investigation and screening. This process is still ongoing.

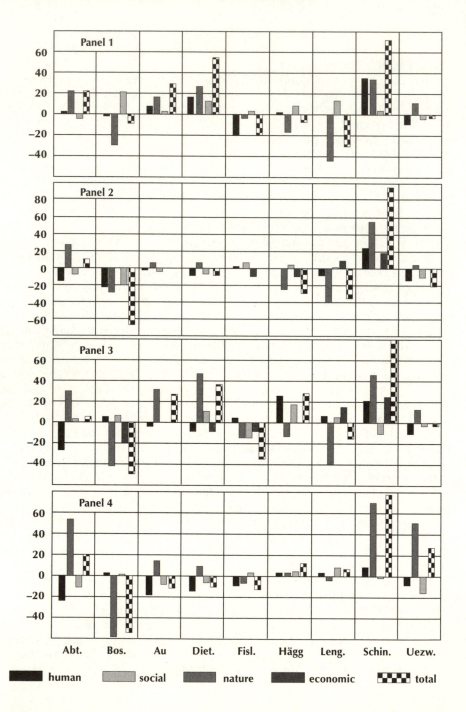

Figure 11.3 *The MAU analysis for each panel and potential site on the four main criteria*

Evaluation of Fairness

Fairness in our model has two components: substantive and procedural fairness. Defining substantive fairness is part of the deliberation process, but our rules require that any deviation from an egalitarian distribution needs justification. Procedural fairness refers to the opportunity of all affected persons to take part in decision making and to make claims and demand justification of claims made by others. There are four fundamental actions that every participant must be free to take: attend, initiate, discuss and decide. These refer in a discourse setting to four essential tasks: selection of participants, agenda setting, rule making, moderation and rule enforcement.

With respect to substantive fairness, we introduced our default option and made it clear that failure to reach a conclusion would mean that each community would be back on its own. Participants intensely discussed these issues. Although most shared the opinion that some communities need to take more risks for the common good, there were clear indications that such an altruistic approach was contingent on several conditions spelled out during the value tree exercises.

All groups placed a fairly high value on distributing burdens on those who produce the highest amount of waste. At the same time, they accepted the criterion that a site that is already burdened by other hazardous facilities should be spared. They opted for a balanced model of equity by contribution and need. (Similar results were obtained in an Austrian case study on hazardous waste disposal: J Linneroth Bayer and K B Fitzgerald 'Conflicting views on fair siting process' *Risk Health Safety and Management*, vol 7, no 2, pp119–134). All groups were convinced that a substantial health risk was unacceptable regardless whether it was distributed equally among all contributors or not. Participants demanded that the risk be reduced to a degree that serious health impacts were avoided. Once they perceived that this point was reached, fairness issues received focal attention. Fairness issues were then selected as indicators in each group, but with varying degrees of relative weights. While groups 1 and 2 placed most emphasis on the technical criteria, groups 3 and 4 assigned fairly high weights to equity considerations. Most differences among the four groups could be explained by the difference in relative weights given to technical versus social criteria (the social criteria included the fairness aspects).

In addition to including some criteria of substantive fairness in the decision tree, the issue of compensation came up during the discussion and was resolved in an unusual manner. Rather than paying monetary compensation to a community or its citizens (which was regarded as distributing bribes), all four panels favoured a model of joint ownership of the facility by the Canton and the selected community. Such joint ownership provides two major benefits for the community: sharing the revenues (the prices for waste disposal are administered in Switzerland, thus assuring some profits for each waste management facility) and sharing control. This suggestion was widely accepted by the groups, although the final decision was left to the representatives of the host community. Since several potential host communities are still under investigation, a final decision on joint ownership has not been made yet.

Judging procedural equity is more complex. The selection process for the panels was different from our model of random sampling. Although we issued clear guidelines for selecting citizens, some towns asked for volunteers, others looked for opinion leaders, and still others asked the politically active to participate. Three communities made the deliberate approach to make a selection according to the degree to which these people might be affected by a landfill. We cannot judge the representativeness of the selection, nor do we know if the selection of represented interests showed any systematic bias. For example, we had less than 20 per cent women among the participants. We also believe that we had better educated people in our panels than one might expect from a random sample. Yet average education levels are much higher in Switzerland than, for example, in the US. Other biases were not obvious.

Fairness within the panels was less of a problem. To protect the participants from unruly behaviour and to enable the panels to have direction and focus, the panels agreed to be run by facilitators from the research team. The citizens agreed to accept the appointed facilitators, but they did not surrender the right to remove the moderator at some latter point in time. None of the moderators was ever replaced. During the first meeting, the research team suggested a list of rules for conduct. These were meant to encourage a safe, non-aggressive, cooperative spirit during the panel discussions. These rules were adopted – out of common sense – by all the citizen participants without objection. They encouraged listening and created a space in which everyone could have their say without fear of being put down. The facilitators made sure that people said what they meant and that others heard what was said.

The rules explicitly included the requirement that each participant had the same rights to make statements and to challenge statements of others. By enforcing this rule and allowing everyone to speak, the facilitator helped create the belief that everyone's opinion or interests were legitimate. Individual interviews with participants revealed that they felt positive about the panel atmosphere: that it was non-hierarchical and cooperative. One person mentioned the beneficial effects of the setting:

> *I really enjoyed coming to these meetings. Although it was a lot of work, I found it refreshing to work in a non-hierarchical atmosphere, which is open and fair. This is so different from my workplace.*

Other anecdotal evidence suggested that a group identity did emerge over the six-month period. For example, during the site visits, a local official commented that he assumed the local citizen representative on the panel would vote against the site. She responded coldly that this was objective work of the panel and she was not there to merely keep the landfill out of her town. It is difficult to verify that she authentically was of that opinion, but it is significant that she thought it important enough to portray herself of that mind before the other panel members and other people from the communities.

Small working groups was another activity that promoted procedural fairness and gave participants the opportunity to discuss substantive aspects of fairness as well. During the evening meetings, small working groups of four to five participants were often used to frame questions for experts, to list potential concerns, to estimate the importance of different values and so on. It is known that working in groups promotes communication and participation. People who do not speak in the plenary often participate in small group settings. These settings also offer people an opportunity to explain in more detail their positions and opinions. During the first meeting we organized working groups to come up with a list of questions for the cantonal representative. The discussions in these groups were intense with every member participating.

Fair procedures should also help to build trust and confidence in all the various actors involved. Citizens' views on trust changed slightly throughout the process. At first, they held a high degree of mistrust for the official from the Building Department, the political institutions, such as the Building Department and 'the Canton' in general. Trust towards the official from the department improved for one-third of the citizens; our interviews revealed that this was because the citizens got to know him on a personal level. Trust for the political institutions did not improve during the process, however. This scepticism was not one-sided. We experienced that many people in government and some experts did not fully trust the citizens either. There was never strong support for this participation process within the Building Department, with the exception of the Director (member of the Canton's government) and the person responsible for the siting process.

Trust for the facilitator improved substantially. We hypothesize that this result was not so much movement of mistrust to trust, but rather removal of suspicion, as people became familiar with individual facilitators. Personal interviews confirmed that many people strongly trusted the facilitators and believed them to have good intentions.

In addition to the structural aspects of fairness, we had the respondents evaluate the fairness of the process in several surveys. To explore the citizens' subjective assessments of aspects of the process which are associated with the major goals of fairness and competence, we asked the participants about their opportunities to bring their values, interests and concerns into the discourse. We handed out written questionnaires to all participants at the beginning of the process, shortly before the final evaluations were made, at the end of the process and six months later. More than 70 per cent returned the first three questionnaires, slightly more than 50 per cent the last questionnaire. Figure 11.4 shows the distribution of ratings for subjective evaluation of fairness in four consecutive surveys. (In the last survey, not a single respondent was convinced that the process was unfair.)

All participants entered the process with high expectations of fairness. Over the six-month period, negative evaluations vanished, while positive evaluations stabilized. However, a more sceptical evaluation was observed immediately before participants made the final selection. They were probably uncertain of how their own

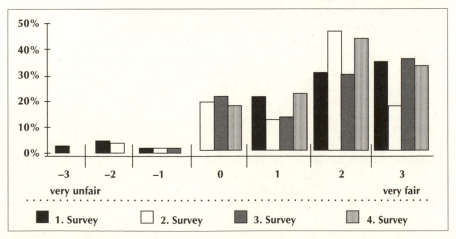

Figure 11.4 *Evaluation of fairness of the participation process by panellists*

home town would be evaluated. Six months after the process, the positive impression was again overwhelming. Nobody questioned the fairness of the process. At the same time, however, extremely positive evaluations became more moderate.

Overall 80 per cent of the respondents of the last survey agreed with the list of priorities that the super panel had suggested. This is rather astounding because 72 per cent of the respondents were originally convinced that their respective home communities were not suitable. All panellists without exception agreed that the list sites they had produced in their respective panel were justified and well selected. In contrast to our expectations, people representing priority sites were even more positive in backing the decisions of the panels. This could be interpreted as a manifestation of avoiding cognitive dissonance, but it could also show a strong degree of commitment to the result of a process to which the respondents developed some faith.

Conclusions

We began this article by pointing out that procedural and substantive fairness have to be integrated in one model of decision making. Our model is inspired by the idea that the default option is equal distribution of resources not the status quo. We leave the selection of one of the substantive fairness principles to the deliberation process, provided that each deviation from egalitarian distribution is justified by arguments. Procedural equity is accomplished through random selection of participants (if this is possible) or at least a selection procedure that guarantees the participation of most interests and values. Fairness demands that each party has the same right to participate and to make claims. Within the discourse setting, moderation, agenda setting, rule creation and rule enforcement are part of the consensual decision-making process. Rules for redeeming claims and for finding agreements need to be established in the beginning of the discourse process by the facilitators to assure competence and an atmosphere of seriousness. But these rules need to be approved by all participants.

Our model of citizen panels is only one of many possible ways to involve the public in decision making and policy designing. It is characterized by several features usually not found in other proposals for citizen involvement.[22] In contrast to joint commissions of experts and citizens, in this model each participating group is assigned a specific function. In contrast to negotiations with stakeholder groups, our model of participation is inspired by the normative goal of a fair and impartial representation of all citizens' values and preferences, be they organized or not. There are, of course, limitations to this approach. Based on our experiences[24] with panels in Germany, the US and the Swiss case study reported here, the following criteria should be used to evaluate the suitability of our proposed procedure:

- **Variability of options:** Do the participants have the choice of selecting one option out or a variety of options that are all feasible in the specific situation? Yes–no situations are likely to be resolved by 'no' because it provides the easiest way to consensus. The default option of egalitarian distribution is, however, a powerful agent to avoid status quo conservatism.
- **Equity of exposure:** Are all groups of the community or the respective constituency exposed in some way to the potential disadvantages of the proposed op-

tions (to avoid a distinction between more or less affected citizens)? The only way to introduce merit or contribution is by changing the opportunity rate for participation. Members of the more affected groups should enjoy a higher probability of being drafted than members of the less affected groups. Although we have tried this selection rule in the past, experiences with stratified samples were not too encouraging (1991).

- **Personal experience:** Do participants have some experience with the problem and do they feel competent about giving recommendations after they are further educated about the problem and the remedial options? Our Swiss example demonstrates that lay people can develop the necessary degree of self-confidence to make competent and prudent judgements. The subject of solid waste is certainly a topic that is simple enough to make the consequences of different choices transparent to non-professionals. Other topics may be more difficult in this respect. Past experience, however, has made us confident about the ability of normal citizens to process complex information and to understand sophisticated problems. People's capability for making prudent judgements is usually underestimated by most analysts as well as politicians. The cognitive limits of a co-operative discourse are yet to be determined. Our case studies in Germany and the US are further proof that lack of knowledge or of intelligibility was never a serious issue (1985 and 1993).
- **Personal relevance:** Do participants judge the problem as serious enough to sacrifice several days of their time to work on solutions? We had an extraordinary commitment in the Swiss case study. Nobody dropped out and all meetings were well attended. This may be caused by the selection process of the participants and the strong tradition for voluntary involvement of citizens within the Swiss political culture. In contrast, our main case study in the US showed a disappointing participation rate for randomly selected citizens (1991).
- **Seriousness and openness of sponsor:** Is the sponsor willing to accept or at least carefully consider the recommendations of the citizen panels or does it pursue hidden agendas? The participants of the Swiss case study suspected the Building Department to have a hidden agenda, but were proved wrong. However, the new policy of the Building Department to ignore the priority order for the top candidates has revitalized some scepticism in the communities.
- **Acceptance by stakeholder groups:** Using randomly selected citizens as jurors in a policy debate depends on the willingness of the various stakeholder groups to accept the outcome of the panel process. Stakeholders may agree to delegate the problem to a group of uncommitted citizens if one of the following conditions is met. First, the stakeholders have the feeling they cannot reach a satisfactory agreement in direct negotiation with other groups or the political authorities. Second, they feel they have more power when directing their arguments to uncommitted citizens rather than to charged administrators or politicians. Third, they feel pressured by public opinion to go along with what the public wants them to do. In all other cases, acceptance of the citizens' judgement is difficult to accomplish.

While one case study cannot validate the long-term effects of our model on participation and fairness, it does illustrate how our model can be used to design and evaluate public participation programmes. So far we have collected case studies in three countries. Evaluation of these cases has taught us that several aspects of the process are instrumental in promoting fairness and competence:

- Giving everyone in the affected population a chance to participate;
- building an atmosphere that encourages people to discuss anything that comes to their minds and to criticize or challenge anything that anyone else says;
- agreeing on a means to resolve disagreements before they arise;
- giving people the right to ask for new discussion leaders or experts and to influence the agenda;
- giving people time between the meetings to discuss the result of each meeting with their constituents, but reserving at least a day or two days for finalizing the recommendations;
- organizing a group delphi to clarify expert certainty and uncertainty;
- providing expert witnesses to educate the participants;
- providing pre-reviewed informational material;
- visiting the potential sites.

The central tenet to keep in mind with public participation projects is that the public is in principle capable and wise in making prudent decisions. Public input is essential to make the right decision, not only strategically necessary to gain acceptance. The rationality of public input depends, however, on the procedure of involvement. Provided citizens are given a conducive and supportive structure for discourse, they are capable to understand and process risk-related information and to articulate well-balanced recommendations. Our model of participation is one attempt to empower citizens to become more competent in making collective decisions, to promote a fair distribution of resources and risks, and to provide a procedure of decision making that provides equal opportunities to all citizens affected by the outcome of such a decision.

References

1. Kristen S Shrader-Frechette (1991) *Risk and Rationality: Philosophical Foundations for Populist Reforms*, University of California Press, Berkeley, pp29ff; George Cvetkovitch, Charles Vlek and Timothy C Earle, 'Designing Technological Hazard Information Programs: Towards a Model of Risk-Adaptive Decision Making' (1989) in *Social Decision Methodology for Technological Project* in C Vlek and C Cvetkovich (eds), pp253, 262ff
2. Niklas Luhmann (1968) 'Soziologie des politischen Systems' in *Kölner Zeitschrift Sozio. & Socialpsych* p705; Tom R Burn and Rainer Ueberhorst (1988) *Creative Democracy: Systematic Conflict Resolution and Policymaking in a World of High Science and Technology*
3. Douglas MacLean (ed) (1986) 'Social Values and the Distribution of Risk' in *Values at Risk*, p75
4. Kristen S Shrader-Frechette (1991) *Risk and Rationality: Philosophical Foundations for Populist Reforms* pp32ff
5. H Peyton Young (1993) *Equity in Theory and Practice*
6. William J Baumol (1986) *Superfairness: Applications and Theory* (1986); *cf* empirical analysis in Robin L Keller and R K Sarin (1988) 'Equity in Social Risk: Some empirical Observations' in *Risk Analysis* no 8, p135

7. Vittorio Hösle (1990) 'The Greatness and Limits of Kant's Practical Philosophy' in *Grad. Faculty Phil. J.* no 13, p13

8 Jürgen Habermas (1991) *Moral Consciousness and Communicative Action*; Karl Otto Appel (1992) 'Normatively Grounding "Critical Theory" Through Recourse to the Lifeworld? A Transcendental-Pragmatic Attempt to Think with Habermas against Habermas' in A Honneth et al (eds) *Philosophical Interventions in the Unfinished Project of Enlightenment*, p125

9. John Rawls (1971) *A Theory of Justice*

10. Eg Jürgen Habermas (1984) *The Theory of Communicative Action: Vol. 1 Reason and the Rationalization of Society*

11. Ortwin Renn et al (1984) 'An Empirical Investigation of Citizens' Preferences Among Four Energy Scenarios' in *Technology Forecasting and Social Change*, no 26, p11; Ortwin Renn et al (1985) *Sozialverträgliche Energiepolitik. Ein Gutachten für die Bundesregierung*; Ortwin Renn, Thomas Webler and Branden Johnson 'Public Participation in Hazard Management: The Use of Citizen Panels in the US' in *Risk* no 2, pp197,198–226; Ortwin Renn et al (1993) 'Public Participation in Decision Making: A Three-Step-Procedure' in *Policy Sciences* no 26, p189

12. Jürgen Habermas (1984) *The Theory of Communicative Action: Vol. 1 Reason and the Rationalization of Society*; Jürgen Habermas (1987) *The Theory of Communicative Action: Vol. 2 System and Lifeworld*; Jürgen Habermas (1990) *The Philosophical Discourse of Modernity*

13. Ortwin Renn (1992) 'Risk Communication: Towards a Rational Dialogue with the Public' in *Journal Hazard Materials*, no 29, p465; Ortwin Renn and Thomas Webler (1992) 'Anticipating Conflicts: Public Participation in Managing the Solid Waste Crisis' in *GAIA Ecol. Persp. Sci. Hum. & Economics* no 1, p84

14. Howard Raiffa (1970) *Decision Analysis*; Ralph L Keeney and Howard Raiffa (1976) *Decisions with Multiple Objectives and Value Tradeoffs*; Detlof von Winterfeldt (1987) 'Value Tree Analysis: An Introduction and an Application to Offshore Oil Drilling' in *Insuring and Managing Hazardous Risks: From Seveso to Bhopal and Beyond* P R Kleindorfer and H C Kunreuther (eds) p439; and Kan Chen and J C Mathes (1989) 'Value Oriented Social Decision Analysis: A Communication Tool for Public Decision Making on Technological Projects' in *Social Decision Methodology for Technological Projects* C Vlek and G Cvetkovich (eds) p111

15. Miley W Merkhorer (1984) 'Comparative Analysis of Formal Decision-Making Approaches' in *Risk Evaluation and Management* V T Covello, J Menkes and J Mumpower (eds) p183

16. Ralph L Keeney et al (1984) *Die Wertbaumanalyse. Entscheidungshilfe für die Politik*

17. Ortwin Renn and Ulrich Kotte (1984) 'Umfassende Bewertung der vier Pfade der Enquete – Kommission auf der Basis eines Indikatorkatalogs' in *Energie im Brennpunkt* G Albrecht and H-U Stegelmann (eds) p190; and Thomas Webler et al (1991) 'The Group Delphi: A Novel Attempt at Reducing Uncertainty' in *Technology Forecasting & Social Change*

18. Peter C Dienel (1978) *Die Planungszelle*; Peter C Dienel (1989) 'Contributing to Social Decision Methodology: Citizen Reports on Technological Projects' in *Social Decision Methodology for Technological Projects* C Vlek and C Cvetkovich (eds) p253

19. Ned Crosby (1986) 'Implementing Citizen Panels: A Ten Year Program of Political Reform' unpublished; Ned Crosby, J M Kelly and P Schaefer (1986) 'Citizen

Panels: A New Approach to Citizen Participation' in *Public Administration Review*, no 46, p170

20. S R Watson (1982) 'Multiattribute Utility Theory for Measuring Safety', *European Journal Operational Research* no 10, p77

21. Detlof von Winterfeldt and Ward Edwards (1986) *Decision Analysis and Behavioral Research*

22. Cf Daniel J Fiorino (1990) 'Citizen Participation and Environmental Risk: A Survey of Institutional Mechanism' in *Sci Tech and Hum Values* no 15, p226; Carol Pateman (1970) *Participation and Democratic Theory*; Stuart Langton (1987) 'Citizen Participation in America: Current Reflections On State Of the Art' in *Citizen Participation in Public Decision Making* J DeSario and S Langton (eds) p1; Michael Pollak (1985) 'Public Participation' in *Regulating Industrial Risk* 76 H Otway and M Peltu (eds); Mary G Kweit and Robert W Kweit (1987) 'The Politics of Policy Analysis: The Role of Citizen Participation in Analytic Decision Making' in *Citizen Participation in Public Decision Making* J DeSario and S Langton (eds) p19

23. *See* note 11

List of Further Reading

Psychometric Paradigm

Gould, L C, G T Gardner, D R DeLuca, A R Tiemann, L W Dobb and J A J Stolwijk (1988) *Perceptions of Technological Risks and Benefits* Russell Sage Foundation, New York.
Kahneman, D and A Tversky (1974) 'Judgment under uncertainty: Heuristics and biases' in *Science*, vol 185, pp1124–1131
Pidgeon, N, C Hood, D Jones, B Turner and R Gibson (1992) 'Risk perception' in Royal Society (ed) *Risk: analysis, perception and management* Royal Society, London
Renn, O (1990) 'Risk perception and risk management: A review, part 1: risk perception' in *Risk Abstracts*, vol 7, pp1–9
White, G F (1961) 'The choice of use in resource management' in *Natural Resource Journal*, vol 1, pp23–40

Social Construction of Risk

Bayerische Ruck (1993) *Risk is a Construct* Bayerische Ruck, Munich, Germany
Wynne, B (1996) 'May the sheep safely graze?,' in S Lash, B Szerszynski and B Wynne (eds) *Risk Environment and Modernity: Toward a New Ecology* Sage, London, pp44–83

Cultural Theory

Douglas, M and A Wildavsky (1982) *Risk and Culture* University of California Press, Berkeley, CA
Grendstad, G (1990) *Europe by Cultures. An Exploration in grid/group analysis* Department of Comparative Politics, Bergen, Norway
Thompson, M, R Ellis and A Wildavsky (1990) *Cultural Theory* Westview Press, Boulder, Colorado

From Risk Perception to Communication

Leiss, W (1996) 'Three phases in the evolution of risk communication practice' in *Annals of the American Academy of Political and Social Science*, vol 545, pp85–94
National Research Council (1989) *Improving Risk Communication* National Academy Press, Washington DC
Stern, P C (1991) 'Learning through conflict: a realistic strategy for risk communication' in *Policy Sciences*, vol 24, pp99–119

Social Amplification of Risk

Kasperson, R E and J X Kasperson (1996) 'The social amplification and attenuation of risk' in *The Annals of the American Academy of Political and Social Science,* vol 545, pp95–105
Machlis, G E and E A Rosa (1989) 'Desired risk and the social amplification of risk framework' in *Risk Analysis,* vol 10, pp161–168

Trust

Barber, B (1983) *The Logic and Limits of Trust* Rutgers University Press, New Brunswick, New Jersey
Earle, T and G Cvetkovich (1995) *Social Trust: Toward a Cosmopolitan Society* Praeger, Westport, CT
Giddens, A (1990) *The Consequences of Modernity* Polity Press, Cambridge
Kasperson, R E, D Golding and S Tuler (1992) 'Siting hazardous facilities and communicating risks under conditions of high social distrust' in *Journal of Social Issues,* vol 48, pp161–172
Misztal, B A (1996) *Trust in Modern Societies* Polity Press, Cambridge
Nye Jr, J S, P D Zelikow and D C King *Why Don't People Trust Government?* Harvard University Press, Cambridge
Renn, O and D Levine (1991) 'Credibility and trust in risk communication' in Kasperson, R E and P M Stallen (eds) *Communicating Risks to the Public: International Perspectives,* Kluwer, Amsterdam
Slovic, P and D MacGregor (1994) *The Social Context of Risk Communication* Decision Research, Eugene, Oregon

Mental Models

Atman, C J, A Bostrom, B Fischhoff and M G Morgan (1994) 'Designing risk communications: completing and correcting mental models of hazardous processes. Part 1' in *Risk Analysis,* vol 14, no 5, pp779–788
Bostrom, A, C J Atman, B Fischhoff and G M Morgan (1994) 'Evaluating risk communications: completing and correcting mental models for hazardous processes. Part 2' in *Risk Analysis,* vol 14, no 5, pp789–799

How Can Social Scientists Contribute to Risk Management?

Kunreuther, H, K Fitzgerald and T D Aarts (1993) 'Siting noxious facilities: A test of the siting credo' in *Risk Analysis,* vol 13, no 3, pp301–318
National Research Council (1996) in P Stern and H Fineberg (eds) *Understanding Risk* National Academy Press, Washington DC
Renn, O, T Webler and P Wiedemann (eds) (1995) *Fairness and Competence in Citizen Participation* Kluwer, Dordrecht

Index